The
McCrays
of
America

Second Edition

Philip Roger M<u>c</u>Cray

HERITAGE BOOKS
2019

HERITAGE BOOKS
AN IMPRINT OF HERITAGE BOOKS, INC.

Books, CDs, and more—Worldwide

For our listing of thousands of titles see our website
at
www.HeritageBooks.com

Published 2019 by
HERITAGE BOOKS, INC.
Publishing Division
5810 Ruatan Street
Berwyn Heights, Md. 20740

International Standard Book Numbers
Paperbound: 978-1-55613-829-4
Clothbound: 978-0-7884-8825-2

To Cely,
My Patient Wife,
Who complements my life.

AND

To Richard, my brother
"He started it!"

"Yet no one is really alone;
Those who live no more echo still
within our thoughts and words,
And what they did is part of
what we have become."

From a Judean prayer

-- P R E F A C E --

    Genealogy is defined in my dictionary as: "A study of family ancestors *and histories*." All too often searchers, after finding names and dates of their ancestors, stop there, forgetting to learn their stories--their histories--and thereby fail to give new life and definition to those people from whom they sprang. Unless we learn what they did in their day, and as far as possible, explain what motivated them, and the environment that modified their actions, all we have done is to make a list, something about as useful and informative as a telephone directory. Genealogy is history, and history is about people just like ourselves, but who lived in a quite different environment and were affected by quite different social, religious, political and geographical forces. It is only when we understand the world they lived in that we can give these long-dead people a new kind of life in our journals.

    We may know that our Scots-Irish ancestors came to America from Ireland some two centuries ago. But why did they come here? What in the world would have persuaded them to board a cramped sailing vessel, probably of questionable seaworthiness, that was intended to transport only bulk commodities such as lumber, cotton, tobacco or spices, and spend two or three months at sea? Then, if they survived the sea journey without medical facilities, privacy, medicines, decent food or safe drinking water, they went ashore in an unknown and vastly different land from the one they left, and where they were generally despised by the Colonial population. Were things that bad in Ireland? And after their arrival here, why didn't they stay on the East Coast with the population there who lived in relative comfort, instead of striking out into the wilderness to the west, to live in danger and discomfort? What sorts of people would deliberately change their lives so drastically?

    We searchers often bemoan the paucity, or complete absence, of records of these long dead people who came before us. A very few of them did leave us treasured records that they themselves wrote, such as the journal that Margaret McCray wrote, describing her relatives, her travels across the prairies, with descriptions of the land and people, and the exciting and dangerous life she lived. How her descendants value this little notebook and bless her for keeping it! Because of it Margaret McCray will be remembered far longer than those who lived at the same time but didn't foresee that they, too, could have been long remembered in this way. In our vanity, we too would want such immortality, and we'd do well to prepare our own autobiography to give our children and grandchildren.

    When I began this revision and expansion of my first book, *The McCrays Of America*, in which I tried to deal with our ancestors against a backdrop of Scotland, Ireland and America of the seventeenth, eighteenth and nineteenth century, I tried to explain the moves of the various McCray families across Great Britain and Colonial America in some detail. To do this it was necessary to re-learn British history from the start of the reign of Henry VIII in 1509 and the Reformation to the reigns of the Hanoverian kings and the first three Georges, and on through the remainder of the nineteenth century. Following the five great migrations of the Scots-Irish from Ireland to America, it was logical to take up American history once more, a subject so badly presented in American public schools that it often instills in children a life-long disinterest in history.

In this volume an attempt has been made to tell something about several Scots-Irish families who came here to America and to relate what they did to the tenor of the times in which they lived. A brief historical background precedes the story of each family, in order to offer plausible explanations for their moves across the face of the globe to the newly emerging American nation, as well as subsequent moves after their arrival here. It is fervently hoped that something both interesting and informative has been wrought, and that it might stimulate similar efforts among others when they undertake ancestor research.

It has long been standard genealogical practice to record only the male line of ancestors. This strikes me as presumptious, sexist, and demeaning of brave and patriotic women whose contribution to the life of our nation and its communities was in every way equal to that of the men. Life today might well be better if women's voices had been raised more forcefully both in legislative halls and in log cabins a couple of centuries ago, and we might be in far worse shape had it not been for the steadying low voices of wives and daughters from behind the scenes to husbands and fathers in authority. Too long have male historians written history as a story of maleness, begrudgingly including women whenever they were Queens Elizabeth I or Joans of Arc. It is time that genealogists give the ladies full time and attention along with the men of their families. It will be noted that this volume does include material on the families of female spouses wherever it was available.

As Martha, a cheerful black cook I once knew in Alabama, said of her husband: "He makes the livin', but I makes the livin' worth while."

I don't doubt this book contains errors in both typing and fact. Every effort has been made to prevent and correct errors. I have come to realize that it would be nice to be a professor in a university, where I would have access to ambitious undergraduate students who could be conscripted to do the tedious details of research and proof-reading for me. This is one of the regrets of my mis-spent youth, although I really did have a lot of fun while ignoring opportunities that lay before me.

However, I have enjoyed some aspects of that status, for most of the delving into gold mines of the archives that are in this book was done by others, wonderfully generous people, who have shared their precious nuggets with me, and trusted me to weave their work into this story of the McCrays. It has been my intention throughout to treat their work with the respect it is due, and to hope that everyone will forgive any inadvertent omissions, errors or apparent slights that may have occurred. It can be seen that this has been a summing of many parts when looking at the following list of those who have made this book possible. Almost all of them are either McCrays or McCray-related, people to whom I am very thankfully related, some closely and others more distantly. I have met but a small fraction of them in person, but most of them I know by letters or that marvelous instrument for human contact, the telephone.

My sincere thanks to these following people:

Mrs. Shirley Bedow, of Union City, PA
Ray Boutwell, of Corry, PA
Mrs. Lucy Botkin, of Head Waters, VA
Betty Buffa, of Pacific Palisades, CA
William E. Carroll, of Oklahoma City, OK
Mrs. Patricia Case, of Santa Barbara, CA
Mrs. Lorena Day, of Chula Vista, CA
Dennis Davis, of Erie, PA
Mrs. H.K. Fosha, of Calhan, CO
Mrs. Cynthia Fletcher, of Weston, OH
Hazel Foster, of Sun Lakes, AZ
Mrs. Ruth Gadbury, of Lometa, TX
Mrs. Dorothy Gray, of Granbury, TX
Mrs. Ilo Grisham, of Pueblo, CO
Mrs. Patrica Heinen, of Mercer, PA
Glenn Hicks, of Dallas, TX
Mrs. Pat Kennedy, of Medford, OR
Francis Lipp, of Frankfort, IN
Mrs. Leland Maryott, of Union City, PA
Mrs. Adele McCray
Miss Cora McCray (Deceased), of Meadville, PA
Douglas James McCray, of Bowling Green, OH
Don McCray, of Madison, WI
Elwin E. McCray, of St. Petersburg, FL
Ernest McCray of (temporarily) Riyadh, Saudi Arabia
Glen M. McCray, of Springfield, MO
Harrison McCray (Deceased), of Charlotte, NC
John F. McCray, of Alexandria, LA
John W. McCray, of Costa Mesa, CA
Joseph & Eleanor McCray, of Corry, PA
Ronald McCray, of Dayton, OH
Richard L. McCray, of Johnson City, TN
Richard N. McCray, of Hendersonville, NC

Mrs. Mary McKinney, of Tucson, AZ
Mrs. Blanche Meritt, of Oceanside, CA
Mrs. Leona Meyer, of Marshall, MO
Robert F. Mitchell, of Erie, PA
Leon Moore, of Alexandria, AR
Alice Morrison, of Titusville, PA
Myles Murray, of Sanibel, FL
Mrs. Frances Nicholas, of Tucson, AZ
Mrs. Diane Olivier, of Metarie, LA
Mrs. Hilda Padgett, of Erwin, TN
Ralph Piper (Deceased), of Derby, KS
Mrs. Nina Pollock, of Union City, PA
H.A. Price, of Waynesboro, VA
Lewis Reed, of Temple City, CA
Franciska Saffran, of SUNY, Fredonia, NY
Mrs. Grant F. Sears, of Frewsburg, NY
Mrs. Pattie Smith, of Spearsville, LA
Mrs. Nina Stillwell, of Nauvoo, IL
H. William Townsley, of Fort Meyers, FL
Mrs. Della A. Upshaw, of Camp Verde, AZ
J. Duane and June Upton, of Hemet, CA
Mrs. Louise Watkins, of Rockford, TN
Mrs. Diana Zimmermann, of Littleton, CO

The following organizations have been of great help:

The Annandale (VA) Branch Genealogy Library, The Church of Jesus
    Christ of The Latter Day Saints
The Connecticut State Library, Hartford, CT
The Corry Area Historical Society, Corry, PA
The Crawford County Historical Society, Meadville, PA
The Cumberland County Historical Society, Carlisle, PA
The Erie County Historical Society, Erie, PA
The Hall of Records, St. John's College, Annapolis, MD
The Historical Society of Charles County, Port Tobacco, MD
The Library of Congress, Washington, D.C.
The Maryland Historical Society, Baltimore, MD
The National Archives of The United States, Washington, D.C.
The National Genealogical Society, Arlington, VA
The Perry Historians, Newport, PA
State Library of Pennsylvania, Harrisburg, PA
The Western Pennsylvania Genealogical Society, Pittsburg, PA

-- C O N T E N T S --

CONTENTS

CHAPTER FIVE

CHAPTER SIX

CHAPTER SEVEN

ADDENDUM

CONTENTS

CHAPTER EIGHT

CHAPTER NINE

CHAPTER TEN

CHAPTER ELEVEN

CONTENTS

CHAPTER TWELVE

CHAPTER THIRTEEN

CONTENTS

MAPS

Correspondence invited

Philip R. McCray
7720 Bock Road
Fort Washington, MD
20744

xiii

THE McCRAYS OF AMERICA

CHAPTER ONE

THE SCOTS-IRISH

Please to remember the Fifth of November,

With gunpowder, treason and plot.

That's about as much of this nursery rhyme most of us can remember. It recalls an event remembered principally by English
schoolboys today, who make and carry around town scarecrow-
like replicas of Guy Fawkes, demanding from passersby, "A
penny for the Guy." Then, on the evening of November the fifth
all the guys are piled up on the common and set alight, while everyone
cheers and, sooner or later, sings with much gusto, "Rule Brittania!"

But nobody cheered in 1605 when the Gunpowder Plot was discovered
just hours before King James and his Parliament would all have been blown
up on the morning of November 5. Guy Fawkes, a Yorkshireman, was literally the "fall guy" for a group of Catholic plotters bent on restoring
the Catholic Church to its powerful place before Henry VIII. Fawkes was
caught red-handed in a cellar underneath the chamber where most of the
members of Parliament were to meet with King James the following morning.
The plotters had stashed thirty-six barrels of gunpowder in the cellar,
and concealed it under faggots of firewood. Iron rods were laid on top
of the barrels to facilitate penetration through the roof and into the
bodies of the men meeting there. Nobody doubted that if the explosion
had occurred, everyone would have been injured or killed. If King James
had died there would never have been any "Scotch-Irish," and who knows
what the outcome of the American Revolution would have been without them?
For that matter, where would we McCrays be today?

Scots, who can be picky about names, point out that "Scotch" is
whisky (spelled without the "e"), and that they are "Scots", not "Scotch,"
so hereafter we will refer to ourselves as "Scots-Irish." We are not a
mixture of Irish and Scots, generally speaking; we rose from Lowland
Scotland, we lived for a time in Ireland, and came to America still Scots.

Scotland before The Reformation

WHEN THE TRUMPETS OF THE REFORMATION blew down the walls of European feudalism, Scotland remained unchanged. Its poverty was of a degree hard for us to imagine. The Lowland forests had all been cut for fires made on the earthen floors of the peasants' primitive huts of stone, sod, straw, and cow manure. There were no minerals, so there was no manufacturing, no commerce, and no shipping. There was no class of wealthy and educated people to support arts and letters. Scots found their sole diversion in warfare, and clans fought clans, barons fought barons, and the lairds fought other lairds. The peasants were the soldiers, and because peasants were too poor to have horses, all fighting was done on foot.

Kings of Scotland had little authority or wealth to wield it if they had it. The nobles of Scotland owned the impregnable castles, and they held themselves above any national laws, and each lord declared the law to be whatever he said it was. These lords took responsibility for the farmer-warriors on their lands, and they took it as a personal insult when raiders took cattle from their vassals, and would immediately launch retaliatory raids to regain the stolen cattle, plus a few extra ones. Unlike most of Europe, Scotland never had a peasants' uprising, because the landowners were ever ready to go to war to defend the peasants' fields and cottages, gaining for them the highest respect. Often there was blood kinship up and down the social and economic ladder, and although a peasant never expected, or received, any familiarities from his remote cousin, the laird, upon whose land he toiled, he nevertheless proudly and fiercely supported him.

Scotland's soil was thin, sour, and rocky, and what farming was done was as badly done as it was during the Dark Ages. Animal manure, instead of being used to fertilize crops, was dried and either burned as fuel or mixed with mud and straw to daub chinks in their miserable huts. Even the upper classes had no elegance. Half of whatever grains reaching maturity in their very short growing season was used for making beer because the water almost everywhere was undrinkable. What grain left was of such poor quality that a quarter of it had to be set aside as seed for the next year.

The typical Scottish farmer's wealth generally consisted of his crudely woven woolen clothes, a windowless sod hut that he built in a few hours, perhaps a half-starved cow or ox, some crude wooden farm implements, some wooden bowls, spear, iron sword, and leather shield. Plows were likely to be the common property of several farmers, and agriculture was practiced at a near-Iron-Age level. The peasant family and his domestic animals all crowded into the dark, stinking hut at night, and not surprisingly, death was to be expected early in life from various filth-related diseases.

Christianity didn't make much headway in Scotland until a Scot, Cuthbert, Bishop of Lindisfarne* began to preach in the seventh century. Religion wasn't a dominant factor in the life of the typical Scot for the next six centuries, but then the Scottish kings, seeking to establish their power, brought in English bishops and gave them large estates and military support to firmly entrench the church. As the power of the church increased, it acquired more and more of whatever wealth resided in Scotland, and by the middle of the sixteenth century it had more wealth and power than the Scottish monarchs and all the nobles.

In Germany Martin Luther had unbeknownst planted the seeds of the Reformation, and Henry VIII asserted his right to dominate the clergy in England. None of these rumblings had the slightest effect on the priests in Scotland. Half of Scottish land and possibly more than half of her wealth was in the hands of the Roman Church, and the clergy were generally corrupt, self-serving, venal, ignorant and indifferent in the extreme to their sworn duties to minister to their flocks. Instead, they bled the peasants by tithes that kept them at near-starvation levels. The church had fallen from its position of scholarly leadership of civilization to a point where some priests could hardly stumble through the words of the Mass. They lived in luxury, growing fat and lazy in rich abbeys and monastaries, surrounded by the very, very poor, who paid for it all.

Nor was the Scottish monarchy all that much a truly Scottish institution. Sixteenth century Scotland was ruled by kings and queens with strong ties to France, England's ancient (and Catholic) enemy. Henry VIII, nervous about having all those French nobles and French soldiers on the island just to his north, made several forays into Scotland to keep the French from becoming too powerful there. James V of Scotland married Mary, of the French Catholic family of Guise, and their daughter became Mary Queen of Scots. She married a French prince, later to become King Francis II of France. For a time she was both queen of Scotland and of France, while her mother ruled Scotland as Queen Mother-Regent, surrounded by French nobles and supported by French troops. Both the clergy and the monarchy ignored the warnings implicit in the growing Reformation movement.

Revolution and Reformation

ON NEW YEAR'S DAY 1559, it all boiled over. A revolutionary manifesto was affixed to the gates of every Scottish religious establish-

* Cuthbert's name is remembered in Scotland in the name of the border shire, Kirkcubright, with the delightful pronunciation, "Coocoobree."

ment. Somewhat reminiscent of our Declaration of Independence, this "Beggars' Summons" began:

> The blind, crooked, lame, widows, orphans, and other poor visited by the hand of God as may not work, to the flocks of all friars within this realm, we wish restitution of wrongs past, and reformation in times coming."

It went on to list specific injustices and complaints in detail, and ended with an ultimatum:

> "Give back what you have stolen from us...betwixt this and the Feast of Whitsunday next...or we shall enter and take possession of our said patrimony, and eject you utterly forth from the same."

Strong words. The clergy was warned, and should have cleaned house. Instead, it appealed for protection from the Queen Regent. Countdown began for the Catholic Church.

In that same year John Knox was released after seventeen years at the oars of galleys. He returned to a Scotland in uproar. Protestant sermons were preached everywhere, and the heretofore docile Scots were ready for revolution. Knox came on the scene as The Man Of the Hour, and all Scotland turned to him. He didn't preach freedom--he was every bit as narrow and bigoted as the church he sought to condemn, but what he said was warmly received everywhere.

In Perth, after Knox had delivered a particularly fiery sermon in a church, the Mass being said by a priest, the service was disrupted by a riot. It isn't certain what started it, but the congregation rose up and wrecked the interior of the building, then swept through the streets of Perth, destroying statues in all the religious houses. The Queen Regent sent an army of French troops to punish Perth, and for this the Protestants raised an army and called upon Queen Elizabeth to send help from England. Before things got completely out of hand, even before any blood was spilled, the opposing sides met on July 6, 1560, and struck a bargain known as the Treaty of Leith, by which the French forces withdrew from Scotland, leaving the Protestants triumphant.

Only four days later, July 10, 1560, Parliament toppled the Church of Rome as the Established Church of Scotland, and that same day drew up three acts which:

1) cast off the Pope,
2) condemned all doctrines and practices of any church but the churches of Protestants, and,
3) forbade the saying of the Mass.

Parliament went on to ask the Protestant ministers to draw up a Confession of Faith, a document of doctrines for a new church. The ministers wrote the First Book of Discipline for the new government and thus was born the Presbyterian Church, the Established Kirk of Scotland, and so it has remained to this day. And wherever the Scots went after that they took with them the Presbyterian Church and planted it wherever they tarried a while.

Mary Queen of Scots, now a widow, returned to Scotland to sit on the throne. She was determined to restore the Catholic faith in Scotland, and she immediately began having trouble with John Knox. After a series of stupid scandals she could easily have avoided, she fled from Scotland, leaving the throne to her small son, King James VI. Mary was imprisoned in England, for she was next in line for the throne of England, and neither Elizabeth nor her ministers could countenance the prospect of another Catholic monarch, such as Mary I, whom Elizabeth had followed to the throne. Elizabeth had experienced the terror of prison in her own youth, and couldn't bring herself to sign her cousin's death warrant, but she did finally do so and Mary Queen of Scots was executed at Fotheringhay Castle. Elizabeth was distressed and vowed that her ministers had tricked her into signing the death warrant.

The boy monarch, James VI, was brought up in Scotland by Calvinist Presbyterian teachers. He was a good scholar, intelligent, and quick to learn the techniques and dangers of court intrigue. He embraced the concept of Protestantism but rejected the Kirk of Scotland because its government was organized as an authoritative body separate from the Crown, an idea which he regarded as a threat to his authority. He waited out his regency as a youth, but upon reaching the age of seventeen he took over the throne and banished the stern Calvinist teachers who had sought to mold him into a royal John Knox clone. He was charming, regal, and a monarch whose homosexuality was generally overlooked as a to-be-expected peculiar privilege of royalty. He made it clear that he was in charge of things, and that he was going to unite Scotland by stopping the incessant wars between clans and nobles. He was also determined to rule the Kirk himself, by installing bishops into its government, claiming that he was put on the throne by God and thereby ruled by God's grace and authority. He insisted upon certain liturgical practices, such as kneeling at prayer, and of ministers wearing surplices in the pulpit, which Presbyterian purists regarded as popish and an abomination.

James was the great great grandson of Henry VII, and next in line to become King of England, a job he thought himself to be eminently fit to do. His claim was favorably regarded by Queen Elizabeth, who was determined that only a devout Protestant could succeed her, and a treaty was drawn up to effect James' succession. Good Queen Bess died in 1603, and James exultantly set out for London and a great welcome by courtiers who were tired of a monarch in skirts.

5

He had thin brown hair, watery blue eyes, and went about with a shambling gait on thin spindly legs, and when he drank, liquid dribbled down his front. The skin on his hands and face was of a strange cast. Actually, it was just dirty, for he never washed. He made coarse scatalogical jokes to ecclesiastics and sang bawdy Scottish songs. Still, to many courtiers, he was a charming man of learning. To all the court he made it abundantly clear that the new man on the block was in charge of things.

He dredged up an ancient concept, The Divine Right of Kings, and let it be known that his authority came from God and was not to be questioned. He summoned Puritans from Commons who were demanding simplification of the English church and abolishment of episcopy and bishops. He firmly put down the royal foot, saying: "No bishops, no king." Both king and bishops stayed. He ended the long war with Spain and put an end to cross-border warfare between England and Scotland. He set out to reform the Scottish church, and opened a non-stop quarrel with Parliament over the royal stipend. He ordered a convocation of divines to Hampton Court in 1604 to prepare a new translation of the Bible that became known as the Authorized, or King James, version of the Bible, thereby insuring his name in Christian history for centuries.

England's old enemy, Spain, was expanding its claims in North America, and James could see that if the English were going to play on that field they'd better get their wickets in place. He gave his name to the Jamestown Colony in Virginia in 1606, replacing the earlier "Lost Colony" of Sir Walter Raleigh during Elizabeth's reign. Later he endorsed the founding of the Plimouth Plantation in Massachusetts, and populated it with Puritans. Closer to home he meditated upon Ireland, un-Reformed and still Catholic Ireland, and not likely to embrace Protestantism. Nine counties in northern Ireland already had several plantations of English landowners, and these counties seemed to be a likely place to begin the conversion of Ireland from Catholicism to Protestantism. These nine counties were known as Ulster, and it is here that the Scots-Irish come onstage.

Ulster: Planting The Stuart Seed of Discontent

JAMES' OPPORTUNITY CAME IN 1607, when the Irish earls of Tyrconnel and Tyrone fled from Ireland, justifiably sensing their lives to be in danger, following an Irish uprising in 1603. With them went nearly a hundred Irish chiefs of six of the nine Ulster counties. They were tried in absentia, and all were found guilty. The finding of guilt on the treason charges permitted James to exercise an ancient legal concept: whenever any land was abandoned, or when its owner didn't pay taxes or was found guilty of treason, the land was escheated to the Crown, and became the property of the king to do with as he pleased. James was

Atlantic
Ocean

DONEGAL

Lough
Foyle
Londonderry

LONDONDERRY

ANTRIM

TYRONE

Lough
Neagh

Lower
Lough
Erne

Belfast

Enniskillen

Strangford
Lough

FERMANAGH

ARMAGH

DOWN

Monaghan

MONAGHAN

Newry

CAVAN

Dundalk

Irish Sea

X

Drogheda

REPUBLIC

OF

IRELAND

River Boyne

Philip R. McCray

1989

Dublin

ULSTER TODAY

indeed pleased. He declared that the Counties Fermanagh, Armagh, Cavan, Donegal, Coleraine (later "Derry"), and Tyrone, were abandoned and escheated. Several Irish sub-chiefs protested, but they were waved aside and were told they were but tenants on the land that had been "owned" by Tyrone and Tyrconnel who had abandoned their lands. There was no appeal from the king's decisions.

James' plan was to plant English, Welsh and Scottish Protestants in Ireland, men of proven loyalty, who would set about to show the errant Irish the spiritual joys and practical advantages of being members of the Established Church of England. But he needed money to do this, for until the Irish had been shown the error of their ways, he'd need troops to persuade them to listen to reason. Parliament had always been stingy when it came to handing over money to its monarchs, and it had repeatedly refused James' pleas for money to maintain the court in a style to which James wished to become accustomed. He knew that if he could gain the assistance of the Scottish lords and lairds and the English lords and gentry, they could use their influence on his behalf. Parliament had gained control of the national purse over a century before, and it used this power to prevent English monarchs from getting too full of themselves and starting wars for unpopular causes.

But Parliament remained stubborn and refused the king's pleas for money. James did some more thinking and came up with a brilliant idea. Knowing something about using ambition to advantage and of man's longing for high station, he created a new heriditary title of "Baronet," a dignity between a barony and a knighthood that did not require that the recipient have royal blood flowing in his veins. For the first time, any well-off gentleman with funds who was confirmed to be a good Protestant could gain a title, be addressed as "Sir," and hang a crest in his great hall. All that was required was that he put up a thousand pounds, and it was put about that the monarch would smile gratefully upon any amounts in excess of that amount that applicants cared to offer. Over two hundred untitled, ambitious English landowner-climbers fattened up the royal exchequer by 225,000 pounds, a quite staggering sum of money in 1611. James announced his Great Plantation plan.

Applications poured in for the land in Ulster, and he began parceling it out to men he felt would administer the great estates in a way to bring Irish Catholicism down, as well as to bring in a great deal of new tax money. Since all the worthwhile land in Ulster was already occupied by Irishmen, the only thing to do was to drive them off the land and turn it over to the new arrivals. It was also necessary to have troops there and to require that the new tenants build forts or castles in order that English law and order be maintained.

The first settlers were from England, Wales and Scotland, but within a few years the greatest number of immigrants to Ireland were Scots. These Scots were exclusively Lowlanders; James didn't open any estates to

Highlanders because too many of them were Catholic or Catholic-inclined.
Besides, the Lowlanders were but a score of miles and a few hours sailing
time from Ireland, and they could better keep in touch with Britain's
main island.

The migrations to Ireland began in 1611 and continued for nearly
a century.

Scots occupied almost all of Counties Donegal and Tyrone; the English controlled Counties Armagh and Derry; Fermanagh and Cavan were a
mixture of Scots and English. Counties Down and Antrim had been planted
with English and Welsh settlers before 1611. Only County Monaghan remained almost exclusively Irish.

The rest of Ulster was parcelled out to three groups of grantees:
Undertakers, Servitors, and native Irish. Undertakers, mostly English,
could lease only to English and Scottish tenants, all of whom had to take
the Oath of Supremacy. Servitors, mainly Scots, were permitted to lease
land to a few Irish tenants, but they had to charge higher rents. A few
native Irishmen "of good merit" were made grantees, but they had to pay
rents twice as high as Undertakers, however they were excused from taking
the Oath. Undertakers and Servitors were required to build "bawns,"
fortified enclosures with a central stone building similar to a castle
keep or a fortified manor house.

Irish landowners were summarily displaced from their holdings, and
their lands were taken over by the newcomers. The Irish had never been
very wealthy, but they were now destitute. They became beggars, thieves,
or guerrillas, living in the hills from which they sallied forth period-
ically on raids against their usurpers. If the new arrivals hadn't heard
before of the Irish fighting spirit they soon learned about it. But the
Scots were accustomed to fending off English raiders during their lives
in Scotland, so there was nothing new about being raided by Irishmen,
and they quickly adapted to living on the green, moist soils of Ulster.

The Scots brought with them habits of hard work and self-discipline,
virtues they learned in Scotland, disregarding discomfort and danger with
stoicism. The Irish farmers had poor work habits and had not properly
cared for their farms. They worked fitfully and shoddily, getting very
poor yields on rich lands in a fine climate that should have made them
prosperous. The poverty of the Irish was equally matched by the poverty
of the Scots, but after a few years in Ireland they showed what hard
work and careful farming could accomplish. The Scots immediately saw
the possibilities in Ulster of having their dreams fulfilled; they would
be able to feed themselves and their families well, and perhaps to even
have some grain and wool left over to sell. Plants of all sorts grew
with enthusiasm, and there was plenty of good grazing land for both sheep
and cattle. The Scot's hunger for land that drove him to Ireland never
left him, and if his conscience was disturbed by driving an Irishman off

of his land and impoverishing him, it didn't bother him enough to prevent
him from doing the same thing later to Indians in America.

Much of northern Ireland then was still quite wild, and the Scots had to
defend themselves not only against the enraged Irish, but also against
a now-extinct species of wolf, a great shaggy predator who would as soon
hunt down a man as a sheep. Even with an offered bounty of six pounds
for heads of female wolves, it was 150 years before the last wolf was
hunted down and the Irish wolfhound became a domestic pet.

Except for a few glitches, the Ulster Plantation was, right from the
start, a huge success, at least from the English viewpoint. Some of the
settlers were incompetent farmers, and their holdings failed. Some English grantees found that they missed English life and culture, so they
hired overseers to manage their Irish estates, and returned home. They
forgot about the people and their problems that they left behind across
the Irish Sea, and were reminded of them only on days when the rent money
arrived. Owner isolation from the day-to-day problems on their estates
made for hard feelings on the part of the farmers who had no one to whom
they could explain problems that required money to solve.

King James and his Privy Council did little to build better relations between England and Ireland. In spite of a number of ways in
which Irish gentry had contributed to the success of the venture by assisting in maintaining peace and good order, they were treated with con-
tempt, and were referred to as "meer Irish." The English government
might well have made it a bit easier for the transplanted Protestants
with some restraint and regard for human natural goodness, but English
policies brought only stiffened Irish resistance.

The Presbyterian Scot

THE STORY OF THE SCOTS-IRISH is inseperable from the story of the
origin and development of the Presbyterian Church. Not all Ulster Scots
may have been Presbyterian, but so great a proportion of them were that
one needs to understand the nature of the early Presbyterian Church to
gain any understanding of the nature of the Ulster Scot. When he came to
America he brought with him not only the church, but a way of thinking
that was associated with subscribers to the Presbyterian faith.

The Presbyterian Church was born in Scotland in fire and blood, and
as in the aftermath of most revolutions, the new church was, if anything,
more intolerant, bigoted and tyrannical than the ancient Roman Catholic
Church it replaced. The early Scottish Presbyterian was a prototype of
the Puritan who later ruled the Plymouth Colony in Massachusetts. He devoted himself totally to the worship of God without the intercession of
priests in a church building deliberately made as unattractive and uncomfortable as possible. Ministers were enjoined to live and dress as

10

simply as possible, and to teach their parishioners to do likewise. No musical instruments were used to accompany hymn-singing, and one of the differences within the church was whether the clergy should wear the black Geneva gown in the pulpit. It was argued that in the strictest sense (and the strictest sense was always the preferred sense) the Geneva gown was decorative, with a vague resemblence to a priest's robe. The gowns won that one.

Jock took to the discipline and tyranny of his kirk with excited enthusiasm. For the first time he was given something for his facile brain to really mull over. All the new and revolutionary religious ideas that swept Europe never disturbed him. Jock heard little about them, never gave them a moment's thought, and probably would have rejected them if he had. All day Sunday he listened to several hours of long sermons, and all week following he and his fellow parishioners discussed and debated them in the greatest detail. A new spirit of rightousness pervaded Scotland, and sin was not only frowned upon but was punished, often as severely as by hanging. Church law was largely based on Old Testament edicts and it included burning of witches. Religious zeal flourished, but the fun of life was gone. Jock earned with a vengeance the term, "dour Scot."

The Scottish Presbyterian was not greatly different from the Puritans, with whom the Kirk had many clashes, ultimately to be cruelly dealt with by the epitome of Puritanism, Oliver Cromwell. Puritans wanted neither bishops nor synods, and for him each man was his own minister. They were characterized by intense zeal for reform, even where common sense would see no need for reform, a zeal to order everything about him including his personal life, family life, worship, church, business, political views, and even recreation, as God would have them do--as they saw what God demanded.

The Kirk set itself toward two goals: to abolish illiteracy and to correct immorality. John Knox declared it was every Christian's duty to learn to read The Word, so he could learn the truth for himself, rather than have it sung to him in Latin at Mass. Wealth seized from the Catholic churches was used to build the world's first free public schools, and Scotland today has some of the finest schools in the western world. The Kirk set out to eliminate all vestiges of Catholicism: clerical robes, the Mass, choirs and choir boys, kneeling at prayer, confession to priests, and the inerrancy of a Pope. It is often said of James I that he had many leanings toward Catholic forms and litany even while protesting his devout Protestantism. As head of the Church of England, he found it useful to have the power to appoint bishops and archbishops, and the sturdy independence of the Kirk irked him, and he repeatedly asserted his authority as head of the Scottish church. He faced open revolt when he tried to introduce white surplices in place of the Genevan gown, kneeling at prayer, and chanting choirs. When he tried to install bishops,

11

bishops whom he appointed, the Scots simply refused to obey any of his
religious edicts. To the new Scot, kneeling at prayer was a popish
abomination. A devout Christian Scot, he believed, should stand fully
erect with face turned heavenward, confessing his sins out loud in his
own words to God, and pleading for forgiveness for his trespasses. Man,
he said, was made in the image of God who never intended that men should
abase themselves by kneeling in prayer.

Many Scottish clergymen couldn't stomach these new "reversions to
popery" which James insisted upon, and they left Scotland to join their
Lowland parishioners in Ulster, where they were welcomed with open arms.
Their arrival spurred more Scots to join the migration, and by 1640 it
has been estimated that over 40,000 of them were in Ulster.

Presbyterian churches and congregations grew rapidly, and the stern
discipline of Presbyterianism became the watchdog of Scottish communities
in Ulster. Church sessions acted not only as discipliners of those in
spiritual error, they had some of the functions of modern police forces
in dealing with some misdemeanors, and they dealt with such things as
debauchery and small theft.

James proclaimed the Church of England to be the Established Church
of Ireland. Puritans held a majority in Parliament, and James had to
make some accommodation to these numerous and powerful men. James named
a number of Puritans to bishoprics and then sent them as Puritan/Episco-
pal bishops to Ulster to direct the Established Church there. Still,
Presbyterians held a decided majority in Ulster, so the bishops and the
Presbyterians reached a curious accommodation; the Presbyterian ministers
accepted ordination from Church of England bishops, and having gone that
far, and no further, in adjustment of their otherwise unassailable Presbyterian scruples, they were then allowed to retain the Presbyterian
liturgy and receive tithes in the names of their sessions. The Church
of England, in turn, quite gravely regarded the Presbyterian clergymen
as equals to the Episcopal clergymen.

King James was in many respects an able leader, although he was
never able to lead Scotland, nor the transplanted Scots in Ulster, to go
along with his notion that all churches in the realm should either be
Anglican or be governed by a church hierarchy that reported to him. He
never trusted Highlanders enough to grant Ulster lands to them because
many of them were Catholic or favored it*. He made a number of attempts
to force, or to lead, Presbyterians into acceptance of Anglican forms

* There may have been exceptions to this, but I believe that we McCrays
may not be really true to our heritage when we sing, "My Heart's In The
Highlands." It remains for someone to prove to me that the McCrays,
McCreas, McCraes, et al are directly related to the Highland MacRaes of
Castle Eilean Donan on the shore of Loch Duich.

and government, but he was too wise to try to "reform" the Kirk by force of arms, thereby risking the failure of the Ulster plantation scheme.

But the Ulster Plantation was succeeding as well as he could hope for, save that Irishmen were still as Catholic as ever and were a more bitter foe than ever. For the Ulster Scot things were going swimmingly; he had a good farm to work, he was learning to read and write, thanks to his beloved Presbyterian Church, and he prospered materially. As he prospered, taxes rolled in from Ulster to the coffers at Whitehall, and both James and Parliament smiled exceedingly as more and more hardworking Scots made their way to Ulster.

Little things sometimes have large effects on the lives of men. History isn't only Hastings in 1066, or Lexington and Concord in 1775. Who would have ever dreamed that the potato, introduced probably into Spanish gardens in mid-sixteenth century from South America as an aphrodesiac, would be instrumental in destroying the last vestiges of feudalism in Europe, and especially in Ireland, where it became known as the "Irish Potato?" The tuber seemed to have found its home in Ireland, where the soil and climate was exactly right for it to thrive, and it became the peasant's ticket to freedom.

Until the potato and its virtues were discovered, feudal peasants and their families barely survived on their crops of grains, of which they kept very little for their own use. Most of it was given to the lord of the manor as rent and to the church as tithes. Because water was often unfit to drink, a good bit of the grain went into home-brewed beer, which was drunk by all the family. Another substantial portion had to be saved as seed for the next year. The amount left for food was generally hardly enough to last until the next harvest, and the peasants would sometimes, in order to prevent starvation, risk summary execution by poaching game or fish from the estates of nobles.

The lowly spud changed all that. For the first time a highly nutritious food became available that was easily raised in quantity by fewer farmers with less effort, and it drove the final nail into the coffin of feudalism by freeing peasants from the full-time slavery of raising subsistence crops. The peasant could now turn his attention to profitable crops that provided cash, and to animal husbandry and cottage industries. By hard work and industry a peasant could now obtain enough money to buy a farm tract and to leave serfdom forever behind him.

Cattle and sheep raising also thrived. Woolen mills and dairy processing plants opened, and this spurred shipbuilding, so goods could be sent to England and the American colonies in Irish bottoms, and return with sugar from the West Indies.

So radically was the average Scot's situation changed by his move to Ulster that he no longer regarded himself as a Scot, but as an Irishman, and he so declared himself to be, although a Protestant Irishman. When he came to America he came as an Irishman, not a Scot, and he was usually so regarded by Colonists. The appellation "Scotch-Irish" was not used until many years after the American Revolution, and was then regarded as a derogatory term. It is unknown today in Britain by most people, and it causes raised eyebrows and questions when Americans use it.

The English Parliament came to regard the Ulster Scot as a colonist and not a true British subject. In the English mind, colonists could sell to Englishmen only things they either didn't want to make themselves, or such raw goods as England needed to make finished goods to sell to Colonists. It was thought that it really wasn't proper for colonists to compete with English merchants, especially if it put the English merchants at a disadvantage. Parliament never could decide just what status to assign to Ireland; it was not quite a colony like the American colonies, nor was it a part of the British nation, as were Wales and Scotland (and they weren't too certain about Scotland). Parliament simply shrugged off its responsibility to deal with the matter of Ireland.

At the death of James I in 1625 the Ulster Plantation scheme was an economic success. As for the original idea of planting Protestantism in Ireland, there were plenty of Protestants in Ulster but they were all Scots and a few English and Welsh people, and almost no Irish had converted to Protestantism, nor was there any indication that they were going to abandon the Roman Church anytime in the foreseeable future.

Charles I, The Unhappy Monarch

CHARLES I BECAME KING OF GREAT BRITAIN only because he couldn't see any way to get out of it. Unlike his father, James I, he did not enjoy ruling or making serious decisions. He had a slight stammer and his shy manner struck observers as being silent and reserved, but his good disposition, courteous manners and lack of vices made him welcome as a relief from his father's crudeness. As a child he had been isolated from his father by his Calvinist teachers, and he grew up as a sickly and lonely young man who had little contact with the common people of Scotland. He made few friends, and many enemies, and the friends he had failed to serve him well.

While he was still Prince of Wales, he and his bosom friend, George Villiers, 1st Duke of Buckingham, made an incognito trip to Spain in search of a suitable wife for Charles. They had in mind the daughter of the king, but the infanta was immediately repelled by Charles--short Charles, who was but five feet, four inches tall--who was, worst of all, a Protestant. Negotiations with the king stalled when the Spanish government made it clear that whoever married the infanta was going to be--had to be--Catholic. Charles and Buckingham, highly offended that anyone would think that the heir to the British monarchy was unsuitable for any European princess, sailed for England in high dudgeon. There, they persuaded James I, now sick and probably a bit deranged, to renew the war with Spain. Later he married Henrietta Marie, a French Catholic.

14

His reign didn't get off to a good start. He managed to get France into the war with Spain, so now England had two enemies to deal with. Puritans, who dominated Parliament, were not pleased with their new king, for he had a Catholic queen, had re-asserted the Divine Right of Kings, demanded, rather than requested, funds, and had brought along Buckingham as his principal advisor, the same Buckingham who had been James I's favorite "pretty boy." The power of the Treasury had been seized by Parliament during Henry VIII's reign, and it had since then always granted the monarch the tax collected by "tonnage and poundage" (custom duties). The year after Charles became king Parliament refused Charles his tonnage and poundage. Charles used the only weapon he had by dissolving Parliament, a strategy he used three more times to stop Parliament from having its way with him. For eleven years he ruled alone, obtaining funds from tonnage and poundage without parliamentary consent.

He had other quarrels with Parliament over religious questions, such as whether the church should preach free will or predestination. Charles preferred high church services that were thought of by Puritans as neo-Catholic. He determined to force the Kirk to conform to episcopal forms of worship and government, and while he realized he could do little against the powerful Puritans, he could bring Presbyterians to heel. There were Presbyterians in Ireland, too, and he targeted them.

Buckingham directed the campaigns against France and Spain, and the Puritans tried more than once to impeach him. Buckingham was assassinated (nobody seemed to know whodunit), Charles was destitute over the loss of his friend, but he soon turned to another friend, Thomas Viscount Wentworth, brought him to court and raised him to the peerage, with the title of Lord President of the Council of the North. While Charles marched off to Scotland, he sent Wentworth to Ireland with the title of Lord Deputy. The title of "Governor" would have done just as well. Wentworth disliked both Presbyterians and Puritans. Charles disliked Wentworth for his crudeness and lack of manners, but he wanted someone in Ireland to enforce episcopy, and also to suppress Irish troublemakers. Wentworth, he knew, would stop at nothing to carry out such an assignment.

Wentworth, a Yorkshireman, was exactly the man Charles needed to enforce his edicts upon the Presbyterians in Ireland. Known as "Black Tom," he had a talent for carrying out dirty work that most men would turn away from. Morality, justice, kindness were foreign to him. All that mattered was that he carry out his orders, and if rape and pillage were the instruments to accomplish his goal, he didn't flinch from using them. Accounts of his day tell of his gout-twisted body, supported by a great stick he always carried. Cavernous eyes blazed out from under shaggy brows, and the skin on his flushed face looked like soiled parchment. He knew all that bribery, intimidation or violence could accomplish for a weak master who never asked how he succeeded, but only if he did succeed. Wentworth's virtues were his total loyalty to his master and his dedication to whatever cruel work he was ordered to do.

He hoped to destroy Presbyteriansim and Catholicism in Ireland and
to make Ireland wealthy in order to enrich his royal master through taxes,
and at the same time to be hatchet man for Archbishop Laud, a kindred
soul, and for him he would enforce conformity to the letter of the Established Church of Ireland (Anglican). He instituted a Star Chamber Court
in Dublin for more expeditious punishment of troublesome Irish Catholics
and Protestant dissidents (read, "Presbyterians."). He issued an edict
that all males in Ireland over age sixteen were required to swear they
would obey all of King Charles' commands, and also that they disapproved
of Scottish rebellion against episcopacy in the Kirk. Anyone could have
predicted that the required oath would generate not a whit of cheerful
obedience, but would only cause a sullen and perfunctory compliance,
with plenty of underground non-conformance.

Wentworth's motive for making Ireland wealthy was not inspired by
his admiration for the Irish, whom he hated, but to fatten the purse at
Whitehall. Whether or not Parliament would pass any of it along to the
King was not his worry. He had already prohibited the manufacture of
woolen cloth in Ireland, allowing only shipment of raw wool to England,
and then seeing that this prohibition, while helping English weavers,
would ruin the rapidly developing and successful industry that had generated considerable tax money, he bought with his own money flax seed
from Holland, built linen mills, and recruited linen workers from the Low
Countries. Two decades of depression settled upon Ireland while the conversion was being made from wool to linen. It eventually prospered greatly, and Irish linen became a much sought-after commodity in the world.

It should be remembered that linen was used far more than was cotton
for cloth. Cotton cloth was a luxury, costly because the only known way
to remove cottonseed was by hand-picking. Linen was used almost uni-
versally for clothing, sails, wall coverings, and wherever cloth was
needed. The invention of the cotton gin in America in 1793 changed this.

Meanwhile, back in England, Charles had need of a churchman holding
his views to help in dealing with Parliament. William Laud suited him
admirably. Laud, Bishop of Bath and Wells, had long advocated the "divine right of kings" theory, and had also taken an early dislike to Puritans. It was an unfortunate choice, for Laud set the stage for the event-
ual execution of his king at Horse Guards Parade in London. He immediately forbad the printing of anything advocating or helping Puritanism,
quoting a law from Queen Elizabeth's reign that required that all books
be approved by the Archbishop of Canterbury, and this was the office given
to him by Charles. He changed the order of Church of England services to
remove aspects of Calvinism and to replace them with high church forms.
He made life so hard for Puritans that more than 20,000 of them fled to
America and joined the Pilgrims there in Massachussetts, which had the
effect of creating a sort of political border between the French in Canada and the English below the Great Lakes. Laud and Charles set out to
reform the Kirk in Scotland, and to force the Kirk to adopt many Anglican
forms.

Wentworth in Ireland and Laud in London made up the terrible two-
some of the time. Both were completely honorable, in that they never conspired against the king or the law, and they never did anything that was
not sanctioned by civil or church law, but this virtue they both turned
into despotism. It was said that "The courtiers hated them for their
virtues and the people for their faults." They prevailed for some time
only because they had the unswerving support of Charles, but their power
eventually was poured out in their blood at Tower Hill.

Charles and Laud, together with four Scottish (Anglican) bishops,
sat down together and prepared a new ritual and a new prayer book based
on the English book of prayer. The new order of service was for the Kirk,
like it or not, to use in Presbyterian services, discarding Knox's *Book
of Common Order*. Treveyland said: "It was an order in no veiled terms that
Scotland should be Scotland no more." The Kirk didn't like it, the Scots
everywhere but in the Highlands didn't like it, and nobody obeyed it. Laud
and Charles tried negotiations and encountered a Scottish stone wall.
After a year of futile dickering, in 1638 Charles decided to conquer
Scotland by arms. This was a case where somebody gave a war and nobody
came. The First Bishops' War was a total failure. Charles rode up and
down from London to Yorkshire trying to rally support, but nobody was interested in this foolishness.

Wentworth in Ireland conceived an idea of how to help his king in
his troubles with Scotland. He raised an army of 9,000 Irish Catholics,
and armed them. His plan was to join with Charles' forces in England and
march against Scotland whenever Charles gave a signal that the invasion
was to begin. When Charles' attempts to raise an English army failed,
he sent word to Wentworth to return to England to act as chief counsellor
for the king. He probably couldn't have chosen a worse helper. He made
Wentworth earl of Strafford; the name "Strafford" has never been forgotten in Ireland, and is brought up whenever Irish people think of their
oppression by England. Parliament was rightfully alarmed about the army
in Ireland that Wentworth had raised and left behind without English
leadership, and they wanted to question him about his way of trying and
imprisoning dissidents in Ireland without following English systems of
fair trial. Bishops sent to Ireland to convert the Irish had enriched
themselves at the expense of the native Irish, and as far as converting
them, the bishops couldn't even speak their language. Wentworth had managed to largely destroy the Irish merchant class in the seacoast cities,
and the domino effect of the decay of shipping and manufacturing soon
caused general depression throughout the land, including Ulster.

Archbishop Laud had single-handedly drained away all joy and meaning
from the Anglican service by making it all ritual and no spirit. His
use of the Court of High Commission, acting as the ecclesiastical arm of
royal authority, had effectively closed down all printing except for that
which pleased him. He took upon himself the tight supervision of all the

17

bishops, looking over their shoulders and questioning their every move. He only wanted to have things rightly done, but he only succeeded in turning his bishops into his enemies. It was later to cost him his life.

Scotland's Kirk was more than an annoyance to Charles for its stubborn refusal to reorganize and become more like the English church. Charles thought the Scots were intractable, they thought Charles was intransigent, and both sides resembled a pair of stubborn mules. When Charles ordered the Kirk to implement Laud's Book of Canons and Liturgy, Scottish leaders formed a National Covenant and swore they would never adopt any popish forms of worship. Charles then swore he'd have his way in Scotland, and marched off with an army for Edinburgh, where a well-trained Scottish army sent the English back across the border in panic.

Charles then recalled Wentworth from Ireland where he had just raised an army of 9,000 Catholic Irishmen, should Charles want to use them against the Scots. Anyone should have guessed what would happen if 9,000 Catholic Irishmen were left unguarded, fully armed, and long hoping for revenge against the English.

Upon his return, Charles elevated Wentworth's rank to earl of Straford, and begged his advice on how to deal with Scotland, and to somehow persuade Parliament to grant Charles a larger purse. The two of them soon discovered that not only did Strafford have no influence with Parliament, but that there wasn't going to be any money forthcoming. Strafford sent out press gangs to raise an army of unwilling English peasants, but they revolted, burned a lot of churches and property and then scattered. A rag-tag English army headed a second time for Scotland and again were ignominiously defeated.

Now Charles was desperate, and called Parliament back to London. He then spoke firmly to them, instructing them in their duty to promptly get up the money he needed to force Scotland to yield and conform. Instead, they impeached Strafford, clapped him in the tower, and when rioting mobs in London demanded his death, they drew up a bill of attainder, and Charles reluctantly signed it. In May, 1641, Strafford watched through a window as workmen erected a scaffold on the green outside the Tower of London upon which he was beheaded. Archbishop Laud suffered the same fate nine months later on the same scaffold.

The Irish Rebellion And Cromwell

IN 1641, AFTER WENTWORTH'S DEATH, while King Charles was embroiled with Puritans in Parliament and with rebellious Scottish Covenanters, Ireland's smoldering anger against the English interlopers came to a head and rebellion erupted. Incited by injustices committed against them by English and Scottish invaders over the previous hundred years, all the seized properties, all the starvation, all the killing, finally goaded the half-wild population finally to unite against it all.

The army Wentworth had raised and armed was the rallying point for thousands of angry Irishmen. The population swarmed out of hillside caves and thatched hovels like angry hornets to take back all of Ireland and to kill and drive out the hated English "heretics. Irish leaders such as Sir Pheline O'Neill and Rory O'More came forth, and from foreign lands where other clan chiefs had fled for their lives, came grim old warriors who were ready to bury old grudges against each other and take up the fight. Their anger was directed mainly toward the English, but it didn't take much persuading to include the Ulster Scots.

Parliament in London responded by subscribing a million pounds to raise a great army, the bonds to be paid back by grants of Irish lands after the rebellion had been suppressed. News of this in Ireland raised anger to new heights, and the following rumor that an army of Scottish Covenenters, who had two years before pledged to root out popery wherever it could be found, was about to embark for Ireland, convinced every Irishman that his land, his religion and his very life was at stake. In fact, such an army was dispatched from Scotland later in the rebellion, which lasted eleven years.

First to feel the wrath of the Irish Catholics were English planters in the south-central parts of Ulster. Hundreds of English Protestants were slaughtered, men, women and children, without mercy. The Scots, who had no use for English Protestants, did not come to their aid, but instead spent time while the English were being killed in preparing their own defenses. When the Irish turned their attention to the Scots in the rest of Ulster they got no help from the English who had themselves escaped the butchery. Estimates of the dead seem to agree that about one-seventh of the Ulster Scots were killed before 1650, when Oliver Cromwell came with an army and showed the Irish what cruelty was all about.

Cromwell, a farmer with no military training, was elected to Parliament from the Borough of Nottingham when he was age 41. The only speech he is known to have made there was an attack upon bishops. From the first he took an active part in any action against any kind of ritualism in churches, and he joined a party to obtain a bill to strip the king of royal prerogatives and to abolish archbishops, bishops and others of the hierarchy of the Church of England.

Relations between King Charles and Parliament went from bad to worse. The two Bishops' Wars had not changed the Kirk a whit, Charles was nearly broke, and all he could do was to go to a hostile Parliament and beg for money. He could have saved his breath, for Parliament was busy preparing a Grand Remonstrance, a long list of complaints of things gone wrong. Parliament demanded control of the large army that had been raised to combat the Irish Rebellion, fearing that the army could be used against Parliament instead. To this Charles exclaimed "By God, not for an hour!". After a failed attempt to have six Parliamentarians arrested in 1642, Charles fled to York, and Queen Henrietta fled to Holland to sell her jewels to buy arms for the Royalist cause.

Cromwell's moment in history came in 1643 when the English Civil War broke out. England was divided between the Royalists and the Parliamentarians, or Roundheads. Detailed accounts of the Civil War can leave students glassy-eyed, but in this account it is sufficient to say that Charles was captured in 1647, tried in Westminster Hall in 1648, and executed on a scaffold in Whitehall in January, 1649. Today's tourists engaged in brainless efforts to coax smiles from young Horse Guards mounted on glossy black horses before the old guardhouse gate to Westminster Palace seldom know that three hundred years before the crowd's attention was opposite, across the street, where the bloody death of the last British monarch by execution occurred, or that the frozen mounted guards were originally Cromwell's guards.

Cromwell was now in charge of things without having been proclaimed, appointed or elected. He just took over because nobody opposed him. He proclaimed a republic, appointed a skeleton government, and set out with a Roundhead army for Ireland to deal with the rebellion there. He wasted no time in "wasting" several garrisons and putting to the sword those who opposed him. His butchery struck terror into the Irish, and they surrendered everywhere without resistance. The cruel violence employed would have been the envy of Adolf Hitler. Over 600,000 had been killed, and over 500,000 of them were Irish. The remainder were Ulster Scots, who had supported King Charles. After the killing stopped, tens of thousands of Irish fled to foreign countries and thousands more were deported to virtual slavery in the sugar plantations of the West Indies.

Cromwell then turned his malevolent eye upon Presbyterians. Some lands were seized, a few were transported, but without explanation, repressive measures were dropped, and by 1660 it was reported that 80,000 Scots were in Ulster, and generally doing very well.

Oliver Cromwell died in 1658, and was interred in Westminster Abbey. His son, Richard, attempted to keep the Protectorate in operation, but it was clear that the English people had had quite enough of Puritanism and the dour lifestyle that it imposed on the land. They wanted a king once more and Charles, son of Charles I, came down to Londontown from Scotland amidst great rejoicing. Taverns rolled out the barrel and the bottle once more, theaters reopened after eleven years of darkness, music and dance was in the land again, and England was once again merry. Puritanism went into decline, and gaity reigned once more in the royal court.

Extremists dug up Cromwell's remains from Westminster Abbey's Poet's Corner and set his head on a pike on London Bridge. After things settled down a bit, his remains were collected and re-interred in Westminster Abbey, where they remain today among England's great. Thus ended Britain's one experiment with the republican form of government.

The Merry Monarch, Charles II

        BY 1640 CHARLES I COULD SEE THAT THE MONARCHY WAS IN TROUBLE, and he
sent his son, Charles Prince of Wales off to France to live, with instruc-
tions to prepare himself to someday return to England as King Charles II.
It was only natural that he would become a Catholic, since Catholicism
was the established faith of France and anyone who was anyone there was
Catholic. He learned to love the life of gaity and sophistication of the
French court, and he also studied kingship and fully intended to one day
be England's monarch. During the Commonwealth he went to Scotland where
he was hailed as the true king, Charles II. Then he waited. He was
called to England in 1660, to the delight of everyone, including himself.

        After the first euphoria cleared Parliament began to look critically
at things in the palace. Charles was not openly Catholic, and nobody
seems to have ever asked him about it, but there was talk...added to the
suspicions about Charles, his brother, James, Duke of York, was openly and
avowedly a Catholic, and more than one bill was brought before Parliament
to prevent James from succeeding to the throne, but Charles managed to
head off these laws. As far as Ireland and the Ulster Scots were concerned, Charles wasn't interested in making things tough for them; while
he was living in Scotland the Presbyterians had unreservedly backed him,
and he may have been grateful for this. At any rate, he left Ulster to
its own devices, and things were going very well there.

        Charles was a patron of the arts and brought Rubens to London to
paint the magnificent ceiling at his Banquetting Hall. He also collected
several mistresses, most notably Nell Gwynn, formerly a sort-of Eliza
Doolittle selling oranges in the streets of London. On May 29 of each
year the military pensioners of the Royal Hospital in Chelsea gather on
the green wearing their distinctive red jackets, with a sprig of oak in
their lapels in rememberance of Charles having hidden in an oak to avoid
capture after the Battle of Worcester. There they give three cheers for
King Charles, founder of their retirement home in Chelsea. They really
should also give three more cheers for Nell Gwynn, for it was she who
persuaded Charles to build the hospital for retired veterans of the Civil
Wars after a ragged old soldier begged alms from her one day on a street
of London.

        In 1673 Parliament enacted the infamous Test Act, "the black charter
of English Protestantism", which forbad anyone who would not take the sac-
rament by the rites of the Church of England to hold civil or military
office. It was intended to sniff out Catholics in public office, which it
did do, at least partly. Among those removed from office was Charles'
brother, the Duke of York, who had commanded the navy as Lord of Admiralty
It was the Duke who threatened to bombard Niew Amsterdam unless the Dutch
handed it over to the British, and it was he who re-named the city New
York, not for the city of York, but for his very own royal self. More on

him later. The Test Act was used against not only Catholics but Presbyterians as well, especially those in Ulster, where most of the civic of-
fice-holders were Presbyterians, and a number of them held military rank
as well.

The prosperity that Ulster was enjoying had its downside. Parliament
was made up mostly of rising merchants and industrialists, and seeing
that Ulster was prospering to the disadvantage of England, it passed laws
forbidding the shipment of finished goods and raw materials to England in
Irish ships. This was a severe blow to Irish shipping interests in Dublin and Belfast, who already had been forbidden to sell finished goods to
any of the colonies. A few years later it was forbidden to ship cattle
from Ireland to England, an act which totally destroyed the thriving cattle
business in Ireland. Although the people on Ulster plantations were
British subjects in every sense, the merchant class of England was more
and more viewing them as colonists, and colonists were not allowed to compete with English businesses.

Still, things were going quite well for the Scots in Ulster. They
were industrious and the Irish soil yielded bountiful crops, and they
prospered economically, even though they had suffered many repressions
because of their stubborn Presbyterianism. But suddenly, things became
very bad for them. King Charles II died in 1685, having been received
into the Roman Catholic faith as he lay dying. In spite of Parliament's
efforts to prevent it, James, Duke of York, became James II.

James II, The Last Catholic English Monarch

BECAUSE CHARLES II DIED WITHOUT SONS OR DAUGHTERS, his brother,
James, succeeded him to the throne. He came to power full of suspicion
of everyone at court, and he expected to find an assassin behind every
door. He was emotionally disturbed, oversexed, arrogant and haughty, and
worst of all for his subjects, openly a Catholic. He was married to Mary
of Modena (Italy), who was a Roman Catholic, and he made it clear from
the start that he intended to make Catholics and Protestant dissenters
equal in all respects to Anglicans.

Parliament, which had done all it could to prevent him from having
the monarchy, was determined to give him a fair trial as king, and voted
him a generous purse. James, rather than being grateful, accepted it as
his due. He systematically replaced Protestant military officers with
Catholic men, in direct violation of the two Test Acts that specifically
forbad it, an act that startled even his supporters in Parliament. His
illigitimate son, the Duke of Monmouth, believing that the country would
refuse to obey a Catholic king, staged an armed revolt, but it was easily
suppressed.

One of James' first acts was to recall James Butler, Duke of Ormonde, and Lord Lieutenant of Ireland, a Protestant who had served Charles I since 1641. He replaced him with his brother-in-law (through his first wife) Henry Hyde, earl of Clarendon, and also a Protestant, but still, sort-of kin, in a manner of speaking. His ultimate goal was, of course, to put Catholics in all important posts, and after thinking it over he recalled Clarendon. He'd found just the man for the job in Ireland.

Richard Talbot, a real hatchet-man, Irish Catholic and earl of Tyrconnell, was James' choice to replace Clarendon. Known around court circles as "Lying Richard," he was disliked and distrusted by everyone at court, but he shared a characteristic with James that attracted them to each other. Neither of them trusted each other nor anyone else. James knew Tyrconnel was the man needed in Ireland to drive out the Protestants. As we sometimes say today: "It takes one to know one."

English statesman and writer Lord Macaulay wrote this colorful description of Tyrconnel and his time:*

> "Tyrconnel sprang from one of those degenerate families of the Pale which were popularly classed with the aboriginal population of Ireland. He sometimes, indeed, in his rants, talked with Norman haughtiness of the Celtic barbarians: but all his sympathies were really with the natives. The Protestant colonists he hated; and they returned his hatred.

> "A royal order came from Whitehall for disarming the population. This order Tyrconnel strictly executed as respected the English (Macaulay included all Scottish, Welsh and English settlers in Ulster). Though the country was infested with predatory bands, a Protestant gentleman could scarcely obtain permission to keep a brace of pistols. The native peasantry, on the other hand, were suffered to retain their weapons.

> "He pushed on the remodelling of the army eagerly and indefatigably. The ranks were completely broken up and recomposed. Four of five hundred soldiers were turned out of a single regiment chiefly on the ground that they were below the proper stature. Yet the most unpractised eye at once perceived that they were taller and better made men than their successors. Orders were given to the new officers that no man of the Protestant religion was to be suffered to enlist.

* *History Of England*, Thomas Babbington, first Baron Macaulay, London 1848.

"Their places were supplied by men who had no recommendations but their religion. Of the new Captains and Lieutenants, it was said, some had been cowherds, some footmen, some noted marauders; some had been so used to wear brogues that they stumbled and shuffled about strangely in their military jackboots. Not a few of the officers who were discarded took refuge in the Dutch service, and enjoyed, four years later, the pleasure of driving their successors before them in ignominious route through the waters of the Boyne.

"'There is work to be done in Ireland', said James, 'which no Englishman will do.' All obstacles were at length removed; and in February, 1687, Tyrconnel began to rule his native country with the power and appointments of Lord Lieutenant, but with the humbler title of Lord Deputy.

"His arrival spread dismay through the whole English population. A large proportion of the most respectable inhabitants of Dublin, together with gentlemen, tradesmen and artificers, went across St. George's Channel. It was said that fifteen hundred families emigrated in a few days. The panic was not unreasonable. The work of putting the colonists down under the feet of the natives went rapidly on. In a short time almost every Privy Councillor, Judge, Sheriff, Mayor, Alderman, and Justice of the Peace was a Celt and a Roman Catholic."

The reign of James II mercifully lasted but three years. He was, in spite of many doubts in the minds of members of Parliament and the general population, given a royal welcome at his accession, but his paranoia led him to suspect it was all a sham to throw him off guard. He seemed bent on self-destruction. He dismissed all Protestant ministers who constituted the government's administration and national defense. He drove Scotland to revolt. Mary Modena, his second queen, and a cadre of priests forced him to dismiss his Protestant mistress, the Countess of Dorchester, which may or may not have had something to do with the fact that Queen Mary bore James a son soon afterward. He quarrelled violently with William of Orange because William refused James' demand that he appoint a Catholic to command British regiments in Holland, and to hand over the Scots and English refugees there who fled to avoid James' wrath. He issued the Edict of Toleration (of Catholics) and imprisoned the Archbishop of Canterbury and six bishops who refused to read the edict from their pulpits.

Of all the things he did to turn the country totally against him, the final straw was his bringing an army of Irish Catholics to England to protect him and to enforce his pro-Catholic edicts. A number of the nobles James had dismissed met secretly and sent an invitation to William, son of William of Orange, in Holland to bring an army and become

24

joint monarch with his wife, Mary, the first daughter born to Anne Hyde, James II's first wife. A second daughter, Anne, was destined to rule as the last Stuart monarch in the next century.

William gathered his army and sailed for England, easily avoiding a fleet out to intercept him, and landed at Torbay, on the English Channel coast, in November of 1688. He encountered no resistance and slowly set out for London, avoiding contact with James' troops. He gambled on the liklihood that their loyalty to James was shaky at best. He took a month to march to London--really, "marching" doesn't describe the event. It was more like strolling. Before he arrived there, James' most valuable man, Churchill, joined William; the navy also threw in with the rebellion, his daughter, Anne, joined the rebellious gentry in Nottingham, and James decided it was time to leave. He slipped down the Thames, but at Rochester was captured by a crowd of angry Kentish men. William, well aware of his "escape" and only wanting to be rid of him, allowed a second escape, and James made his way to Dover and crossed to France. Treasure hunters still seek the jewel-encrusted Royal Scepter James took with him and clumsily dropped overboard in the Thames.

Tyrconnel in Ireland kept the pot boiling. He sent a proposal to James in France that James should collect an army of French Catholics and sail to Ireland. There they would conquer the Protestants in Ireland, enlarge their joint forces with thousands of Irish Catholics who, he assured James, would flock to their colors. James thought it was a smashing idea, and he then persuaded the French King Louis XIV to help make Ireland a totally Catholic nation once more.

Leaders of Parliament had supposed that William would serve as consort or regent, but William made it clear that he would be King William III or nothing. Mary's claim to the throne was unquestioned, but thinking of Elizabeth a century before, stated she would not reign alone, but only jointly with William, keeping in mind Paul's admonition; "Wives, be obedient to your husbands in all things." It was a done deal. James sent word from France that he disowned her. Her father's act so deeply distressed her that she was almost immediately aged. This shows in her final portraits, and at age 33 she died of smallpox, after only four years as Queen.

Tyrconnel recruited more Catholic Irishmen into his army and started marching north. The Ulster Protestants had been getting rumors that a new Irish rebellion was about to erupt, and they had gathered, with all the arms, food and medicines they had, into Einskillen and Londonderry. As they left their farms and moved into these walled cities they burned everything that could be used by invaders. They placed cannons at the ports in the walls, deployed their men, and waited.

James and a French army landed at Dublin and marched off to join Tyrconnel's troops who had surrounded Londonderry, and the seige was on. The city and its Protestant beseiged people were outgunned and outnumbered, but they fought grimly on, day after day. Many died and much of Londonderry was destroyed by shot, shell and fire, and still they resisted. The world has wondered how they managed to hold out for 105 days; they were eventually reduced to eating cats, dogs, and even rats, and they were clearly trapped behind the city walls, with no friendly troops to come to their aid anywhere in Ireland. They were determined, if it came to it, to die rather than surrender, for they knew that if they surrendered they would probably all die in a horrible massacre.

It seemed almost a miracle that on the 106th day, several English warships, loaded with food and arms, sailed into Lough Foyle, ran a gauntlet of Irish cannons along the banks of the River Foyle, smashed through a log-and-chain barrier placed across the river, and entered the city through watergates in the walls, saving the city in a manner so dramatic that only Hollywood would have written such a script! Descendants of the men and women who fought at Londonderry* still proudly tell their children about the battle.

A few weeks later, William landed a thousand well-trained men in County Down and marched south in pursuit of the now retreating Irish army. A few miles west of Dublin, the Protestant English army engaged the Catholic Irish army at the River Boyne, and for two days they fought. The English soundly defeated the Irish, and the Treaty of Limerick ended the last religious war in Ireland. None of the wars, misery and privation had anything to do with religion--it was all over the power of the state vs. the power of the Church. Jesus, Mary and all the angels probably wept.

William III returned to England, now firmly on the throne with Queen Mary in a Protestant England. James II's son, James, technically in line for the throne, actually never had a chance. He spent his life wandering around Europe in a futile quest for support. England would never again allow a Catholic to even come near the throne, and Parliament passed a law to back it up. For any future king, the concept of the Divine Right of Kings was something to be learned about in school as a peculiarity of royal thought. Parliament now took firm control of the royal purse, so no king could get into a pet with some foreign king over a trivial slight and plunge the nation into war. Beginning with William, kings would rule with the consent of Parliament. Ireland was brought into the ethnic family of Great Britain, including Wales. Scotland was also included in Great Britain in 1707. It was a quite different England. Religious tolerance was even adopted as state policy.

* In 1984 the City Council changed back the name of Londonderry to its ancient Irish name, Derry. English undertakers had changed it in 1611.

William, Mary and Ireland

PEACE CAME TO GREAT BRITAIN WITH WILLIAM AND MARY, and with peace, Ulster once again began to prosper. Included in the army that triumphed at the River Boyne were a number of Protestant French Huguenots, and in gratitude for their help, William opened Ulster to them for settlement. They were welcomed by the Ulster Scots, for like them, they were indus- strious and thrifty, and they brought with them skills needed in proces- sing flax. The growth of flax in large quantities made new crops in County Antrim and Tyrone, and Belfast became a manufacturing center for linen. Ulster's climate was just right for sheep production, and wool and wool cloth became a booming industry as well. Ulster's success got it into trouble once more with English weavers, who petitioned Parlia- ment for relief. Parliament passed it over to William, and he ordered the Irish Parliament to devise and pass the Woollen Act of 1699. The act restricted the exportation of woolen goods from Ireland to anyplace except Wales and England. The colonies could obtain woolen goods only from England, which permitted English merchants to set prices without having to compete in lower priced markets. The Irish woolen industry was dev- astated, but with the linen business booming, the overall effect was that Ulster was far better off than it had been.

Demand for labor in the linen industry created a new freedom for women in Ireland. There was more work in the mills than there was labor or machines to meet the demand, so some of the handwork was farmed out to housewives. This created a great new cottage industry that gave paid employment to women to do at home. It was especially a boon to widows with children, who heretofore were reduced to extreme poverty when their husbands died. It also created subtle changes in domestic life, as women became somewhat less dependent upon husbands, as well as improving the family's income. It also tended to shift Scots' dependence upon agri- culture for the family living to a manufacturing employment. This un- fortunately put their lives more into the hands of the English and Irish Parliaments, for they controlled manufacturing and marketing to always favor English interests, so that booms in Ulster were always certain to be cut down whenever English merchants protested.

However, they could take comfort in being able to live without the fear of having soldiers come to harrass them. They were left alone to be as Presbyterian as they liked.

Queen Mary died of smallpox in 1694. William provided for the accession of James' daughter, Anne, after his death. He suffered a fall when his horse stepped into a molehole and within a few days he died on March 8, 1702. It is thought that William's health declined due to overwork, and had he been in better health the injury should not have caused his death.

27

Exodus And The Migrations

AT THE DAWN OF THE EIGHTEENTH CENTURY, Ulster was a success. The
economy was up, the Irish were down, and the Presbyterians thrived in
peace. It was just too good to last. During the first two decades of
the new century the roof caved in. The English and Irish Parliaments
rose against Ulster almost as though they were compelled to hate some religious group, it didn't make much difference which one, and the Presbyterians were handy. Nature seemed to have conspired to destroy everything growing in Ulster that had been planted by the Ulster Scots, and
the very lantation ystem which delivered them into Ulster drove them
off the land and beggared them. By 1730 more than ten thousand Scots-
Irish had fled to America, never to return.

Queen Anne, last of the Stuart monarchs, seemed to have little interest in Ulster, but was instead caught up in the War of the Spanish
Succession for most of her reign, during which John Churchill was elevated to Duke of Marlborough and led Britain and her allies to the great
victories at Blenheim and Gibraltar. She emerged from these wars in
1810 the most powerful nation in Europe. Anne left the administration of
the colonies to her ministers, who were largely high-church bisnops with
low-voltage minds. They were hangers-on from the bad old days of
Charles II and James II who never heard the modern admonition: "If it
ain't busted, don't fix it."

Parliament never could make up its mind about what status to assign
Ulster. It came to accomodation with Scotland in 1707 and made it equal
to Wales and a sister kingdom to England, but although the monarch's
title included Ireland, Parliament just couldn't see its way to make
Ulster a full partner, but regarded it as more of a colony of hewers
and drawers of water who should be glad to serve and pay taxes, but not
to get any notions that they were in any way equal to Englishmen. And it
was about time that they joined the Church, too.

The bishops declared that all civil officers in Ireland must take
the sacraments of the Established Church, and they ordered the subser-
vient, all-Protestant Irish Parliament to re-draw the infamous Test
Act to make it apply to all non-Anglican holders of civil or military
office. Most civil offices in Ulster had been filled by better-educated
Presbyterian laymen and ministers. Now, Presbyterians and Catholics were
to be held equally excluded from public or military service. Worse than
that, Presbyterian ministers were ordered out of their pulpits unless
they would, in effect, become Anglican. Priests were considered to be
properly ordained in the Catholic faith, but Presbyterian ministers were
not. Entire town and city councils were removed from office, to be replaced by inexperienced men, often of low repute, who filled only one
requirement for office, that of being Catholic. Everyone, Catholic,

Presbyterian, any other denomination, and non-believers, all had to pay a tithe to the Anglican Church. Non-payment, or refusal to pay, meant seizure of the offender's property.

But the most cruel and offensive of all was the stipulation that all children born of marriages solemnized in Presbyterian services were bastards and non-persons. Bishops' courts actually prosecuted honest men for fornicating with their wives! Presbyterian schools were closed, and other schools, excepting Catholic schools, refused to register children of families who refused the Black Oath, the oath taken to confirm belief in the rites of the Established Church. Funerals were forbidden except wherever rites of the Established Church were read.

Life for the Ulster Scot farmers was made miserable by "Rack-Renting," a term used perhaps in reference to the instrument of torture still in use then. Tenants in 1700 usually occupied the same tract that had been worked by their fathers and grandfathers; each thirty-one years the lease was renewed, so that after three generations of one-family occupancy of a tract, the tenant understandably had a sense of ownership of the farm. Because of the length of the leases and the familial sense of belonging to the farm, the tenant built barns, fences, drainage ditches, and other improvements. Oftentimes the undertaker who owned the complex of farms lived in England and never came to Ireland to oversee his properties. His overseer collected the rents and sent them to the owner, who had no other interest in his holdings in Ulster, and he judged his overseer by the amount of increase in rent money he collected. Because of the Irish Rebellion and the rush of new immigrants following the Treaty of Limerick in 1691, an unusual number of leases came up for renewal in 1717 to 1723. Overseers, upon inspecting the farms and seeing all the improvement that had been made, saw that the value of the farm had increased also, so up went the rent. Some farmers were shocked to learn that their rents had doubled or tripled.

After about 1710 there were several years of extreme drought and especially cold, wet winters. Crops failed everywhere, cattle died, food prices went up, and whatever savings the farmers may have accumulated were spent on food. When they were confronted with rack-renting, they were unable to raise the money demanded. Worse yet, the tenant may have found himself bidding against others, sometimes even Irishmen, for his lease. Hundreds, perhaps thousands of Ulster families were turned out onto the roads, penniless and dispossesed. Because the wool industry was booming, some overseers abandoned farming and turned to cattle and sheep grazing, which required only a few shepherds or milkers, so the leases on many tracts were not renewed. On top of all these calamities, a malignant epidemic of smallpox descended upon Ireland and thousands died. It was time to leave, and they left--thousands of them.

The political injustices visited upon Ulster were without any justification. Although Scots in Ulster hadn't always meekly obeyed every letter of the laws that Parliament passed, some of which were hardly more than harrassment, they had always been loyal subjects and had supported the monarchy throughout the Civil War. They had strongly protested the execution of King Charles I. They had risked their lives assisting the suppression of the Irish during the Irish Rebellion, and they had proven themselves to be diligent and creative workers in making the Plantation of Ulster a tremendous success. Yet, Queen Anne never questioned her ministers about why it was necessary for them to so persecute the Scottish Presbyterians.

Rack renting, the Test Act, discriminatory laws causing failure of the wool industry, drought, disease, and despair, combined to make Ulster seem to have been visited by plague, and Scots began to talk of immigrating to America. A few did leave. Almost every colony had some Scots-Irish that had come to America during the last half of the seventeenth century, mostly in the Mid-Atlantic colonies of New Jersey, Pennsylvania, Virginia and North Carolina. Word came back from America of its wonders; fertile soil, mild climate, cheap or even free land, vast timberlands, and almost complete freedom of religion. It was said that anyone wanting to work could take his pick of employers, and tradesmen of any kind were guaranteed a good living for life.

Getting there presented problems. It wasn't a Mediterranean cruise. Ships were small and made to carry freight, not passengers, so there was little or no privacy, poor ventilation below decks, inadequate sanitation, and poor food and water. The voyage lasted two months if nothing went wrong, and could take three months. Epidemics sometimes broke out and children often died from various causes. If a birth occurred on board it was not likely that a live infant would be taken ashore in America. And it cost money, something many dispossessed Scots didn't have.

But there was a way for the destitute and determined. A person with no funds could sell his services to a master in America for a period of usually seven years, during which he was required to do whatever his master ordered him to do. American colonists seeking a man, woman, or even a family, could contract with an agent to find servants in Ulster. The agents sailed to Ulster and spread the word that they were seeking people willing to indenture themselves to a master who would pay for their passage. At the end of the indenture, the servant was free to go wherever he wished, and he usually was given new clothes, some money, and basic agricultural hand tools : a shovel, axe, and mattock. During the indenture he was legally bound to the master and could not leave, no matter how hard he was required to work or at what tasks, provided they did not involve moral turpitude. Sexual abuse of female servants could result in severe punishment for a master, and neighbors of the offender would shun him. Shunning was a severe punishment in a country where everyone needed to be on good terms with his neighbors. The servant was required to be given decent clothing, adequate food, and at least minimal sleeping accommodations, although there were no standards, and courts usually favored the master. The kind of treatment often depended upon the colony in which the indenture was served; indentured servants in the Carolinas were usually field hands and life was hard for them, but in Pennsylvania they were protected by the most comprehensive laws and customs regarding indentured servants.

Abuse of indentured servants could and did happen, as evidenced by the number of posters in crossroads and taverns, advertising rewards for return of indentured runaways. All people were required by law to return any known indentured runaway to his master, and bounty hunters made a living running down and returning runaways. Apprehended servants could be returned in chains like runaway slaves, and when back under his master he could be worked very hard as punishment, and was likely to have his period of indenture extended by twice the length of his absence.

Lacking a sponsor in America, a person or family could sign on with a ship's captain, who would sell the indenture to the highest bidder in an American port. An advantage of this was that the captain would try to have adequate supplies of food and potable water in order to be able to offer healthy-looking servants to prospective bidders. On the other hand, captains sold indentures to whomever bid highest. The immigrant might find himself or herself on a wagon headed for service as a fieldhand in a Carolina cotton field. A bidder might want just the husband or just the mother, or even just the children, and families were sometimes broken up and never re-united again. Only the most flinty-hearted captains would allow this sort of thing, though.

Sometimes a master would turn out to be a decent and religious man who took entire families of indentured Scots into his household almost as family members. Some indentured children were adopted by their masters and reared as members of the family. A widower would occasionally marry an indentured woman and have a family with her. Some were apprenticed into a trade, guaranteeing the servant a good living after his indenture was served.

Although they could be sold to other masters, they were not held as slaves, for they had some recourse at law for gross mistreatment by masters. A cruel master might work his slaves to death, but in fear of what his neighbors would say, he might give his white indentured servants better treatment. Killing an indentured servant was murder, but a slave was a piece of property at the mercy of his owner.

A colonist might be granted a tract of several thousand acres by a colonial governor, with a proviso that within a stated number of years there be a stated minimum number of families settled on the land. The grantee might send an agent to Ulster to recruit likely-appearing families and pay their passage to America, even providing horses or wagon transportation to the grant of land. There he would be given 150 or 200 acres, and to a poor man in Ireland, it was truly a grand thing indeed.

A period of indenture could provide an interval of time during which new arrivals could learn where the best prospects were for settlers in America. If their master permitted, they might even save a bit of money for a grubstake when they were free. A master was entitled to take possession of any money or property that came to his servant during his or her indenture; however, whatever he owned before the indenture could not be taken from him.

Thousands of Scots came to America under indenture, but nobody knows how many. By no means did they all come here indentured, for some represented Ireland's best people who had done quite well in wool, linen, or agriculture. Many of them had means to buy passage for themselves and family, with money left over to buy American land. Only those who had been evicted from their land, or who had their assets seized by the crown or the church, or who had been visited by any of several natural calamities, were forced to take the indenture route.

The first waves of immigrants contained the highest percentages of indentured Scots-Irish. Estimates were that from sixty-five to ninety percent were indentured, and these would have been the most poor and desperate.

In 1717 sheep died by thousands of "sheep rot" disease, following four years of drought and inflated food prices. People began to gather in groups and talk about leaving Ulster and going to America. They learned about the cost of ship passage, what they needed to carry aboard, and where they could go after arrival in America. Almost like lemmings, they spontaneously abandoned everything they could not sell or take with them and streamed by hundreds to Irish seaports. Roads from the interior were filled with people, walking, riding horses or wagons, pushing carts, carrying small children, on their way to Newry, Belfast, Londonderry, Larne and other seaports. There they dickered with ship owners for passage, and sailed as soon as winds and tides were favorable.

Ships leaving as early as May of 1717 were able to make two crossings loaded with passengers before the end of September. Probably as many as two thousand people made the trip that summer. Only brave or foolhardy captains would risk their life and ship after September because of Atlantic hurricanes off the coast of the Colonies. Fierce winter storms and spring gales kept them in port until late April or May.

That winter a severe epidemic of smallpox killed thousands of people in Ireland, and as soon as they could find ships to carry them, more left in 1818. The first wave of immigrants probably amounted to more than five thousand Scots-Irish.

The flow of outbound people continued every year after 1818, and in 1725 the movement swelled to a new wave as many leases expired and rack-renting impoverished hundreds more farmers. Entire villages emptied out.

This wave began to recede in 1729, but immigration*continued each year thereafter. Archbishop King wrote to the Archbishop of Canterbury urging him to use his good offices to warn the nation. Leyburn (Op Cit, p. 169-170) quoted from the letter:

"I find likewise that your Parliament is destroying the little Trade that is left us. These & other Discouragements are driving away the few Protestants that are amongst us. ...No Papists stir except young men that go abroad to be trained in arms, with intention to return with the Pretender (James II's son, James, "The Old Pretender") The Papists being already five or six to one & breeding People, you may imagine in what conditions we are like to be."

Without naming the Ulster Scots, King was pointing out that only Presbyterian Protestants were leaving. The Irish, hoping to regain their land that was being abondoned, were glad to be rid of the Scots. The English Parliament yawned and asked how the king, George I, was getting on with his mistresses. The Irish Parliament predicted the Presbyterian immigrants were going to starve in America.

The flow of Scots-Irish across the Atlantic swelled to another great wave in 1740 and 1741, as famine again visited Ireland, causing an estimated 400,000 deaths. This time the wave subsided only a little, and thousands more came during the next ten years. By then all the available land in Pennsylvania had been taken up as far west as the Allegheny Mountains, and the path of migration turned south into Virginia and the Shenandoah Valley. The Alleghenies were a formidable barrier to westward bound pioneers. Steep slopes at right angle to progress were covered with huge boulders, trees and vines. Diamondback rattlers lurked by every stone, and the valleys were Indian hunting grounds that were fiercely protected. There was plenty of good land to the south along the eastern side of the mountains, and the path was easy.

* The term "immigrant," as used here, does not imply the usual usage of the word: a person leaving one nation and going to live in another nation. The immigrants treated here were always British subjects travelling *within* British jurisdiction, and never having the status of being foreigners. The German religious refugees who immigrated to the Colonies were foreigners, and as such, their names were recorded in official ledgers, many of which have been preserved. The arrival of the Scots-Irish went unrecorded, as far as we have been able to learn, and no one set down their names in any official documents. Ships' passenger lists were kept only after the founding of the United States.

Pennsylvania's population had increased markedly at this time by thousands of minority religious sects fleeing persecution in Germany. These gentle people were made welcome because they were excellent farmers with stable families, and like the Quakers, lovers of peace. Their descendants still farm the rich limestone earth in the Great Valley, and many farms have remained continuously in one family. When the Scots-Irish began to arrive in numbers, the German settlers had taken up all the good land north and west of Philadelphia to the Susquehanna River.

The fourth great wave, 1754-1755 was largely caused by letters from Scots-Irish Americans to relatives and friends back in Ulster, especially those from a successive line of Scots-Irish governors of North Carolina appealing for settlers in their western frontier. Many of those arriving at Philadelphia were persuaded by the dearth of land in Pennsylvania to head west and south through the Valley of Virginia into the Carolinas.

Near the end of 1754 immigration slowed dramatically as the French and Indian War broke out, followed by Pontiac's War, and for ten years there was but a trickle of westward-bound Scots-Irish. The slowdown was aided by economic recovery of Ulster's industries and an increase of population there. The prosperity was only temporary.

By 1770 the people of Ulster were typically very poor, especially those whose living depended on farming. Greedy landlords had repeatedly divided the little farms to crowd in more families on each estate, thereby obtaining more rent money. They had also reduced the manpower required to operate the estate profitably by taking much land out of production to graze sheep. Farms became too small to provide but a bare living for the farmer and his family, whose diet consisted largely of potatoes, oats and milk.

In 1771, scores of leases ran out on the great estate of the Marquis of Donegal in County Antrim. He raised rents beyond the means of most of his tenants to pay, so they were summarily evicted from farm plots they and even their forefathers had worked for years. Word of the marquis' cruel injustices sped all over Ulster, arousing so much anger and resentment that thousands of them sold what goods they could spare to pay passage to America, and marched to the nearest seaport to book passage to America. They were still streaming into America's seaports up to the time of Lexington and Concord, in numbers estimated to exceed 18,000.

This last migration brought a number of skilled tradesmen from Ireland's linen industry, as well as some rather well-to-do Scots-Irish who brought with them considerable cash, thereby depleting valuable manpower and Irish currency. Not so apparent at that time was that in a few years a great number of angry Scots-Irishmen would have an opportunity to avenge themselves as they lined up the sights of their rifles on British Redcoats during the American Revolution.

In a little village in Massachussets one morning in 1775 a detachment of British soldiers fired on a small group of unmilitary farmers
who stood their ground and defied the troops to search their houses for
their small supplies of arms and gunpowder. This incident marked the
abrupt end of immigration of Scots-Irish to America for the next eight
years. After 1783, newly arrived Scots-Irish did not come as British
subjects, but as foreigners, immigrants seeking American citizenship.
The Colonies never were the same, nor was the world.

The American Scots-Irish

THE NUMBER OF SCOTS-IRISH that came to America before the Revolution
has been estimated to be from as few as 100,000 to as many as 500,000.
Conservative scholars, using all sources of information, have agreed,
more or less, that the number came to about 250,000. Some have made an
estimate by counting Scottish names in the first U.S. Census of 1790,
but they failed to take into account the number of Irish names that were
made Scottish (O'Donnel to MacDonald) and Scottish names made Irish
(McCrea to McCree), as well as other mix-ups of English, Irish and Scottish, and even Welsh and French Huguenots. Colonial scribes also did
some creative spelling of names given to them verbally. Also, it would
be difficult to account for the increase in numbers of Scots-Irish up
to 1790 because of the fecundity of these folk; they customarily would
have ten or more children in a family.

The first arrivals of Scots-Irish in the Colonies were welcomed, as
were all newcomers. They were given approval for their good work habits,
thrift, religion and strength of body. After the arrival of many
thousands of them, the Colonists began having second thoughts. There
were a tremendous number of them and their numbers threatened the suprem_
acy of the Quakers in Pennsylvania. In fact, in 1749 there were more
Presbyterians in Pennsylvania than any other sect, including Quakers.
And no doubt about it--they were a difficult lot to deal with and get
along with. They were viewed by the peaceful Quakers of Pennsylvania as
loudly quarrelsome and dirty, always with a chip on their shoulders, and
they weren't always very moderate with drink. But they could fight, and
that was a talent to be admired in the relatively primitive society of
the American frontier. In quiet council the Quakers found a solution:
give them land on the northern frontier where they could fight Indians
who appeared to be preparing for trouble with white invaders.

After William Penn died, his sons succeeded to his proprietorship
of Pennsylvania. They lacked their father's scrupulous honesty and respect in dealing with the Indians, and had cheated the Indians in a land
purchase deal. The terms agreed on for the sale was to sell to the
white men as much land as a man could encircle in a day's walk. The
Indians knew rather closely how much land this would be, but the day of

35

the measuring walk came and the "walkers" turned out to be trained athletes, runners, who set off on a dead run. When they had completed their circuit, they had encircled about twice as much land as a true walker would have done. Indians didn't cheat on deals, and after that trust of white men was replaced by anger and suspicion.

The Quakers reasoned that these contentious "Irish"* would provide a buffer between the Iroquois on the north and the Delawares on the west, and the white people in Philadelphia. The Scots-Irish named their gift of land, "Donegall." Wherever they went they remembered the soft, green land from whence they came, naming townships "Antrim," "Toboyne," "Lurgan," and "Letterkenny."

They were a people of independent spirit who seldom sought advice from others, but preferred to make their own decisions. It was a characteristic that stood them in good stead in their frontier homes, but as soldiers in the Revolution they didn't really take to discipline and taking orders, especially if they thought the orders given were stupid. But as soldiers, how they could fight! They came out of the wilderness with their long Pennsylvania rifles and joined with a will the fight to free the American Colonies from their old adversary, the English.

Unlike other great mass movements of people across the face of the globe, the Scots-Irish had no Moses to lead them to a promised land. No one organized them and shepherded them to America. A quarter of a million of them organized their own journeys across five thousand miles of nearly unknown ocean without being harangued by a great leader saying, "Arise and follow me," nor were they inspired to come here to follow a great figure of the time.

Intermarriage: Did They Or Didn't They?

WERE THE SCOTS-IRISH A MIXTURE of Irish and Scottish? Some scholars maintain that the animosity between the native Catholic Irish and the invading and conquering Presbyterian Scots was too great for them to ever allow one of *them* to marry one of *those*. The Catholic clergy warned the Irish about endangering their immortal souls by getting too close to the Presbyterians, while the Presbyterians were bent on stamping out everything Irish and Catholic. Therefore, it is argued, they both stayed at

---

* The Scots-Irish came to America, not as Scots, but as Irish. They had, during their lives, lived in Ireland, and they thought of themselves as Irish, not Scots. The Colonists referred to them as Irish, too. They later were branded with the pejorative "Scotch-Irish," a badge of shame. Only in the last hundred years have we Scots-Irish come out of the closet and become proud of our ancestry.

arms length from each other.

Others argue that they were not segregated at all, that the Scots needed workers in their fields and helpers in their homes, and that they frequently hired Irish men and women to work for them in circumstances that brought them close together, almost in intimacy. Surely, they point out, there must have been many times that a laddie noted the soft curve of a cheek on a maid, and a colleen admired the tall, young Scot out of the corner of her eye. Laws, customs and prejudices are forgotten when that mysterious, wonderful magnetism draws men and women together, and they must be together as man and wife for the rest of their lives, and they will have their way, no matter what.

It seems inevitable that there was some, perhaps much, intermarriage, but in the main, the Scots left Ireland with only Scottish blood in their veins. No matter. For whatever Irish genes we carry, we're the better for them, and a little blarney never hurt anyone.

CHAPTER TWO

THE McCREAS

ONE OF THE FIRST THINGS we McCrays find when we begin to seriously research our families is that everyone thinks we don't spell our name correctly, and that it should be McCrea. I've actually been told I don't spell my name correctly! This was told me by a lady whose name was Shyma Gerohristodoulos, so what would she know? Just because the McCreas got to America before the McCrays (I think), and they were first-order begatters and spread themselves all over the place, doesn't mean that the McCrays, McCraws, McCraes, et all who came a few years later don't know how to spell their names. By the time the McCrays began arriving here, public scribes had learned the name McCrea, and they saw no need to learn another spelling for what sounds like the same name. When I first began casting into the genealogical pool, it was logical to begin with eighteenth century records on the Atlantic seaboard. Right away I ran into this McCrea business, and soon afterward I discovered that many people known to be McCrays had been recorded, "McCrea."

Were the McCrays and McCreas related? Undoubtedly! It is almost certain that they were all one great family in the early eighteenth century in Ayreshire (now Strathclyde), Scotland. In 1984 we drove through England, Scotland and Wales, and in almost every village and town we searched telephone books for McCrays -- "we" being myself and Cely, who signs checks as "Mrs. Cecelia McCray." We found McCreas in almost all phone books, sometimes scores of them in the area around Glasgow, but in all of Britain we found but four McCrays listed, and two of them we rang up had no idea at all who their ancestors were, and it seemed clear, couldn't imagine why anyone would care. Many of the Scots living in Ireland changed the spelling of their names, probably to circumvent repressive laws by appearing to be Irish. For example: "Macdonald" might become "O'Donnell."

The spelling "McCray" may have evolved after they left Ireland for America. The earliest records of them in America, written about five years after their arrival, are spelled "McCrea," and all the records of Cumberland County up through 1795 are similarly in that spelling. Some of the family who migrated later to Forest and Warren Counties, Pennsylvania, used that spelling in the nineteenth century, and may still use it today. Or, it may be that the scribes in Carlisle, Pennsylvania already knew the spelling, "McCrea," and used it in Cumberland County records.

The McCreas were clustered around the northern parts of Ayreshire just above Glasgow and south of Loch Lomond. Their location made it

38

easy for them to make their way by boat down the River Clyde, through the protected waters west of Ayreshire, and offshore from Mull of Kintyre strike out across the Irish Sea for a landing on the northeast coast of County Tyrone, Ireland.

An early reference to the McCreas in Ireland tells of John Glenn, of Donaghdry, Strabane, Tyrone, born, 1665, died before 1740, who married Jannett McCrea. They had three children: James, born about 1693, died 1733-39, in Jamaica; Joseph, born about 1695, removed to Mill Creek Hundred, New Castle County, Delaware, in 1736, and died there before 1740; and Robert, born about 1697-1700, who also went to Mill Creek Hundred in 1740.*

Another account in the same magazine has Doctor William Archibald McCrea marrying Margaret Elinor Norwood, April 6, 1784, in Old Swedes (Presbyterian) Church, Wilmington, Delaware. They had three children: Frances B., who married John Hankinson of New Jersey: Edith Ruston, who married Colonel Peter P. Schuyler, of Albany, New York; and Margaret, who married John Campbell, a major in the War of 1812. Doctor McCrea's mother married three times; (1) David Chambers, an Elder in the Second Presbyterian Church of Philadelphia,(2) to ------- McCrea, father of Doctor Archibald McCrea, who was divorced by his wife at Philadelphia. He died in Georgia, March 25, 1802. Her third marriage was to ------ Ruston. Note that Doctor McCrea's second child was named Edith Ruston.

The Calander of Wills, New Castle, Delaware, p. 35, lists Thomas McCrea, will recorded June 10, 1745; wife, Esther McCrea; son, Thomas McCrea. On page 147, Sam'l Platt, M.D., recorded 1798; daughter, Margaret McCrea.

These McCreas were gentlefolk of substance; doctors, merchants, shipbuilders, and Presbyterian clergymen. The family quickly spread out into Philadelphia and the neighboring counties of Bucks, Chester and York. They were leaders in their communities, so a number of them are still to be found in record books.

William McCrea, who was born in 1705 and died in 1763, owned considerable property along the Delaware River. Another William, apparently his son, had a wife Margaret, who died in 1790. One of these Williams was a major in a company of militia in White Clay Creek Hundred, and the elder William was an elder in the White Clay Creek Hundred Presbyterian Church, known as "Old Swedes," a landmark in downtown Wilmington today. It was built in 1695 by Swedish settlers, the first white settlers in the area. New Sweden was the only attempt at colonization by Swedes, who were driven out by Peter Stuyvesant's Dutch troops, sent down from Nieuw

Amsterdam. The Dutch, in turn, were conquered by the English, under the command of the Duke of York, later to become King James II.

The "Hundred" referred to here, is an ancient unit of government between the village and the county, and is still used today in Pennsylvania, Delaware and Virginia. Also called "Wopentake" and "Wards," hundreds courts once were open-air courts where disputes were settled and minor criminal offenses were tried.

I became interested in the McCrea families because I hoped I might find that their son, James McCrea, a Presbyterian minister of some note, would turn out to be my ancestor, James McCray, and I was rather sorry to have to conclude that he wasn't. It's always nice to have a respectable clergyman in the family tree. He was one of the first to be graduated from William Tennent's "Log College" in 1739. Tennent was a Presbyterian minister at Neshaminy, Pennsylvania, who was born in Ireland and educated at the University of Edinburgh. Concerned because of the scarcity of Scottish-trained clergymen, he founded his "Log College" in 1736 to educate and train Presbyterian clergymen in the Colonies. Until then only men who had the benefit of an education in a Scottish university were ordained to serve in the Colonies, and at the rate that Scots-Irish Presbyterians were arriving in the Colonies there were far too few ministers to serve the new arrivals. The Log College, as the name implies, was a log building, and in this primitive structure the Reverend Tennent instructed students in Greek, Latin, Hebrew and Scriptures. It was a lineal ancestor of Princeton University.

James McCrea, the year after his ordination in 1939, married Mary Graham of Monmouth, New Jersey on April 8, 1740. She bore James seven children before her death in 1752, at age 32. James remarried sometime later to Catherine Rosbrugh, and they had five children.

The Reverend James McCrea was pastor of a Presbyterian Church at Bedminster (now "Lamington"), New Jersey, and served his ministry there until his death in 1769. His gravestone can be seen today in the churchyard there. He was spared the distress of seeing his family divided by mounting tensions that exploded into the War for American Independence in 1775. Five of his sons took up arms in the American cause, and three of them remained loyal to the Crown. The first-born, John McCrea, was a colonel in the British Colonial Militia, and his half-brother, Creighton, also held a commission in the British cause. When the war ended, Creighton sailed to England and remained in royal service, eventually being named governor of the Isle of Guernsey.

Another of the sons, Stephen, a physician and surgeon, became the highly valued chief surgeon in the Northern Continental Army, and both Generals Horatio Gates and Benedict Arnold wrote to Continental headquarters in Philadelphia, praising Stephen's abilities and dedication to the American cause. Philip McCrea, another son, was also an officer in the Continental Army.

A daughter, Jane McCrea, earned a rather considerable measure of fame by the nature of her tragic death. She was engaged to a British officer, David Jones, and when she was nineteen, left her home in Bedminster and journeyed to the home of her brother, Col. John McCrea, near Fort Edward, New York, several miles north of Albany, where her brother and her sweetheart were both stationed. While she was preparing for her wedding at Fort Edward, her fiance sent a party of friendly Indians to escort her safely through the forests to the fort. Meanwhile, another band of Indians allied to the British, were returning from raids on American farms and isolated settlers in the region, and they burst into the house and seized both Jane and another woman and took them captive, intending to deliver them to Fort Edward as prisoners. The two parties of Indians met on the trail to the fort, a quarrel broke out over custody of the two women, and an enraged Indian shot and scalped both women.

The story of the murder spread throughout New England, and in a curious twist, it became distorted and poor Jane was portrayed as an American victim of British brutality. It so inflamed the local population that recruitment into the Continental Army swelled, contributing in no small way to the defeat of General John ("Gentleman Johnnie") Burgoyne at the Battle of Saratoga. It was the first significant victory for the Continental forces, and not only did it give hope to the discouraged Americans but it was the deciding factor in persuading the French to send assistance to the Americans.

Someone should write a book about this most interesting family!

Samuel and John McCrea Of Cumberland County

SAMUEL McCREA LIVED IN CHESTER COUNTY, Pennsylvania, just outside of Philadelphia. He had no idea that he was going to make trouble for me some 250 years later when he placed an advertisement in Benjamin Franklin's *Pennsylvania Gazette*, announcing the sale of his Chester County plantation in 1749. It is conjecture on my part, but I believe he was the same Samuel McCrea who appeared on the tax rolls of Cumberland County in 1750, the year that Cumberland County was carved out of sprawling Lancaster County, partly to notify Maryland of Pennsylvania's claims of lands on the disputed boundary of the two colonies, and partly to establish a governmental presence in the newly developing frontier. Samuel McCrea's name was joined the next year by John McCrea's name, and surely they were relatives, and very likely brothers. They were listed living in Middleton Township, now in Adams County, on the Pennsylvania-Maryland border. Pennsylvania also had a quarrel with Virginia over the border further west.

The trouble he made for me was that not only did he settle in Cumberland County, where my earliest known ancestor, James McCray, also settled, but he also used bad judgement by naming several of his children

41

the same as did James McCray. This was before I had learned for certain
the names of James McCray's children, and I still was on rather shaky
ground about just who my ancestors really were. For several months I
tried to fit Samuel and John McCrea and their children into my family
tree without success. It was when I found a map locating the various
townships of eastern Cumberland County, and found that Samuel and John
lived about fifty miles south of Toboyne Township, where James and his
family settled, that I was able to determine that Samuel and John were
really McCreas and not McCrays.

The difficulty of using a modern map of Pennsylvania to learn where
these townships were is that the boundaries of the counties have been
changed many times since the first counties were laid out. Today, Cumberland County is a rather small county approximately in the center of
Pennsylvania. In 1750, the year of its creation, it embraced nearly all
of southwestern Pennsylvania from the Susquehanna River to the Ohio line,
and south of a line very roughly along the east-west direction of the
middle of the state. Above this line was territory "owned" by the Iroquois Nation. Indians did not own land in the sense that we do; an area
was occupied by a tribe or nation, and the land used for light agriculture, while the animals were hunted for food. The land itself was regarded as the mother of all life, and therefore could not be owned any
more than a person can own his or her mother. This concept was the
source of much of the hostility between white men and Indians.

As white men encroached upon Indian lands, moving further and further westward, Cumberland County was divided, sub-divided, and then
divided again, until finally "Mother Cumberland" had given birth to
thirty-five counties. The last major subdivision occurred in 1800, when
Allegheny County was divided into eleven counties: Adams, Allegheny,
Armstrong, Beaver, Butler, Centre, Crawford, Erie, Mercer, Venango and
Warren. Some of these were further subdivided later.

Many McCreas still live around the area of Carlisle and Chambersburg, and there is a village just west of Carlisle named "McCrea." I
was told that no McCreas live today in the village, although they are
plentiful all around it. Newville, in particular, has many McCreas
living there today, and the churchyard of Big Spring Presbyterian Church
there has several McCrea graves of pre-Revolutionary War period. George
Washington once reportedly worshipped there.

A branch of the McCrea family, not closely related to any of the
previously discussed McCreas, lives in Venango County, Pennsylvania,
today. Their story in America began with two McCrea soldiers who came
to America as officers under Lord Cornwallis during the Revolution.
Michael McCray was a captain, and his son, Dr. Patrick McCrea, both served in the Light Horse Troop. Michael was killed in the Battle of Brandywine. Michael either stayed in America after the war, or else returned
to Ireland, where he was born, and later came back to the United States.

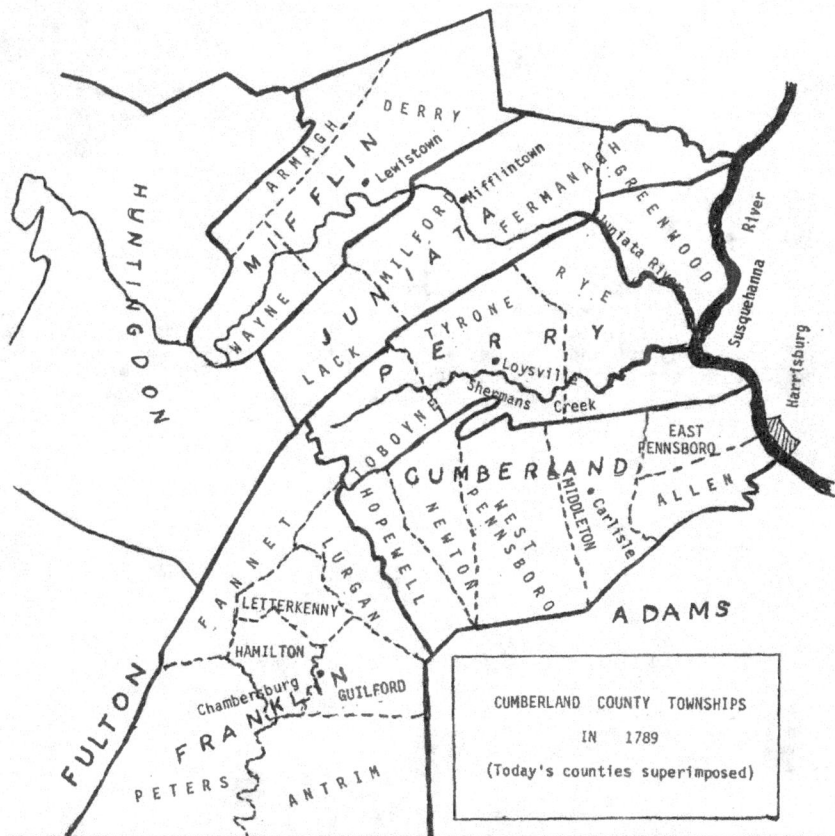

CUMBERLAND COUNTY TOWNSHIPS

IN 1789

(Today's counties superimposed)

Maryland Border

Philip R. McCray
1985

He settled in Richmond, Virginia, for a while. In 1797 he joined the land rush to northwestern Pennsylvania, and settled in Eagle Rock, Venango County. In 1902 he married Flora McGerald, daughter of Hugh McGerald. Their son, Hugh McCrea, married Patience McGuire, a native of Erie, Pennsylvania. Their daughter, Charity McCrea, married Patrick Masterson, and their son, John W. Masterson, was born in 1872 at Eagle Rock and was still living there at the time Reisman's book (see footnote, p. 42) was written.

-0-

Although this book is about the McCrays of America, there is reason to believe that the spelling of the name "McCray" was spelled "McCrea" when they lived in Scotland. Scottish church records* prior to the year 1800 do not contain any McCrays, but they do have many McCreas, McCraes, McCrees, McCraiths and other variant spellings. The name, McCray, is a rarity today in Scotland, England and Wales, but is not uncommon in Ulster. When I once inquired of a red-haired lass in a petrol station near Glasgow about the location of a cemetery wherein some McCrays were said to have been buried, she responded: "Oo, 'tis an unuusual spelling now, isn't it?"

Tax records found at the Cumberland County Historical Society in Carlisle, Pennsylvania, show that my family spelled it McCrea, and sometimes McCree, over the years of 1787 to 1792. One of the McCray men of that time used the McCrea spelling, and many of his descendants still use it today. Early records in other places in the United States, written before 1800, show the McCrea spelling was mostly used for people who today spell it McCray.

I am not now persuaded that the name McCrea or McCray is a variant of MacRae. To my knowledge no one has presented any evidence that the Lowland McCreas are related to, or descended from, the Highland Clan MacRae. Similarity of pronunciation of the two names is no evidence of kinship. My wife's maiden name was Cecelia Spear, from the English name, Speare, but other Spears in America descended from a German family, the Speers. The only thing they have in common is pronunciation.

However, on occasion I wear a Clan MacRae hunting tartan necktie, and on cold evenings I may warm my legs with a wool "rug" woven in the MacRae dress tartan design. Just in case, y'know.

*The Old Parochial Register of Scottish Names and Parishes, available in libraries of the Church of Jesus Christ of The Latter Day Saints, commonly called, "The LDS Libraries."

CHAPTER THREE

THE FIRST McCRAYS IN AMERICA

EVERY ONE OF THE FIFTY UNITED STATES of America undoubtedly has a
share of the McCray clan living within its boundaries today. There may
be as many as hundreds of thousands of them altogether. Open almost any
telephone directory anywhere in the United States and you're likely to
find at least one of them, and some communities have large clusters of
McCrays.

All of these McCrays seem to have descended from a handful of ancestors, perhaps so few in number that they could be counted on the fingers
of one hand--well, maybe two hands, making certain that some of them are
not duplicated.

The earliest McCray in America we have encountered was Alexander
McCray, in the Valley of Virginia in 1750. He was at that time well
enough established in the Colonies to be appointed by a probate court to
be one of three assessors of an estate, so he must have lived in America
for a few years before 1750 to have attained status as a reliable citizen.
Nothing beyond this single fact has turned up about Alexander, but he may
have been the progenitor of several McCray families whose names were recorded in records of the Valley of Virginia within the next quarter-
century.

McCrays in Colonial America were found in Connecticut, New Jersey,
New York, Pennsylvania, Maryland, Virginia and South Carolina. William
and Margaret McCray were living in Hartford, Connecticut, in 1754, and
Robert McCray bought two lots in Maryland in 1758. Still awaiting research as some McCrays who lived in New Jersey before the Revolution.

Mrs. Irene Titus, of Indiana, prefaced her *History of the McCray
Family* with this terse summary:

"So tradition goes, Samuel McCray I, immigrated from Scotland with at least four sons -- Samuel McCray II, John McCray,
William McCray who drowned, and James McCray who sickened and
died."

Mrs. Titus' family legend seems to be more or less supported by a
biography of John McCray, of Fayette County, Pennsylvania, reproduced on
Page 188. John's grandfather, John McCray, was born in Ireland and was
a weaver by trade, "...came to America, and with three of his brothers
served under Washington in the Revolutionary War."

45

This theme of the earliest McCrays having come to America as a group of brothers, or as a father and some sons, is found in other family legends of McCray clans in various parts of the United States.

Ronald McCray, of Dayton, Ohio, sent a copy of a letter written by Christy McCray about their ancestor's family who came from the Valley of Virginia to Ohio in 1813:

> "John and Samuel McCray came from Scotland after the Revolutionary War, the year being unknown. Both went to the State of Pennsylvania. Samuel was the older and soon went to the State of Virginia settling in the Shenandoah Valley. The location was close to the mouth of the Roanoke River ("source", rather than "mouth")."

Blanche Meritt, of Oceanside, California, sent a remarkable and lengthy letter, written in 1890 by her great grandfather, Thomas Hamilton McCray, a grandson of Daniel McCray of Virginia and Tennessee. He wrote at the top of the letter, "My hands are very shaky and my memory bad."

> "There is a tradition that some time in the 17th (probably intended to be 18th) century three brothers, McCrays, landed on this continent from Scotland and subsequently, one of them located in the east, probably in Rhode Island. Another located in North Carolina, and the third, my grandfather in Virginia, where father was born. They, all my grandfather's family moved to Tennessee, and settled on what is now known as the City of Franklin.

> "If one will sit down who knows something of the McCray descendants, with some data of the numerical strength of the McCrays and their kinfolk and will count up and continue to count up, and continue to count up for three or four days, or a week, one will quit in disgust, and exclaim, in Gods name, How many are there? The truth is, the fecundity of the McCrays, the world over is proverbial. Both hes and shes are renowed for tneir ability to increase their species.

> "And now for stock. There is as much difference in people as there is in any other animal. There are fine blooded horses, fine cattle, fine hogs, fine sheep and so on even to fine game chickens. And we have fine and coarse blooded people, or I may say common stock. The original McCrays, those who came from Scotland, were of that class and I found that my father's family were naturally ahead of any of them. And I attribute it all to my little mother..."

46

McCrays were never noted for shyness or lack of opinion about themselves--or of others.

Lewis Reed, of Temple City, California, reported that as a result of anti-Presbyterian feeling, during which a church was burned in New Hampshire, one Samuel McCray left New Hampshire for Pennsylvania. He gave no dates for his journey. He was one of about five Samuel McCrays who lived in Colonial days, according to Mr. Reed.

Mr. Reed is descended from this Samuel McCray, whom he describes as a squatter on what was known as Ten Mile Country, Pennsylvania. It is an area around Ten Mile Creek, on the line between Washington and Greene Counties, south of Pittsburgh. He believes that this Samuel McCray is the same pioneer who founded the line of McCrays from whom Irene Titus is descended. Mrs. Titus said that her Samuel was from eastern Pennsylvania. Mr. Reed disagrees with some of Mrs. Titus' research, as do some others, but there is no disagreement on the names of children of Samuel McCray.

Death Of A Child In Massachusetts

COLONIAL RECORDS TOO OFTEN CONTAIN mentions of people who bore variant names of McCrea, but always with no accompanying information which could be used to further identify them.

In *The New England Historic and Genealogy Register* (volume and page number I failed to record) there is a sad little entry about the death of two of the daughters of John Gram and Elizabeth Cocke, in 1764. John Gram's will lists ten children, and it was recorded therein that their ninth and tenth daughters, Elizabeth, age three, and Catherin (sic), age one, died of a violent flux, and that they had been infected by Allen, son of Allen Macrea. It mournfully added that Elizabeth had been their "comliest child," and had died four days after having become ill.

It is sometimes mistakenly said that people of ancient times died at very early ages. The statistical death of people of long ago was quite low because it was an average of death of all people, children and adults. It was common for half the children in a family to die before reaching age ten. Those who lived to adulthood usually lived to at least their fifties and sixties, and it wasn't unusual for some to live into their eighties and nineties. Their deaths were brought about by rather much the same causes as we do today, in spite of limited medical knowledge and lack of modern sanitation. Examination of genealogical charts giving ages at death, supports this argument.

The Scots-Irish In New England

WHEREVER THE SCOTS-IRISH WENT IN NEW ENGLAND the inhabitants made it abundantly clear to them that they were unwelcome. For that matter, all newcomers who weren't English and Puritan were unwelcome. The Scots-Irish were not at all pleased to find, after making the arduous voyage to avoid English repression and tithes to the Established Church, that in New England they were forced to tithe to the Puritan Church. Bostonians were contemptuous of the newcomers, describing them as dirty, uncouth, and worst of all, Presbyterians. The concept of freedom of religion was still to be conceived; such a notion would everywhere be regarded as wild-eyed, radical, revolutionary, and dangerous to good order and certain to make kingdoms unmanageable.

The first large migration of Ulster Scots to New England in 1718 was about eight hundred people on five ships who had been led to believe they would be welcomed there. Instead they were coldly told that citizenship in a Puritan colony was granted only to members of the Puritan Church. All but a few stayed only one cold winter; some went to Maine, then part of Massachusetts, but most went up the Merrimac into what is now southern New Hampshire and founded their own churches and schools. They spread out and during the next fifty years, founded ten other settlements in New Hampshire, Vermont, northern Pennsylvania, and Nova Scotia.

Some who didn't stick out that first winter along the New England coast, left for Worcester on the frontier, where at first they were welcomed as reinforcements for the fort that was often attacked by Indians, but they soon had differences over religion with Worcester Puritans who commanded them to pay tithes to the Puritan Church. When they tried to build a Presbyterian church, Puritans tore it down, burned some materials, and took the rest for their own use. The Scots-Irish took the hint and left in a body. They founded a number of New England towns.

Word went back to Ulster Scots in Ireland about the cold weather and the even colder reception they could expect in New England, so only a total of about sixty thousand or so ever went there. Many of those who did go didn't stay, but moved southward into Pennsylvania, where the social and religious climate was considerably warmer.

A few went to Newport, Rhode Island, the colony founded by Roger Williams, who shared the Scots-Irish's dislike of Massachusetts. Some McCrays who lived near Hartford, Connecticut, two decades later may possibly have been part of this group.

The Connecticut Connection

WILLIAM AND MARGARET McCRAY WERE LIVING in Hartford on April 25, 1752, on the day their daughter, Elizabeth, was recorded as having been born that day. If this was the "William who drowned," he had three more children before his unfortunate demise. They were: Ruben McCray, born March 3, 1754; David McCray, born December 22, 1755; and Sarah McCray, born October 23, 1763.

In Vernon, a few miles east of Hartford (later, North Bolton, or Bolton, and today, North Vernon), a Presbyterian church was built in 1764. The next year, on February 10, 1765, the name "John, son of John Mcray," was recorded in the church register. Other names recorded there were:

Nov. 2, 1766, Rebecka, daughter of John Mcray
Dec. 12, 1767, Jane, daughter of John Mcray
Aug. 4, 1771, Sarah, daughter of John Mcray
Aug. 22, 1773, Elenor, daughter of John Mcray
July 16, 1775, Eleazor, son of John Mcray
Apl. 22, 1793, John McCray, aged 70 years   (Did he change the
    spelling, or did they finally get it right?)
Apriel 3 Anno Dom 1796, Polly and John, daughter and son of
    John McCray and his wife Polly
Sept. 3, 1797, Eleazor McCray to Eunice Ladd
Augt. 12, 1798 Eunice, daughter of Eleazor McCray
Sept. 14, 1806, Eleazor McCray and wife Eunice from Malborough*
March 24, 1809, child, 1 mo., 2 da., child of Dr. McCray (Eleazor)

At nearby Enfield, Roxanna Hill and Isaac McCray of Ellington, were married on May 28, 1792, at the Congregational Church there. She later married ----Holbrook, of Medway, Massachusetts. Roxanna's sister, Sarah, married ---- McCray, of Ellington, after first marriage to ---- Rogers.

At Ellington, Calvin and Betsey McCray had a son, Horatio, born April 25, 1789, and Calvin, Jr., on June 6, 1791. Betsey was born to them April 22, 1795, but seems to have died, for they named another daughter "Betsey", upon her birth July 19, 1801.

There doesn't seem to be any connection of these McCrays with any other McCrays in other parts of America. Their names have disappeared from Connecticut records after about 1800.

* Apparently, Eleazor and Eunice were being re-admitted after living for a time in Marlborough, Connecticut, south of Vernon.

Maryland and The McCrays

A FEW THOUSAND SCOTS AND SCOTS-IRISH came to Maryland near the end
of the seventeenth century, and were accepted as casually as were all
other colonists. Probably Marylanders were too busy with their own concerns to care very much that the newcomers were Presbyterians, for Maryland was the first American colony to guarantee religious freedom for
all, having passed its "Act Concerning Religion" in 1649. However there
was precious little toleration of Anglicans, Presbyterians, Catholics, or
Jews, all of whom were under as severe repressions as have ever occurred
in America during the next ten years under Cromwell. But to the colonists
of Maryland, the people from Ireland were no threat, but instead were an
asset because of their industriousness and willingness to work hard and
make money growing and exporting tobacco to England.

Although Maryland's charter was granted in 1632 by Charles I to a
Catholic, Cecil Calvert, second baron Baltimore, no attempt was made to
establish the Catholic Church in Maryland. Baltimore rightly sensed that
attempts to enforce Catholicism as an established church would probably
have brought on violent revolution, for there was strong anti-papist
feeling throughout Maryland. At the year 1775, six Lords Baltimore had
ruled Maryland. The names "Baltimore" and "Calvert" are remembered all
over Maryland today as the names of its second-largest city and Calvert*
County, as well as any number of commercial enterprises.

At Snowhill, on the long eastern peninsula bounding the waters of
the Chesapeake Bay, known as "Eastern Shore," there was in the early
eighteenth century a thriving Scottish community that boasted five Presbyterian churches**. When America's first Presbyterian synod was formed
in 1717 in Philadelphia, Snowhill was a very large presbytery. They
slowly shrank as the people drifted away to other places in the growing
colonies, and no one thought to write down anything about why or how
this migration occurred.

Charles A. Dana wrote:

"Concerning the early congregations in Maryland, very
little is known beyond the fact that about 1670, Colonel Nin-
ean Beall emigrated to that colony, settling between the Potomac and the Patuxent. During the next twenty years he induced
a number of his friends (most accounts place the number at

* Pronounced "Cawl-vert" in these parts.

** *The Scotch-Irish, Or, The Scot in North Britain, North Ireland and
North America*, Charles A. Dana, 2 vols.,G.P. Putnams' Sons; New York
and London, 1902.

50

about two hundred) to join him. They founded the Presbyterian congregation at Upper Marlborough (today, "Marlboro"),
which was the first under the care of Rev. Nathanial Taylor."

Not more than a tenth of all the Scots-Irish immigrants went to
Maryland. By far the majority of them went to Pennsylvania, probably
because the Quakers of Pennsylvania did a superior job of recruiting in
Ireland. Maryland was a producer of tobacco, a field crop, so the planters of Maryland wanted field hands, rather than skilled linen workers or
farmers who had developed a sense of worth as independent farmers. The
Scots-Irish who were forced to indenture themselves to pay their way here
would, given a choice, have preferred to go to Pennyslvania. William
Penn's agents stressed to the people in Ulster that their rights as indentured servants would be protected, and they would not be treated as
slaves as they might in the colonies to the south. There, when crops
failed, a plantation owner could sell off some un-needed slaves, and the
indentured hands were sometimes driven away without any funds or means
of earning a living.

Nor was Maryland's freedom from religious conformity a particular
advantage in recruitment among Europe's religiously oppressed, for Pennsylvania not only just tolerated but welcomed people of all faiths.

Best estimates are that Scots-Irish were ten percent of the arrivals
in Maryland who came ashore at Port Tobacco, St. Mary's City, Annapolis
and Baltimore, but nobody ever recorded their numbers so it is unknown
which of the Maryland ports was most favored. Port Tobacco, as the
name implies, was well on the way to becoming Maryland's principal city,
but the city was built at the estuary of a small creek, and development
of the land there resulted in the port becoming silted up and ships could
no longer get to the docks. St. Mary's City was the first port to be
encountered by ships entering the Chesapeake Bay, and it thrived for many
years, but it, too, failed. Annapolis and Baltimore developed as more
cosmopolitan cities, and were located further inland, reducing the difficulty of transporting goods out from the ports.

Both Port Tobacco and St. Mary's City shrank to almost invisibility,
but both are now being rebuilt, with buildings duplicating the original
ones, and developers hope to make them tourist attractions. St Mary's
City tells its story in daily costumed stage productions, and handicraft
and food vendors are dressed in appropriate seventeenth century costumes.
One can see today a hint of what Port Tobacco once amounted to in the
beautiful large Catholic church on a hilltop overlooking the confluence
of the creek and the Potomac River. Local history and archeology buffs
have uncovered the ballast brick foundations of several large buildings
and have reconstructed a municipal building. They're looking for a very
rich angel to finance the restoration of Port Tobacco.

The McCrays Of Maryland

ONE OF THE FAMILY LEGENDS OF THE McCRAYS OF PENNSYLVANIA relates
that the first of the clan landed at Baltimore and made his way north
along the Susquehanna River to a valley just north of Carlisle, Pennsylvania. I once suffered from a vain supposition that we McCrays of northwestern Pennsylvania were unique in America, and that in all the world
there could be but one Philip McCray. The occasional McCray who turned up
denying that he or his family were natives of Pennsylvania -- well, he
just must have forgotten.

My perspective was suddenly widened when I found my name listed in
the index of a history of Charles County, Maryland, in our local library.
To say that I was startled would understate it. How could this BE???
As I turned to the page indicated I sensed that perhaps some ghostly
presence was laughing from behind the stacks. And it was true: there it
was printed that Philip and Henry McCray lived two hundred years ago in
Port Tobacco, just down the Potomac River a few miles from this very
spot, this county where I had lived for more than half of my life, Prince
George's County. Their names were printed in a census taken in 1776 by
Constable Peter Griffith, listing the able-bodied men capable of bearing arms in the Revolutionary War. They lived in East Hundred, Charles
County. In another book I found Henry again, this time as witness to a
will of Zachariah Low, February 5, 1776. In La Plata, the county seat
of Charles County, a few days later, I found a Jesse McCray, who had
transferred title of a tract of land in consideration of nineteen pounds,
eleven shillings, thruppence and one-and-a-half pence, "current money,"
to Christopher Robinson, on May 30, 1789. Philip was also listed in the
1790 Federal Census as head of a household in Charles County, consisting
of three free white females and one slave.

At the Maryland Historical Society in Baltimore I learned that the
McCrays had also lived almost in my backyard. I found this in some
Prince George's County records:

"In the November term (of the Prince George's County court
in 1768) an order was passed to pay Dr. James Lopier three pounds
for attending the last illness of Martha McCray. "

Also in a list of Maryland marriages I learned that Farquire McCray
married Susan Ferguson, April 21, 1781, in Prince George's County, with

the Reverend Osborne Sprigg officiating. In 1796, Farquire was listed in the county's tax records as "delinquent."

Encouraged, I took myself off to Annapolis and the Hall of Records, Maryland's depository of state archives at St. John's College, where I found the earliest record of a Maryland McCray. Two land patents were granted to Robert McCray, one for 266 acres in Cecil County in 1758, and the other, in 1760, for forty acres in Worcester County. No further mention of this Robert turned up, but in the 1790 Federal Census, Robert McCray was listed in Fairfax County, Virginia. There is no known connection between these two McCrays.

An advertisement appeared in Benjamin Franklin's *Pennsylvania Gazette* in 1752, seeking, "Runaway apprentice, William Clifton, age 17, whose mother, Sarah Clifton, lives in Dorset County, Maryland, runaway from William McCrea, Shipjoiner." This was probably William McCrea, mentioned in the preceeding chapter on McCreas.   This item, not concerning the McCrays really, but an interesting tidbit.

There are several McCrays in Prince Georges County today, but none that I contacted knows anything about a possible link to these early McCrays.

At the same time that these McCrays of Maryland were being recorded in records, a few miles upstream of the Potomac River, Daniel McCray turned up in Loudoun County, Virginia. From Port Tobacco to Loudoun County, Virginia, is a distance of about sixty miles via the river. The Potomac and the Shenandoah Rivers were highways into the interior of Virginia, and there was always a stream of hunters, trappers and settlers going upstream on these rivers. It seems quite unlikely that the McCrays of southern Maryland and Daniel McCray were not at least aware of each other, and some gamblers might give odds that they were closely related, perhaps even brothers.

Thomas McCray is also listed in the *General Index, Land Records, Cecil County (Maryland)*, p. 450, as having transferred a plot of land to Peter Springer.

In Chapter Five of this book, John McCray, who lived several years in Maryland and had children there, will be dealt with. He apparently was not a native of that state.

CHAPTER FOUR

VIRGINIA

The Settlement Of Virginia's Backwoods

BETWEEN THE BLUE RIDGE ON THE EAST AND THE ALLEGHENEY MOUNTAINS on the west lies a beautiful and wonderfully rich place called the Valley of Virginia. Native Americans travelled the length of it, but never occupied it, leaving it undisturbed for their game preserve. Deer, elk, bear, beaver, and the huge eastern bison, the "woods buffalo," roamed freely there, and were harvested in the late fall for winter food. In the spring they burned off the valley to destroy tree seedlings, keeping the valley covered with dark green grass that grew waist high by fall.

The northern one hundred and fifty miles of the Valley of Virginia is referred to as the Shenandoah Valley, and strictly speaking, it is that part drained by the Shenandoah River, which joins with the Potomac River at Harper's Ferry, West Virginia. The two rivers were major waterways for access to the interior from tidal regions of Virginia and Maryland until roads, canals and railroads came. People today have extended the Shenandoah Valley to include Rockingham and Rockbridge Counties, even though the valley doesn't tilt north there.

William Gooch became governor of Virginia about the time that Scots-Irish and German settlers were beginning to filter down into the Shenandoah Valley from Pennsylvania in 1730. He determined to open the Shenandoah Valley to settlers, thereby not only to increase Virginia's farming prosperity, but to plant well-armed men in sufficient numbers to make a military deterrent. Both France and England claimed the land west of the Allegheny Mountains; Virginia's charter included all the territory from the Atlantic to the Mississippi River, but France claimed the western parts of Virginia's claim. With France and England at each other's throats almost daily, the French and Indian War was almost inevitable.

To get things started, Governor Gooch awarded forty thousand acres in northern Virginia, comprising today's Jefferson (West Virginia), Frederick and Clarke Counties to John and Isaac Van Meter, who sold their warrant to Joist Hight. He brought in large numbers of German settlers, descendants of whom have annual German festivals in the region today. With all the good intentions in the world, he gave away land that had already been granted to Lord Fairfax by Charles II. Charles didn't do his homework. Inevitably, confrontations and litigation resulted which lasted long after the principals were in their graves.

In 1736 he granted two more huge tracts in the Shenandoah Valley,

54

this time to William Beverley and Benjamin Borden. Much of the land in both tracts was already settled upon by both German and Scots-Irish squatters. This Manor of Beverley was 118,491 acres, located in present-day Rockingham and Augusta Counties, including the cities of Staunton* and Waynesboro. A Scots-Irish settler, one John Lewis, was already in the area when the Beverley Manor grant was made. He had fled from Ireland after having killed a landlord, probably over rack-renting. Lewis became one of the valley's leaders. Among others who settled there, McCrays appeared soon after the Manor of Beverley was opened for settlement.

Benjamin Borden, of New Jersey, received a grant of nearly a half-million acres that embraced most of Rockbridge County and some of Augusta County, shortly after Beverley's grant. A stipulation applied to both grants that a hundred families must be settled on the land before clear title would be given. The goal was reached in 1739. Neither Borden nor Beverley had any trouble fulfilling the requirements for title. Both tracts were liberally sprinkled with cabins of squatting settlers who had come there before 1736, and they were taken in as part of the specified one hundred families. There was some haggling and grumbling, but they worked out payments with everyone. Borden's tract had so many Scots-Irish settlers that it became known as"The Irish Tract."

Lewis was visited by Ephriam McDowell** an Ulster Scot from eastern Pennsylvania, whom Lewis introduced to Borden. Borden was impressed with McDowell, and offered to make him overseer of his tract. John McDowell, Ephriam's son, surveyed all of Borden's allotments. Ephriam's descendants produced a line of leaders that included a governor of Virginia, a U.S. Senator, a Civil War general, a famed surgeon and numerous local leaders. There are several counties in southern Appalachian states that bear the name McDowell. When I tried to impress my son, Thomas, with this litany of greatness, and pointed out to him that he had some pretty good genes in his body, he looked at me with a twinkle in his eye and asked, "What happened?"

Travel through the Valley of Virginia was relatively easy in early days (disregarding occasional Indian attacks), because there was already a well-used Indian trail on the floor of the valley and no forests to contend with. The grass attracted hordes of game that provided the Indians with meat, hide, bones, and sinew--all essential for Indian life and culture. As one might expect, when white men began erecting fences,

* Originally spelled "Stanton" and still so pronounced. Native Virginians quickly spot outlanders when they pronounce it "Stawnton."

** My mother, Marion Louise McDowell, is probably descended from a contemporary of Ephriam McDowell; both came from eastern Pennsylvania, but the common link has not been found to date.

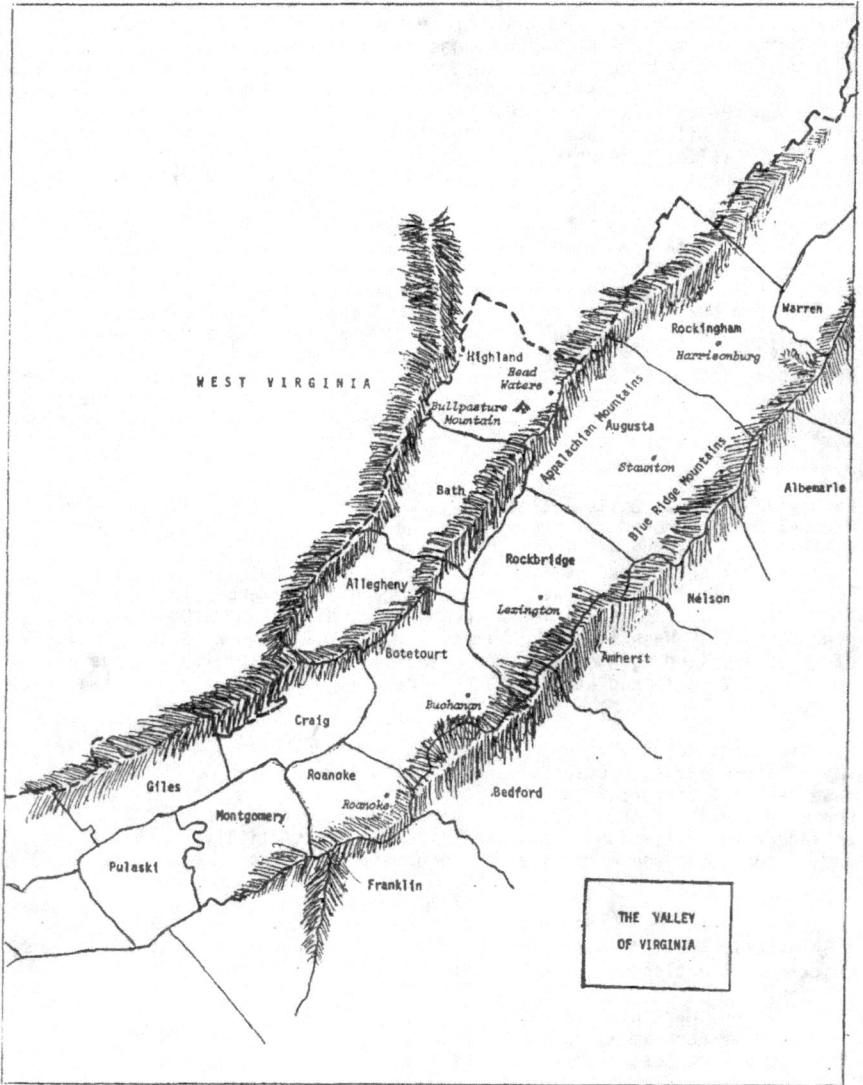

WEST VIRGINIA

Highland
Head
Waters

Bullpasture
Mountain

Warren

Rockingham
Harrisonburg

Appalachian Mountains

Augusta

Staunton

Bath

Blue Ridge Mountains

Albemarle

Rockbridge

Allegheny

Lexington

Nelson

Botetourt

Amherst

Craig

Buchanan

Giles

Roanoke

Roanoke

Bedford

Montgomery

Pulaski

Franklin

THE VALLEY
OF VIRGINIA

56

building dams, putting up cabins, and plowing the soil, they became most
unwelcome, and the Tuscarora and Shawnee Indians didn't give up the fight
until they were hopelessly outnumbered. But for a long time after the
settlement in Paris of the French and Indian War, the natives would occasionally come down from the western heights, take some scalps, burn a
few cabins, kill cattle, and generally spread terror.

The Scots-Irish caused problems for the Government at Williamsburg,
but they generally governed themselves quite well, and from the viewpoint
of the gentry on the coast, drove out the Indians as well. More importantly, they were insatiable buyers of land, especially after the third
great wave of immigrants from Ireland in 1740.

In 1738 Augusta County was taken out of Orange County; in 1769,
Botetourt County was taken from Augusta; in 1778 Rockbridge County was
born of Augusta and that same year Augusta and Botetourt were divided
some more to make Rockingham County. Highland County was taken out of
Bath and Pendleton Counties in 1847, and Pendleton County, once part of
Augusta and Hardy Counties, was created in 1787.

Prior to 1700, Virginia was a vast country that extended over today's
West Virginia and Kentucky, known as Fincastle County. In 1776 Fincastle
County was renamed Kentucky and it became a state in 1792.

When the Civil War came the nation was split by strife, and Virginia
itself was split, geographically. The Allegheny Mountains had always provided a cultural barrier, with those west of the mountains being predom-
inently pioneer stock of German and Scots-Irish extraction. Virginians
east of the Blue Ridge Mountains were mostly Episcopalians of English
descent, and the Episcopal Church was, until 1787, Virginia's established
church, complete with compulsory tithes. The Scots-Irish had left the
British Isles partly to get away from tithes to churches not of their
choice, and conflict began the day the first Scots-Irish came into the
Shenandoah Valley about 1730.

These sturdy folk living in the mountains and valleys of the Alleghenies were mostly Union sympathizers, so in 1861 they met and decided
that if Virginia could secede from the Union, then they could just up and
secede from Virginia, which they did, calling themselves "Kanawha," but
in 1863, it was taken into the Union as West Virginia.

Whatever political and cultural differences that may have existed
then are now quite blurred and the people of the two states in adjoining
counties proudly call themselves "Mountaineers."

In the following section on other McCrays of Rockbridge County, it
is shown that McCray/Armstrong marriages began before the Highland County
McCrays began leaving recorded evidence of their lives and loves. It
rather strongly suggests there is a link between the two clans.

57

Alexander, A Very Early McCray

IN AN ASSORTED LOT OF COURT ACTIONS taken in Augusta County on a spring day of 1750 was the following:*

"Page 246--22nd May, 1750. Archibald Clendenning's appraisment, by Hugh Coffee, Alex. McCray, John Cartmel. Books."

And,

"Page 148--13th December, 1748. Archibald Clendenning (of Cowpastui , will--wife, Esther; son John; etc."

This 1750 date is the earliest one that has turned up so far for a McCray in America, although on page 49 it is recorded that Elizabeth McCray was born in 1752 in Hartford, Connecticut, and it is anyone's guess how long her parents, William and Margaret McCray, had been living in Connectuct before Elizabeth was born. And for Alexander McCray to have been appointed by a court to appraise an estate suggests that he had been living in the area long enough to have learned local values of books, probably at least two years.

Augusta County, formed in 1745, included all the land in today's Botetourt, Rockbridge and Rockingham Counties, and parts of Bath, Highland, Alleghany, Montgomery and Roanoke Counties. It would be impossible to guess where the Clendenning land was located had not the clerk inserted the parenthetical, "(of Cowpasture)," when he recorded Clendenning's will. In today's Bath County, then in Augusta County, is the Little Cowpasture Creek, and it would be safe to say that Clendenning's land lay thereabouts, and we may wonder if perhaps Alexander didn't also live there.

Geographers probably smile at some pioneer's wit when preparing maps of Highland and Bath Counties, for Bullpasture River flows down from Highland County where it merges with Cowpasture Creek in Bath County, and the combined waters continue on into Rockbridge County where Calfpasture River adds its bovine waters, and the whole mixture then joins with the James River at Lexington. The possibilities for jokes here seem endless.

* *Chronicles of the Scotch-Irish Settlement of Virginia,* extracted from the original court records of Augusta County, Virginia, in 1745-1800; Lyman Chalkley, Genealogical Publishing Company, Baltimore, 1974. Pp 12 & 17.

It is also tempting to wonder if Alexander McCray was the progenitor of some of the McCrays who lived in Rockbridge County, especially because Cowpasture Creek was, until Bath County was created in 1790, within the bounds of Rockbridge County. The idea loses credence, however, because there were, as far as records show, no later Alexander McCrays. Scots-Irish families almost always named alternate generations of males with the child's grandfather's name. Alexander McCray was listed later as a taxpayer in Louisa County between 1782 and 1787. Louisa County is about 125-150 miles east of Cowpasture Creek.

Joseph McCray, of Rockbridge County

ROCKBRIDGE COUNTY TAXPAYERS between 1782 and 1787 included:

> James McCray
> Joseph McCray
> Robert McCray

We have no solid information about who these McCrays were, or what their relationship was to each other. One branch of the McCray family, many of whom still live in the area of Bullpasture Mountain, in Highland County, have traced their line back to a Robert McCray, but they have been unable to learn whether or not this Robert is their ancestor. (See p. 78)

James McCray, of this tax list, is very likely the James McCrea who, along with Joseph McCrea, was listed as serving in John Paxton's Rockbridge County company of militia. On "Je 27, 1814, Daniel L. Burford and wife Ruth, sold for $600, 117 acres of land to Jas. McCrae." according to Amherst County records. That's all anyone has found about this James McCray, and the last item is questionable, at that.

Lorena Day, of Chula Vista, California, and Mrs. Mary McKinney, of Tucson, Arizona, are both descended from Joseph McCray, and both have done their research carefully and conservatively. Neither has found any positive connection between the Joseph McCray listed in the earliest records of Rockbridge County and two others, father and son, who followed. Quite naturally, they suspect that the earliest one is the progenitor of the others, upon whom Mrs. McKinney and Mrs. Day have accumulated a great deal of documented data.

Joseph McCray died in Rockbridge County in 1785. Mrs. McKinney does believe that the first Joseph McCray MAY (italics mine) have married Jean Armstrong of Augusta County. This would have been prior to 1778, when Rockbridge County was taken out of Augusta. Joseph is known to have had a son, other than the almost-certain Joseph (II?), and two daughters the names of all of them being unknown. Joseph died in 1785, and his will was recorded in Rockbridge County between May and June, 1785.

Joseph McCray, believed to be the son of the Joseph above, was born August 23, 1785, about three months after the death of the first Joseph. He married Sophia Burford, daughter of James and Mary (Rucker) Burford, on December 20, 1808, in Amherst County, Virginia. Their children included:**

> Joseph W. McCray
> Rueben McCray
> Sophia McCray
> John McCray
> Probably six others

In June, 1827, Joseph and Sophia sold their land "on Harris Creek" in Rockbridge County to Ambrose Rucker, the brother of Sophia's mother, Mary (Rucker), on June 23, 1827. They also sold another tract of land to Matthew Davidson. The McCrays and Davidsons seem to have had a close relationship. *The Virginia Genealogist*, listed Rockbridge County marriages from 1778 to 1805, and among the items were these:

> "DAVIDSON, John and Sally McCrea, dau. of Jos. McCrea, dec'd. Bond: John Davidson, Hugh Paxton. Consent of William Davidson for son John to marry Sally McCrea who is a daughter to my wife Elizabeth. 6 Jan. 1801."

> "DAVIDSON, William and Elizabeth McCrea, widow. Bond: William Davidson and James Carruthers, Esq. 19 Jan. 1792."

The first of these two items would indicate that William Davidson married the widow, Elizabeth McCray, in 1792, and that she had a daughter, Sally. No records have turned up to shed light upon which McCrea/McCray Elizabeth married.

** The Federal Census listed five sons and five daughters, un-named.

Mrs. McKinney believes that Joseph I was her ancestor, and that his wife was Jean Armstrong. Her belief is rather strongly supported by the will of Archibald Armstrong, filed in the year 1800, in which he left bequests to a grandson, Archibald Armstrong McCray, and to a daughter, Jean McCray. We may safely suppose that Archibald Armstrong McCray is the son of Jean (and Joseph?) McCray, but the will doesn't make this clear. *Chronicles*, in obvious error, reports, "to grandson, Margaret McCray," which should read "granddaughter." We may suppose that Archibald and Margaret were brother and sister, but again, it isn't made clear in the will as reported.

After disposing of their land in Rockbridge County, Joseph and Sophia loaded up their possessions and moved to Deer Creek Township, Madison County, Ohio, where they were enumerated in the 1830 Federal Census. Madison County is located in the center of Ohio, adjacent to Franklin County; Columbus, the capital, sprawls over most of Franklin County today. The Federal Census of 1830 revealed that Joseph and Sophia had then twelve children. It was recorded that the first-born, Joseph W. McCray, was born on October 26, 1809, a year after the marriage. The next child whose name was preserved was Sophia, born in 1823. John was born in 1825, and Rueben A. was born in 1827. Eight children were born between 1809 and 1823, roughly one every one and three-quarters years. Unfortunately, the names of none of them has been kept.

It was the Federal Census of 1850 that told us the ages and place of birth of the known children. Sophia was age sixty-one, Sophia (daughter) was 27, John, 25, and Rueben A., 22.

Joseph, the father, died on May 28, 1848, at age sixty-three, in Franklin County. The Joseph McCray family had moved to Franklin County between 1830 and 1840. After his death in 1848, Sophia took the family remaining with her back to Madison County. She died there, date unknown.

Joseph W. McCray married seventeen-year old Mary Ann Frederick on January 26, 1835, when he was age 26, in Madison County, Ohio. She was born on December 23, 1818. A son, James, was born to them on October 26 1835, but he didn't quite live out his first year of life, dying on October 11, 1836. Elizabeth Jane, John Calvin, and Margaret C. were born next. The family moved to Franklin County, but they didn't stay there very long, for in 1842, Joseph packed up their possessions and they moved to a farm near Fairbank, Iowa. Fairbank is about fifteen miles northeast of Waterloo on the Wapsipinicon River. They had seven more children in Iowa. Mary Ann died on April 8, 1862, and Joseph W. died

61

on October 26, 1878, on his farm near Fairbank, Iowa.

The Notebook Of Margaret C. McCray

EVERYONE SHOULD KEEP A JOURNAL of their life and their family, complete with dates and places. Margaret C. McCray, daughter of Joseph W. McCray, kept a notebook during her life which is a family treasure today. In it she jotted down the birthdays, deaths, marriages, and important dates--dates important to the family. She is remembered and spoken of with endearment as "Grandma Estey."

Margaret McCray was two years old when she came to Iowa with her family, and she grew up there. Her family believes that she was educated by her father, a graduate of Amherst College (University, today). She often talked of her father and his office which was filled with books. Mrs. Lorena Day, a descendant from Margaret, described how her mother showed "the case of books her father had in their farm home in Nebraska, about 1895, to her teacher, who was amazed to see so many books in a private home." Some of the books were related to his college studies, but somehow nobody ever thought to find out what his major studies were.

In 1858, Margaret married Elam Jones, a native of England, born there in 1833. Shortly after their marriage they went to Omaha and joined a wagon train across the Territory of Nebraska to the burgeoning town of Denver, where gold had been discovered a few years before. Denver was then in the Territory of Colorado. Permanent white settlers had come to the new territory only three or four years before, and several new settlements there were becoming modest towns.

An article in the *Fremont* (Nebraska) *Tribune* of March 28, 1967, described life on wagon trains and on the western frontier. Most of the article was written by Margaret, but there seemed to have been some input to it from her son. Mrs. Day wrote concerning this: "Margaret went by the name of Maggie and her son much later assumed her name was Magdelina." Margaret is referred to in the article as "Magdelina McCray." The article also refers to her husband as "Judson" Jones, rather than Elam Jones.

"There were 40 wagons in the ox train as no one was allowed to leave Omaha without there being enough wagons together to protect them from the Indians.

"There were only a few houses in Omaha then, and nothing clear across the plains to Denver, Colo., except Indians and Buffaloes. There was quite a stream running at the foot of Capitol Hill in Omaha (probably Papio Creek). I don't know what they did with it but I know it was there because our train camped by it over Sunday.

62

"My it was lonesome country. No houses, railroads, tele-
graph or telephones as we see them now (1915). No trains or
stations except a stage station every 30 miles where the stage
horses were kept.

"Lincoln had not been heard of then (Lincoln, Neb.), or any
of the towns except Fremont. There were only three or four
houses in Fremont, and Dr. Abbott was the only doctor between
there and Denver. There was no Grand Island, except the Grand
Island in the Platte River from which the town took its name."

She gave no details of their life in Denver, but a year later they
returned to Nebraska to operate the Overland State Station on the (Fort)
Kearney reservation. The *Tribune's* lead of the story described the
terror of an ordeal she went through there:

"A small enclosure, crudely constructed of tall weeds and
willows intertwined, caught the attention of the bride of a year
as she loped her horse over the bottom-land prairie. She rode
to it. Dismounting, she peered into the enclosure, wondering
who had built it and why. As her eyes adjusted to the darkness
of the enclosure, where the sun failed to penetrate, she dis-
cerned the body of a white man, her husband--dead. It was
the work of Indians.

"Stunned and terrorized by what she saw, the young woman
hurriedly scanned the countryside for possible redmen as she
remounted her horse and rode hurriedly away, back to her home
at Ft. Kearney Station.

"So I was left among strangers with my three little children but my uncle (Rueben McCray), who was visiting us, took
the children and me back to Iowa, where my parents lived. Two
years after that I came back but our horses were scattered no
one knows where. Houses were being built along the roads and
the country was already beginning to change.

"However, marriageable women were still scarce on the
frontier. Stationed at Ft. Kearney was a young soldier who had
never forgotten the vivacious young Widow Jones. He was William A. Esty (Estey)."

William Estey's ancestors didn't catch the voyage of the Mayflower
to the coast of Massachusetts, but Jeffrey Estey and his son, Isaac, got
there in 1636. Isaac grew up and married Mary Towne, who later was ac-
cused of witchcraft, tried, condemned and hanged in 1692. Aaron Estey,
William's great grandfather, who was then living in Vermont and New Hampshire, served in the American Revolution.

63

In 1855 William A. Estey was a young man living in Sheboygan County, Wisconsin. He went for a walk one day and walked until he stopped "where Sioux City now stands." On May 22, 1861, he married Mrs. Mary (McGuire) Cloud in Woodbury County, Iowa. She was the stepdaughter of J.M. Townsley* of Woodbury. Mary achieved a dubious distinction in the social history of Woodbury County when she divorced her husband, Jonathan M. Cloud, in the county's first divorce case.

William and Mary (McGuire)(Cloud) Estey sold their farm five months after their wedding and moved westward across Iowa to a site near Fort Kearney, in the Nebraska Territory. The fort was in the middle of the territory, situated along the Platte River, just west of the junction of the Mormon Trail (U.S. Highway 30 today), and the Oregon Route. The Civil War was being fought then, and Indians were not welcoming settlers, and Fort Kearney was an active military installation. It was also a station for the Pony Express and the Overland Stage routes. Similar stations were spaced along the route every thirty miles, primarily for the exchange of fresh horses. The town of Kearney grew up around Fort Kearney and it is today the county seat of Buffalo County.

The Esteys lived there for five years, and during this time Estey served with the Union troops as a scout. Mary Estey died in 1866, and fifty years later in 1916, someone found her grave on the prairie near Kearney, and the D.A.R. moved the body to Kearney Cemetery. Hers is the oldest grave in the cemetery.

William Estey must have had a happy marriage and was sold on the institution, for he wasted no time in courting and wedding the pretty widow, Margaret (McCray) Jones, living in the family home near Fairbank, Iowa. The couple returned to Fort Kearney, where he completed his Army service, mustered out, and they built a home along the busy wagon trail about ten miles east of the fort along the Platte River, near where the town of Gibbon now stands. The *Fremont Tribune* article continued:

"We kept a ranch and store for travelers, but think what it would cost us to have our provisions brought from Omaha. We gave $12 for a sack of flour, $4 for potatoes, and everything else in proportion. But it was 100 miles west of us to the next place where travellers could buy grain so they had to buy from our store.

"The Union Pacific Railroad was built through central Nebraska while the Esteys lived in the Gibbon area. 'It was quite

* John Townsley, in some way related to my gr gr gr Grandmother, Eleanor Townsley, migrated from Cumberland County, Pennsylvania to Ohio, in 1794. No relationship is known between J.M. and John Townsley, but it does not appear to be an accidental similarity.

an exciting time,' she wrote. 'Soldiers were kept with the trains. The Indians derailed one train and thought they had destroyed it and all the men on it, but when other soldiers came they found one man who had been scalped and left for dead was still alive. They brought him to our house and we took care of him until the stage came from the west the next day. They brought him to Omaha and as far as I know he is still alive.'"

It cost a fortune to ship fruit to Nebraska, so it was almost non-existent there. The Esteys decided to supply some of the demand themselves from their own orchards. Knowing that fruit trees could not be grown where they were located, they sold out their ranch and store and moved back eastward to Fremont, a few miles west of Sioux City, Iowa, found some land along the Platte River, and dug out a sort of cave-like home in the riverbank. A few years later, in 1878 they built a "soddy", a house of "prairie brick", which was prairie sod, a common building material of the time. It wasn't much for looks, but as my grandfther, Grant McCray would say about his Model "T" Ford, "It ain't much for looks but it's hell for strong."

They had fruit trees shipped to them and developed a truck farm which was, according to the *Tribune*, successful to a high degree. They worked very hard and began taking vegetables, sweet corn and melons, and later, fruit, to Fremont where everything was eagerly bought up. Their success attracted neighbors who also built soddies.

Margaret wrote about living in sod houses:

"They were very comfortable quarters, but occasionally a rattlesnake would attempt to take up his abode in the same quarters, at which time a peculiar chilly feeling would come over us which was hard to overcome." Indeed!

As it was among pioneers living in log cabins, the test of quality of the pioneering family was how soon they built themselves better accomodations. The Esteys built a large modern frame house to replace their soddy. Just across the river the town of Leshara was growing. The nearest postoffice was twelve miles away, so the Esteys founded a post-office in their home, and mail began arriving more frequently because stormy weather prevented trips to pick up mail, and there was no delivery at that time. They named the postoffice "Estina."

Estey was a community leader; he built the first schoolhouse in the area which served the community of Leshara until it grew large enough to build a schoolhouse for the surrounding area. He also gave the money and a lot of labor to build a Methodist church in Leshara. He was an ardent Prohibitionist, and used his considerable influence to keep Leshara dry during his lifetime.

Margaret became the area's angel of mercy, a nurse who could be relied upon to saddle up her pony any time and go to the aid of mothers delivering babies, splinting broken bones, treating snake-bite and gunshot
wounds, and treating the sick. An epidemic of diphtheria descended upon
the community and she was on the go constantly, doing what she could
with what she had, which wasn't much. There was no positive treatment
for diphtheria, and thousands of children died of the disease every year.
Somone asked her if she wasn't fearful that she herself would be struck
down, and she calmly replied that God would not allow that to happen.
The Estey family was the only family in the community that didn't have
at least one case of diphtheria. Margaret would have said that wonderful things can be done with faith.

Rueben McCray, Wagon Driver of the Prairies

ROMANTIC FIGURES ABOUNDED IN THE WEST. Gunslingers, cowboys, gold
miners--all were glorified and written up in Eastern newspapers and mag-
azines, with not much said about the fact that most of their lives were
spent in dull drudgery, with occasional highlights of danger and excitement. Wagon drivers who skillfully handled the freight wagons pulled by
spans of horses, and sometimes by four or even six horses, were not only
romantic figures to writers, but they delivered the goods out where the
railroads didn't go. Rueben McCray was a wagon driver.

Rueben A. McCray was a brother of Joseph W. McCray, born in Madison
County, Ohio, in 1827. As far as we know he never married, but he probably would have made a lousy husband and father, so it's just as well
he didn't. We have no details of his childhood and upbringing, but his
educated father apparently wasn't able to instill a love for the life of
a scholar in his son. Life in frontier towns wasn't conducive to book-
ish interests anyway, and boys' heroes usually were men of action and
muscle who could ride, shoot and fight--men like Daniel Boone, Michael
Cresap, and Simon Kenton. A boy of that time might hope for a career as
a wagon driver--a muleskinner-- in the same way that today's lad might
aspire to become a spacecraft pilot.

We might imagine Rueben as a barefoot boy, hanging around stables
where the great dusty wagons came to change horses, learning to crack a
long blacksnake whip, carefully studying harness and hitching techniques.
Perhaps he carried buckets of water to the huge draft animals, and listened to fantastic yarns, some true, about adventures on prairie roads.
As an older lad he may have gone along with his heroes on shorter trips
and learned the craft of managing horses under harness, getting the feel
of the messages through the reins from each horse that told the driver
how each animal differed from the others.

66

So he became a driver of freight wagons, a romantic, envied figure of the early West. He was called "Uncle Mac" by his family. He managed to make fairly frequent stops at Fort Kearney to visit his neice, Margaret (McCray) Jones and her husband, Elam and their children. He just happened to be there when Indians, intent on stealing Elam's horses, killed him. Rueben was helpful in getting the body of Elam Jones buried and then he took Margaret and her children back to the farm of his brother, Joseph W. McCray, near Fairbank, Iowa.

Mrs. H.K. (Margaret Anne Gammon) Fosha, of Calhan, Colorado, wrote to Mrs. Day about the Ohio McCrays from whom she is descended. She is the granddaughter of Roxie Green Gammon, whose mother was Sophia Green, sister of Rueben A. McCray. She said that there are papers of the Gammon family that tell of Rueben McCray coming to the Pike's Peak region in 1858. In the 1850s he drove wagon trains in the fur trade between Denver and Leavenworth, Kansas.* She wrote:

"In 1874 R. McCray and Julien Gammon received territorial brand certificates and settled in a dugout on Big Sandy Creek, acquiring more land and starting in the cattle business. Soon after, this was part of the OZ Ranch, postoffice and store (a couple of miles west of the present town of Ramah, Colo.).

"In 1876 R. McCray brought his widowed sister, Sophia Green, and her two daughters, Roxie Anne (age 16) and Rosalie from Cedar Rapids, Iowa to live at OZ.

"In 1876 Roxie Green and Julien Gammon were married there by Rueben McCray--a Justice of Peace.

"Notes show that R. McCray died at the home of Julien and Roxie at 3H Ranch (formerly OZ) on Jan. 1, 1897, and was taken by train to Colorado Springs and buried in the Gammon family plot in Evergreen Cemetery."

The wail of the locomotive's whistle drowned out the crack of the driver's whip in 1869 when a golden spike was driven in a crosstie to herald the completion of coast-to-coast railroad service. But Rueben McCray was there at the right time and place when the trumpet sounded. He had his day. Few of us get things timed so nicely!

* She believes there are records in the Gilpin County, Colorado, courthouse at Central City of business dealings in the 1860s, and in the Douglas County, Colorado courthouse at Castle Koch, or the Pioneer Museum in Colorado Springs, which might shed some further light on Rueben McCray.

The Family and Descendants from

Joseph McCray of Virginia

Generation I   Generation II

Joseph McCray | Joseph McCray*
b. ? | b. 23 Aug., 1785, Rockbridge Co., Va.
d. 1785, Rockbridge | d. 28 May, 1848, Franklin Co., Ohio
County, Va. | m. Sophia Burford, on 20 Dec., 1803, in
m. Jane (Armstrong | Amherst Co., Va. Dau. of James Burford
   of Augusta Co., | and Mary Rucker.   10 ch.
   Virginia?) | b. 1789
                                 | d. ? in Deer Creek Twp., Madison Co.
                                 | Ohio.

Mrs. Lorena Day, of Chula Vista CA wrote that her grandmother, Margaret
C. McCray, stated that the family name is correctly spelled "MacRae."

* It is not confirmed that this Joseph McCray was the son of the
  Joseph McCray of Generation I above.

Generation I   Generation III

Joseph McCray | Joseph W. McCray #
     & | b. 26 Oct., 1809, Rockbridge Co., Va.
Jane (Armstrong?) | d. 15 July, 1878, Fairbank, Buchanan Co. Iowa#
                                     ──| m. Mary Ann Frederick, on 26 Jan., 1835, 10 ch
                                       | b. 23 Dec., 1818
                                       | d. 8 April, 1862

                                       | Reuben McCray
                                       | b. ca 1828, in Deer Creek Twp., Madison Co.
                                       | Ohio.
                                     ──| d. 1 Jan., 1897, nr. Ramah, Colo.
                                       | buried, Evergreen Cemetery, Colorado Springs,
                                       | Colorado.
                                       | Never married.

Generation II

Joseph McCray | Sophia McCray
     & | b. ca 1823, Rockbridge Co., Va.
Sophia Burford   ──| d. ?
                                       | m. (1) ------- Green   10 ch
                                       | (2) Julien Gammon, in 1878

                                       | John McCray
                                       | b. ca 1825, in Rockbridge Co., Va.
                                     ──| d. ?
                                       | m. ?

Dates taken from Margaret C. McCray's notebook.

69

Generation I   Generation IV

Joseph McCray   James McCray
     &   b. Oct. 26, 1835#
Jane (Armstrong?)   d. Oct. 11, 1836#

                                     Elizabeth Jane McCray
                                     b. 18 Feb., 1837, in Ohio#
                                     d. 20 July, 1918, in Oelwein, Iowa
     Generation II   m. William Bentley, on 23 March, 1861#
                                        b. 1838
                                        d. 1922
Joseph McCray II   He was a blacksmith in Oelwein.
     &
Sophia Burford   John Calvin McCray
                                     b. 9 Oct., 1838, in Ohio
                                     d. March 1863 (May, 1863#) He was a hemo-
                                        philiac; his little finger was shot off
                                        and he bled to death. Civil War.

     Generation III   Margaret C. McCray
                                     b. 16 Dec., 1840 (15 Dec.#)
                                     d. 16 April, 1923, in Leshara, Saunders Co.,
Joseph W. McCray   Nebraska
     &   m. (1) Elam (Judson) Jones, on 26 Jan., 1858
Mary Ann Frederick   in Fairbank, Iowa   2 ch
                                        (2) William Andrew Estey, ca 1867
                                        b. 1835, in Summit Co., Ohio
                                        d. 1913, in Saunders Co., Nebraska

                                     son, b/d 23 Dec., 1842

                                     Mary (May Ellen?) McCray
                                     b. 12 Dec., 1843
                                     d. 7 Aug., 1844

                                     Sophia Caroline McCray
                                     b. 11 Aug., 1845#
                                     d. 21 Sept., 1879#
                                     m. John Jones, on Oct. 1, 1866 (Oct. 11#)

These dates taken from Margaret C. McCray's notebook

Sarah McCray
b. 23 April, 1848#
d. 28 Dec., 1921, in Fairbank, Iowa
m. (1) John Potts, on 23 Mar., 1868
   (2) L.J. Deitz.

Mary M. McCray
b. 8 Dec., 1850#
d. ?
m. (1) John Campbell, on 8 April, 1868#
      b. 14 June, 1846
      d. Sept. 5, 1871
   (2) ------- Goodnight   2 ch

Amanda McCray
b. 23 April, 1853#
d. ?
m. Charles Jones, on Sept, 11, 1869#

daughter
b. April 18, 1856
d. May 6, 1856

George W. McCray
b. 27 June, 1857
d. 14 July, 1859

These dates taken from Margaret C. McCray's notebook

Generation I

Joseph McCray
&
Jane (Armstrong?)

Generation II

Joseph McCray II
&
Sophia Burford

Generation III

Joseph W. McCray
&
Mary Ann Frederick

Generation IV

Margaret C. McCray
&
(1)Elam Jones

(2)William Andrew Estey

Generation V

Josephine B. Jones
b. 10-11-1857, in Iowa
d.
m. Charles Wallace

Harry Judson Jones
b. 3-12-1861, in Nebraska
d.
He was a deputy sheriff in Oklahoma.

William Walter Estey
b. 1870
d. 1950
m. (1) Anna Cadwallader, 3 ch
   (2) Leone Leigh (Fratt) Hultgren
                              3 ch

Herbert Eugene Estey
b. ca 1872
d. 1963, in Fremont, Nebraska

Mable Estey
b. 1877
d. ? in Valley, Nebraska.
m. William Schocknessee, no ch

Ray S. Estey
b. 1878
d. 1969, in Chula Vista, Calif.
m. Lorena Mary Wilson, 4 ch

Marjorie Estey
b. 1884
d. 1977, in Chula Vista, Calif.
b. Jesse A. Sutton, 4 ch

72

Generation V   (Cont.)

Robert Elvin Estey
b. 1881
d. in 1960's, in Craig, Colo.
m. Olive Rose Saddoris, 3 ch

Ernest C. Estey
b. ca 1874
d. in 1960's
m. ?   no ch.

Generation I   Generation VI

Joseph McCray
      &
Jane (Armstrong?)

   Generation II

Joseph McCray II   Marjorie Patricia Estey
      &   b.
Sophia Burford   d.
                            m. unmarried

   Generation III
                            Kathleen Ellen Estey
Joseph McCray III   b.
      &   d.
Mary Ann Frederick   m. Joseph Seamann, 3 ch

   Generation IV   Michael William Estey
                            b.
Margeret McCray   d.
      &   m. unmarried
William Andrew Estey

                            Noreen Leone Estey
   Generation V   b.
                            d.
William Walter Estey   m. James Tanner
      &
Leone Leigh Hultgren
                            Mary Agnes Estey
                            b.
                            d.
                            m. William C. McKinney, 5 ch

74

Generation I	Generation VI
Joseph McCray	
&	
Jane (Armstrong?)	Lorena Margery Estey
	b. 10-19-1916, in Delta, Colo.
	d.
Generation II	m. Merrill LeVerne Day, 6-20-1940,
	at York, Nebraska
Joseph McCray II	b. 6-24-1920
&	d. 11-7-1970 in San Diego CA
Sophia Burford	bur. at Glen Abbey, Chula Vista CA
Generation III	
	Irma Ree Estey
Joseph W. McCray	b. 2-4-1918, York, Neb.
&	d.
Mary Ann Frederick	m. Melbourne Johnson
Generation IV	
	Roberta Lucille Estey
Margaret C. McCray	b. 10-18-1920, York, Neb.
&	d.
(1) Elam Jones	m. Thomas McClure, 1942, in York, Neb.
(2) William Andrew Estey	
Generation V	Sylvia Lenore Estey
	b. 6-24-1920
Ray S. Estey	d.
&	m. Walter B. Carroll, 1944, in York ,
Lorena Mary Wilson	Neb.

Generation I   Generation VIII

Joseph McCray
    &
Jane (Armstrong?)

    Generation II
                                          Darlene Elaine Day
Joseph McCray II   b. 12-4-1943, Chula Vista, CA
    &   d.
Sophia Burford   m.

    Generation III

Joseph W. McCray
    &
Mary Ann Frederick

                                          Marilyn Elaine Day
    Generation IV   b. 5-20-1947, at Chula Vista CA
                                          d.
Margaret C. McCray   m. Carl Martin Jensen, on 2-1-1969
    &   in San Diego, CA
(1) Elam Jones
(2) William Andrew Estey

    Generation V

Ray S. Estey
    &
Lorena Mary Wilson

    Generation VIII

Lorena Estey
    &
Merrill Day

76

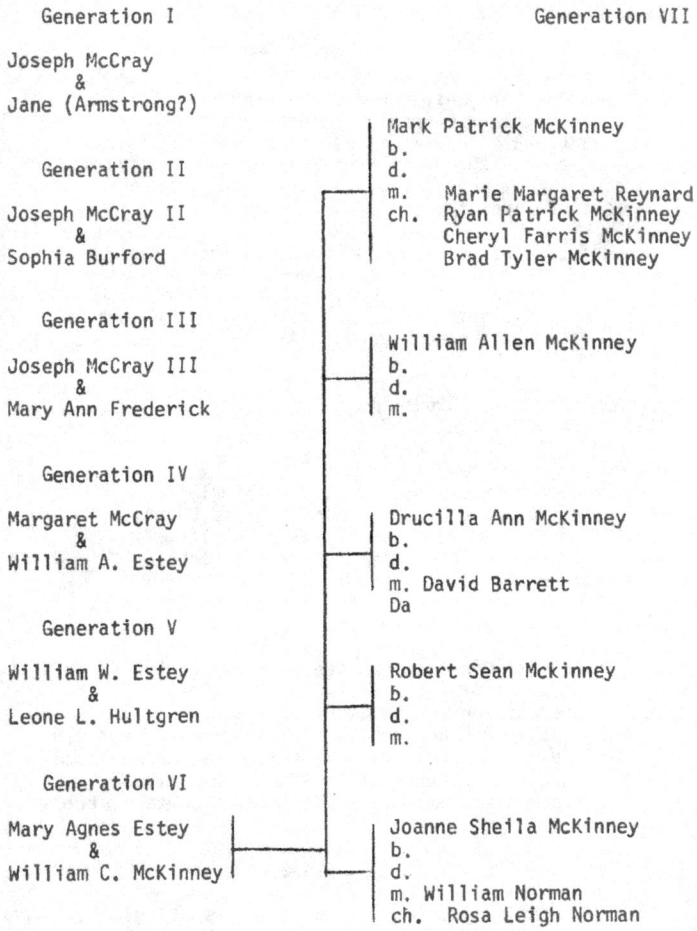

Generation I

Joseph McCray
&
Jane (Armstrong?)

Generation II

Joseph McCray II
&
Sophia Burford

Generation III

Joseph McCray III
&
Mary Ann Frederick

Generation IV

Margaret McCray
&
William A. Estey

Generation V

William W. Estey
&
Leone L. Hultgren

Generation VI

Mary Agnes Estey
&
William C. McKinney

Generation VII

Mark Patrick McKinney
b.
d.
m.   Marie Margaret Reynard
ch. Ryan Patrick McKinney
     Cheryl Farris McKinney
     Brad Tyler McKinney

William Allen McKinney
b.
d.
m.

Drucilla Ann McKinney
b.
d.
m. David Barrett
Da

Robert Sean Mckinney
b.
d.
m.

Joanne Sheila McKinney
b.
d.
m. William Norman
ch. Rosa Leigh Norman

77

The McCrays of Highland County, Virginia, and of West Virginia

ROBERT McCRAY (I) IS KNOWN TO HAVE BEEN BORN BEFORE 1776, but nothing else is known about him or his origins. He was the progenitor of a clan of McCrays living today in Highland County, Virginia, and in central West Virginia. Little is known of his wife, other than that she was from a family of Douglases. They had three children whom we know today, whose birthdates are still sought. Of them, Mary, Elizabeth and Sinclair, only Sinclair's name is in records today.

Sinclair's first wife, Kate, last name unknown, is the object of considerable unsuccessful research by his descendants. They had five children before Kate's death after the birth of Barbara, their fifth child. Sinclair wasted no time in marrying Margaret Simmons, and their son, Joshua, or Josiah, was born the next year, 1843. Sinclair's nine children were:

Robert McCray, born 1833, died 1904*
St. Clair McCray, born 1834, died 1864 in battle
Joseph McCray, Born 1836, died 1864 in battle
Ellen Jean/Jane McCray, born 1840, died 1933
Barbara, born 1842, died ? in Lewis County, West Virginia
Josiah (Joshua) McCray, born 1843, died ? in Highland County
Thomas McCray, born 1844, died 1864, possibly in battle
James Nicholas McCray, born 1846, death unknown. A bachelor
Alexander McCray, born 1848, death unknown
Sally McCray, birth and death unknown. Not listed in 1850 Census, so she may have been born after that date.

Because "Sinclair" and "St. Clair" were used interchangably in early records, some family genealogical material shows that St. Clair, Sinclair's son, married Margaret Simmons on December 20, 1840. Since he was born in 1834, he would have been age eight in 1940, marriage for him was a not too likely a circumstance. His marital status is unknown. He died while serving with Confederate forces at the Battle of Bethesda Church in 1864, and he was probably buried in a mass grave on the battlefield.

The people who supplied information for this section are:

1) Mrs. Lucy Henrietta (McCray) Botkin, of Head Waters, Virginia, in Highland County, granddaughter of Robert and Mary (Hodge) McCray.

* The dates of birth were derived from ages given in the 1850 Census, and dates of death were supplied by Mrs. Botkin.

2) Hermon A. Price, of Waynesboro, Virginia, a descendant from William A. Hodge and the father of Mary Hodge, above. Mr. Price's primary interest has been focused on the Hodge family, who are known to have been in Rockbridge County in the last half of the eighteenth century. There has been some intermarriage between the Hodge and McCray families over the last nearly two hundred years.

3) Mrs. Pattie Lee (Norman) Smith, of Spearsville, Louisiana, a West Virginia native, who is descended from Joseph and Elizabeth (Leach) McCray. Joseph was Sinclair's and Kate's third child. Mrs. Smith whimsically describes herself as a domestic engineer.

Do you recall, Reader, the people who warned you that digging into family history would reveal an ancestor who was hanged as a horse thief? It does really happen. Hermon Price noted: "The story is told that Bob (Robert McCray II) was chased out of West Virginia because he stole a horse." If the story is true, he apparently escaped the noose. The yarn is a bit suspect, however, because West Virginia wasn't created until 1863, and if Robert was still alive then, he would not likely have been active enough to have taken up horse rustling.

Mrs. Botkin wrote that Robert McCray I and his wife, the Douglas lady, lived on Bullpasture Mountain, Virginia (elevation 3200 feet), about thirty miles northwest of Staunton, Virginia. Many McCray families still live in that area. Head Waters is within hiking distance of Bullpasture Mountain, hard by Bullpasture River. There's also a Cowpasture and a Calfpasture River nearby, perhaps so named to remind flatlanders of the agricultural nature of these mountain people. A business of Head Waters is the manufacture of maple syrup and sugar products. It's all high country; to reach it one must cross the first range of the Shenandoah Mountains at 3700 feet, and then descend into a valley, still at 3000 feet, where Head Waters lies.

West Virginia was created when it threw in its lot with the Union cause and became the thirty-fifth of the United States. The new state boundaries placed Pendleton County into West Virginia, while Highland County remained in Confederate Virginia. Joseph and Elizabeth (Leach) McCray had moved to Pendleton County well before the outbreak of the Civil War, and they then found themselves split from other family members for the duration. It was a far larger Pendleton County at the time of the birth of Sinclair's children than it is today. It then included much of Shenandoah Valley, and when it was broken up in 1848, Highland County was one of the new, smaller, counties to emerge. Robert McCray I's firstborn child, Mary McCray, who married James Bodkin (sic) was probably the first McCray to join the Botkin lineage down to Mrs. Botkin. She says the McCray family has lived in the Head Waters area since the very early nineteenth century, which is as far back in time as she has been able to go in her research.

"My great grandmother, Kate McCray, lived at Shaw's Fork, which is now Head Waters, Va. I haven't found out where she came from or who her husband was (now she knows). She had two children, Robert (I) and Sally McCray. Robert married Mary Hodge and Sally married John Burke, and they built the log house where we were all born.

"My father always told us he was Scotch-Irish, a Presbyterian and Republican. My brother, Earl McCray and I still own the old McCray house at Head Waters."

St. Clair McCray joined the Confederate forces when the Civil War erupted, and was a private in Company B., Regiment 31, Virginia Infantry, and was killed in action at Bethesda Church, May 30, 1864. His brother, Joseph M. McCray, also took up arms for Virginia, and he also was killed, June 8, 1862. Of the thousands of tragic deaths of that Civil War, this family had more than its share. Not only did three of Sinclair and Margaret (Simmons) McCray's sons, Joseph, St. Clair and probably Thomas, die in battle, but Joseph McCray's father-in-law, John Leach, and Joseph's wife's brother, were also killed in the same Battle of Port Republic. None of the bodies was recovered for family burial, but were probably buried on the battlefield in mass graves.

Thomas D. McCray served in the Second Company of G, 18th Virginia Cavalry. He died in 1864, but whether or not he died in battle isn't certain. Joshua McCray, another of this family, enlisted in the same infantry company with St. Clair and Joseph, and he was with Joseph when he was killed. Later, he had second thoughts about the war and he deserted to the Union side, and served with enough distinction to be awarded a medal. Whatever were the circumstances of his change of heart, his decision and defection didn't turn his family against him, for they buried him along with other family members in the cemetery at Bullpasture Mountain.

Mrs. Botkin wrote that Ellen Jane McCray never married, and lived near the state line in Pendleton County, West Virginia, and died in 1933, at age ninety-three.

Here is Mrs. Botkin's family history, written in about 1982:

"My grandfather, Robert McCray, married Mary Hodge in 1833. They lived in a cábin on the Shenandoah Mountains until 1860, when they moved to Head Waters (then known as Shaw's Fork). They came to live with his sister, Sally McCray Burke. Her husband, John Burke, drowned in a flash flood. Sally Burke died January 8, 1872, and the McCray family has lived here since then.

"Robert and Mary McCray had the following children: George, Ellen Jane, Henry, Peter, William, Owen Reese, Sarah, Mary Ann and Elizabeth. All of them married and left home but George.

"In 1909, Owen Reese McCray married Louie Viola Armstrong
of Doe Hill, Virginia. They came to live with George and his
mother, who was now blind. Reese and Lou McCray had the following children: Porter Anderson, Ogretta Mae, Lucy Henrietta,
Geneva Gertrude, Leo Marsh, Charles Clifton, William Petton,
Elizabeth Evelyn, Earl Howard and Anna Lou.

"My mother and father were both postmasters until they
retired, and also had the toll gate here for several years.
It was moved here from the Marshall Place at the death of Sissy
Marshall in 1917.

"My father worked for the United States Forest Service for
many years. During fire season, he stayed at the lookout tower
on Shenandoah Mountain known as Signal Core. My mother would
take all of us to visit him on Sundays (from the top of the
mountain it was about three miles out the trail). He would
cook our dinner, and late in the evening he would put all the
kids on "Old Sam," our horse, and bring us home.

"My parents also played string music at local dances for
many years; my dad, the violin, my mother, the banjo, and our
brother, Peyton, played the guitar.

"My mother learned to play the banjo at a very early age
(eight years). In later years, her greatest enjoyment was
playing music with her friends. She had been to the Grand Ole
Opry several times, and played with Grandpa Jones, Roy Acuff,
Stringbean, Oswald and other musicians there.

"She had a banjo that was autographed and sent her by the
musicians in Nashville--we hope some time it will be returned
to Nashville and placed in the Music Hall of Fame.

"She was also a wonderful cook and homemaker. I will
never forget her ham, buckwheat cakes and custard pies!

"Our father worked away from home a great deal during our
early years, so our Uncle George was a great influence on all
of us. He always chewed Bloodhound tobacco. When any of us
got a sting, bite or cut, he would put a little tobacco juice
on it.

"He was a grand old man, always doing things for us. He

could mend shoes and fix anything around the home. Whenever he
went to pick apples, go to the mill, get wood, or work on the
farm, he always had all of us children on the wagon with him.
He was loved and treated the same as our parents.

Earl McCray still lives at the old home place at Head
Waters. We have no idea how old the house is, or who built it."

-0-

Mrs. Pattie Lee (Norman) Smith has traced her family back to
Joseph M. McCray, third son of Sinclair and Kate McCray. He was born in
Pendleton County, Virginia, in 1836. He married twenty-year old Elizabeth Leach, daughter of John and Margaret (Pierson) Leach, on December
29, 1855. John came to America from Ireland under indenture, which he
served out under one David Bell, completing his term of indenture in
1796. Margaret Pierson, his wife, was also from Ireland, and they
probably married in America. John and Margaret's daughter, Elizabeth,
was born in 1835 in that part of Pendleton County, Virginia, that would
become Highland County in 1848. John Leach died in 1834.

Joseph and Elizabeth had three children: James C. McCray, born
in 1854, Robert McCray, born in 1856, and Margaret Jane McCray, born
April 22, 1858.

Joseph joined the Confederate army soon after the shelling of
Fort Monroe in South Carolina opened the Civil War. He was in Company
B, Regiment 31, Virginia Infantry, and the war had been under way less
than a year when he was killed in action on June 8, 1862, at Port Republic, Virginia, in Rockingham County, not far from his home in Highland County. Elizabeth died of tuberculosis in Lewis County, West Virginia, where she had moved after the close of the Civil War.

Joseph and Elizabeth (Leach) McCray's daughter, Margaret Jane
McCray, married a native American, Nathaniel Theodore Watson, known as
"Ponty" Watson. He was born in 1856, and was a veteran of service in
the Confederate army, having served in Company F, 7th Virginia Infantry.
He died on July 12, 1925 in Weston, West Virginia, and his wife, Margaret Jane, died six months later, December 18, 1925. They had twelve
children between 1875 and 1898. John Edward Watson, Mrs. Smith's grandfather, was born in 1883, and he married Bertie Ellen McCartney. Both
were natives of Lewis County, West Virginia. Their ninth child of ten
was Rilla Mae Watson, born in 1925, who married James Edward Norman, to
whom were born Sharon Louis, in 1946, and Pattie Lee, in 1954. Pattie
Lee Norman married Arthur Claud Smith in 1983, and they have two sons,
James Stacy Smith and Derrick Clinton Smith.

Sue Morfit Shanklin, of Panama City, Florida, contributed these two items about some McCrays who lived in northern Virginia in that area destined to become West Virginia. No connection between these McCrays and other McCrays is known. Perhaps some future researcher can produce the family from which these people came.

"William McCray and his wife, Martha, who had a son, George McCray, was born in 1780, in Monangalia County* West Virginia. They also had: Andrew E. McCray, B. 1795, John McCray, b. 1787, Sarah, Jane, and possibly more. John McCray married Phoebe Brown, and their child was John Ellet (Elliot) McCray, b. 1816. Some have said that Martha was an Ellet or Elliot, but no proof has been supplied."

"Margaret McCray and George Nixon married February 12, 1807, probably in Harrison County, Virginia. Her tombstone gives her birth as February 10, 1786, and her death, February 19, 1843, in Marion County, West Virginia. She had several children, one named Ellet McCray Nixon. Location of the tombstones wasn't given, but it was probably in Marion County. Both Harrison and Marion Counties are now in West Virginia."

There appears to be a familial connection between these two items. Note that in the first one there is John Ellet McCray, and in the next there is Ellet McCray Nixon. These Scots-Irish were forever naming children for close relatives and passing on the same names over and over. Having these McCrays bearing names such as William, George, John and Margaret yields only confusion, rather than clues, for was there ever a McCray family that didn't have dozens of Williams, Georges, Johns, Janes, Sarahs and Margarets?

* West Virginians spell it "Monangalia," Pennsylvanians spell it "Monongehela." It's "Alleghany" in Virginia, "Allegheny" in Pennsylvania, but when you get to New York it's "Allegany." That's why we call our nation The United States.

83

Generation I   Generation II

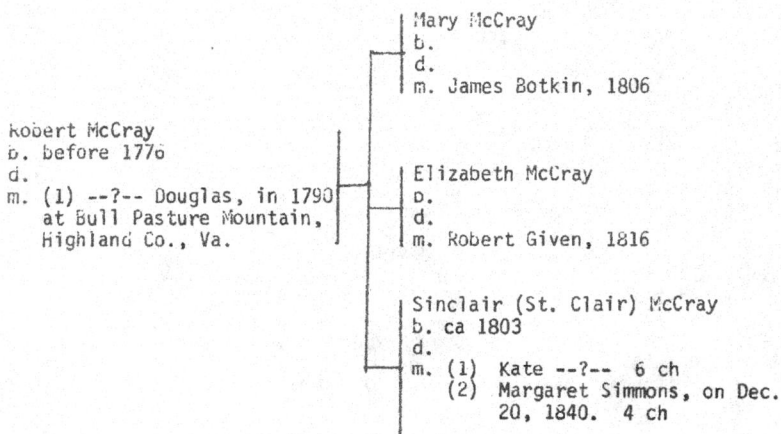

```
                                        | Mary McCray
                                        | b.
                                       /| d.
                                      / | m. James Botkin, 1806
                                     /  |
Robert McCray                        |
b. before 1776                       |
d.                                   |
m. (1) --?-- Douglas, in 1790        | Elizabeth McCray
   at Bull Pasture Mountain,         | b.
   Highland Co., Va.                \| d.
                                     \| m. Robert Given, 1816
                                      \
                                       \| Sinclair (St. Clair) McCray
                                        | b. ca 1803
                                        | d.
                                        | m. (1)  Kate --?--  6 ch
                                        |    (2)  Margaret Simmons, on Dec.
                                        |         20, 1840.  4 ch
```

84

·Generation I   Generation III

Robert McCray   Robert McCray
      &   b. 1833, in Pendleton Co., Va.
--?-- Douglas   d. 1904, at Head Water, Va.
                                       m. Mary Hodge, 12 Nov., 1850   9 ch

                                       St. Clair McCray
   Generation II   b. 1834, in Pendleton Co., Va.
                                       d. May 30, 1864 at Battle of Bethesda
Sinclair McCray   Church in Virginia
      &   m. ?
(1) Kate --?--

(2) Margaret Simmons   Joseph M, McCray
                                       b. 1836 in Pendleton Co., Va.
                                       d. May 30, 1864 at Battle of Port
                                           Republic, Va.
                                       m. Elizabeth Leach, Dec. 27, 1855. 3 ch
                                           Dau of John and Margaret (Pierson)
                                           Leach, both of Ireland

                                       Ellen Jean/Jane McCray
                                       b. 1840 in Pendleton Co., Va.
                                       d. 1933
                                       m. unmarried. had dau, Dollie McCray

                                       Barbara McCray
                                       b. 1842 in Pendleton Co., Va.
                                       d. ? in Lewis Co., W. Va.
                                       m. John Brady

                                       Josiah (Joshua) McCray
                                       b. 1843 in Pendleton Co., Va.
                                       d. ? Buried in Highland Co. Va.
                                       m. Maria McCray; 5 ch; Joshua, Clinton,
                                           Alice, Sinclair, Thomas

                                       Thomas McCray
                                       b. 1844 in Pendleton Co., Va.
                                       d. Nov., 1864, possibly in battle
                                       m.

James Nocholas McCray
b. 1846 in Pendleton Co., Va.
d.
m. bachelor

Alexander McCray
b. 1848 in Highland Co., Va.
d.
m. Mary A. Losh

Sally McCray
b. ? possibly after 1850
d.
m. John Burke

(Sally's parentage not certain. She
may have been Kate's child.)

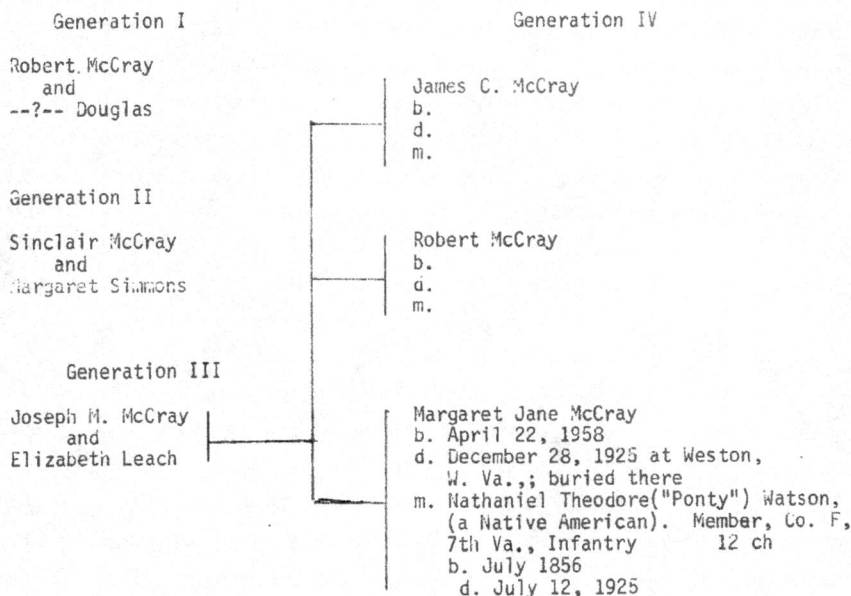

Generation I

Robert McCray
    and
--?-- Douglas

Generation II

Sinclair McCray
    and
Margaret Simmons

        Generation III

Joseph M. McCray
    and
Elizabeth Leach

Generation IV

James C. McCray
b.
d.
m.

Robert McCray
b.
d.
m.

Margaret Jane McCray
b. April 22, 1958
d. December 28, 1925 at Weston,
   W. Va.,; buried there
m. Nathaniel Theodore("Ponty") Watson,
   (a Native American). Member, Co. F,
   7th Va., Infantry   12 ch
   b. July 1856
    d. July 12, 1925

Generation I

Robert McCray
and
--?-- Douglas

Generation II

Sinclair McCray
and
Margaret Simmons

Generation III

Joseph M. McCray
and
Elizabeth Leach

Generation IV

Margaret Jane McCray
and
Nathaniel T. Watson

Generation V

Melvina Watson
b. 1875
d.
m.

Roda A. Watson
b. 1878
d.
m.

Tintie A.E. Watson
b. April, 1880
d.
m.

Jessie L. Watson
b. December 18, 1881
d.
m.

John Edward Watson
b. April 22, 1883 in Lewis Co. W. Va.
d. July 27, 1962, buried Kinkaid
   Cemetery, Ireland, W. Va.
m. Bertie Ellen McCartney, in Lewis
   co. W. Va.   10 ch
   b. March 2, 1886
   d. April 5, 1950
   Dau. Adam Patrick and Susan M
   (Ballard) McCartney, of Lewis Co.

Mary Ellen Watson
b. Aug., 1885
d.
m.

William Cleveland Watson
b. 1888
d.
m.

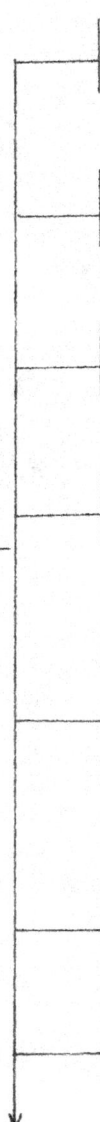

88

Generation V, Cont.

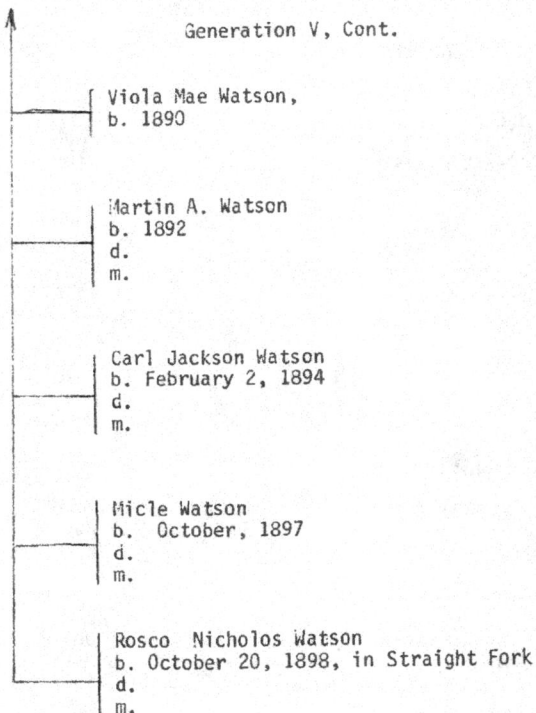

Viola Mae Watson,
b. 1890

Martin A. Watson
b. 1892
d.
m.

Carl Jackson Watson
b. February 2, 1894
d.
m.

Micle Watson
b. October, 1897
d.
m.

Rosco Nicholos Watson
b. October 20, 1898, in Straight Fork
d.
m.

Generation I	Generation VI

Generation I

Robert McCray
and
--?-- Douglas

Generation VI

Walter Lee Watson
b. 1904
d. 1922, killed in mining accident
m.

Generation II

Sinclair McCray
and
Margaret Simmons

Eula Manerva Watson
b. 1905 (was blind)
d. 1927
m.

Generation III

Joseph M. McCray
and
Elizabeth Leach

Chlowie Sawilla Watson
b. May 27, 1907 (was blind)
d. October 10, 1970
m.

Generation IV

Margaret Jane McCray
and
Nathaniel T. Watson

Raymond Clyde Watson
b. August 17, 1909
d.   (was blind)
m.

Warder Harrison Watson
b. April 29, 1912
d. 1955
m.

Generation V

John E. Watson
and
Bertie Ellen McCartney

Willard Edward Watson
b. 1916   (was blind)
d. December, 1990

Reva Vermell Watson
b. April 22, 1919
d. January 9, 1948

Anna Grace Watson
b. April 19, 1922
d.

Rilla Mae Watson
b. July 12, 1925
d.
m. James Edward Norman on Oct. 24,
1946. (Div.) 2 ch
Son of James C. and Leanna (Allman)
Norman.
b. Nov. 7, 1926

Virginia Watson
b.
d. at seven months; buried in
Roanoke, Va.

Generation I

Robert McCray
and
--?-- Douglas

Generation II

Sinclair McCray
and
Margaret Simmons

Generation III

Joseph M. McCray
and
Elizabeth Leach

Generation IV

Margaret Jane McCray
and
Nathaniel T. Watson

Generation V

John E. Watson
and
Bertie Ellen McCartney

Generation VI

Rilla Mae Watson
and
James Edward Norman

Generation VII

Sharon Louis Norman
b. July 1, 1946
d.
m Robert Nickial Huskin, on Jan. 19,
   1963. one child, Robert Lee Huskin
   b. June 13, 1964

Pattie Lee Norman
b. June 23, 1964
d.
m. Arthur Claud Smith, on Oct. 23, 1983
   b. Aug. 5, 1950
   d.
   Two children:
      James Stacy Smith
      b. Oct. 8, 1984

      Derrick Clinton Smith
      b. Feb. 25, 1989

92

Generation I

Robert McCray
    and
--?-- Douglas

Generation II

Sinclair McCray
    and
(1) Unknown woman
(2) Margaret Simmons

Generation III

Robert McCray
    and
Mary Hodge

Sources for the next
four pages;
Lucy McCray Botkin, of
Headwaters, Va., and
Hermon A. Price, of
Waynesboro, Va.

Generation IV

Ellen Jean (Jane) McCray
b.
d. at age 20 of tuberculosis
m. unmarried

George Grant McCray
b. January 15, 1866
d. 1948
m. unmarried

Elizabeth McCray
b.
d.
m. George Armstrong, 1885
    Ch: Arlie, Ernest, Lacy

Mary Ann ("Molly") McCray
b.
d.
m. Bryscen Lamb, at Parkersburg,
    W. Va.

Sara ("Sally") McCray
b.
d.
m. (1) George Crummett, 1893
    (2) Bob Drummond, at Clarksburg
        W. Va.
    Ch: William Kennedy, Owen, Oral,
        Ogretta, Otha

Henry McCray
b. 1860
d.
m. (1) Rebecca Killingsworth, 1882
    Ch: Lula, m. --?-- Thomas
    (2) Kate Armstrong, in 1889
    Ch: William McCray, b. 1900,
        died in Illinois, 1966

Peter Franklin McCray
b. 1871
d. 1949
m. Clara Snodgrass, d. 1955

93

William McCray
b.
d. killed by lightning at Headwaters, Va.
m. Unmarried

Owen Reese McCray
b. 1876, at Headwaters Va.
d. 1953, at Headwaters, Va.
m. Louie Viola Armstrong, Jan. 27,
   1907- or 1909 10 ch.
   b. 1899
   d. 1975, at Headwaters, Va.
   Dau. of Will and Susan (Botkin)
   Armstrong, of Doe Hill, Va.
   Both buried in Hodge Cemetery on the
   Hill, in Headwaters, Va.

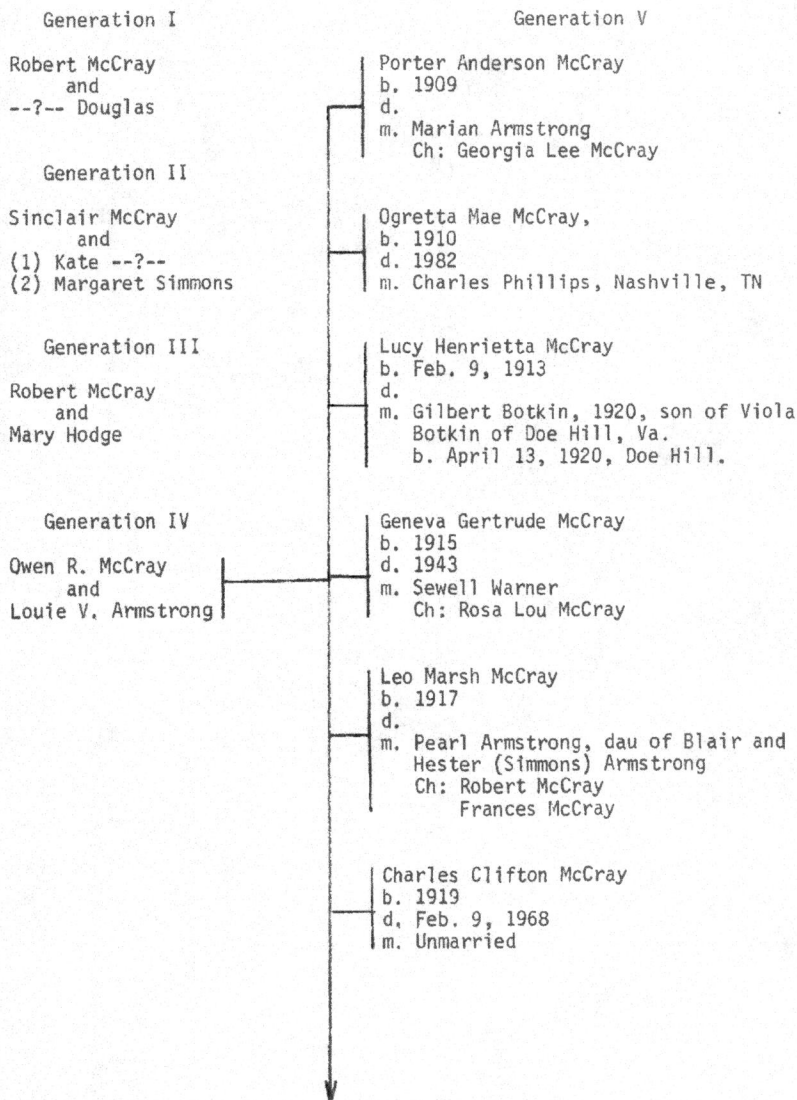

Generation I

Robert McCray
    and
--?-- Douglas

Generation II

Sinclair McCray
    and
(1) Kate --?--
(2) Margaret Simmons

Generation III

Robert McCray
    and
Mary Hodge

Generation IV

Owen R. McCray
    and
Louie V. Armstrong

Generation V

Porter Anderson McCray
b. 1909
d.
m. Marian Armstrong
    Ch: Georgia Lee McCray

Ogretta Mae McCray,
b. 1910
d. 1982
m. Charles Phillips, Nashville, TN

Lucy Henrietta McCray
b. Feb. 9, 1913
d.
m. Gilbert Botkin, 1920, son of Viola
    Botkin of Doe Hill, Va.
    b. April 13, 1920, Doe Hill.

Geneva Gertrude McCray
b. 1915
d. 1943
m. Sewell Warner
    Ch: Rosa Lou McCray

Leo Marsh McCray
b. 1917
d.
m. Pearl Armstrong, dau of Blair and
    Hester (Simmons) Armstrong
    Ch: Robert McCray
        Frances McCray

Charles Clifton McCray
b. 1919
d. Feb. 9, 1968
m. Unmarried

95

Generation V (Cont.)

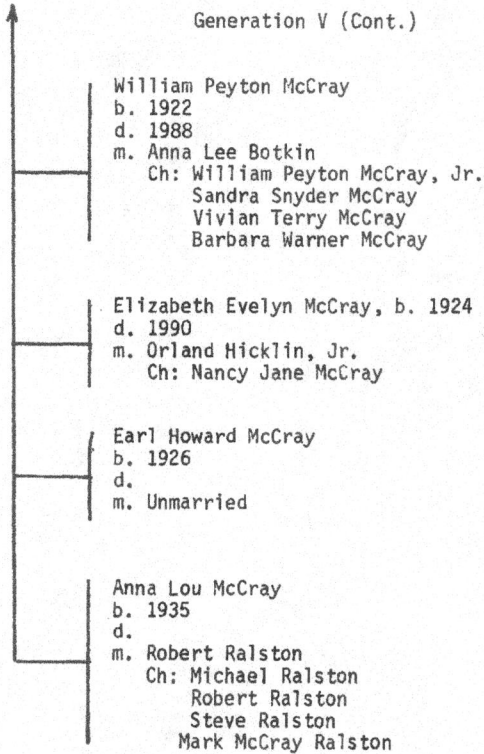

William Peyton McCray
b. 1922
d. 1988
m. Anna Lee Botkin
    Ch: William Peyton McCray, Jr.
        Sandra Snyder McCray
        Vivian Terry McCray
        Barbara Warner McCray

Elizabeth Evelyn McCray, b. 1924
d. 1990
m. Orland Hicklin, Jr.
    Ch: Nancy Jane McCray

Earl Howard McCray
b. 1926
d.
m. Unmarried

Anna Lou McCray
b. 1935
d.
m. Robert Ralston
    Ch: Michael Ralston
        Robert Ralston
        Steve Ralston
        Mark McCray Ralston

CHAPTER FIVE

THE McCRAYS OF OHIO AND INDIANA

BY THE YEAR 1800, many of the Scots-Irish living in the western part
of Pennsylvania, Maryland, Virginia and the Carolinas were beginning to
feel restless and crowded. All the good land was occupied, the Indians
had either moved west or had given up trying to drive settlers away.
Most of the land between Canada and the Gulf of Mexico and west to the
Mississippi River was in the United States. For the Scots-Irish, it was
time to move on--always westward, settling just a year or two behind the
trappers and hunters who were the vanguard, the blazers of trails that
would become wagon roads.

Many settlers had already come to Tennessee, Kentucky and southern
Ohio. The British still controlled much of the area around the Great
Lakes, even though they had agreed to withdraw under terms of the Treaty
of Paris at the end of the Revolution. They just hadn't gotten around to
pulling out yet, perhaps hoping that they could somehow gain back the
entire Great Lakes region for Britain, and their Indian allies were still
ready to take an American scalp or two if any of them should come in
with an idea of settling. But the British did withdraw from all United
States territory after the War of 1812.

Kentucky and southern Ohio were popular territories to migrate into
because the Ohio River was the great water highway from Pennsylvania and
northern Virginia. Several families would buy a sixty-foot river boat
at Pittsburgh or Wheeling, load up their goods, horses and cattle, and
shove off. The Ohio River did the rest, its flow providing the motive
power. The craft was rather easily kept between banks and headed downstream by one man at the sweep at the boat's stern. When the party arrived at its destination, the boat could either be sold, broken up for
its timbers and planks, or just abandoned if no buyers turned up.

Those Samuel McCrays

WHAT CAST OF DICE or whimsy of the gods of chance, brought together
two McCray families, each headed by a Samuel, and each having a Samuel,
Junior, to the southwest corner of Ohio to settle within a day's walk of
each other? Or *was* it a chance happening? Even though one family came
to Ohio from Virginia, and the other came from Pennsylvania by way of
Kentucky, who can deny that they may have agreed to move there to together? It is a challenge for anyone to find answers to these questions.

Counties Of Ohio and Indiana Where McCrays Settled

Since there is a problem of identification when writing or speaking of one of these four Samuel McCrays, let us arbitrarily call one father and son pair, "Samuel 1" and his son, "Samuel 1a." The other father and son will be likewise designated, "Samuel 2" and "Samuel 2a."

Samuel 1 has been researched by Irene (McDaniel) Titus, of Indianapolis, Lewis Reed, of Temple City, California, Francis Lipp, of Frankfort, Kentucky, and by Hazel (McCray) Foster, of Sun Lakes, Arizona.

Lewis Reed wrote: "I have a computer print-out listing 132 McCrays between 1790-1819 (some duplications), with 13 Samuels and 9 Jameses (also with duplications). There were a lot of McCrays, and each left hundreds of descendents wondering which one was theirs." To which I can add: "Amen, Cousin Lewis!"

Samuel McCray 1, according to the D.A.R. Index for Pennsylvania, was born in Pennsylvania in c1740, and died in 1791. However, it is recorded that he died on October 14, 1817, and his will was filed in the Warren County (Ohio) Probate Court (Record 1, page 103: Box 10, #1). It would be of interest to learn where it is recorded that he was born in Pennsylvania, and where in Pennsylvania. If any McCrays were born in Pennsylvania as early as 1740, it is a well-kept secret. A history of Warren County, Ohio, not identified, supplied by Mr. Lipp, Says:

"Samuel McCray and his wife, Rebecca Douglass, came to Warren County from Jefferson County, Va. (now West Virginia) in 1799. After spending the winter of 1799 and 1800 at Bedle's Station, they removed to what was called Smalley's Settlement on Todd's Fork, and in the spring of 1801 they settled on the west side of the Little Miami, opposite the mouth of Todd's Fork. Mr. McCray afterwards resided in Lebanon, and still later owned the mill now known as the Zimri Stubbs Mill. He was an early sheriff of Warren County."

Before moving to Ohio, they lived in Washington County, Pennsylvania. Mrs. Titus wrote that "he entered the War of Independence while living in the County of Washington. He became a Private 8th Class of the 1st Battalion, Class Role A, of Captain Andrew Fereley's Company, Washington County, Pennsylvania." This is puzzling because Washington County did not exist during the Revolution; it was formed in 1781, the same year as the Battle of Yorktown. In this same paragraph she also wrote: "The Pennsylvania Militia of 1790-1800, lists this Samuel McCray as being between the ages of 18-45 years of age, and residing within the bounds of 3rd Battalion, Cumberland County Militia." This item of information was taken from the Pennsylvania Archives, and my notes show that not only Samuel was listed, but also James and George McCrea. The "bounds of the 3rd Battalion" were located about two hundred miles from Washington County in the area just north of Carlisle, Pennsylvania, and these three "McCreas" were sons of my gr gr gr gr grandparents, James and Ellen (Bell) McCray, who lived in Shermans Valley in today's Perry County.

Before Washington County was created in 1781 southwestern Pennsylvania had been since 1772 designated Westmoreland County. Mrs. Titus's ancestors owned a 300-acre tract known as Ten-Mile Creek Farm. Lewis Reed found that Ten Mile Creek is the boundary between today's Washington and Greene Counties. It was in this area that Samuel and Rebecca (Douglas) McCray lived before moving on westward. Samuel McCray was listed as a taxpayer in Morgan Township, Washington County, married, and owning 100 acres, 2 horses, 2 cows, 1 sheep, and paid a tax of 55 shillings. Cheap. Fifty-five shillings today wouldn't buy a bag of hamburgers.

Mrs. Titus wrote that Samuel and Rebecca next moved to Kentucky, but the few sentences from a history of Warren County, Ohio (see above) said nothing about their having lived in Kentucky. Information for the item was no doubt supplied by Samuel and Rebecca's descendents who probably had heard the story of migrations many times. There doesn't seem to be any doubt that Samuel and Rebecca's first son, Phineas McCray, lived for a while in Kentucky, but it may be that more research is needed on the McCrays in Kentucky. If the land they bought there was sold in 1792, and the deed showed that Samuel's wife was Mary, not Rebecca, it is something needing clarification, for there is no doubt at all that Samuel 1's wife was Rebecca Douglas, so this land transfer described in the deed may have involved another Samuel McCray. In view of the fact that there were at least three other Samuel McCrays who could possibly have owned land there, some questions remain about this Kentucky business.

By 1801 they had moved to the Territory of Ohio. Mrs. Titus says Samuel was a commissioner of Warren County in 1801, but that is unlikely because there was no Warren County until Ohio became a state in 1803. Samuel and Phineas paid taxes on land in Butler County, Ohio, in 1810, and Phineas bought and sold land in Butler County. In 1814, Phineas moved to Fayette County, Indiana, which is separated from Butler County, Ohio, by Union County, Indiana, and he made his home there until his death in 1832.

On page 280 of the *History of Warren County* is an account of the construction of the courthouse for Warren County at Lebanon:

"On March 25, 1805, the Commissioners agreed upon a plan for a court house. The building was to be constructed of brick, and to be thirty-six feet square and two stories high--the first story twelve feet high, the second ten feet high. The floor was to be constructed of tile or brick twelve inches square and four inches thick. There were to be eight windows in each story, with black walnut frames, twenty-four glasses in each window of the lower story, and twenty in the upper story, a fireplace five and one-half feet wide in the lower story, and two fireplaces four and one-half feet wide in the upper story. Two summers (horizontal beams, also *summertree*) were to extend through the house and an upright post to be placed in the middle

of each summer. The building was to be ornamented with a handsome gutter cornice. The contract for the erection of the
building was let, April 27, 1805, to Samuel McCray, at $1450;
and on January 3, 1806, the house was accepted from the contrac-
tor. Six years later, a cupola was placed on the house."

Samuel "saved" enough out of the building costs to buy a lot upon
which he built a brick house. Nobody seemed to object to his drawing up
a contract for more money than he used, and then pocketing the surplus,
or to the fact that there might have been a conflict of interest in his
being awarded the contract in the first place.

Samuel and Rebecca (Douglas) McCray's children were: (Mrs. Titus'
data , page three of her McCray family history):

> Phineas McCray, 1762-1839   Samuel McCray 1775-1862 (Sam'l 1a)
> Shaphet McCray   Catherine McCray Heaton
> Martin McCray, 17-- -1836   Prisilla McCray Call
> William McCray   John McCray, 1778-1847
> Mary McCray Brannon   Margaret McCray Cox
>   James McCray; not certain that he was of this family

The children of Samuel and Rebecca moved into Indiana and settled
in several Indiana counties. Since Mrs. Titus' ancestor was Phineas Mc-
Cray, it is understandable that she devoted considerable attention to him.
She recorded this remembrance: (page 4)

> "Mary McCray Reeves of Greenfield, Indiana, a grand-daugh-
> ter of Phineas McCray was 18 years old when her grandfather
> died, and she remembers him as "a very fine old man, quite
> queer, a little crusty and very much the master of his house-
> hold." While her grandmother, Sarah Jane "was a very lovely,
> quiet, meek and obeying old lady." Aunt Polly and Aunt Peggy
> (Mary and Margaret McCray) often visited in the Moses McCray
> home and were well remembered as very lovely ladies."

Phineas McCray was born October 21, 1762, in Berks County, Pennsylvania, and his wife, Sarah Jane Peters, whom he married in Pennsylvania
were charter members of Village Creek Baptist Church in Connersville
Township, Fayette County, Indiana, when it was founded on July 24, 1824.
They lived out their lives there.

Shaphet McCray, the next son, was also born in Berks County in 1763
or 1764, married Catherine Yoky in Bourbon County, Kentucky. They settled in Wayne Township, Henry County, Indiana, in 1819 or 1820 in a settlement that became Knightstown.

Martin McCray's birth was unrecorded. Mr. Reed pointed out that
because Martin was not listed as a member of the Pennsylvania Militia in

1778, he must have been under age sixteen. "He signed a deed as a witness in 1800, so presumably he was 21 then. Thus he was born between 1762 and 1779. His age bracket in the Federal Census of 1820 was 'over 45', so that narrows it down to born before 1775."

"Martyn McGrea" was named in a history of Montgomery County, Ohio, as one of a group of "Kentuckians" who squatted in 1798 on some land in what later became Germantown Township. These men were hunters, living in shelters, the story related, who came from Kentucky, Pennsylvania, Virginia and the Carolinas.

Martin married a lady, believed to have been Hannah, the latter being named administratrix of Martin's estate at his death in 1836. Martin's grandson, Warren McCray, became governor of Indiana, and his footnote in history was that in 1921 he was the only governor of a state to be impeached on charges that he had his hand in the state's cookie jar. Martin and Hannah seem to have lived in Franklin County, Indiana, although they bought land in Montgomery County, and on the deed Martin gave his residence as Franklin County, located on the opposite side of Indiana bordering on Ohio. His will was probated in Union County, adjacent to Franklin County.

William McCray married Elizabeth Saingore on November 22, 1793, in Bourbon County, Kentucky, and later settled at Todd's Fork, Warren County Ohio. Their descendants lived in Indiana, but it isn't known whether William and Elizabeth moved there as did other members of the family.

Mary McCray married James Brannon and later was "taken apart from her husband" and lived out her life in Franklin County as a single lady.

Margaret McCray married John Cox, whose grave is in the Mount Jackson Cemetery in Indianapolis.

Samuel McCray, son of Samuel and Rebecca (Douglas) McCray, was born in January, 1775, "probably on the old homestead in Pennsylvania." He married Rebecca Hedges, born March 3, 1775, near "Fredricksburg"* Maryland, in 1795 and they lived in or near Middletown, Kentucky for a time. By 1839 they had located in Putnam County, Indiana. They had ten children. Samuel died September 11, 1862, and is buried in Brick Chapel Cemetery, north of Greencastle, Putnam County, Indiana.

Catherine McCray married Abraham Heaton (or Eaton), and they settled first in Wayne County, Indiana, and later built and operated a grist mill at the mouth of Buck Creek, near Knightstown, Henry County, Indiana.

* It's Frederick, Maryland, or Fredricksburg, Virginia. Even natives of this area get them confused.

He became superintendent of schools. Catherine Heaton is buried in a cemetery in Knightsville. Her headstone reads: "In memory of Catherine Heaton, born Aug. 16, 1781, and departed this life March 26, 1831."

The life of Prisilla McCray is relatively unknown, but she may have married John Call.

Mrs. Titus did not find that Samuel and Rebecca (Douglas) McCray had a son named James McCray, but a Mrs. Peck wrote a history of the Harlin* family and in it wrote that Samuel and Rebecca had a son named James, born February 23, 1806, who married Mary Harlan in 1829 in Ohio. It is unlikely that Rebecca could have conceived again in 1806, forty-four years after the birth of her first child, Phineas, in 1762. Even if she had married at age fourteen, she would have been fifty-eight in 1806. However, Mrs. Titus found there was a James McCray in 1785 in Bourbon County, Kentucky, who owned eight thousand acres of land. She also found in the 1850 Census a James McCray of Waterloo Township, Fayette County, who was born in 1801, married to "Mary", born in 1809. They had eleven children when the census was taken. Mrs. Titus doubted they were of the Samuel McCray 1 family, but with all those other McCrays rattling around Fayette County in those days I could believe they fitted into Samuel 1's family somewhere.

Mrs. Titus's ancestral line is here outlined:

Samuel and Rebecca (Douglas) M^{C}Cray

Phineas and Sarah Jane (Peters) McCray

Moses and Jane (Sparks) McCray

Martha (McCray) and Jacob Alexander McDaniel

James Bryan and Ora Anne (Sommerville) McDaniel

Minnie Irene McDaniel, b. 9-25-1896; married Walter Mitchel Titus, born 5-26-1886

* Also spelled "Harland" and "Harlan."

103

Samuel McCray 2, and Samuel McCray 2a

MOST OF WHAT WE KNOW about this family has been written by Samuel 2's
great grandson, Christy McCray, who wrote accounts of the family. One,
written in 1929, was probably written, unedited, by him, and at least two
others were obviously written by someone else, probably as Christy told
it to them. I like his literary style. He used words so sparingly one
might think he had to buy each one he wrote, but it would be nice if he'd
recklessly bought enough more words and numbers to supply dates and just
a few more details. However, this is what he wrote:

"April 6, 1929
On the farm, Clarksville O.

"History of the M'Cray family as I know it.

"There were 2 brothers, John and Samuel, who came over from
Scotland and settled in Reading, Pennsylvania. Samuel later
went over into Virginia and settled in the Shenandoah Valley on
the Roanoke River. Samuel married twice. His first wife's name
was Porter and their children were Samuel, Robert, Mary.

"Samuel's second wife's name was Jeanette Weir, who came from
Ireland. Their children were Stephen, William, Thomas, Ann,
Margaret, James, Matthew, Hugh, John, Daniel, Christy, Joseph,
Andrew and Armstrong.*

"After the death of her husband Jeanette Weir started with 5
sons and 1 daughter, in a covered wagon on Christmas eve, 1813
and drove over the mountains to Ohio. They arrived in March
and settled near Clarksville. One of these sons who came over
in the covered wagon was Christy. He was born in 1795. He married Nancy Urton from Culpepper County, Virginia. Their children were Joseph, 1821, Thomas, 1823, Lucinda 1825, Jane, 1828,
Samuel Adams, May 26, 1830, Nancy, 1833, Leanor 1835, and
Christy, 1837. Samuel Adams married Lydia Nacholson and their
children were Atwell, January 28, 1878, Alfred, May 2, 1882, and
Linny, October 20, 1884. Alfred married Mary Latta of Ludlow,
Kentucky and their children were Samuel Adams, August 19, 1913,
and Taylor Latta, August 1, 1916.

"Samuel was the first to come here. John, William and Hugh
came later when Samuel died. Jeanette brought the children,

*Christy re-arranged these names with a pencil, presumably put-
ting them into chronological order. However, they were not
born in that order.

104

Daniel, Christy, Joseph, Andrew and Armstrong came to
Ohio. Christy married Nancy Urton in 1820. The other children
died in childhood.

"Robert left Virginia before father was born. He was a lieutenant in Wilkinson's army. He went to Vicksburg and married a
southern woman and died in the south.

"Mary came to Ohio. She married a man by the name of Kessler
near here. Jeanette settled in the Sewill neighborhood near
Clarksville--then the next spring they went to the Baker bottoms
near Morrow and lived there a couple of years and then bought
this place from Murphy. Part of this house was on it then. It
was moved here and the rest built to it. I was a little over
three years old when they did that.

"Daniel married a Skinner. They had two boys, Theodore, father
of Daniel J. One of them belonged to the 17th Ohio in the Civil
War. At battle of Hoover's Gap he was frightened.

    "Andrew and Armstrong both stayed around here. Armstrong
was a teamster. On the way to Wilmington his team ran away and
he was killed. Eliza Ann is one of his children.

"Joseph died in March after they got here. Oldest child was
Daniel about 21. Christy was next. Took from Christmas to
March to come over mountains in wagon. Boys slept in a linen
tent. Horses were never unharnessed. Uncle Andrew used to say
about horses--"They ain't such horses as we brought to Virginia".

"My father was a strong temperance and antislavery man. Was an
agent of the underground railway.

"Uncle Tom was very strong. There was a big rock that only he
and one other man ever lifted. He tried it again and started
nose bleeding and he was never strong again. They sent to
Alexandria, Va.* (60 miles) for a doctor. He only lived about
two years afterward.

"In the Civil War I was only in 100 days service. I was 27
years old. Mother objected. I was in the 146th. Sam was in
the 19th. He served in Tenn. and Georgia. He was sick at At-
lanta and was sent back to Chattanooga. He was in 3 years. I
was out four months. We were in West Virginia. I had measles
very bad. They didn't come out on me till I read news of bat-

*Obviously not Alexandria, Virginia, but Kentucky, just across
the Ohio River from Cincinnati.

tle of Risoca (?). I read of so many boys I knew that the excitement, I guess, brought them out. Sam's company was not in
the fight. They were on guard duty. He was in many battles."

Christy McCray "

Christy's signature was so shaky that it was almost illegible. The
document he signed was partly in script that didn't match the signature,
and partly typed, so he obviously had help on it. He was age ninety-
two at the time.

In an earlier history, dated "Sunday, July, 1926," he gave some more
information, part of which conflicts with things written by Mrs. Titus
in her account preceding, for Christy said:

"Samuel, that is the second Samuel, came to Ohio and built
the first Lebanon Court House. It cost $400. He was later
sheriff of Warren County."

Two men, both named Samuel McCray, lived in the two counties just
north of Cincinnati, Hamilton County. Mrs. Titus' Samuel settled in Butler County, which abuts Indiana on the west side, in 1810. Christy
McCray's Samuel settled in Warren County, adjacent to Butler County's
eastern border, sometime before 1800, and was a county commissioner when
Ohio and its counties became a state in 1803. Mrs. Titus states that her
Samuel built the Warren County courthouse, but then, Christy made the
same claim. There was only one courthouse built, and the Samuel of Warren County was in an admirable position to obtain the building contract.
Also, he later became sheriff of Warren County, and died there in 1839.
Mrs. Hazel Foster (see p. 113) is descended from the Warren County Sam-
uel McCray, and her great great grandfather, Francis Dill, was a Warren
County commissioner and signer of the contract for building the courthouse. Circumstantial evidence strongly suggests that it was Christy's
Samuel McCray who was the courthouse builder.

Christy's earlier family history contains enough information not
included in the above that it should also be presented:

"John and Samuel McCray came from Scotland after the Revolutionary War, the year being unknown. Both went to the State of
Pennsylvania. Samuel was the elder and soon went to the State
of Virginia, settling in the Shenandoah Valley. The location
was close to the mouth of the Roanoke River. Samuel married
a woman whose name was Porter, there being three children, Samuel, Robert and Mary. Samuel, that is the second Samuel, came
to Ohio and built the first Lebanon Court House. It cost $400.
He later became Sheriff of Warren County. Robert, remaining in
Virginia, enlisted in the United States Regular Army and
became a lieutenant. He was with General Wilkinson, in what was

106

known as Burr Campaign and later went to Vicksburg, Mississippi.
Robert later lived there at Vicksburg, having no children except Samuel (!). Samuel McCray, of Lebanon, had one daughter,
Nancy, who later became Nancy Jones, having a son Clint Jones
who died some time after 1912. Nancy Jones first married Hay-
wood and then Jones. Samuel McCray, of Virginia, had a daughter Mary who also came to Ohio. She was Mary Kessler and
raised Joseph Nickleson, Grandfather of Alfred McCray; and she
died at Joseph Nickleson's home. Samuel McCray of Virginia,
married Jeannette Weir for his second wife (Porter for the
first wife). Jeannette Weir came from the Roanoke River country
in Virginia. Samuel McCray and Jeannette Weir had 16 children.
(Christy McCray, Alfred McCray's Grandfather was one.) Stephen,
William, Thomas, Hugh, John (this John lived near what was
known as Kackensack, Warren Co. later removed to Iowa--his
children, Samuel, Jonothan, David and Job of Centerville) Daniel (Theodore's father, Dan, John's Grandfather) Christy, Joseph (died enroute to settlement while near Clarksville) Peggy,
Andy and Hugh never married and lived together. Jeannette Weir
McCray, five boys and Peggy left Roanoke River on Dec. 24,
1813 with a 6-horse team & wagon and arrived at Clarksville
Ohio March 1814. Joseph died in the Summer of 1814; they then
moved to what is known as the Baker Bottoms just south of Morrow, Ohio. Jeannette Weir McCray and family lived on what is
known as Joseph Nickleson's home farm (owned in July 1926 by
Joseph Nickleson). Living on Christy McCray's present farm
(1926) when Christy McCray and Nancy Urton were married. This
must have been in 1820. Joseph McCray, their son, was born in
1821. Nancy Urton's Father was Thomas Urton, of Culpepper
County, Virginia. Nancy Urton's Mother's name was Leanor Fur
(Fir it may be) of Culpepper County, but she lived in Fauquier
County, when they came to Ohio. Fur's (Fir's) lived in the
adjoining county to Alexandria, Va. Known ("No one") had to go
for Doctor 20 or 40 miles in a certain case of sickness. Do
not know what Thomas Urton's Father's name was. Christy McCray
born March 7, 1795, died Sept. 2, 1839. Nancy Urton McCray
born May 4, 1795, died May 30, 1870. "

Christy said that Samuel married twice, and that his first wife's
name was Porter. At the L.D.S. Library* in Annandale, Virginia, I wrote
in my notebook several years ago that Samuel McCrea married Jane Porter in
Philadelphia on February 16, 1765 (Batch A184730 Sh 0816). Mrs. Hazel
Foster, of Sun Lakes, Arizona also recorded this same information in her
notebook. This probably was the wedding of Samuel 2.

* Genealogical libraries of the Church of Jesus Christ of the Latter Day
  Saints in most major cities of the United States.

It is probably significant, and certainly interesting, that on that same day, February 16, 1765, James McCree married Ann Porter , somewhere in Pennsylvania. Forget that one was "McCree" and the other was "McCrea"; I'd bet the rent that Samuel and James McCray, brothers, married the sisters, Ann and Jane Porter, in a double wedding ceremony in Philadelphia. But just to stir the pot a bit, four years later, James McCray married Ann Porter in Hunterdon County, New Jersey, on March 22, 1769!* I'll take no bets on that one!

Christy McCray, the author of the family history, apparently didn't know that Samuel spent several years in Maryland, and may have been born there, before he lived in Virginia and Ohio. Indeed, in a history of Warren County by the ubiquitous Beers, on page 1047, under an account of Thomas McCray, son of Christy and Nancy (Urton) McCray, appeared this:

"Christy's parents were Samuel and Jenette McCray *natives* (italics mine) respectively of Virginia and Maryland."

Of course, it should have read "...natives respectively of Maryland and Virginia," but Beers' county histories were more notable for the money they generated than for their accuracy.

The Federal Census of 1850 revealed that William McCray, age 72, Margaret McCray, age 70, Hugh McCray, age 61, and Daniel McCray, age 58, all reported the place of their birth as Maryland. **William's age, 72, and Daniel's age, 58, means that Samuel McCray lived in Maryland AT LEAST from 1778 to 1792.** Christy said that Samuel McCray married Jeanette Weir, who lived on the Roanoke River, after the Revolution. If Christy got it right, it is hard to avoid the conclusion that Samuel married Jeanette after 1792, and that William, Margaret, Hugh and Daniel, and probably John (more later), were children either of his first wife, Jane Porter, or children of a second wife, and Jeanette would then have been his third wife. John McCray, who wasn't visited by the 1850 census-taker because he had died in 1836, would then very likely have been the child of Jane (Porter) McCray.

Andrew and Armstrong McCray were also visited by the census-taker in 1850, and both gave their place of birth as Virginia; Andrew was then age 50 and Armstrong was 48. Christy was born, according to the later Christy in 1795, but didn't say whether he was born in Virginia, Maryland or Ohio. It can be concluded then that Samuel married Jeanette before the year 1801, when Andrew was born, and after 1792. The alternative is that Christy got it wrong and Samuel married Jeanette before the Revolution, and before 1770, when John was born.

By examination of all the data at hand, this is how the children of Samuel 2 are arranged in chronological order, following the three children of his first wife, Jane Porter, who were Samuel 2a, Robert and Mary:

John McCray, 1770-1836, born in Maryland?

William McCray, 1778-after 1850, born in Maryland

Margaret McCray, 1780-after 1850, born in Maryland

Hugh McCray, 1789-after 1850, born in Maryland

Daniel McCray, 1792-   born in Maryland

Christy McCray, 1795-1839, born in Virginia?

Andrew McCray, 1800-   born in Virginia ?

Armstrong McCray, 1801 or 1802-1849, born in Virginia ?

Joseph McCray,   d. 1814 born in ?

Stephen McCray

Thomas McCray }
James McCray } These probably were the children
                 said by Christy to have died in
                 childhood. Birth or death years
Matthew McCray} unknown.

Christy wrote in his 1926 account that Robert McCray, Samuel's second son by his first wife, left Virginia "before his father was born"," (a sentence that is the despair of teachers of English Comp). Robert was according to Christy, a lieutenant with General Wilkinson "in what was known as the Burr campaign..." General Wilkinson served in the Revolutionary War, and afterward settled in Kentucky. There he engaged in some double-dealing with the Spanish government, meanwhile planning to turn over to Spain all the western settlements of the United States. For his skullduggery he was awarded a Spanish pension. Although his enemies insisted he would have helped Spain gain the settlements along the Mississippi River, he was never charged nor tried. Commissioned a lieutenant-colonel in the Army, he was appointed to be one of the commissioners to receive the lands purchased by President Jefferson that were the Louisiana Purchase. He cooked up a deal with Aaron Burr who was in Philadelphia avoiding warrants for his arrest for killing Alexander Hamilton in a duel (these two worthies really deserved each other!) to take over the Southwest, but he then betrayed Burr and rode out with Army troops to capture Burr and deliver him up for trial. His own duplicity was examined

109

in several courts-martial, but he escaped conviction, and even managed to gain a promotion to the rank of major general. Eventually, however, his career ended in disgrace, and he died in Mexico City.

Burr escaped conviction on charges of treason, went to France, and tried to persuade Napoleon to aid him in conquering Florida, but Napoleon wasn't interested. Burr returned to America in 1812 and opened a law office in New York, N.Y. At age 77 he married a widow about twenty years younger, and three years later, in 1836, they were divorced. The divorce papers were delivered to him on the day of his death. Burr spent most of his life going the wrong direction, it seems, but let us give him some points for his views on the ladies, which probably didn't gain him very much approbation in his day. He said:

> "I happen to think that woman is a glorious species, but contrary to the fiction held by many men, women are men's intellectual equals, and if it were not for discrimination against them in education, and by custom, they would match us in every endeavor, except perhaps war. I see no reason why we should continue to value grace, allure, frivolity and vacuity in a woman above skills, acumen and intellect."

It may be that Robert McCray served under Wilkinson at Vicksburg when the scandalous Burr campaign was under way. He married a lady who lived in Vicksburg, and after retirement he returned there to live. Christy wrote that he had a son he named Samuel McCray, but it wasn't clear whether his son was born to the lady from Vicksburg or not. He probably died sometime after 1810.

We can only speculate about the nature of some dramatic event that occurred that made it necessary for the widow, Jeanette McCray, to leave Virginia. Christy said that she left after Samuel's death, but not that she left because of his death. He may have died some years before and she was forced to leave because the house burned. She must have left under duress, for surely no one would undertake such a trip just as winter was setting in unless a great emergency made it necessary. On Christmas Eve, 1813, she loaded up six children and all the food and clothing, feed for the horses, and absolutely necessary supplies that could be packed into the wagon, and set off on a journey to Ohio that was to take two and a half months to complete. Such a journey would have been difficult enough in the summer, what with the lack of good roads, and in some areas, no roads at all, only wide paths, and winter in the mountains of West Virginia can be very bitter and snowy.

To say: "Took from Christmas to March to come over mountains in wagon," is really reducing a story to its very basic elements. It says a lot, though, about the kinds of people of that day, for one just didn't mess around in those stony, heavily forested mountains that lie between the Valley of Virginia and the Ohio River. Roads were poorly maintained, and travellers often had to repair roads in order to proceed past some spots. Erosion and large boulders in wagon tracks could test the resolve of horses, people and wagons. Having six horses hitched to the wagon was probably necessary to pull the vehicle up some of the hills, and it took a skilled driver to handle that large a hitch. Armstrong, the youngest member of the party, learned the handling of multiple hitches on this trip, for he worked as a teamster when they got to Ohio. It was customary for members of travelling parties to walk beside the wagon, instead of riding, and it was very probably necessary to walk for much of the time to avoid freezing. But then, probably people of those times didn't think that such a trip was as arduous as we would. Walking was how you got there.

Christy said that the children of Jeanette who accompaned her to Ohio were Margaret, Daniel, Christy, Joseph, Andrew and Armstrong. Joseph became ill on the trip and died on the wagon almost within sight of their destination at Clarksville. He added, "Other children died in childhood." William, Hugh and John McCray arrived later in Ohio, so counting those three, plus the six that came by wagon, it appears that Stephen, James and Matthew were the "other children." Mary McCray somehow got to Ohio, too, and she may have come with William, Hugh and John when they came later. She married a man named Kessler in Ohio.

Local and county histories were produced all over the United States at the latter part of the nineteenth century. Most notable of these biographers was Beers Publishers in Chicago, who published under a variety of publishing firm names, but always with the name "Beers" in the title. Scholarship had little to do with them; their purpose was to generate profits for the publisher by producing books about citizens within a given county that were written primarily to sell to those who were interviewed for the books, and never was said a discouraging word about any of the subjects, and no attempt was made to confirm the truth of what the interviewer was told. Nevertheless the Beers county history series are a very valuable resource for genealogists today because they often contain information that didn't get printed elsewhere.

From *History of Warren County, Ohio,* page 692 this extract is given:

"Settlement of Todd's Fork of Little Miami River & Montgomery Road. The McCRAY family, from Virginia, settled in the vicinity in 1813. There were 7 brothers: *Hugh, Daniel, Christy, Joseph, Andrew, Armstrong & William,* the latter coming some years previous. (Beers didn't bother with dates much of the time.) They settled at different points SE of the Creek and were industrious and useful citizens. Thomas URTON, a Revolutionary soldier, came from Culpepper Co., VA., in 1818 to where Thomas McCray (mother was a URTON) now lives on the Bull Skin Road."

111

On page 689 of the same volume was:

"Timothy Titus settled in 1806, on the north side of the
Chillicothe Road, which James Melow now owns, in a half-faced
camp. As soon as he got matters a little regulated, he set
up a blacksmith shop. This was the first snop of the kind in
the township except for Nebo Gaunt's. It is supposed William
McCRAY settled in the vicinity the same year."

Further along, on page 1047:

"THOMAS McCRAY, farmer; P.O. Clarksville; was born in Washington Township April 21, 1824; he is a son of Christy and
Nancy (Orton) McCray, who were natives of Botetourt and Culpepper Counties, Va. respectively. The former was born March
7, 1795, and the latter May 4, 1794. Mr. McCray's parents,
Samuel and Jenette McCray were natives of Virginia and Maryland, and came and settled in Union Township, Warren Co., in
1814, and subsequently in Washington Township, where Mr.
McCray died September 25, 1839, and Mrs. McCray May 30, 1870.
Thomas, our subject, was reared on a farm and obtained his education in the common schools, principally under the preceptor-
ship of his father, who was one of the 'old pioneer school
teachers.' Mr. McCray was married Sep. 5, 1852, to Mary Madden, a daughter of Solomon and Ruth (Robbins) Madden, natives
of North Carolina. Mrs. McCray was born in Clinton Co., Ohio,
Jan. 4, 1830. This union was blest with one child--Alice,
born Aug. 9, 1853. She married Dec. 6, 1873, to Elwood Hampton and died July 24, 1876, leaving one little daughter--Blanche
M., who was born June 3, 1875. Mrs. McCray is a member of the
Society of Friends, and Mr. McCray is a Republican; he owns a
farm of 116 acres and follows general farming. Mrs. McCray's
father was born in 1793 and died Nov. 3, 1849; her mother was
born Aug. 9, 1800. They came to Clinton Co., in a very early
day, and to this county in 1849. Mrs. McCray's grandfather,
George Madden, served eighteen months in the Revolutionary War."

In a local history, *City of Dayton and Montgomery County, Ohio;* edit-
ed by Frank Conover, of Dayton; A.W. Bowen & Co., 1897; p. 1014;

"ORVILLE McCRAY, M.D., of West Carrollton, Montgomery
County, Ohio, is a native son of Ohio, born in Clinton County
on 2 April, 1868, and was a son of Samuel and Samantha (Wright)
McCray, and paternally is of Scotch descent. Armstrong McCray
his grandfather, was a native of Maryland, but with his wife,
Jane, came from Virginia to Ohio, settled in Warren County,
where Armstrong became a farmer among the pioneers and was
prominent in local affairs. The maternal grandfather was Mitchell Wright of Virginia, and pioneer farmer of Clinton County.

112

"Samuel McCray, father of the doctor, is a native of Ohio,
and is now proprietor of a flouring mill in Charlesville. Orville is a graduate of the University of Louisville, 1893. He
started practice in Clarksville, but moved to West Carrollton.
He married Marietta Flack, daughter of Adam and Nancy (McCray)
Flack, on 6 May, 1894. They have a daughter, Buleah."

An excerpt from *History of Clinton County, Ohio*, (publisher and
author not given), 1882. Washington Township, p. 1145:

"Samuel McCray, a miller of Cuba, is a son of Armstrong
and Jane (Urton) McCray. He was born in Washington Township,
Warren County, on 2 June, 1839. His father was born October,
1801, and his mother in June, 1801. They went to Warren County
with their parents when young. Armstrong was killed by a team
running away, 28 December, 1849. She died August, 1851. Samuel was the second son and fourth child of five children. In
October, 1875 he bought the Cuba Mill. He married in October,
1861, to Mary E. Osborn, daughter of William and Hannah Osborn.
She died Sept. 1862, leaving a child, Emily, now deceased. Samuel married Samantha A. Wright, daughter of John M. and Penel-
ope Wright, in September, 1868. She was born in Marion Township in September of 1844. They have two children, Orville
and Nellie."

John and Sarah (Dill) McCray

MRS. HAZEL (McCRAY) FOSTER, of Sun Lakes, Arizona, is examining the
possibility that Christy was mistaken in naming John as a son of Samuel2,
and she thinks there is a possibility that John was the brother of Samuel, who once lived in Reading Pennsylvania. Christy's history is open
to question, as it has been shown that he apparently was unaware that at
least five of Samuel's children were born in Maryland, not Virginia, as
he thought. He gave us an account of his ancestors, probably based
largely on his recollections of things told him long ago. Nothing in his
history suggests that he used written records as his sources, but rather
he had probably depended solely upon his memory and that of relatives,
and all of them were two generations removed from the pioneer ancestors.
Christy wrote concerning John McCray, Mrs. Foster's ancestor:

"This John lived near what was known as Kackensack, Warren Co. later removed to Iowa--his children, Samuel, Jonathan,
David and Job of Centerville."

John didn't move to Iowa. He died and was buried in Lebanon, Ohio.
There are Centervilles in Ohio and Montana. Christy didn't know about

two Centervilles. Mrs. Foster has all the names in her lineage, and Job McCray was her grandfather, Samuel McCray was her great grandfather, and John McCray was her great great grandfather. Samuel 2 married Jane Porter in February of 1765, so it is biologically possible that she bore Samuel 2a, Robert, Mary and John by 1770, and that Christy was incorrect in naming John as a son of Jeanette (Weir) McCray.

Mrs. Foster supplied a chart of the generations from John to herself. John married Sarah ("Sally") Dill, daughter of Francis and Anne (Dunlap) Dill. They had six children:

> Ann McCray, m. Garett Jefferys
> Francis McCray, unmarried
> Samuel McCray, m. Sharlott (sic) Clevenger, Oct. 30, 1833
> Joseph McCray
> Jane McCray, m. Elam Bone, Feb. 2, 1837
> John McCray, unmarried

John died in 1836 and is buried with his wife, Sarah, in the Old Presbyterian Cemetery, in Lebanon, Warren County. His will was probated* in Lebanon, with Sally named as his wife. She asked the court to appoint her son, Francis, to be administrator instead of herself. Among the items presented were debts to the estate; David McCray, her grandson, owed $90, and Francis, another grandson, owed $65. Here is how the estate was divided:

> | | |
> |---|---|
> | Sarah McCray | $521.20 |
> | Samuel and Charlotte (Clevenger) McCray | 168.48 |
> | Jane (McCray) and Elam Bone | 168.48 |
> | Joseph McCray | 168.48 |

Mrs. Foster supplied much of the material used in this chapter about the family of Samuel and Jeanette (Weir) McCray. Ronald McCray, of Dayton, Ohio, and Francis Lipp, of Frankfort, Kentucky, also contributed much useful material.

Daniel and Harriet (Skinner) MCCray

DANIEL McCRAY WAS BORN IN 1792, the son of Samuel and Jeanette McCray, somewhere in Maryland. He was living in Virginia when, at age twenty-one, he and his widowed mother and five siblings moved across the western Virginia mountains to Clarksville, Ohio. This was in the winter

* Will Book 7, page 692, Box 79 #17

114

of 1813. On January 30, 1818, he married twenty-four year old Harriet Skinner, daughter of Cornelius, Jr., and Sarah (McMakin) Skinner, of New Jersey; Harriet was born in Virginia. The Skinners, both Senior and Junior, lived in New Jersey, then later in Loudoun County, Virginia.*

Daniel and Harriet are recorded in the 1850 Federal Census (what would we do without the 1850 Census?) in Salem Township, Warren County, Ohio, with four children, Margaret, 21, Samuel C., 19, Theodore M., 14, and John F., 8. Another daughter, Mary Jane McCray, who was 29 in 1850, and not living in Samuel's household, married James W. Longstreth in April, 1841, when they were both age twenty. By 1860 Samuel C. McCray was married to Sarah E.--?-- and they then had two children; Mary, 7, and Alonzo H., 5.

Elizabeth Longstreth married Richard McCray. Just where Richard fits into the McCray clan isn't known, but he lived in Salem Township, Warren County, so he probably is a descendant from Samuel 2 McCray. Elizabeth was born in 1822 and he was born in 1818. They had two children; George, born in 1843, and Daniel M. Daniel was a Civil War veteran from Illinois.

Theodore M. McCray, a son of Daniel and Harriet (Skinner) McCray, was born in 1835. He married Nancy C. Moore, born September 8, 1841, on June 17, 1875, in Midland City, Clinton County, Ohio. Their son, David Jesse McCray, was born May 18, 1878, and he married Grace Flossie Taylor on October 15, 1899, at Cregonia, Clinton County, Ohio. Grace was the daughter of Isaac J. and Emma (Beecham) Taylor. She was born January 28, 1883. Theodore was a blacksmith.

Their son, Clyde Edward McCray, Sr., was born March 8, 1808, and on December 24, 1830, he married Mable Grace Rodgers at New Holland, Ohio. She was born August 15,1814, daughter of Jess Franklin and Blanche Cordelia (Campbell) Rodgers.

Ronald Lee McCray, who supplied much of the material for this chapter, was born June 24, 1941. He is a teacher of Chemistry in a Dayton, Ohio, high school.

William, Margaret, Hugh, Christy and Andrew McCray

WILLIAM McCRAY, AGE 72, was living in the household of John B. and Julie Ann (also Juliann) (Curtis) McCray, who probably was his son, when the census-taker came a'calling in 1850. Listed underneath his name was his wife's name, Nancy, age 56, who said she was born in Virginia. Wil-

*Could there be a relationship there between the famous actress, Cornelia Otis Skinner, born in 1901, and these Skinners?

115

liam told the census-taker that he was born in Maryland. Nancy was listed below him, at age 56. Sometime between 1850 and 1860 they separated,
but why is not known. In the 1860 Census, Nancy is living in the household of Thomas and Mary (Madden) McCray. Thomas was a son of Armstrong
McCray. William, then age 82, was living in the household of William F.
McCray, another son of Armstrong McCray. One would expect that the
couple would have been living with their son, John B. McCray, but instead,
Andrew McCray, still a bachelor at age 60, was living with John B. and
Julie Ann (Curtis) McCray.

Christy McCray was born March 7, 1795 in Virginia. He married Nancy
Urton, in 1820, in Virginia. She was a daughter of Thomas and Leanor
(Fur, or Fir) Urton, of Culpepper County, Virginia. In a biography of
Thomas McCray it was stated that Christy was a native of Botetourt County, Virginia, and this is the only statement that indicates where Samuel
and Jeanette (Weir) McCray lived in Virginia. (The biography can be
found four pages before this.)

Christy died September 2, 1839, at age 44. His widow, Nancy, declined being appointed administratrix and asked the court to appoint
Christy's brother, Daniel, as administrator. Letters of administration
were signed by Armstrong McCray, another brother of Christy's. Daniel
was "assigned" $256.30 for expenses by William Guttery on August 12, 1844.

116

Family Chart Of

SAMUEL McCRAY OF PENNSYLVANIA,

MARYLAND, VIRGINIA AND OHIO

Generation I

John McCray, who accompanied his brother, Samuel, from Scotland, and both settled in Reading, Pennsylvania, according to a family history by Christy McCray.

James McCray, who married Ann Porter in Philadelphia on the same day that Samuel McCray married Jane Porter, according to published records. An unproven assumption is that James and Samuel were brothers who married sisters, Ann and Jane Porter, in a double wedding ceremony.

Samuel McCray, born c1750 in Scotland. After his marriage to Jane Porter, according to the family history, they had three children, and then Samuel married Jeanette Weir, and they had thirteen children. Census records show that five of the children were born in Maryland. Christy's family history implies, but does not state, that Samuel and Jeanette's children were born in Virginia. Three children died in childhood. A Warren County, Ohio, county history mentions that Samuel was a native of Maryland. Samuel died before 1813. The remaining family living in Virginia settled in Warren County, Ohio, in 1814.

Jeanette Weir was, according to Christy, a native of Ireland, but the above-mentioned county history says she was a native of Virginia. She was born in 1755.

Generation I   Generation II

Samuel McCray   Samuel McCray
    and   b. Prob. before 1770
(1) Jane Porter   d.
(2) Jeanette Weir   m. ?   Had dau, Nancy, m. --?-- Hay-
                                       wood, then --?-- Jones. Ch.
                                       Clint Jones;d. after 1912

                                 Robert McCray
                                 b. Prob. before 1770
                                 m. --?--, who lived in Vicksburg, MS
                                    Ch, Samuel McCray

                                 Mary McCray
                                 b. Prob. before 1770
Dotted lines indicate   d.
Jane Porter may have   m. --?-- Kessler
been mother of these
five children.   John McCray
                                 b. 1773, prob. in MD
                                 d. 1839 in Lebanon, Ohio @ age 66.
                                 m. Sarah ("Sally") Dill, dau of Francis
                                    and Ann (Dunlap) Dill. 6 ch

                                 William McCray
                                 b. 1778, in Maryland
                                 d. after 1860
                                 m. Nancy --?--

                                 Margaret McCray
                                 b. 1880, in MD
                                 d. after 1850
                                 m. unmarried

                                 Hugh McCray
                                 b.1789 in MD
                                 d. after 1850
                                 m. unmarried

                                 Daniel McCray
                                 b. 1792 in MD
                                 d. Oct. 1, 1857in Clarksville, Ohio
                                 m. Harriet Skinner, dau of Cornelius
                                    and Sarah (McMakin) Skinner.8 ch

118

Generation II (Cont.)

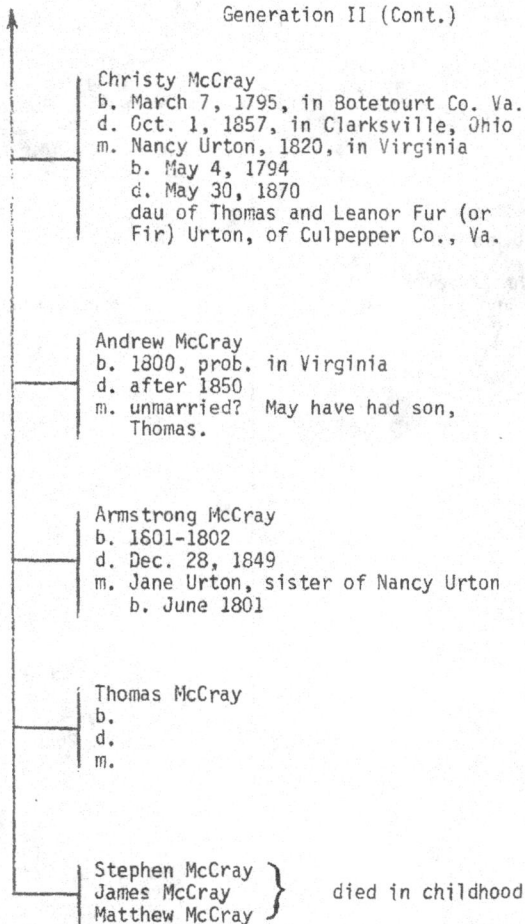

Christy McCray
b. March 7, 1795, in Botetourt Co. Va.
d. Oct. 1, 1857, in Clarksville, Ohio
m. Nancy Urton, 1820, in Virginia
　　b. May 4, 1794
　　d. May 30, 1870
　　dau of Thomas and Leanor Fur (or
　　Fir) Urton, of Culpepper Co., Va.

Andrew McCray
b. 1800, prob. in Virginia
d. after 1850
m. unmarried? May have had son,
　　Thomas.

Armstrong McCray
b. 1801-1802
d. Dec. 28, 1849
m. Jane Urton, sister of Nancy Urton
　　b. June 1801

Thomas McCray
b.
d.
m.

Stephen McCray ⎫
James McCray ⎬ died in childhood
Matthew McCray ⎭

119

Generation I   Generation III

Samuel McCray   Samuel McCray
   and   b. 1809 in Ohio
(1) Jane Porter   d. bet. 1880 and 1890
(2) Jeanette Weir   m Sharlott Clevenger, Oct. 30, 1833
                                         b. 1814 in New Jersey
                                         d.

Generatiaon II   Ann McCray
                                      b.
John McCray   d.
   and   m. Garett Jefferys
Sarah Dill

                                      Francis McCray
                                      b.
                                      d.
                                      m. bachelor

                                      Joseph McCray
                                      b.
                                      d.
                                      m.

                                      Jane E. McCray
                                      b.
                                      d.
                                      m. Elam Bone, Feb. 2, 1837

                                      John McCray
                                      b.
                                      d. ? buried in Lebanon Cemetery
                                      m. unmarried

120

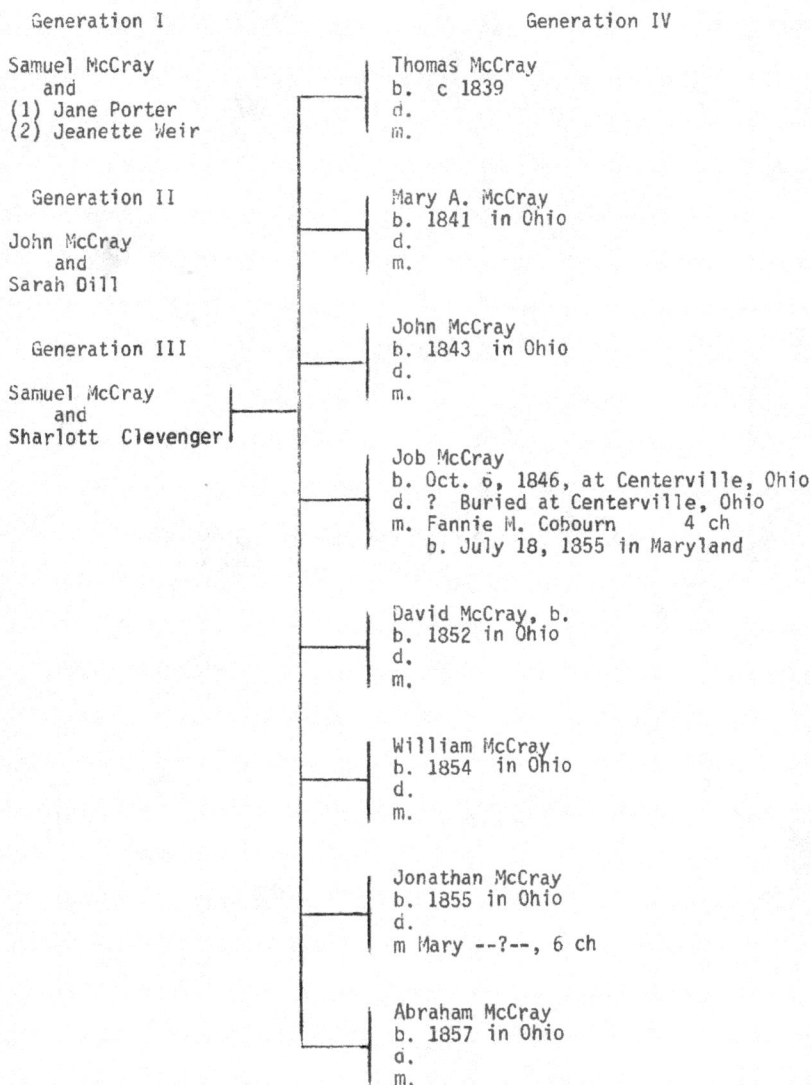

Generation I	Generation IV
Samuel McCray and (1) Jane Porter (2) Jeanette Weir	Thomas McCray b. c 1839 d. m.
Generation II John McCray and Sarah Dill	Mary A. McCray b. 1841 in Ohio d. m.
Generation III Samuel McCray and Sharlott Clevenger	John McCray b. 1843 in Ohio d. m.
	Job McCray b. Oct. 6, 1846, at Centerville, Ohio d. ? Buried at Centerville, Ohio m. Fannie M. Cobourn 4 ch b. July 18, 1855 in Maryland
	David McCray, b. b. 1852 in Ohio d. m.
	William McCray b. 1854 in Ohio d. m.
	Jonathan McCray b. 1855 in Ohio d. m Mary --?--, 6 ch
	Abraham McCray b. 1857 in Ohio d. m.

121

Generation I

Samuel McCray
    and
(1) Jane Porter
(2) Jeanette Weir

Generation II

John McCray
    and
Sarah Dill

Generation III

Samuel McCray
    and
Sharlotte Clevenger

Generation IV

Job McCray
    and
Fannie M. Cobourn

Generation V

Clarence McCray
b. July, 1876
d. ? Buried at Centerville, Ohio
m. Maude --?--

Edgar McCray
b. Mar. 13, 1879, in Centerville, Ohio
d. Oct. 1954, Phoenix, AZ
m. Cecil M. Longman, June 30, 1910
    dau of Albertus A and Mary E
    (Robeson) Longman, both of MD
    b. Mar. 3, 1888
    d. Mar. 10, 1978

Lulu McCray
b. Dec. 1877
d.
m.   George Weller, 1 ch. Catherine
     Weller, m. Lowell Thomas

Joseph McCray
b. Jan., 1884
d.
m. Dorah --?-- , 3 ch.

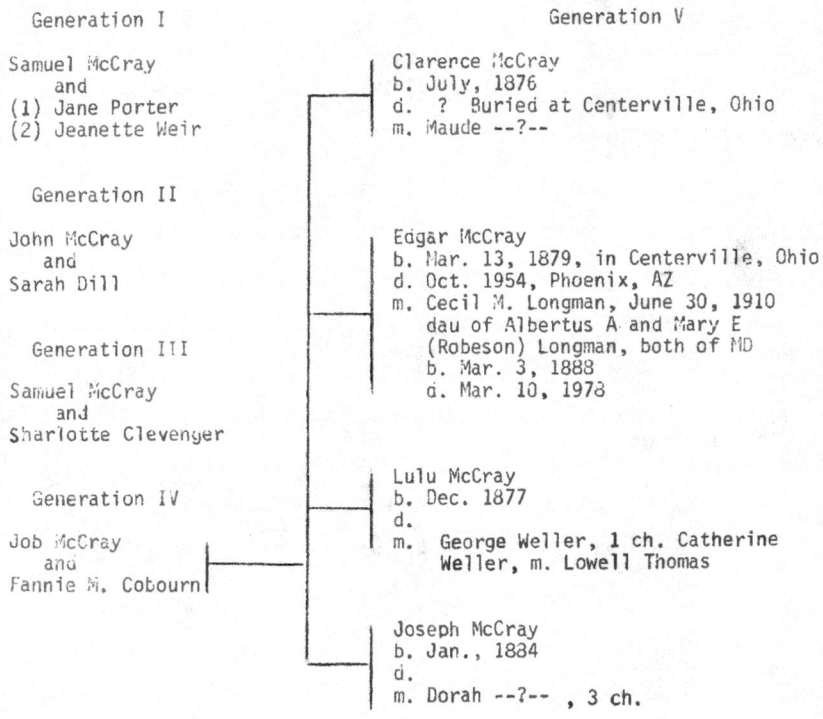

122

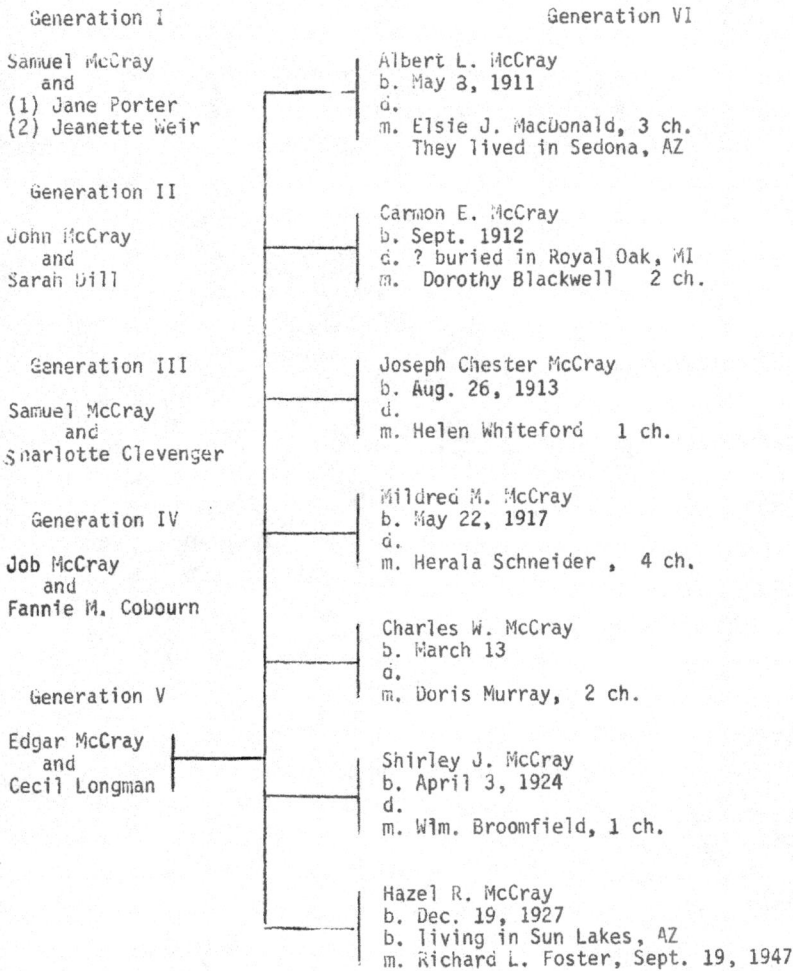

Generation I

Samuel McCray
and
(1) Jane Porter
(2) Jeanette Weir

Generation II

John McCray
and
Sarah Dill

Generation III

Samuel McCray
and
Sharlotte Clevenger

Generation IV

Job McCray
and
Fannie M. Cobourn

Generation V

Edgar McCray
and
Cecil Longman

Generation VI

Albert L. McCray
b. May 3, 1911
d.
m. Elsie J. MacDonald, 3 ch.
 They lived in Sedona, AZ

Carmon E. McCray
b. Sept. 1912
d. ? buried in Royal Oak, MI
m. Dorothy Blackwell   2 ch.

Joseph Chester McCray
b. Aug. 26, 1913
d.
m. Helen Whiteford   1 ch.

Mildred M. McCray
b. May 22, 1917
d.
m. Herala Schneider ,   4 ch.

Charles W. McCray
b. March 13
d.
m. Doris Murray, 2 ch.

Shirley J. McCray
b. April 3, 1924
d.
m. Wlm. Broomfield, 1 ch.

Hazel R. McCray
b. Dec. 19, 1927
b. living in Sun Lakes, AZ
m. Richard L. Foster, Sept. 19, 1947

123

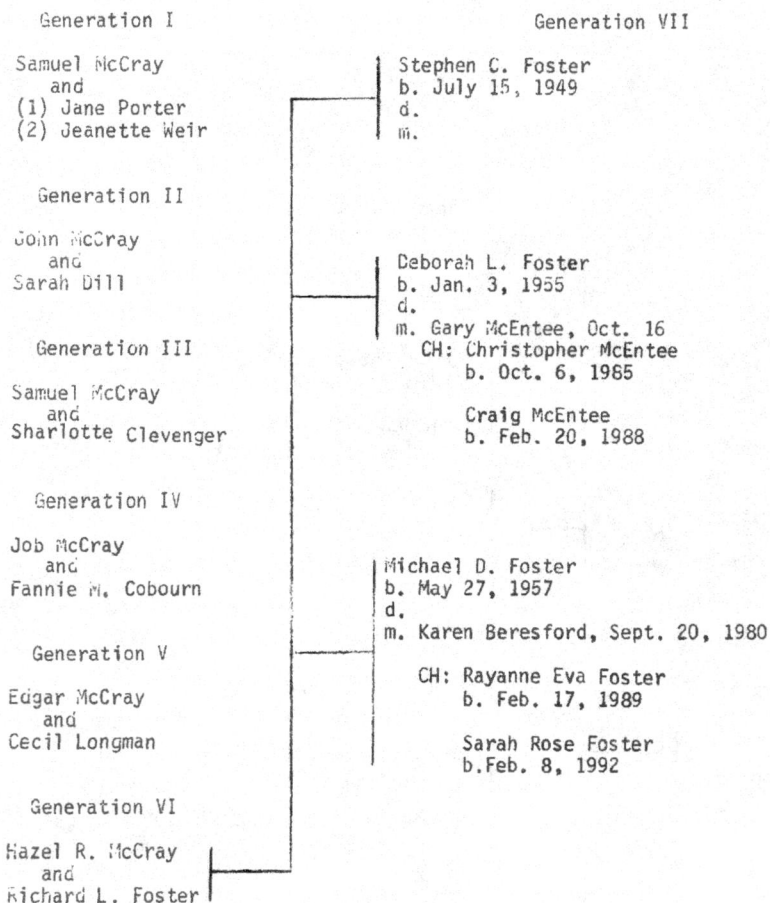

Generation I

Samuel McCray
    and
(1) Jane Porter
(2) Jeanette Weir

Generation II

John McCray
    and
Sarah Dill

Generation III

Samuel McCray
    and
Sharlotte Clevenger

Generation IV

Job McCray
    and
Fannie M. Cobourn

Generation V

Edgar McCray
    and
Cecil Longman

Generation VI

Hazel R. McCray
    and
Richard L. Foster

Generation VII

Stephen C. Foster
b. July 15, 1949
d.
m.

Deborah L. Foster
b. Jan. 3, 1955
d.
m. Gary McEntee, Oct. 16
    CH: Christopher McEntee
        b. Oct. 6, 1985

        Craig McEntee
        b. Feb. 20, 1988

Michael D. Foster
b. May 27, 1957
d.
m. Karen Beresford, Sept. 20, 1980

    CH: Rayanne Eva Foster
        b. Feb. 17, 1989

        Sarah Rose Foster
        b.Feb. 8, 1992

```
Generation I                           Generation III


Samuel McCray              Joseph McCray
      &                    b. 1821
Jeanette Weir              d.
                           m.  ?
                              Ch. Mary Luella (Molly)
                                  Flora McCray Stanfield
                                  Albert McCray - went to Kansas
                                  Arthur McCray -  •    "    "


                           Thomas McCray
                           b. April 21, 1824, Washington Twp., Warren Co.,
                           d.                                            OH
                           m. Mary Madden, dau. Solomon and Ruth(Robbins)
                              Madden, on Sept. 5, 1852
                              b. Jan 4, 1830, in Clinton Co. OH
                           Ch.  Alice McCray
    Generation II              b. Aug. 9, 1853
                               d. July 25, 1876
                               m. Elwood Hampton, Dec. 6, 1873
Christy McCray                 Ch.  Blanch Hampton
      &                             b. June 3, 1875
Nancy Urton


                           Jane McCray
                           b.
                           d.
                           m. ------- Madden
                              Ch. Douglas, Will, Clinton, Christy, Nancy,
                                                                   Adeline


                           Samuel Adams McCray
                           b. May 26, 1830
                           d.
                           m. Lydia Nacholson
                              Ch. Atwell, Alfred, Linny.


                           Lucinda McCray
                           b.  ?  d  ?
                           unmarried


                           Leanna Jeanette McCray
                           b.  ?  d.  ?
                           m. ------- Bowman, 3 ch.


                              125
```

Nancy McCray
b. ? d.   ?
m. ------- Flack, 4 ch.

Christy McCray, Jr.
b. 1837?
d. May 18, 1931; "92 yrs., 8 mo., 27d". His
birthdate would then be: Sept. 21, 1838.
    bachelor

Alexander McMakin   Cornelius and Elizabeth Skinner
                                    b. 1717, Woodbridge, N.J.
                                    d. 1814, Loudoun Co., Va.

Sarah McMakin, m. March 9, 1786   Cornelius Skinner, Jr.
b. Nov. 8, 1765, in Loudoun Co.,Va. b. Feb. 27, 1757, Peapack, Somerset
d. Dec. 29, 1847, Warren Co., OH   Co., NJ
                                    d. Mar. 21, 1812, Aldie or Lees-
                                    burg, Loudoun Co., VA

Samuel McCray and Jane Porter, or,
b. c1750, Scotland Jeanette Weir
d. bef. 1813

Daniel McCray   m. Jan. 30, 1818   Harriet Skinner
b. 1792, in MD   b. June 29, 1800
                                    d. Aug. 18, 1863

Theodore M. McCray m. June 17, 1875 Nancy C. Moore
b. 1835, Salem Twp., Warren Co., OH b. Sept. 8, 1841, New Antioch OH
d. Sept. 10, 1906   d. July 14, 1921, Morrow OH

Daniel Jesse McCray   m. Oct. 15, 1899 Grace Flossie Taylor
b. May 18, 1878, Midland City, OH   b. Jan. 28, 1883, Jamestown OH
d. Sept. 1, 1938, Columbus, OH   d. March 26, 1922, nr. Lebanon
                                                OH

Clyde Edward McCray m. Dec. 24, 1930   Mable Grace Rodgers
b. March 8, 1908, nr. Lebanon, OH   b. Aug. 15, 1914
d. June 11, 1976

Ronald Lee McCray
b. June 24, 1941
living in Dayton, Ohio

CHAPTER SIX

THE BIRTH OF TENNESSEE AND MISSOURI

IN 1784, WILLIAM NODDING, SR., led a caravan of wagons from the Maryland side of the Potomac River westward along the river until it reached the junction of the Shenandoah River. There he fired his musket into the air, and in response, Robert Harper sent his ferryboat across to bring the party over to the Virginia side. They landed next to Harper's mill, powered by the Shenandoah River, and set off from that point into the northern entrance to the storied Shenandoah Valley.

Robert Harper had operated the ferry and his mill at this very important point since 1747, when settlers began pouring into the Shenandoah Valley. It was at the town that sprang up on the hillside there, named Harper's Ferry, that the Civil War began, when John Brown tried to seize the arsenal.

The narrow gorge of the Shenandoah River soon widened out into the beautiful Shenandoah Valley. On their left were the Blue Ridge Mountains and the even grander Shenandoah Mountain lay on their right. They followed a well-marked road, formerly an Indian trail, that became in this century U.S. Highway 11. The valley's floor was already well filled with settler's log houses and a number of large villages were springing up at Harrisonburg and Stanton, now "Staunton," but still pronounced as originally spelled. At some undefined point where the lands no longer drain into the Shenandoah River, the valley is called The Valley of Virginia. The party continued through the valley until they reached a part of western North Carolina that is today Tennessee.

All of today's Tennessee was then called Washington County, North Carolina, extending clear to the Mississippi River. The colony's government in Raleigh, well to the east, regarded the vast interior as a source of wealth in furs, gathered by the half-savage (they thought) frontiersmen, and delivered to the East packed on the backs of horses. Whatever problems the trappers might have had with Indians was of little concern to the Colonial government. And troubles they did indeed have, for the Cherokee nation, whose land the trappers and settlers were invading, regarded these white strangers as a troublesome lot who would eventually destroy and take over their ancient hunting grounds. Their response was to kill settlers and cattle and burn buildings and fences.

The settlers petitioned the government many times to send soldiers to protect them. The governor and his aides yawned into their mint juleps, and remarked that the settlers were indeed a cheeky lot, especially since they objected to paying taxes. The frontiersmen said they gave them nothing in return for the taxes they had paid, and besides, they had no money. The government decided to rid itself of these contentious folk, and offered all of Washington County to the Federal Government, but Congress didn't even so much as acknowledge the offer.

The settlers, seeing that neither Congress nor North Carolina had any interest in them, met at Jonesboro (nowJonesborough) and chose delegates to a convention to form a new state, to be known as "Franklin." North Carolina's government, upon hearing of this, thought things over and realized they may have been just a mite hasty; although Washington County wasn't producing much revenue now, but sometime in the future, well, things would be better. So, they offered to make Washington County a Judicial District. The settlers weren't impressed, and went on with their plans for the new state of Franklin, and in 1785, they elected a governor and set up a code of laws to implement a state government. They then petitioned Congress to recognize Franklin as a state. While Congress droned over this new problem, North Carolina pressed its suit, wooing Franklin to forget and forgive and come on back into its fold. For a time, two governments claimed jurisdiction over Washington County, or Franklin, depending upon who was talking. In 1788 the first and only Franklin governor's term of office expired, and no one was elected to replace him, so the State of Franklin died a quiet and unmourned death.

In 1790, North Carolina again ceded the huge tract to the United States, and this time Congress accepted it as a territory. Six years later a census of the territory showed the requisite 60,000 inhabitants had settled there, and it became the State of Tennessee, the third new state to join the original thirteen states.

The Noddings and their McCray in-laws arrived and settled near Jonesboro just as things were heating up, and they undoubtedly took part in the events of those exciting times.

The Louisiana Purchase and Western Expansion

The Noddings and McCrays settled in as citizens of Washington County, and produced a new generation. Their children displayed the same Scots-Irish restlessness that had brought their parents to Tennessee. They listened in fascination to stories told by adventurers and trappers about the vast, rolling lands beyond the mighty Mississippi River, itself more than a mile wide in some places, and they longed to go, to be among the first to get there and claim the best lands. The trouble was that these fabled lands were foreign territory, and Americans were forbidden entry there.

At the turn of the nineteenth century, France, the United States' former friend and ally, had become a problem to our new nation. Napoleon Bonaparte had just taken Louisiana from Spain, and was planning to

129

create a vast new French empire in North America to compensate for the loss of French Canada at the end of the Seven Years' War. Louisiana was a large territory extending roughly from the Gulf of Mexico to Canada, and from the Mississippi River to the Pacific Ocean. New Spain, or Mexico, jutted up into what is now part of the southwestern United States. A French empire to the west of the United States was viewed as a military threat and an obstacle to America's expansion.

Napoleon's plans, however, ran into trouble. His European conquests and ultimate failure in Russia nearly bankrupted France, and Louisiana was not now as attractive to him as it had been. President Thomas Jefferson sent James Monroe to France to offer Napoleon a mutually beneficial deal--U.S. cash for Napoleon in exchange for Louisiana for the U.S. A deal was struck, and in 1804 the United States suddenly owned more than twice as much territory, and only Russia had more contiguous territory. The $15,000,000 Louisiana Purchase was surely one of the best and largest real estate deals ever, and it was accomplished without violence. It contained enough land to create fifteen new states, and cost less than three cents an acre for all the rich soil and mineral deposits of which nations could only dream.

This was great good news to the restless Scots-Irish people whose westward moves had been frustrated by the Mississippi River barrier, for Spain had made it very clear that American settlers were not welcome in Louisiana. Heretofore, Spain wouldn't even allow American ships that descended the river with raw materials to land at New Orleans. Napoleon conquered Spain and took possession of Louisiana. Now the United States owned not only both banks of the Mississippi but a lot of fine land beyond it. Embittered Spain charged Jefferson with trafficking in stolen goods, but ruefully had to concede that a deal's a deal.

Missouri became a territory in 1812 and settlers began following Lewis and Clark's path up the Missouri River. Steamboats appeared on the river in 1819, while the Missouri Compromise was being hammered out in Washington. In 1821 it became the State of Missouri.

Crop failures in Europe in 1816 created a great demand for foodstuffs which the United States was happy to supply. When the War of 1812 ended, British cotton manufacturers ordered tons of cotton, and orders rolled in for wheat, sugar, tobacco, beef and pork. Cotton production in Alabama and Mississippi shot up spectacularly when the price of cotton doubled. Prices for other commodites doubled and redoubled within a year and a half.

Americans, with their pockets happily stuffed with greenbacks, went on a binge of speculation in land, much of it west of the Mississippi. One could buy United States government land for two dollars an acre, payable over five years, in tracts of 320 acres. Congress rocketed the land rush by changing the law to permit purchase of as little as eighty

acres, and hordes of small farmers and settlers put their meagre savings
into land contracts, and soon speculators owed the government more than
the worth of the annual production of all the land west of the Allegheny Mountains. The nation teetered on the edge of financial instability.

National financial stability was further eroded by large-scale lending by banks who issued great quantities of notes far in excess of their
assets. Bankers engaged in corrupt practices, such as lending great sums
to themselves with no collateral, simply because there were no laws
against such practices.

In 1818, European farmers reaped good harvests and prices fell to
below former steady levels. Prices collapsed and people were unable to
either sell their land or to pay off their loans, and the Panic of 1819
ensued. In the West, land that had been selling for $50 an acre could
not be sold for $2. Western migration slowed, but didn't stop entirely.

Louisiana and Arkansas were part of the Missouri Territory until
1836, when both became states. Oklahoma was Indian Territory. Americans
in Texas revolted against Mexican rule in 1836 and made it a republic,
but then joined the United States in 1845, the only state having the
right to divide itself into several states whenever it pleases. Texans,
firmly believing Texas to be the Promised Land, were then and now ever
ready to tell any and all about the glories of Texas and of being Texans.
Frederick Law Olmstead travelled through Texas, and in 1850 published
A Journey Through Texas. He wrote:

> "So anxious is every one in Texas to give all strangers a
> favourable impression, that all statements as to the extreme
> profit and healthfulness of lands must be taken with a grain
> of allowance. We found it very difficult, without impertinent
> persistence, to obtain any unfavourable facts."

Daniel And Sarah (Nodding) McCray

DANIEL McCRAY WAS BORN IN SCOTLAND about 1744-46. His arrival in
America is unrecorded, but he first appeared in official records in 1771
when he settled in Loudoun County, Virginia, and married Sarah Nodding,
daughter of William and Mary Nodding, Sr., of Montgomery County, Maryland, who lived on a tract beside the Potomac River about a mile upstream
from Great Falls of the Potomac, a series of low falls and dangerous
rapids that mark the upstream limit of navigation. The late Ida Lucille
McCray, of Washington, D.C., has done considerable research in Scotland
on the McCrays and the Noddings, and she believed the McCrays came from
Ayrshire and the Noddings lived in Yorkshire, England.

In 1770 or thereabouts, William Nodding, Sr., witnessed a "Lease

131

for lives" of 300 acres of land in Loudoun County, Virginia, which is located opposite Montgomery County, Maryland. The lease included a life interest for his son, Charles McCray, indicating that Daniel had married Sarah a year or more before the lease. The Potomac River at that point is placid, about two-hundred yards wide, and therefore an easy crossing in a skiff for visits between the Noddings and McCrays. Loudoun County today is an area of exploding development near Dulles Airport, and is less than a dozen miles from the District of Columbia.

We have no information on parents or brothers and sisters of Daniel McCray, but there were other McCrays* living nearby at the same time. Daniel McCray, of the Ohio McCrays, married Harriet Skinner, who lived in Loudoun County, Virginia. While there is nothing to indicate that any of these various McCrays were related, or even knew the other was on the face of the planet, the possibility exists that some of them were related to this Daniel McCray. From Port Tobacco to Loudoun County was an easy paddle by canoe of about forty miles, with an easy portage around Great Falls, and there was much traffic on the river upstream into the Valley of Virginia.

The Noddings seem to have been people of some substance, for one of William Nodding's daughters, Elizabeth, married William Calvert, and the Calverts of Maryland had been movers and shakers since Lord George Calvert, the first proprietor, was granted the enormous tract of land which Lord Calvert named "Maryland" in honor of Henrietta Marie, Charles I's queen. Maryland's first governor was Leonard Calvert, nephew of Lord George Calvert, and William and Elizabeth (Calvert) named one of their boys, Leonard. Sarah Nodding's sister, Mary, married Samuel Bayles (also "Bayless"), while living in Montgomery County, Maryland.

The Nodding caravan arrived in Washington County, North Carolina, in 1784 and set about making homes for them all. William Nodding and Daniel McCray were listed as taxpayers and voters in Washington County in 1785. By then, their new home was in the embryonic state, "Franklin." William and Mary Nodding, Daniel and Sarah (Nodding) McCray, and Samuel and Mary (Nodding) Bayless, were all original covent signatories at the founding of the Cherokee Baptist Church at Cherokee Creek, in eastern North Carolina, for by then Franklin had expired and the territory was again Washington County, North Carolina, in 1793.

Sarah (Nodding) McCray died May 8, 1809, and sometime after that Daniel McCray married Polly Pretchard (or Pritchard). They had no child-

* See Chapter Five, Samuel McCray, "The McCrays of Ohio and Indiana", and Chapter Three, the references to McCrays at Port Tobacco, Maryland.)

132

ren. Daniel McCray died in Washington County, which by then was in the
new state of Tennessee, in 1819. By then their family had already begun
to scatter westward, following the ever-expanding western horizon.

That Other Daniel McCray

Daniel and Sarah (Nodding) McCray had ten and possibly eleven children. We know something about most of them except their first son, Charles, born in 1869 in Loudoun County, Virginia, is an enigma. We only know that he married Elizabeth Deakins, but the names of any children of theirs have not come down to us. There was a Daniel McCray, who lived in Washington County at the turn of the nineteenth century, and several researchers, although baffled about his origins, believe he probably was a son of Charles and Elizabeth (Deakins) McCray. But not all of them think that. Mrs. Patricia Case, of Santa Barbara, California, a descendant of Daniel and Sarah (Nodding) McCray and their son, Elisha and Rebecca (Tilson) McCray, wrote about this Daniel:

"I believe that Daniel McCray who married Sarah Bogart was the younger brother of my Elisha McCray, because the two families appear to have moved to Missouri together, and Daniel appeared at the estate sale of my Elisha and is listed as a purchaser of some items."

Mrs. Louise Watkins, of Rockford, Tennessee, also a descendant of Daniel and Sarah (Nodding) McCray, wrote:

" Ralph Piper (of Derby Kansas)...was of the opinion, and I agree, that he was the son of Charles McCray who married Betsey Deakins in Washington County, TN in 1788. "

Whoever he was, he lived in the community with the other siblings of Daniel and Sarah (Nodding) McCray, and he married Sarah Bogart. Having two Daniels married to Sarahs probably caused no problems in their day, since everyone knew which ones were which just by looking, but things are different today. All we have are names on paper.

Jane McCray, daughter of Daniel and Sarah (Nodding) McCray married George Jinkins, and their son, Elijah Jinkins married Mary McCray, daughter of Daniel and Sarah (Bogart) McCray. Got that? Confused? It becomes a bit clearer by looking at the abbreviated family chart below.

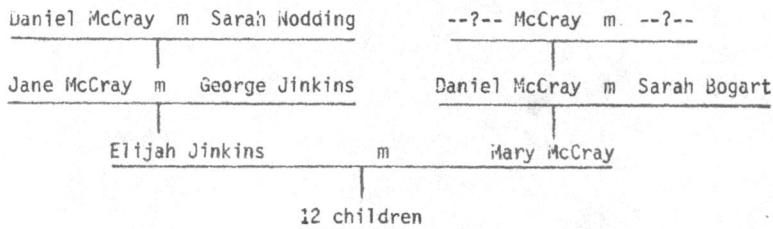

```
Daniel McCray  m  Sarah Nodding        --?-- McCray  m  --?--
        |                                      |
Jane McCray  m   George Jinkins        Daniel McCray  m  Sarah Bogart
        |                                      |
    Elijah Jinkins          m         Mary McCray
                            |
                       12 children
```

Three years after their marriage in 1818, Daniel and Sarah (Bogart) McCray migrated from Washington County, Tennessee, to Howard County, Missouri. Before leaving Tennessee, probably well aware of the brevity of life on the frontier, and the sometimes suddenness of death, Daniel filed his will, which he dictated to someone, for he signed it with his mark. In 1833 they moved on to Ray County and still later they moved again to Buchanan County, where they probably found contentment and lived out their lives there. Sarah died in 1377 and Daniel died in 1881, and both are buried in Elder Cemetery in Tremont Township, Buchanan County. Looking at a map of Missouri it is clear that they used the Missouri River as they moved from one place to another. Buchanan County lies just south of today's St. Joseph, on the east bank of the Missouri River.

Daniel McCray's will, found in Will Book, Volume I, page 165, Washington County, Tennessee reads (verbatim):

"Daniel McCray -- March 1, 1819. It is the request of DANIEL McCRAY that JANE JINKENS shall have my three beds and sids and furniture and pots and chest and hackle and smothen iron and forty dolars for SALLY HARRIS (she was Sarah McCray, daughter of Daniel and Sarah (Nodding) McCray) this being her part for horse beast that she ought to of had. know all men of the COUNTY OF WASHINGTON and State of Tennessee, that I DANIEL McCRAY I do certify this to be my last will and testament that after lawful dets be paid that my Negro man, ELLECK shall have the choosing of his own master and mistress amongst my children and he shall not sel and run him out of the County and whosoever he chooses for master it be more than thur share he must pay to the others as I allow all my children to have an equal share of what I have. I leave HENRY McCRAY and THOMAS McCRAY to be my executors, and I leave --?-- ten dollars.

signed DANIEL McCRAY "D" mark

"wit: GEORGE HAYS
CHARLES JINKINS X mark
JOSEPH JINKINS X mark

"The forgoing will was proven in court by the oaths of CHARLES JINKINS and JOSEPH JINKINS two of the subscribing witnesses thare to at ____ session and ____ records.

"HENRY McCRAY and THOMAS McCRAY quallified as exucutors of the fore going will. "

- - - - - - -

Jane McCray and George Jinkins

Jane McCray, daughter of Daniel and Sarah (Nodding) McCray, married
George Jinkins (later spelled "Jinkens" and Jenkins") in Washington
County, Tennessee. We know a good deal about this George Jinkins, most
of which was gleaned from an 1889 book of Texas biographical sketches*,
a copy of which was supplied by Blanche Meritt, of Oceanside, California, as follows:

> "George Jinkens...came from an old Virginia family, and he
> himself was a native of the 'Old Dominion.' He settled in
> East Tennessee when that country was a wilderness, became the
> owner of a large and fertile farm in Washington County, and
> there, by industry, good management and the intelligent use of
> slave labor, amassed a considerable fortune. He was a large
> planter, an extensive stock grower, and a general producer. He
> made all his own wagons and farming implements, and to some ex-
> tent supplied the local trade. He was also a distiller, and
> sold the products of the still for miles around. He was like-
> wise a large hog raiser, and hauled off great quantities of
> bacon every year. His live stock he drove south and sold to
> the cotton planters of Georgia, his nearest city market then
> being Augusta. Subsequently he moved to Kentucky and settled
> on Barren River in Monroe county, where after a long life of
> great activity and considerable usefulness he died in 1842."

> "The wife of the preceding and mother of the subject of
> this sketch was Jane McCray, daughter of Daniel McCray, native
> of Scotland who settled in east Tennessee when that territory was
> first opened to settlement and while it was yet overrun by sav-
> ages. He brought with him the characteristics of his race--
> great industry, economy and practical sagacity. He lived the life
> of the pioneer and died in the State of his adoption.

> "The children of George and Jane Jinkins were--Charles,
> Joseph, Elijah, George M., Nancy, Sallie and Achsa.

> "The fourth of these, George M., was born in Washington
> County, Tennessee, April 16, 1816, and was reared in Tennessee
> and Kentucky. He was married in the latter State October 4,
> 1837, the maiden name of his wife being Sarah K. Andrews, daughter
> of William Andrews, a native of Virginia and early settler of
> Kentucky. Mr. Jinkins left Kentucky in the year 1844 for Texas,

---

* *Biographical Souvenir of the State of Texas,* F.A. Battey & Co,
Chicago, 1889. pp 457, 458.

starting down the Cumberland river from Monroe county on a flatboat. He had aboard his primitive craft his wife, two children, a young lady friend, all their household goods, and a small quantity of saddles, harness and leather, the latter of which he intended to dispose of in the West. On reaching Nashville, he decided that the journey by that means would be too tedious, and he embarked his goods, chattels and merchandise, and took passage on the then noted steamer, "John O'Fallen." Those were the days of reckless steamboating, and below Nashville there occurred a collision between the "O'Fallen" and another steamer called the "Empress," in consequence of the recklessness of those in charge, which was then distinguished as one of the most disastrous of the times, and one which those aboard the two vessels have not forgotten and never will forget. The "O'Fallen," which had on board over 400 passengers, was struck and parted midway by the "Empress," and at the same time driven onto a sand-bar. In the uproar and confusion which followed Mr. Jinkens was separated from his family, but afterward found and rescued all but one of them. While the vessel was filling with water, his oldest child, then about five years old, became lost, but seizing on to a stovepipe was afterward found by a passenger on board and saved before the boat went down, although badly burned and unconscious from strangulation. In this catastrophe Mr. Jinkens lost all his earthly possessions. He made his way to Texas as best he could, reaching the State two years later and locating in Grayson County.

"He came West for a lung trouble, and, the advice of his physician being to live in the open air as much as possible, after locating a claim, he shouldered his gun and put out for the timber. For many years he was almost constantly in the wilds, hunting and fishing, and game being plentiful then and grazing fine, he lived literally on the fat of the land. He bought a large tract of land, but did little farming in the earlier days. He has since settled some of his children off on the old homestead, but has over two hundred acres left. He has always been a great lover of horse-flesh and has never been without good stock on his place. Everybody who knows "Uncle George Jinkens," knows of him as a good judge of horses, and many of the farmers of Grayson county are indebted to him for the improved strains in their stock.

"Mr. Jinkens, although past the age where he could be required to render military service, nevertheless joined the Confederate army at the breaking out of the war and was in the service down to the close, soldiering mostly in Texas on outpost and frontier duty.

"Mr. Jinkens has raised a family of five children, all of whom reached maturity and most of whom are now living, settled in life and are themselves fathers and mothers. The Christian names of his children are--Elizabeth, Mary, Martha, Emma and William A. Mr. Jinkens has been a member of the Christian church for many years and has brought his family up in the knowledge of the gospel truths as expounded and laid down by the first great teacher. "

Philip McCray

Philip McCray was born about 1793 in Washington County, Tennessee, son of Daniel and Sarah (Nodding) McCray. We know practically nothing of his early life, but he seems to have remained a bachelor until he was nearly 40 years old, when he married Mary Ann Murry on February 7, 1831, in Yancey, North Carolina. Mary Ann Murry was born in 1810, so she was age 21 at her marriage.

Most of what we know about Philip can be gleaned from records generated from his service in the Tennessee militia. He made a sworn statement before the county clerk in Buchanan County, Missouri, on April 6, 1850, "for the purpose of obtaining the bounty land to which he may be entitled..." and he gave his age as 58, thus making his birth year 1792. The clerk's scrawled and sometimes illegible handwriting is so poorly done that details of Philip's military service are obscured in many places.

After his death on February 28, 1864, his widow filed a claim for a veteran's widow's pension, and in it she gave several details of Philip's life. She said he was born in Washington County, Tennessee, and that he had been a farmer for 18 years. The paper did not clarify whether the 18 years of farming was prior to the War of 1812, but it is hard to draw any other conclusion, except that he would have had to start farming at age two, a not too likely circumstance. If Mary meant to imply that he had lived on a farm for 18 years he would have been born in 1794. The claim was filed on January 31, 1879, at which time she was 69 years old, and her memory may not have been as good as was Philip's at age 58, for she gave his superior officer's name as "Captain Isaac Hartsell." Second-in-command below Captain Jacob Hartsell was Lieutenant Isaac Hartsell, who we may assume was Jacob's son, whimsically so named by Bible-reading parents. Widow Mary McCray also stated that her husband held the rate of "sergent," a station he may have been promoted to during some of his later tours of duty.

Philip gave his enlistment date as "on or about the ninth(?) of October, A.D. 1812...for a term of service of thirteen(?) months." He was honorably discharged at the end of the war at Mobile, Alabama, but he both re-enlisted and was drafted again for terms of a few months. One of these tours of duty was apparently served in place of one Zubin Lyons in a company commanded by John Hambilton (sic).

Mary McCray described Philip as "Highth 5 feet 7 in. Hair black Eyes gray Complex. fair." She said that neither of them had been previously married, so that Philip waited a rather long time to seek and find a bride, for he married Mary Ann Murry, aged "16 years, 11 months, 22 days," on February 7, 1831. This would have been just eight days before her 17th birthday, so she was born January 30, 1815. However, that same day she told the clerk of the circuit court of Buchanan County, Missouri, that she was 58 years old, which would make her birth year 1821, not 1815. If the clerk was fully awake he must have realized the lady was telling the old,

old fib about her age that a gentleman never challenges. She also told
the clerk that she was married in Yancey County, North Carolina in 1831,
but Yancey County wasn't formed until 1833. She said the wedding ceremony was performed by "Rice", and that she had "no opportunity of proving
my marriage by testimony of eye witnefses to my marriage as none are known
to me or dead."

Philip and Mary Ann (Murry) McCray lived together in Washington
County, Tennessee, after their marriage, until 1842, and then moved to
Buchanan County, Missouri, apparently to live near the other members of
the McCray family who had earlier moved to that part of Missouri. Philip
petitioned for a grant of land and it was granted to them. He was given
160 acres of homestead, or bounty, land, which he farmed until his death,
February 28, 1864. Mary Ann applied for a widow's pension the year after
Congress authorized them in 1878, and was granted $12 a month for the
rest of her life. The pension was terminated on November 4, 1891, which
may or may not be the date of her death.

Thomas McCray Of Washington County, Tennessee

Go into any library's reference room where someone is doing genealogical research on Scottish families, and you will almost certainly hear
muttered curses from behind that person's stack of books and pamphlets.
Their distress is almost certainly caused by finding fathers, sons,
cousins, uncles, grandfathers and nephews, all bearing the same first and
last names. In some clans, especially those of the Lowland Scots, the
male members will be predominantly James, William, Samuel, Thomas, or
Daniel, throughout six successive generations, sometimes in alternate
generations, but just as often, in successive generations.

Take, for example, "Daniel McCray." He had six sons, none of whom
he named "Daniel." But all six of these sons named one of their sons,
"Daniel." Surely some of them could have found some other way to "Honor
thy father and thy mother," especially since the Bible doesn't actually
require that we honor our grandparents equally with parents.

Daniel's (the first one) son Thomas didn't name any of his sons
"Thomas," but his son, Daniel, did, naming his son, "Thomas H. McCray."
Thomas's (not Thomas H.) brother, Henry McCray, not only named sons Daniel
and Henry, and named a daughter, Sarah, but he also named a son, "Thomas
H. McCray." "Thomas G. McCray" would have been close enough for practical
purposes, but it had to be exactly "Thomas H. McCray." Well, what's done
is done, but whenever you talk or write about any person with a Scottish
name, just keep in mind that it isn't enough to give the first and last
name, even when you throw in a middle name or initial -- you must add in
the person's parents, *including the mother's maiden name!*

Now, about Thomas McCray:

Thomas McCray was born in Washington County, Tennessee, on December 2, 1781. He was a son of Daniel and Sarah (Nodding) McCray. He grew up in eastern Tennessee and married Jane Moore, who was five years younger than he. Jane Moore's family came from South Carolina. They probably married sometime before 1805, as evidenced by the birth of a child, Achsah McCray, on September 14, 1805. However, they had three children whose birthdays are unknown and who may have been born before Achsah.

William Hicks, of Dallas Texas, is descended from Thomas and Jane (Moore) McCray, through a son, Daniel McCray, born March, 1816. Daniel married Louisa Jane Gilbreath on July 22, 1838. She was the daughter of John Fisher and Isabella (Eddington) Gilbreath, who seem to have been close friends of the Thomas and Henry McCray families. Louisa's sister, Angelinea Gilbreath, married Thomas H. McCray, son of Henry and Mary (Moore) McCray.

Sometime after about 1835 and before July, 1838, Thomas and Jane (Moore) McCray moved with their family to Monroe County, Missouri, as indicated by the date of the marriage of Daniel and Louisa Jane (Gilbreath) McCray in Monroe County, Missouri, on July 22, 1838. Since Daniel was born in 1816, and probably didn't marry before he was age 19, in 1835, the move must have taken place during those three years.

Thomas McCray died in Missouri in 1867, and his wife, Jane, died seven years later in 1874. Their son, Daniel, and his wife, Louise Jane, moved from Monroe County to Greene County, in the southwestern part of Missouri, where Daniel died in 1862.

Thomas Henry McCray, son of Daniel and Louisa Jane (Gilbreath) McCray grew up and at age 23 he married Charlotte Elizabeth McSpadden in Greene County on October 22, 1871. They moved to the part of Texas that borders on Oklahoma, probably first to Cooke County, for Thomas's widowed mother is buried there. She probably didn't move to Texas until after Daniel's death in 1862. Just when Thomas and Charlotte (McSpadden) McCray moved to Texas isn't given.

Thomas and Charlotte seem to have moved from Cooke County to adjacent Montague County where Thomas died in 1910 at age 62. Charlotte lived to age 91, and died July 23, 1945, in Cotton County, Oklahoma. Cotton County is but one county away from Montague County, Texas, and is just across the Texas-New Mexico border.

Glenn Hicks, of Dallas, Texas, supplied a chart of the lineage of his family from Daniel and Sarah (Nodding) McCray, on his mother's side, and from Thomas McSpadden, born probably early in the eighteenth century, down through Charlotte Elizabeth McSpadden, who married Thomas Henry McCray in Greene County, Missouri.

Cordie McCray was born to Thomas and Charlotte on August 10, 1894, in Montague County, Texas. She married Joseph Arthur Hicks, also of Montague County on August 11, 1912, the day after Cordie's eighteenth birthday. Their son, Glenn Melvin Hicks, was born October 24, 1917.

For lovers of unusual statistics, Thomas and Jane (Moore) McCray had nine children; Daniel and Louisa (Gilbreath) McCray, the next generation, had nine children, and Thomas, Henry and Charlotte McCray, also had nine.

Henry And Mary (Moore) McCray

Mrs. Louise H. Watkins, of Rockford, Tennessee, a descendant of Henry and Mary (Moore) McCray, graciously granted permission to copy her account of the family of her ancestor, which has also been reproduced in a journal of the Watauga Association of Genealogists, Upper East Tennessee.

HENRY McCRAY
and
MARY MOORE McCRAY

Henry McCray, born circa 1775 in Virginia, migrated to Washington County (then in North Carolina) with his parents, Daniel and Sarah Nodding McCray, during the Revolutionary War period. He grew up on Little Limestone and Cherokee Creeks near Jonesborough, Tennessee.

About 1795, Henry moved west to Davidson County, where a deed in that county dated 1798 gave his location as being on the Big Harpeth River on the original purchase of James Robertson. He had returned to Washington County to marry Mary Moore 19 September, 1796. Other land transactions place him on the Big Harpeth River in part of Davidson bounty that became Williamson County in October 1799. In 1806, Henry deeded part of his acreage to his brother, Thomas McCray, who had married his wife's sister, Jane Moore, in 1803. Both Henry and Thomas McCray had disposed of their Williamson County holdings and had returned to Washington County by late 1806.

In August, 1809, Henry McCray bought the McCray homestead of his father, Daniel, on Little Limestone Creek. Henry's mother, Sarah Nodding McCray, had died in May 1809. From Washington County deeds, Henry lived on this land until he moved in 1838 from Washington County to Chattooga County, Georgia, where he died in 1847. In 1810, Henry McCray was appointed Captain of the First Regiment of East Tennessee Militia. He served in the War of 1812 as Captain under Colonel Ewen Allison's regiment. He was a Justice of the Peace and a member of the County Court of Washington County until his removal to Chattooga County, Georgia. By 1830, Henry was the only son of Daniel McCray remaining in Washington County. He and his wife, Mary Moore McCray, were the parents of six sons and seven daughters. After the death of Mary Moore McCray circa 1825-30, Henry married secondly Elizabeth _____ ; one daughter of this marriage. The children of Henry and Mary Moore McCray: (1) William, born circa 1797, died November 1836, married Hannah L. Taylor, daughter of Henry Taylor (ancestor of Richard L. McCray); (2) Sarah, married Thomas Brown 1819 Washington County, Tennessee; (3) John; died 1842 Chattooga County, Georgia; (4) Henry, Jr.; (5) Levi: (6) Achsah, born 1805, married D.C. Hunter 23 March 1830, to Chattooga County, Georgia and Anderson County, Palestine, Texas; (7) Priscilla, born 1803, married 1836 John McCrosky of Monroe County, Tennessee; (8) Mary "Polly", married Skelton Taylor, son of Henry Taylor:(9) Elizabeth, married Abraham Taylor, son of Henry Taylor: (10) Daniel, born 1814, died 1878, married Malinda McCrosky, daughter of John McCrosky of Monroe County, Tennessee -- moved to Chattooga County, Georgia and California; (11) Louisa Jane, born 21 March 1820,died December 1856, married 1838 Joshua H. King of Knox County, Tennessee (ancestor of Louise H Watkins); (12) Julia, married Dr. DeBard in Palestine, Texas; (13) Thomas H. married Algelina Gilbreath of Monroe County, Tennessee -- moved to Texas and Chicago, Illinois. Thomas was a Confederate Brigadier General in the Civil War (ancestor of Blanche Merritt, Oceanside, California). The daughter of Henry and Elizabeth _____ McCray; (14) Lucy, born circa 1828, married Benjamin King, Chattooga County, Georgia.

In 1838, Henry McCray migrated to the newly-formed Chattooga County, Georgia, along with most of his sons and daughters and their families. They lived in and near the town of Summerville, where Henry's son, Daniel, was sheriff of that county and his son-in-law, D.C. Hunter, was County Surveyor. The will of Henry McCray, recorded in Chattooga County, Georgia, names all of his surviving sons and his daughter's husbands.

After Henry McCray's death in1847, all of his children who were living in Georgia moved on elsewhere, except daughter Lucy. The descendants of his son, William, and daughter, Elizabeth, who married Abraham Taylor are those of Washington County, Tennessee today.

- 0 -

Mrs. Blanche Meritt of Oceanside, California, is a descendant of Thomas Hamilton McCray, son of Henry and Mary (Moore) McCray. She wrote:

" THOMAS H. McCRAY was probably the thirteenth and last child of Henry McCray and Mary Moore. He was born circa 1825 in Jonesboro, Washington County, Tennessee. He was married to Angeline Gilbreath in Monroe County, Tennessee, 11 October, 1845. Their marriage ended in divorce in January 1855. They had two daughters:

1. MARY BELLE, born 9 Sept. 1846 -- died 14 March, 1918. m. 23 June, 1870, to Dr. J.J. Harrison, Loudon Co. Tenn. They had 10 children.

2. ALICE JULIA, born 17 Sept., 1849 -- d. 7 Sept., 1931. m. John M. Cole in Monroe County, Tennessee, 17 June, 1869. They had nine children.

142

"Thomas H. McCray eventually went to Bell County, Texas, circa 1855-1858, where he built a textile mill and was a 'General Commission Merchant,' dealing in cotton factors, farm machinery and related goods. He was postmaster at Tellico, Texas, in 1857.

"At the beginning of the Civil War he went to Wittenburg, Arkansas, and enlisted in the Confederate Service as a 1st lieutenant, on 10 June, 1862. This battalion later became the 31st Regiment, Arkansas Infantry. It is recorded that he served with "valor and distinction" throughout the conflict. He was serving as Review Brigade Commander under Gen. Jeff Thompson in Arkansas when the war ended and they surrendered, 11 May, 1865.

"He probably returned to Texas when the war ended. At some time, it is believed he was married to Wife Number 2, "Vance" (nickname)*. It is not known if there were children of that marriage.

"Family recollections indicate he was associated with McCormick-Deering Company after the war. Later he went to Chicago, Illinois, and probably was still associated with McCormick-Deering until his death in 1890."

The Gilbreath and McCray families apparently were more than just friends, for their son, Thomas, married Angelina Gilbreath, and son Daniel married Louisa Gilbreath, and their daughter, Jane, married Thomas Gilbreath. How Angelina, Thomas and Louisa were related isn't known.

Henry and Mary (Moore) McCray had fourteen children; Daniel, born in 1814 in Jonesborough, Tennessee, married Malinda McCrosky in 1837, and they had nine children. "Dan" and his brother, Thomas Hamilton McCray went to Montague County, Texas. Later, Dan and Malinda moved to Montgomery and Anderson Counties in eastern Texas.

One of their sons, James Monroe McCray, born in 1840, married Mary Ann Agee, and they had eight children, one of whom was Albert Julian McCray, born in 1871. He married Miranda Elizabeth Freeman in Olney, Young County, Texas, and later they homesteaded near Portales, New Mexico astride the western Texas border. Later still they lived in Oklahoma and then ended their wandering days in Long Beach, California. One of the four children of Albert and Miranda was Eshcol McCray, who supplied this data about descendants from David and Louisa (Gilbreath) McCray. She married William W. Chambers, who died in 1980. She lives in Roswell, New Mexico as of 1988.

* Referred to in a letter from Achsah to Daniel in 1858. "Vance" was a widow with a small daughter (no other name known). See marriage of T.H. McCray to ? Mrs. ? in 1857-8, Bell County, Texas. Mrs. Meritt's footnote.

143

Five of the sons of Daniel and Sarah (Nodding) McCray served in the War of 1812. They were: First Lieutenant Elisha McCray, Captain Henry McCray, Sergeant Philip McCray, Ensign Thomas McCray, and Sergeant William McCray. Second Lieutenant Samuel Bayles and Private Leonard Calvert, son-in-law of William Nodding, Sr., also served in the company of militia of East Tennessee in which Philip McCray was enrolled.

The company was under the command of Captain Jacob Hartsell; the company was in the "ridgement" commanded by Colonel William Lillard. Captain Hartsell kept a journal which was printed in *Publication* , the journal of the East Tennessee Historical Society, No. 11, pp. 93-98, 1940. Mrs. Patricia Case, of Santa Barbara, California, provided parts of it.

Captain Hartsell's journal is an utterly charming account of the monotony of day-to-day doings of the military. His innovative spelling is a reminder that Noah Webster's first *American Dictionary of the English Language* was still fifteen years or more away, and standardized spelling was but a dream of pedants. We can hear the rich Appalachian accents in the phonic words he formed that have the taste of cornbread and red-eye gravy. You can still hear it today in the mountainous mining communities well away from the interstates. Ignorant comics sometimes do imitations of the mountain dialect which many scholars believe is pretty much unchanged since the days of Queen Elizabeth I.

The journal, while supplying little information about the people of eastern Washington County, disclosed that military organizations then were humanized by the same sorts of personalities and petty tyrannies that have always characterized the profession of arms. Concerning a visit by General Thomas Pinckney to the Volunteer Company of East Tennessee, he wrote, in part:

When all was Colected we marched to the Generals tent and beet Jefersons liberty ("Jefferson's Liberty March", a popular air) and marched Round the tent and halted in abrest, Expecting the General to Come and Selute us or reed Some leter. We stood about one minit and the General Did not appair. the(y) sent in to his tent for to See what was the mater. the(y) found the General asliep when the(y) entered his tent. we stood there tell he got on his Close, when the General Came out and Did not Comedate us in the Least. he said Gentele men Come tordes the fiere. the officer ordered to the rigt tebout face, Dismissed, which was Capt Hambileton from paules value (Powell's Valley) the officers was much Displeases about it. To think that the(y) Shold Expose ther Selves to march in the cold So long to bee faced to the Right about and be dismissed at the Generals tent, when he Did not pay aney adresses to the officers when the(y) Came to his tent In order agreeabele to his order. Capt. McLing and Captain McLoney and Capt Mckees and Capt Dick and my selfe which was on loine as we marched we Joined and made one file when we was faced to the Right about and dismissed we went to our tents verey Cold and not pleases well.

144

Another entry in Captain Hartsell's journal:

November 30 day 1813--Capt Mc Loney Company, Capt M Lings
Camped Below me, Capt Dicks above. My Companey was formed in
the Senter, the other Companey formed on Each wing, in one
Straight Line which Composed one pretalion (battalion). when all
the Men was Colected and Compleateley Everey man armed, It made
the best Show that I ever Saw. agedent Wm Nolen Came and
Driled the Deferent Companeys. The agedent Sad was Don in high
Stile. It much plaised him to See men So well Dicipelened, and
I believe there was not one musket in the hole Loine. I think
that it was the tretyeth Muster that I ever Saw with my eys.
Jacob Hartsell, Capt

"Volunteer Company" doesn't seem to have been a completely accurate
designation for this troop, although most of its members may truly have
volunteered for service. Captain Hartsell wrote opposite the name of
"Samuel Bayles 2 lieut, a wagon and teeme presed into the United States
Servise." Philip McCray certified many years later that he had both
volunteered and had been drafted into the company's service.

Muster rolls recorded by Captain Hartsell included men who were
either sons-in-law or grandsons of Daniel and Sarah (Nodding) McCray.
They were:

> Samuel Bayles, Second Lieutenant
> "Bayles George private
> Calvert Lenard, private
> McCray philip."

A muster roll dated November 14, 1813, listed 37 men as deserters,
and among them were George Bayles and Philip McCray. On the same list,
"got off by aplying to fisition october 28 1813" were twelve men, including Lenard Calvert. This seems to be a shockingly high number of deserters from one company, but the term "deserter" did not always carry the
same connotations then that it does today. Soldiers frequently just
walked away from military life temporarily, and returned to their farms
to do essential chores that had to be done to keep their families from
starving the next year. When they returned, usually within a week or two,
military order yielded to pragmatism, and the lapse was quietly overlooked.

Sarah (Nodding) McCray died May 8, 1809, and Daniel sometime later
remarried, this time to Polly Pretchard in Washington County, Tennessee.
Polly probably died before 1819, for in that year Daniel dictated a
nuncupative will, to which he affixed his mark, "D." Spoken or dictated
wills were usually recorded when a person was in extremis, so it is
possible that Daniel died shortly after making his will. Polly was not
named in his will; rather, he left bequests to two of his daughters,
Sally and Jane, and named his sons, Henry and Thomas, to be executors.

145

Nancy J. Jenkins, daughter of Elijah and Mary Jenkins, married Benjamin Piper in 1866. Ralph H. Piper, great grandson of Benjamin and Julia Ann (Fahenstock) Piper, supplied the genealogical information on his ancestors back to Daniel and Sarah (Nodding) McCray. Shortly after publication of the first edition of *The McCrays of America*, I received a letter from Mrs. Ralph Piper, in which she said that Mr. Piper died at age 82 on April 12, 1988.

Joe Walker, The Westering Man

AFTER THERE WAS NO MORE WILDERNESS beyond the frontier east of the Mississippi, the tough and adventuresome souls who wanted to live beyond the settlements were forced ever westward, ultimately into the Rockies. They were the half-savage "Mountain Men," the last of their kind in the world, save possibly for a few similar men in Australia's Outback.

Joe Walker was probably the most famous and glamorous of the Mountain men. He was the grandson of John Walker, a Scots-Irishman who brought his family to America in the first quarter of the eighteenth century and made his way to the Shenandoah Valley, and there squatted on a tract before the area was granted by Governor Gooch as part of the grant to Benjamin Borden. *Westering Man,** by Bil Gilbert, the biography of Joseph Walker, is a factual account of his life that began in Virginia when it was already becoming uncomfortably crowded in the eyes of the men who would wander away from civilization for months at a time, living off the land much as the Indians did.

The Walkers were typical Scots-Irish pioneers, and Joe, the subject of Gilbert's biography, came to Tennessee near the end of the eighteenth century, and settled along the Emory River, near today's Oak Ridge. Also living nearby were his brothers, John, James and Samuel, and two of his sisters, Barbara McLelland, and Katherine Scott. Among them they had forty children. Author Gilbert wrote that the Walkers were connected by blood or marriage to just about everyone who was anybody in Tennessee.

Migrations across the Mississippi River into the vast western empire that was acquired in 1803 by the most extraordinary president the United States is ever likely to be blessed with began in eastern Tennessee. It was made up of pioneers who had started westward from Atlantic ports, travelling westward through the Cumberland and Potomac Valleys into the Valley of Virginia, thence southwest into Tennessee, the western Carolinas, Georgia and Alabama, stopping only as they approached Spanish territories. Many of them regarded the settlements they made as only temporary. A remarkable number of the first to move further west were from eastern Tennessee, close to the western North Carolina border. Their organization, methods of travel and style of settlements showed with remarkable clarity how closely knit the travellers were. As they fanned out through Missouri and Arkansas they established new communities in which everyone knew everyone else because of kinship, marriage or lifelong association.

* *Westering Man*, by Bil Gilbert, Atheneum, New York, 1983, and simultaneously in Canada by McClelland and Stewart Ltd.

(Captain Hartsell's journal contains the name, "John Walker." Could
this be Joe's brother, John Walker?)

Gilbert went on with an account of a military expedition, under the
command of Andrew Jackson, "Old Hickory," into Alabama and Florida,
against a tribe of Creeks making a final stand against the white invaders
from the east. The expeditionary forces consisted of several companies
of Tennessee militia (remember Capt. Hartsell's company of militia?).
They made two excursions into Alabama, the first in the fall of 1813,
and the second in the spring of 1814, engaging the Indians finally at
Horseshoe Bend on the Tallapoosa River, fated to be the last great battle
of the eastern Indian wars.

Some 800 Creeks were killed, and about 150 Tennessee militiamen
died. A body of the Indians escaped and made their way to Florida and
joined some scattered tribes that had been joined by escaped slaves who
had banded together in common cause. They were called "Seminoles" (Runaways), and for fifty years they kept the U.S. military busy with their
successful guerrilla tactics. Andrew Jackson returned against the Seminoles in 1818, and Joseph Walker and his brother, Joel, were part of
the campaign. Joe Walker later told friends that they had spent some
time in Alabama and Mississippi, presumably while they were chasing Seminoles with Jackson.

You will recall that Philip McCray certified he had been honorably
discharged at Mobile, Alabama. Why was he discharged in Mobile instead
of Jonesboro? How did he happen to be in Alabama when his term of enlistment was up? Philip McCray may well have been part of that army,
and if he was, he must have known the legendary Joe Walker, the Mountain
Man.

Walker retraced part of Lewis and Clark's expedition up the Missouri
River to live in and explore the hitherto unknown west and the Rocky
Mountains. Philip also followed the Missouri upstream and settled in
western Missouri.

148

THE FAMILY OF DANIEL McCRAY

(Of Virginia & Tennessee)

Generation II

Charles McCray
b. ca 1769, prob. in Loudoun Co. VA
d. May 14, 1812, in Washington Co. TN
m. Elizabeth (Betsey) Deakins, on
    Mar. 25, 1788

Henry McCray
b. ca 1770-80, prob. in Loudoun Co VA
d. Feb. 7 - July 31, 1847, in Chatooga
    Co., GA
m. (1) Mary Moore, on Sept. 19, 1796
    (2) Elizabeth __?__   13 ch.
        1 ch.

Generation I

Daniel McCray
    &
(1) Sarah Nodding

(2) Polly Pretchard
    on May 8, 1809
    in Wash'n Co., TN
    No issue

Thomas McCray
b. ca 1780-90, in Tennessee
d. ca 1867, in Lawrence Co., MO
m. Jane Moore
    d. in Lawrence Co., MO

William McCray
b. April 23, 1789, in Wash'n Co, TN
d. March 13, 1849, in Grundy Co., MO
m. Mariah Koontz, on July 1, 1807 in
    Wash'n Co., TN
He married 4 times.

Elisha McCray
b. 1789-1790, prob. in MD
d. Aug. 13, 1834, in Ray Co., MO
m. Rebecca Tilson, in 1812. 8 ch.
    b. ca 1770-80, in Erwin, TN
    d. ca 1827, in Ray Co., MO

149

Jane (Jean, Jennie) McCray
b. 1770-1785
d.
m. George M. Jinkins, 12 ch.
   b.
   d. 1842, in Monroe Co., KY

They lived for a while in Wash'n Co.,
TN, and in Monroe Co., KY

Sarah (Sally) McCray
b.
d.
m. ---?--- Harris

Philip McCray
b. 1792-94, in Wash'n Co., TN
d. 28 Feb., 1864, in Buchanan Co, MO
m. Mary Ann Murry, on Feb. 7, 1831,
   in Yancey Co., N.C.
   b. Jan. 30, 1815
   d. abt 1891-93

Rebecca McCray
b.
d.
m.

Priscilla McCray
b. ca Jan. 18, 1783
d. Oct. 11, 1835, in Wash'n Co., TN,
   and is buried at Cherokee Baptist
   Church there.
m. (1) Samuel Templin
   (2) William Cox

150

Sarah McCray
b.
d.
m. Thomas Brown on Aug. 9, 1819 in Washington
Co. TN

Generation I

Daniel McCray
&
Sarah Nodding

Mary ("Polly") McCray
b.
d.
m. Skelton Taylor, on 19 Oct., 1824, in
Washington Co., TN

Generation II

Henry McCray
&
(1) Mary Moore

(2) Elizabeth

Elizabeth McCray
b.
d.
m. Abraham Taylor, on 10 Feb., 1831, in
Washington, Co.TN. Son of Henry Taylor.

Achsah McCray
b. 14 Sept. 1805
d. 15 Feb., 1882; is buried at Palestine
Anderson Co, TX
m. David C. Hunter, on March 23, 1830, in
Washington, Co., TN. Son of Henry Taylor.

Priscilla McCray
b. Dec. 28, 1808, in Washington Co., TN
d. Nov. 23, 1879, in Monroe Co., TN
m. John McCrosky, on Jan. 13, 1836, in
Washington, Co., TN

Louisa Jane McCray
b. March 21, 1820
d. Dec, 9, 1856. Buried in Hickory Creek
Cemetery, Hardin Valley, Knox Co., TN
m. Joshua King, in 1838. 13 ch.

151

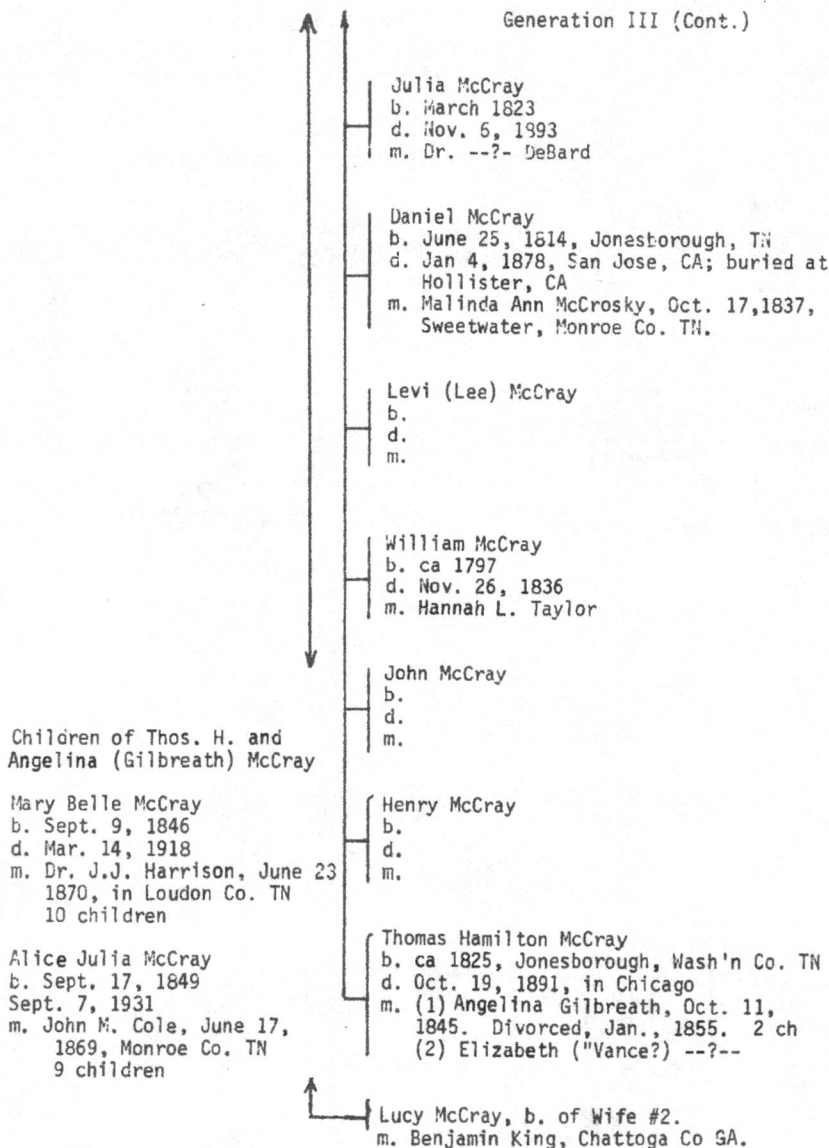

Julia McCray
b. March 1823
d. Nov. 6, 1993
m. Dr. --?- DeBard

Daniel McCray
b. June 25, 1814, Jonesborough, TN
d. Jan 4, 1878, San Jose, CA; buried at
   Hollister, CA
m. Malinda Ann McCrosky, Oct. 17,1837,
   Sweetwater, Monroe Co. TN.

Levi (Lee) McCray
b.
d.
m.

William McCray
b. ca 1797
d. Nov. 26, 1836
m. Hannah L. Taylor

John McCray
b.
d.
m.

**Children of Thos. H. and
Angelina (Gilbreath) McCray**

Mary Belle McCray
b. Sept. 9, 1846
d. Mar. 14, 1918
m. Dr. J.J. Harrison, June 23
   1870, in Loudon Co. TN
   10 children

Henry McCray
b.
d.
m.

Alice Julia McCray
b. Sept. 17, 1849
Sept. 7, 1931
m. John M. Cole, June 17,
   1869, Monroe Co. TN
   9 children

Thomas Hamilton McCray
b. ca 1825, Jonesborough, Wash'n Co. TN
d. Oct. 19, 1891, in Chicago
m. (1) Angelina Gilbreath, Oct. 11,
   1845. Divorced, Jan., 1855. 2 ch
   (2) Elizabeth ("Vance?") --?--

Lucy McCray, b. of Wife #2.
m. Benjamin King, Chattoga Co GA.

152

Generation III

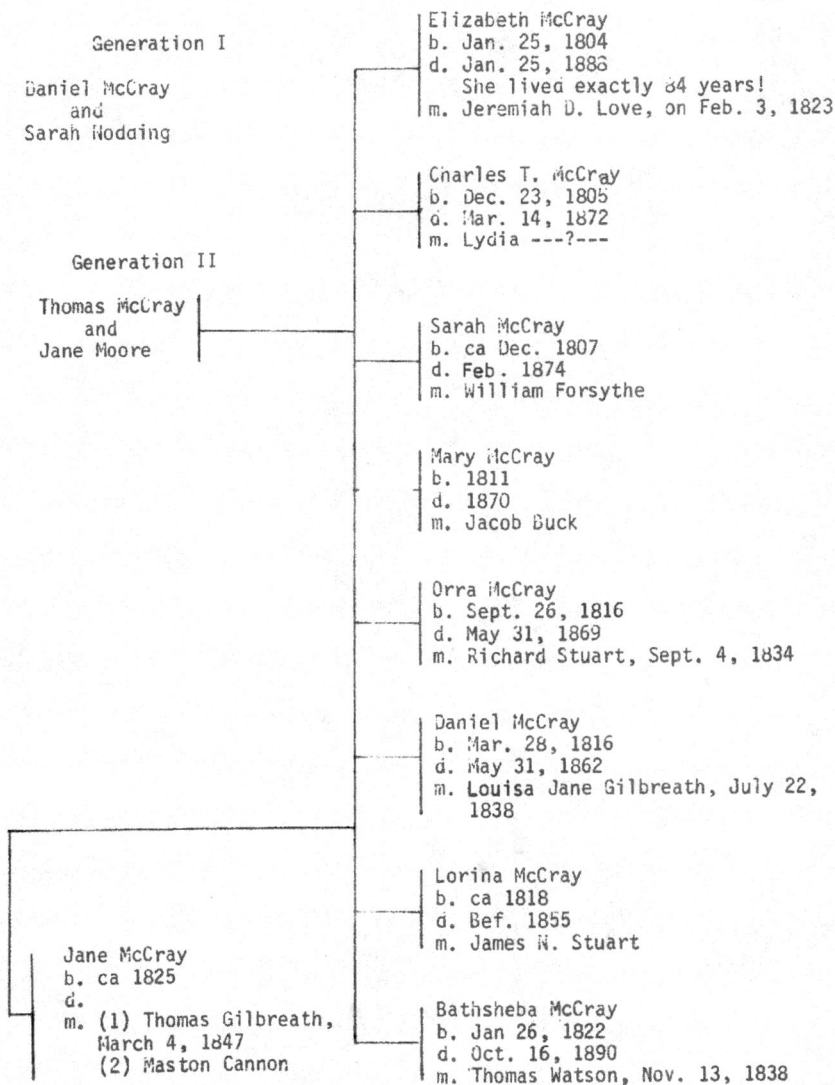

Generation I

Daniel McCray
and
Sarah Nodding

Generation II

Thomas McCray
and
Jane Moore

Jane McCray
b. ca 1825
d.
m. (1) Thomas Gilbreath,
March 4, 1847
(2) Maston Cannon

Elizabeth McCray
b. Jan. 25, 1804
d. Jan. 25, 1888
  She lived exactly 84 years!
m. Jeremiah D. Love, on Feb. 3, 1823

Charles T. McCray
b. Dec. 23, 1805
d. Mar. 14, 1872
m. Lydia ---?---

Sarah McCray
b. ca Dec. 1807
d. Feb. 1874
m. William Forsythe

Mary McCray
b. 1811
d. 1870
m. Jacob Buck

Orra McCray
b. Sept. 26, 1816
d. May 31, 1869
m. Richard Stuart, Sept. 4, 1834

Daniel McCray
b. Mar. 28, 1816
d. May 31, 1862
m. Louisa Jane Gilbreath, July 22,
  1838

Lorina McCray
b. ca 1818
d. Bef. 1855
m. James N. Stuart

Bathsheba McCray
b. Jan 26, 1822
d. Oct. 16, 1890
m. Thomas Watson, Nov. 13, 1838

Generation I   Generation IV

Daniel McCray   James Monroe McCray
    and   b. Aug. 27, 1840
Sarah Nodding   d. Sept. 3, 1923, bur. Prospect TX
                                  m. Mary Ann (also Martha) Agee,
  Generation II   Sept. 11, 1870
                                     d. 1931
Thomas McCray
    and   Martha McCray
Jane Moore   b. May 29, 1843
                                  d. Jan. 1, 1933
  Generation III   m. Samuel L. Mower

Daniel McCray   Isabella Angeline McCray
    and   b. Jan 11, 1846
Louisa J. Gilbreath   d. Dec. 22, 1926
                                  m. Daniel Cooper, Oct. 22, 1871

                                  Thomas H. McCray
                                  b. May 7, 1848
                                  d. June 16, 1910
                                  m. Charlotte E. McSpadden, Oct. 22,
                                     1871.

                                  Jane McCray,
                                  b. abt. 1850
                                  d.
                                  m. Charles Troutwine

                                  Sarah Elizabeth McCray
                                  b. 1852
                                  d. Nov. 3, 1890
                                  m. John F. Patrick

                                  John B. McCray
                                  b. March 24, 1857
                                  d. June 17, 1869
                                  m. unmarried.

Daniel Bruce McCray   Charles Wesley McCray
b. June 8, 1862   b. March 1860
d. Nov. 21, 1939   d. Jan. 1935
m. (1) --?--   m. unmarried.
   (2) Lillie Mae Downey
      Jan. 24, 1892

Generation I	Generation V

Generation I

Daniel McCray
and
Sarah Nodding

Generation II

Thomas McCray
and
Jane Moore

Generation III

Daniel McCray
and
Louisa J. Gilbreath

Generation IV

Thomas H. McCray
and
Charlotte McSpadden

Generation V

Luella McCray
b. Jan. 27, 1874
d. June 24, 1909
m. Charles Davenport on March 4, 1894

Marcella McCray
b. Aug. 1, 1877
d. March 12, 1948
m. Leander Cheddix on Dec. 29, 1895

Leora McCray
b. Augs. 19, 1880
d. Nov. 28, 1965
m. Lawrence Teakell on Oct. 29, 1898

Susan Bird McCray
b. March 7, 1883
d. Jan. 23, 1981, age 98
m. Enoch Davis on Sept. 14, 1902

Henry L. McCray
b. March 9, 1886
d. July 3, 1957
m. Essie Pierce on Nov. 25, 1906

Mary A. McCray
b. Dec. 30, 1888
d. Oct. 14, 1981, age 91
m. Walter Gill on Sept. 13, 1914

Della McCray
b. Sept. 5, 1891
d. June 21, 1981, age 90
m. Grissom Prather on July 21, 1915

Cordie McCray*
b. Aug. 10, 1894
d. Sept. 12, 1978
m. Joseph A. Hicks on Aug. 11, 1912

Ola McCray
b. Jan. 17, 1898
d. Aug. 15, 1982
m. William Goldsmith on Sept. 9, 1917

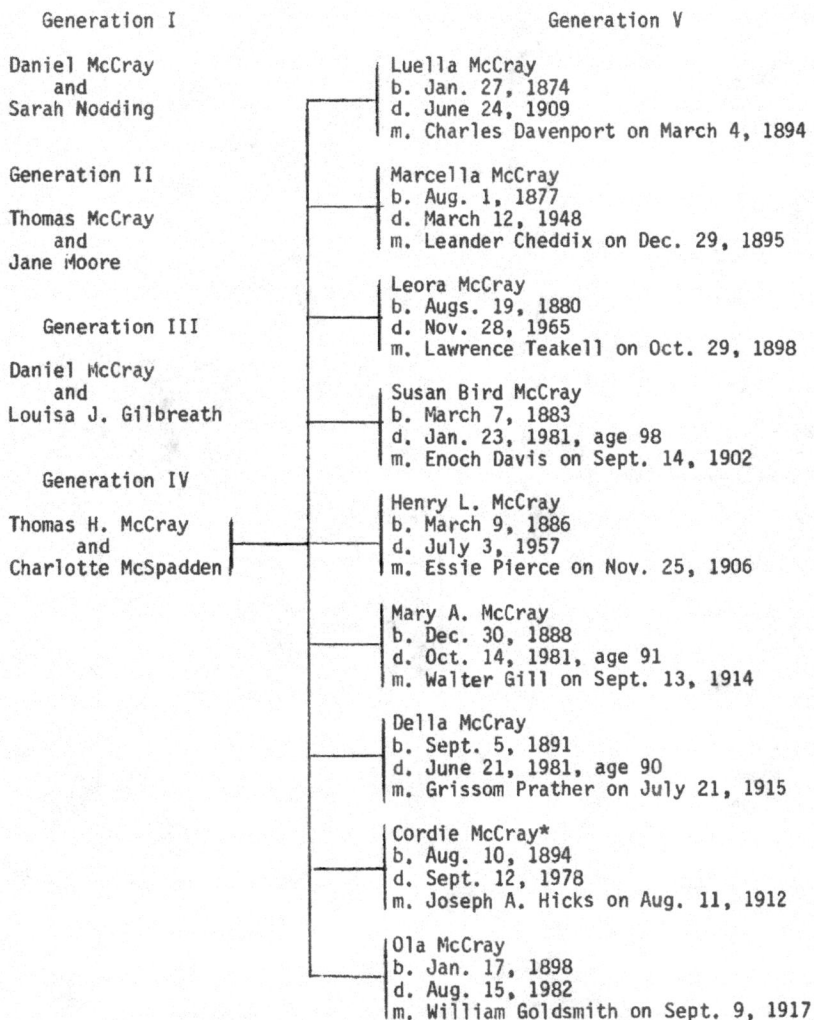

* Glenn Melvin Hicks, b. Oct. 24, 1917, a resident of Dallas, TX,
supplied this lineage. He is a son of Cordie and Joseph Hicks.

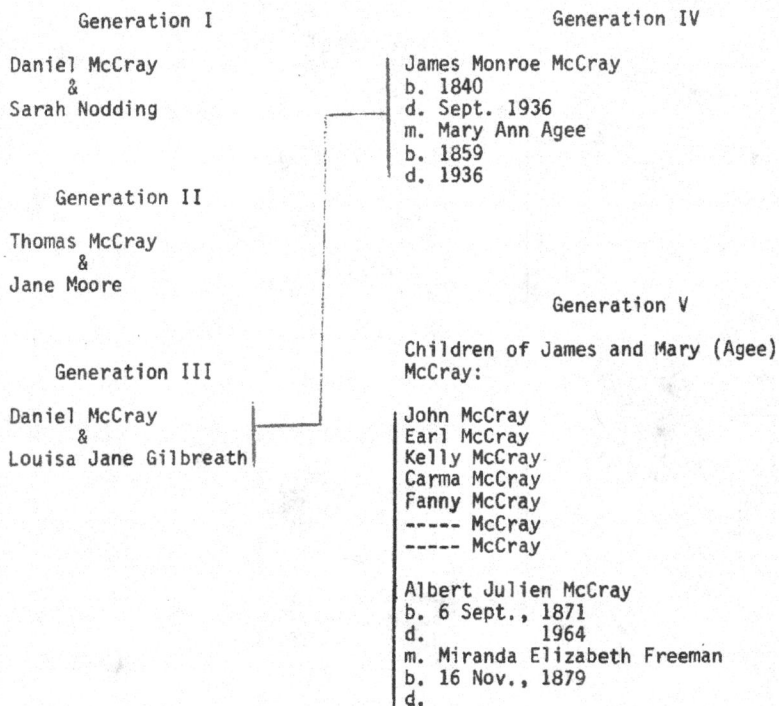

Generation I

Daniel McCray
&
Sarah Nodding

Generation II

Thomas McCray
&
Jane Moore

Generation III

Daniel McCray
&
Louisa Jane Gilbreath

Generation IV

James Monroe McCray
b. 1840
d. Sept. 1936
m. Mary Ann Agee
b. 1859
d. 1936

Generation V

Children of James and Mary (Agee)
McCray:

John McCray
Earl McCray
Kelly McCray
Carma McCray
Fanny McCray
----- McCray
----- McCray

Albert Julien McCray
b. 6 Sept., 1871
d.   1964
m. Miranda Elizabeth Freeman
b. 16 Nov., 1879
d.

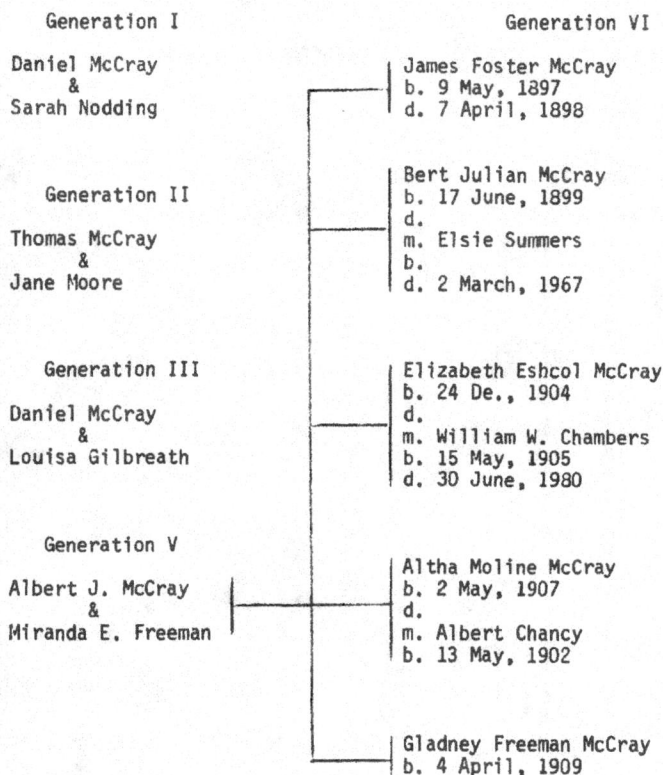

Generation I

Daniel McCray
&
Sarah Nodding

Generation II

Thomas McCray
&
Jane Moore

Generation III

Daniel McCray
&
Louisa Gilbreath

Generation V

Albert J. McCray
&
Miranda E. Freeman

Generation VI

James Foster McCray
b. 9 May, 1897
d. 7 April, 1898

Bert Julian McCray
b. 17 June, 1899
d.
m. Elsie Summers
b.
d. 2 March, 1967

Elizabeth Eshcol McCray
b. 24 De., 1904
d.
m. William W. Chambers
b. 15 May, 1905
d. 30 June, 1980

Altha Moline McCray
b. 2 May, 1907
d.
m. Albert Chancy
b. 13 May, 1902

Gladney Freeman McCray
b. 4 April, 1909

155b

Generation I

Daniel McCray
&
Sarah Nodding

Generation III

| | Daniel McCray
b. 1839

| | James P. McCray
b. 1844

Generation II

Philip McCray
&
Mary Ann Murry

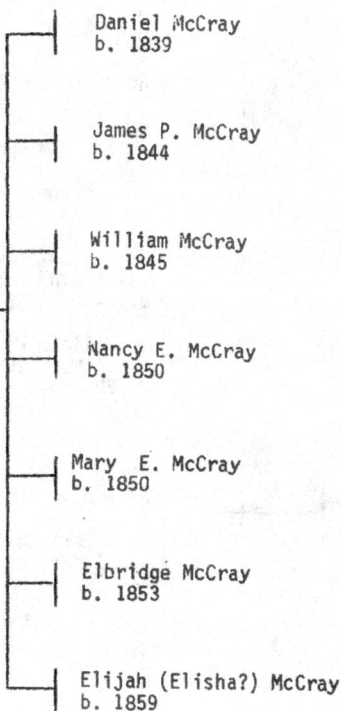

| | William McCray
b. 1845

| | Nancy E. McCray
b. 1850

| | Mary E. McCray
b. 1850

| | Elbridge McCray
b. 1853

| | Elijah (Elisha?) McCray
b. 1859

156

Generation I	Generation III

Generation I

Daniel McCray
&
Sarah Nodding

Generation III

Charles McCray
b. ca 1811, nr. Erwin, Wash'n Co. TN
d.
m.

William McCray
b. 1813
d.
m.

Generation II

Elisha McCray
&
Rebecca Tilson

Elizabeth (Betsey) McCray
b. ca 1815
d.
m. Pittman Clevenger, in Ray Co. MO on Feb.
26, 1835

Ruth McCray
b. ca 1815
d.
m. Archibald W. Dickie, on Feb. 12, 1835

Charity McCray
b. ca 1819
d. believed died in childhood

Achsah (Axie) McCray
b. ca 1821
d. believed died in infancy or childhood.

Nancy McCray
b. June 28, 1823
d.
m. William Washington Smith on Sept. 10,
1844, in Ray Co. MO

∧

└─┤ Daniel McCray
  ─┤ b.1825-27

Note: The children of Nancy McCray and William Washington Smith (on
previous sheet) were: Jeremiah, Martha, Ruth Elizabeth, Thomas Benton,
Phoebe Trephosa, Pitman, Solomon Hampton, and Archibald Washington.
Information on this line of descent from Daniel McCray to Mrs. Patricia
Case, of Santa Barbara, CA, was supplied by her. She asked that the
chart stop here since: "...further lines are documented and copyrighted
 in the Smith-McCray Family Newsletter" Anyone seeking further
information on this line may write to her:

    Mrs. Patricia Case
    1002 San Antonio Creek Road
    Santa Barbara, CA 93111

Generation I

Daniel McCray

Generation II

Charles McCray
(possibly)

Generation III *

Daniel McCray
b. Feb., 1798, in
Wash'n Co., TN
d. June 4, 1881

m
Sarah Bogart, on Jan.
22, 1818, in Wash'n
Co., TN

* No known proof that this
Daniel McCray is either
the son of Charles, or the
grandson of Daniel I, but
some evidence points to it.

Generation IV

Charles McCray
b. Jan. 6, 1819, in Illinois
d. ?
m. Eliza H. Whorton, on Nov. 3, 1842 in
   Clinton Co., MO

Girl, unknown
b. Oct. 5, 1820 - 1825

Mary McCray
b. April 11, 1823, in Ray Co., MO
d. June 27, 1902, Avenue City, Andrew Co. MO
   Buried at High Prairie Cem. Andrew Co., MO
m. Elijah Jenkins (Jinkins), on Aug. 1, 1838,
   in Clinton Co., MO
   b. Feb. 10, 1814, in Wash'n Co. TN
   d. April 28, 1887, in Andrews Co., MO
      Buried in High Prairie, Andrew Co. MO

Nancy McCray
b. Aug. 20, 1825, in Mo
d. July 4, 1902, in Andrew Co. Mo
   Buried NE of Rosendale, Andrew Co. MO
m. James Christie, on Feb. 6, 1845, in Buchanan
   Co., MO

Boy, unknown, listed in 1830 Census, age 5

Girl, unknown, listed in 1840 Census, age 10-15

Salena McCray
b. Mar. 1, 1833, in MO
d. Sept. 4, 1910, buried at Valley Falls
   Jefferson Co., KS
m Zachariah S. Miller on Sept. 4, 1851
   in Buchanan Co., MO

Elisha McCray
b. July 3, 1834, in MO
d. April 29, 1857, in Buchanan Co. MO
    Buried, Elder Cemetery, Buchanan Co. MO
m. Caroline McGauhy on Jan. 3, 1856, in
    Buchanan Co. MO

Philip McCray (Is in 1850 Census as member
of Daniel McCray's family)
b. 1838

Daniel McCray
b. ca 1838 in MO
d. July 5, 1863 in CSA hospital in Miss-
    issippi (?)
(Listed in 1850 Census as of Daniel McCray
family.)

Generation I   Generation III

(Unknown, but possibly)   Charles Jinkens
                                          b. April 30, 1799
Daniel McCray   d. Feb. 9, 1855
       &   m. Elizabeth -----
Sarah Nodding   b. Aug. 16, 1802
                                             d. April 10, 1867

                                          Joseph Jinkins
        Generation II   b. Nov. 4, 1803
                                          d. Feb. 6, 1869   2 ch
Jane McCray
       &
George M. Jinkins   Elijah Jenkins
                                          b. Feb. 10, 1814
                                          d. April 28, 1887, in Andrew Co.,MO
                                          m. Mary E. McCray, on Aug. 1, 1838
                                             in Clinton Co., MO. Dau. of
                                             Daniel and Sarah (Bogart) McCray
                                             12 ch.
                                             b. April 11, 1823, in Ray Co, MO
Note: regarding the spelling   d. June 27, 1902, Avenue City,
of "Jenkins/Jinkins" --   Andrew Co., MO
George M. Jinkins's father was
George Jinkins, and his son
was Elijah Jenkins. Also   George M. Jinkens
spelled "Jinkens".   b. April 16, 1816
                                          d. ·Aug..21, 1891
                                          m. Sarah K. Andrews, on Oct. 4,
                                             1837. 5 ch
                                          They lived in Grayson County, TX

                                          Nancy Jinkins

                                          Sally Jinkins

                                          Achsa Jinkins

John M. Jenkins
b. Aug. 7, 1839
d. July 22, 1845

Generation III

Daniel McCray
&
Sarah Bogart

Dugan Jenkins
b. Jan. 12, 1841
d. Jan. 14, 1906
    (bachelor)

Generation IV

Mary McCray
&
Elijah Jenkins

Nancy J. Jenkins
b. Aug. 8, 1843
d. April 18, 1913 at Edmond, Oklahoma Co.
    Oklahoma. Buried at Edmond.
m. Benjamin B. Piper, on Oct. 24, 1866 8 ch
    (son of John and Julia Fahenstock Piper)
    b. June 16, 1834, Scott Co. IL
    d. Feb. 20, 1896, Cosby Co., MO
        Buried, Bethel Baptist Churchyard

Sarah E. Jenkins
b. Aug. 8, 1845
d. Aug. 14, 1846

Daniel B. Jenkins
b. July 19, 1847
d. 1929
m. (twice) Mrs. Catherine B. Orcutt

Henry Jenkins
b. Nov. 4, 1849
d. Dec. 13, 1826
    (bachelor)

George W. Jenkins
b. Feb. 4, 1852
d. Sept. 24, 1914
m. Alice Maughmer on Feb. 18, 1877
   b. 1854
   d. 1931

Mary E. Jenkins
b. Jan. 29, 1854
d. Sept. 24, 1914
m. Joseph S. Gant on Jan. 20, 1876

Joseph B. Jenkins
b. May 26, 1856
d. Dec. 30, 1860

Margaret S. Jenkins
b. June 19, 1858
d. March, 1925
m. Bony W. Tate on Jan. 19, 1881

Emma F. Jenkins
b. Dec. 15, 1860
d. March, 1928
m. Dr. George F. Boone, Aug. 2, 1882

Martha Jenkins
b. May 15, 1866
d. Aug. 5, 1953
m. John D. Conway on Mar. 4, 1896

Generation III	Generation VI

Generation III

Daniel McCray
&
Sarah Bogart

Generation VI

Minnie May Piper
b. Jan. 29, 1867
d. Sept. 8, 1887

Generation IV

Mary McCray
&
Elijah Jenkins

Julia F. (Kitty) Piper
b. March 29, 1869
d. May 2, 1904
m. William H. Stewart, on Feb. 15, 1903

Effie S. Piper
b. Oct. 4,1871
d. March 28, 1888

Generation V

Benjamin B. Piper
&
Nancy J. Jenkins

Homer Lee Piper
b. July 12, 1873
d. Juen 6, 1934
m. Hattie Rena Morford, on Dec. 25, 1901

Nora Simona Piper
b. Aug. 4, 1875
d. Jan. 26, 1921
m. William Eugene Connor,on March 21, 1908

Martha Emma Piper
b. March 18, 1877
d. Jan. 7, 1919
m. Benjamin B. Reppert, on Dec. 24, 1901

John Jenkins Piper
b. Jan.28, 1879
d. Jan. 17, 1954

Oliver D. Piper
b. April 3, 1882
d. Feb. 14, 1933

164

Generation VII

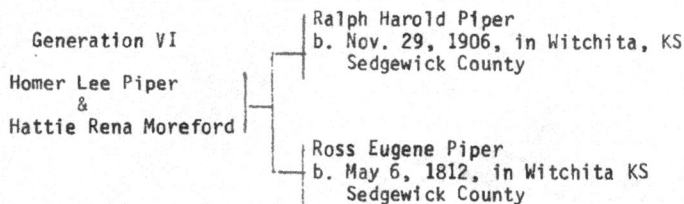

Generation VI

Homer Lee Piper
&
Hattie Rena Moreford

Ralph Harold Piper
b. Nov. 29, 1906, in Witchita, KS
    Sedgewick County

Ross Eugene Piper
b. May 6, 1812, in Witchita KS
    Sedgewick County

I received a letter from Mrs. Ralph
H. Piper in March of 1989, in which
she said that Mr. Piper died on
April 12, 1988, at age 82.

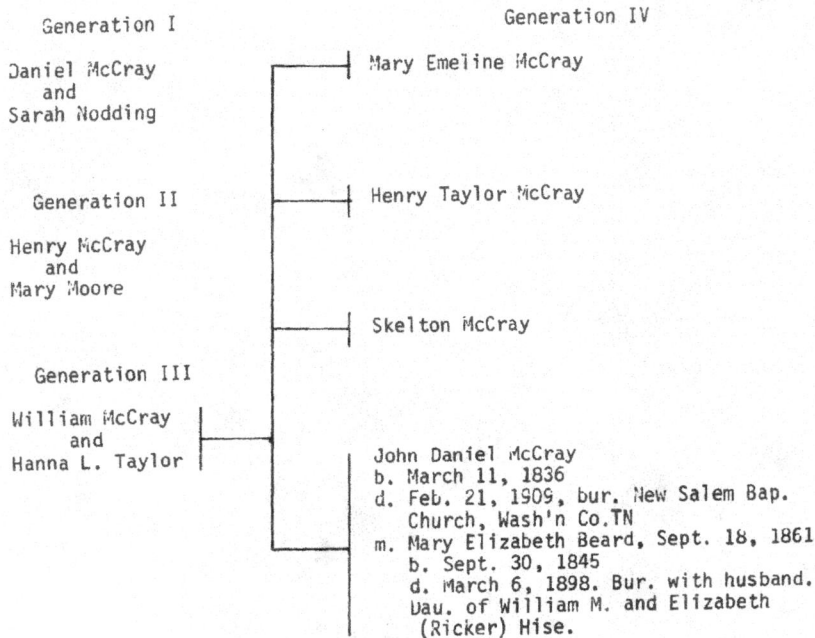

Generation I

Daniel McCray
and
Sarah Nodding

Generation II

Henry McCray
and
Mary Moore

Generation III

William McCray
and
Hanna L. Taylor

Generation IV

Mary Emeline McCray

Henry Taylor McCray

Skelton McCray

John Daniel McCray
b. March 11, 1836
d. Feb. 21, 1909, bur. New Salem Bap.
   Church, Wash'n Co.TN
m. Mary Elizabeth Beard, Sept. 18, 1861
   b. Sept. 30, 1845
   d. March 6, 1898. Bur. with husband.
   Dau. of William M. and Elizabeth
   (Ricker) Hise.

166

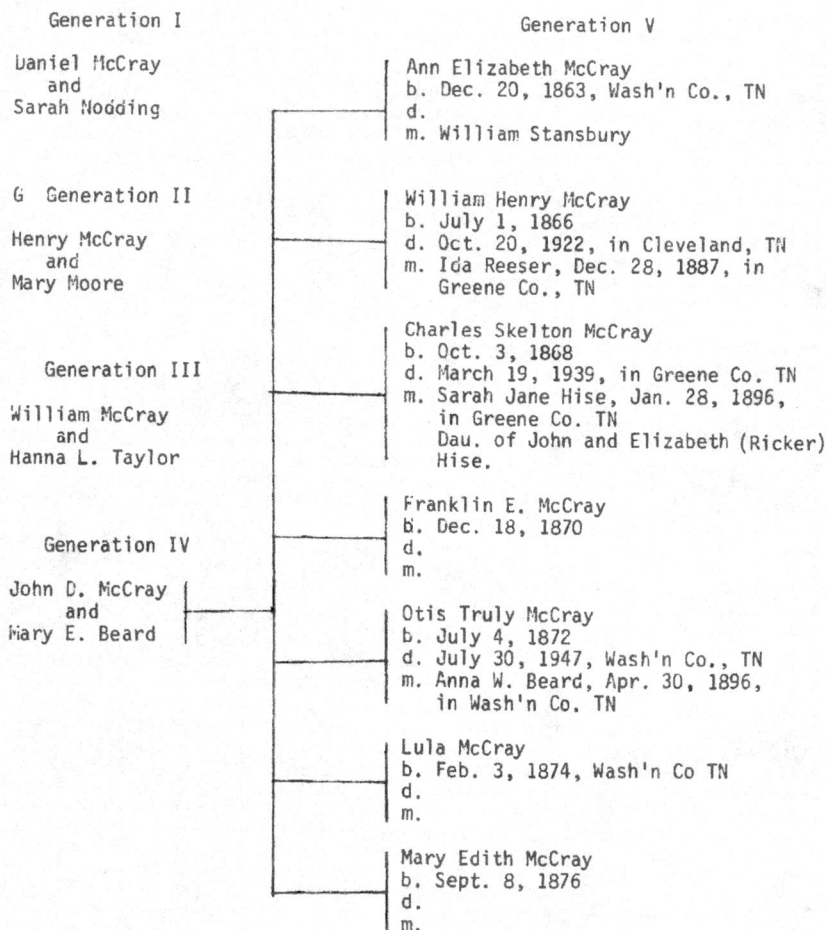

Generation I

Daniel McCray
and
Sarah Nodding

G Generation II

Henry McCray
and
Mary Moore

Generation III

William McCray
and
Hanna L. Taylor

Generation IV

John D. McCray
and
Mary E. Beard

Generation V

Ann Elizabeth McCray
b. Dec. 20, 1863, Wash'n Co., TN
d.
m. William Stansbury

William Henry McCray
b. July 1, 1866
d. Oct. 20, 1922, in Cleveland, TN
m. Ida Reeser, Dec. 28, 1887, in
   Greene Co., TN

Charles Skelton McCray
b. Oct. 3, 1868
d. March 19, 1939, in Greene Co. TN
m. Sarah Jane Hise, Jan. 28, 1896,
   in Greene Co. TN
   Dau. of John and Elizabeth (Ricker)
   Hise.

Franklin E. McCray
b. Dec. 18, 1870
d.
m.

Otis Truly McCray
b. July 4, 1872
d. July 30, 1947, Wash'n Co., TN
m. Anna W. Beard, Apr. 30, 1896,
   in Wash'n Co. TN

Lula McCray
b. Feb. 3, 1874, Wash'n Co TN
d.
m.

Mary Edith McCray
b. Sept. 8, 1876
d.
m.

Generation I   Generation VI

Daniel McCray   Glenna E. McCray
   and   b. Nov. 16, 1896, Wash'n Co. TN
Sarah Nodding   d. Nov. 25, 1981, Greene Co TN.
                                 m. Carl Brown Wilhoit, Greene Co TN.

Generation II

Henry McCray   Ross Dewey McCray
   and   b. July 20, 1898, Wash'n Co. TN
Mary Moore   d. Nov. 2, 1958, Bristol, TN
                                 m. Ona Davis

Generation III

William McCray   Della Edith McCray
   and   b. Nov. 20, 1900, Wash'n Co. TN.
Hanna L. Taylor   d. Nov. 28, 1910, Greene Co. TN.
                                 m.

Generation IV

John D. McCray   Ralph Skelton McCray
   and   b. Oct. 15, 1902, Wash'n Co TN.
Mary E. Beard   d.
                                 m. Ethel Estelle Morelock, Nov. 6,
                                    1925, Bristol, TN.
Generation V   Dau. of Hale and Elizabeth (Collins)
                                    Morelock, of Bristol, TN.
Charles S. McCray
   and
Sarah J. Hise

168

Generation I

Daniel McCray
and
Sarah Nodding

Generation II

Henry McCray
and
Mary Moore

Generation III

William McCray
and
Hanna L. Taylor

Generation IV

John D. McCray
and
Mary E. Beard

Generation V

Charles S. McCray
and
Sarah J. Hise

Generation VI

Ralph S. McCray
and
Ethel E. Morelock

Generation VII

William Ross McCray
b. Dec. 25, 1925, Bristol, TN.
d.
m. Helen Sharp, Nov. 18, 1947, in
     Sullivan Co., TN

John Deliva McCray
b. April 4, 1928, Bristol TN.
d.
m. Barbara Elizabeth Doan, April 15,
     1949, in Sullivan Co., TN.

Richard Lee McCray*
b. Sept. 19, 1929, Bristol, TN.
d.
m. Florence Purel Whitaker, Aug. 24,
     1951, in Corinth, MS.
     Dau. of Rufus B. and Annie Jones
     Hodges, of Deroan, AR.

Joyce Estelle McCray
b. July 12, 1933, Bristol, TN.
d.
m. Ralph G. Smith, Dec. 19, 1952.

James Hale McCray
b. May 8, 1935, Sullivan Co TN.
d. May 8, 1935.
m.

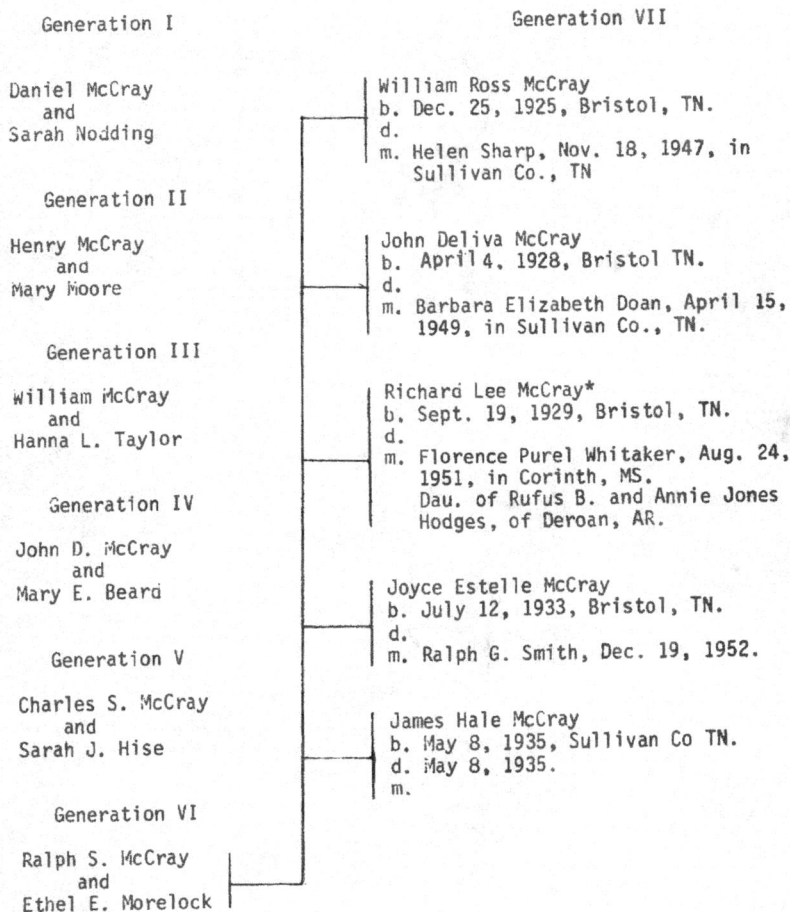

* Richard Lee McCray contributed his family data, as well as considerable
data on Daniel and Sarah (Nodding) McCray and Henry and Mary (Moore) McCray.

169

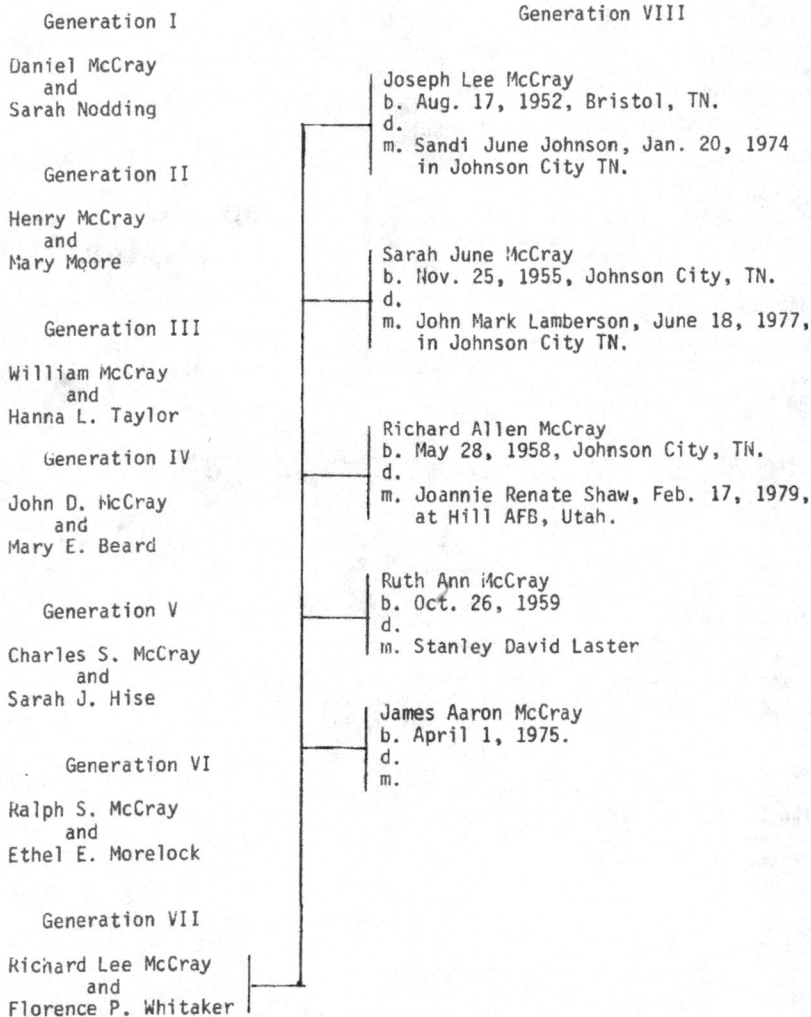

Generation I

Daniel McCray
    and
Sarah Nodding

Generation II

Henry McCray
    and
Mary Moore

Generation III

William McCray
    and
Hanna L. Taylor

Generation IV

John D. McCray
    and
Mary E. Beard

Generation V

Charles S. McCray
    and
Sarah J. Hise

Generation VI

Ralph S. McCray
    and
Ethel E. Morelock

Generation VII

Richard Lee McCray
        and
Florence P. Whitaker

Generation VIII

Joseph Lee McCray
b. Aug. 17, 1952, Bristol, TN.
d.
m. Sandi June Johnson, Jan. 20, 1974
   in Johnson City TN.

Sarah June McCray
b. Nov. 25, 1955, Johnson City, TN.
d.
m. John Mark Lamberson, June 18, 1977,
   in Johnson City TN.

Richard Allen McCray
b. May 28, 1958, Johnson City, TN.
d.
m. Joannie Renate Shaw, Feb. 17, 1979,
   at Hill AFB, Utah.

Ruth Ann McCray
b. Oct. 26, 1959
d.
m. Stanley David Laster

James Aaron McCray
b. April 1, 1975.
d.
m.

170

CHAPTER SEVEN

THE McCRAYS OF ALABAMA AND ARKANSAS

PRIOR TO 1763, only a few Spanish and French white settlers came to
the southeastern region that comprises Alabama and Mississippi today.
Spain gave up Mobile in 1763 with the signing of the Treaty of Paris that .
ended what Europeans called the Seven Years War, and which the Americans
called the French and Indian War. Spain continued its hold on everything
west of the Mississippi River.

The first Anglo settlers in any numbers in Alabama came when the
American colonies revolted against England in 1775. They were Georgians
whose sympathies were with England. When the Colonies gained independence in 1783, Spain again took back a coastal fringe and Mobile, but a
wave of planters came in from Georgia, the Carolinas and Virginia, and
settled in northern Alabama. Scots-Irish from Tennessee came down and
settled the rich lands of the Valley of the Tennessee River. Other settlers slowly took over central and western Alabama.

The Colonies astonished the world by organizing themselves into a
republic, the like of which the rest of the planet had never dreamed of.
As soon as the United States of America got its feet on the road toward
real nationhood, it elected a man from Virginia to its Presidency; he was
a man of many talents, not the least of which was that of a shrewd real
estate investor. Thomas Jefferson and a few canny Yankees negotiated
the Louisiana Purchase, undoubtedly one of the greatest non-violent land
transfers ever pulled off, and for a measly fifteen million dollars, too.

During the War of 1812, Spain held onto Mobile and a coastal fringe ,
which did nothing for its popularity among Americans, who had designs on
that area. The Shawnee chief, Tecumseh, persuaded the Alabama Creeks to
go on the warpath for England against settlers, and in a three-day battle
at Fort Mims they slaughtered over 250 settlers who had fled behind the
log walls of the fort. When the war ended in 1814, the United States
firmly controlled all the south, except Texas, Oklahoma, New Mexico and
Arizona, which Spain still held.

Now, Alabama became the goal of madly rushing settlers, and by 1817
it was organized into the Territory of Alabama, and as the population
grew exponentially, it was taken into the United States as its twenty-
second state in 1819 with twenty-two counties.

171

The Family Of Henry McCray of South Carolina And Arkansas

HENRY McCRAY, LISTED IN THE 1790 CENSUS as "Henrey McCray," lived in the Ninety-sixth District of Spartensburgh County, South Carolina, and his family then consisted of three free white males, age sixteen and older, including himself. No positive connection has been established between him and Henry Newton McCray, but the latter was born in South Carolina in 1811, so he was not one of the three white males noted in the 1790 First Federal Census.

The census enumeration is the sole evidence that Henry, or Henrey, McCray existed, but it is generally accepted among his descendents that he was the father of Henry Newton McCray, and a daughter, Narcissa McCray, and possibly other sons, the other two free white males. Henry Newton was born in South Carolina on August 16, 1811, and Narcissa was born in 1809.

In York County, South Carolina, adjacent to Spartensburgh County, lived the family of Matthew and Margaret Carroll, who had a son, John, and a daughter, Elizabeth, as well as eight other children. The Carrolls and the McCrays were close friends, as later events well bear out.

The Carrolls and the McCrays moved to St. Clair County, Alabama, adjacent to Jefferson County and the city of Birmingham, to the south-west. The move was sometime after 1811 and 1824, and it isn't certain that the two families made up a joint caravan for the move. There, Thomas, John, Ruth, Delilah, Jane and Elizabeth Carroll were married. More to the point of this account, John Carroll married Narcissa McCray on January 26, 1831, and four years later, Henry Newton McCray married Elizabeth Carroll on November 12, 1835.

No more had they gotten settled into married life than they packed up and both families left Alabama and moved on to Arkansas. This was in 1836, as evidenced by the fact, brought out in the 1850 Census, that Elizabeth delivered her first-born child, John Franklin McCray, in Mississippi, en route to Arkansas, in 1836. There is no evidence that they ever settled in Mississippi.*

Arkansas was then a new Promised Land and population was growing at a fast rate, although in 1790 there were fewer than four hundred white people in the area. The Panic of 1837 caused a very large movement of settlers out of southeastern United States westward to Louisiana and Arkansas. Hundreds of farmers in Alabama, Georgia, Tennessee and the Carolinas were wiped out by the severe depression of the banking system and many of them abandoned their farms and went west to make a new start in Arkansas. Like Alabama, Arkansas swiftly became a territory and then a state, becoming the 25th state in 1836.

* William E. Carroll, of Oklahoma City, supplied the McCray-Carroll data.

The inseparable McCrays and Carrolls took up farms in Union Township, Saline County, Arkansas. located in approximately the center of the state. Henry and Elizabeth (Carroll) McCray had eight children:

John Franklin McCray, born 1836. He called himself "Franklin."

Delphia A. McCray, born 1841-42. m. Lauderdale Harris, 1868.
                Had son, Adison O. Harris, b. Sept. 1869, Beaver
                Township, Saline County; m. Frances --?--. 4 ch.

Henry N. McCray, Jr., born 1844. m. Frances --?--, b. 1847, 4 ch.
    Sometimes listed as "Henry H. McCray."

Jasper, or Joseph, McCray, born 1847

Elizabeth McCray, born 1850

David S. McCray, born 1850-52. m. Anna M. Adams, age 16, Oct. 5
                                         1875
Martha McCray, born 1854
Canthis (Kaugus) (Demaris) McCray, born 1858-59. m. Samuel F/T
                  Scott, using name "Demaris McCray.", on
                  Feb. 15, 1877.

Elizabeth (Carroll) McCray died February 11, 1865, and Henry died three years later on March 27, 1886, in Benton, Arkansas.

Henry N. McCray, Jr., married the twice-widowed Olivia (Donohoo) (Wills) McAdoo in 1867, when he was about age fifty-six. She was age 45 when she married Henry. Olivia's story is a bit complicated, and today it would get a splash in a checkout-counter magazine. Let Ltc. Leon R. Moore, of Alexander, Arkansas, tell you about her.

"Henry Donohoo died about 1826 leaving a widow, Eda, and three children and one unborn son. Calvin, Bettsy Ann, Olivia and the unborn William. Eda married Benjamin Wills, of Virginia, in St. Clair County, Alabama, in 1834. Benjamin Wills, Sr., and first wife, Lurana's son, James Maclin Wills, married his step-sister, Olivia Donohoo, in 1839, in Saline County, Arkansas. He was a sheriff of Saline County in 1848 to 1850 and was elected to the state legislature for Hot Spring and Saline County, Arkansas, in 1852, but died in September before the legislature was in session. He died intestate and his widow, Olivia Donahoo, was appointed Administratrix and must not have done a very good job by reviewing the probate records. John A. McAdoo was appointed administrator of the estate and was able to straighten things out. John A. married Olivia in 1855, and they had three children; Olivia, Jefferson Davis, and Josephine. John McAdoo served in the CSA during the Civil War,

173

and was killed in Mississippi in 1864.

"Olivia and her Wills' daughters were very active in supporting the Southern cause. Her daughter, Susan L. Wills, had married Henry James, a young lawyer from Little Rock, Arkansas, about a year prior to the beginning of the Civil War. Henry joined the CSA as a lieutenant, and Susan and her infant son moved in with her mother, Olivia. During the Federal occupation of Benton (Arkansas) her daughter, Susan, had been sweeping the gallery when a Union soldier exposed himself indecently while walking by the house and she shot at him twice with a small pistol. The soldier ran away, and later a friend of theirs found out that the Union army was on the way to arrest her and send her to prison for shooting at the soldier. With the help of some Confederate soldiers that were sent to slip her out before the Federals came, she was able to escape.

"Olivia was arrested by the Union troops in Benton for stealing cotton and aiding the Confederates. She was taken from her home in Benton and marched in her gown, bare-footed to a Federal wagon. After they were leaving and had gotten about a mile toward Little Rock, the soldiers began to curse her and told her to look back at her home, and she saw they had set fire to it. They told her:'Your damned rebel young one is burned up.' (He wasn't.) The Chief Justice of the State Supreme Court was a family friend, and he intervened and got a permit from General Steele to allow Olivia to stay as a prisoner with him until the matter was settled in court. The court finally let her off for lack of evidence.

"It is not clear when she moved to Arkadelphia, Arkansas, but it is assumed that it was right after her release from Little Rock, because her home had been destroyed and the Feds were still in Benton. While in Arkadelphia she ran a boarding house or tavern until the war was over.

"After her husband, John A. McAdoo, was killed in the Civil War, she married Henry Newton McCray in Benton, on January 29, 1867. They had one child, William Newton--"Willie"-- who was born in March, 1868. Olivia filed a bill of equity against Henry N. McCray on February, 1874, and Henry was ordered to pay Olivia $400 and to relinquish all right to property that Olivia owned before their marriage. The final settlement decreed that Olivia was to pay $42.60, or give credit (against the $400 awarded earlier) to Henry. Henry was to furnish Olivia with one year's support or family supplies,"such as his circumstance and means will authorize and warrant and her degree in life requires and justifies." She was to get all his household and kitchen furniture and all the property that he had

before marriage. Olivia and Henry N. McCray were divorced on
the 23rd day of January, 1879."

Olivia never remarried, but Henry wasn't at all deterred by his marital troubles with Olivia. Like many people as feisty as Olivia, she
went serenely on her way and lived until May 4, 1901. She was buried in
Rosemount Cemetery, Saline County.

On August 23, 1882, William N. McCray, at age 69, married Mrs.
Margaret Reid, in Pulaski County, Arkansas. Shortly after their marriage,
a guardian was appointed over Henry because he was judged to be insane.
He died on March 27, 1885, and was buried in Old Union Cemetery in Bland
Township, Saline County, next to his first wife, Elizabeth.

Henry and Olivia's son, William, or "Willie," married Emma Lulu Shoppack, in Benton. Leon Moore showed that there had been a neighborly
relationship between them:

> "Olivia McCray, age 57, with Jeff D. McAdoo, age 17, living
> next door to her daughter, Josephine McAdoo, age 25, and her
> husband Columbus Vann, age 27, who lived next door to Freder-
> ick Shopack, age 31, and his wife Sophronia, age 31, daughter
> Emma, age 10, son John F., age 8, and Robert F. Homan, age 1, a
> nephew."

Mr. William Carroll, of Oklahoma City, found the marriage record of
John E. McCray to Mary E. Pelton, on February 27, 1862, and then again,
John F. McCray married Lou J. Homan, on December 26, 1867. John F.
McCray was, of course, the son of Henry Newton and Elizabeth (Carroll)
McCray.

William ("Willie") Newton McCray, Jr., married Emma Lulu Shoppack
on June 27, 1894, in Benton. One of their children was William Frederick
McCray, who married Emily Florence Jones. One of their children was
John Fred McCray, born on May 12, 1932. He has a son, John Stephen Mc-
Cray, and two grandson, John Wesley and Bradley Stephen..

Narcissa (McCray) Carroll and her husband, John, were part of the
migration into central Arkansas. By 1850 their family consisted of Narcissa and five children. John Carroll died on January 7, 1850, so when
the census-taker enumerated the family Narcissa was a widow. Their
children were:

Henry Carroll, born 1832

Jane Carroll, born 1834

Ervin Carroll, born 1839

Thomas Carroll, born 1842

Mary A. Carroll, born 1845

Henry Newton McCray's biography was printed in one of those popular county histories that proliferated in the late nineteenth century*, reproduced here:

"Henry H. McCray, one of the pioneer settlers of Saline County, was born here in 1844, being the son of H.N. and Elizabeth (Carroll) McCray, the father a native of South Carolina, and the mother of Alabama. H.N. McCray was married when a young man, and removed to what is now Union Township, Saline County, A k., in 1837, there entering land and partly improving it, when he sold out and went to what is now Grant County. He bought a claim and improved it, but some years after returned to Saline County, and settled in Union Township, the second time in 1842. Later he bought a farm on Saline River. His remaining days were spent in Benton, his death occurring March 27, 1886. He was a member of Benton Lodge No. 34, A.F.& A.M. His wife died in 1865. Henry H. McCray passed his boyhood days on the farm, and was educated in the subscription schools of Saline County. He enlisted at Little Rock, in 1862, in Col. Crawford's regiment for three years or during the war, and was engaged in scouting, being transferred to Col. Hawthorn's regiment of infantry, where he was principally engaged in Texas. He was paroled at Marshall, Tex., in May, 1865, when he returned to Saline County, becoming engaged in farming. He married in November, 1868, Miss A. J. Frances Pelton, a native of Saline County, and daughter of James and Arrilla (Williams) Pelton, of Illinois. Mr. Pelton came to the Louisiana Territory when a young man, was married here and settled in what is now Beaver Township, Saline County, Ark. He settled on a claim of eighty acres given by the territory to actual settlers, where he made his home until his death in 1846. His esteemed wife survived until 1876. Grandfather Berry Williams was a native of North Carolina, was in the War of 1812, and at a very early day came to Arkansas. His death occurred in what is now Grant County, in 1854. Mr. McCray settled in 1872 upon a farm, where he now resides, which is one of the oldest settled places in

* *Biographical and Historical Memoirs of Pulaski, Jefferson, Lonoke, Faulkner, Grant, Saline, Perry, Garland and Hot Springs Counties, Arkansas;* The Goodspeed Publishing Company, 1889, Chicago, Nashville and St. Louis. pp286, 287.

Saline County. He has also opened up considerable land, and
has now about 100 acres under cultivation, owning besides 475
acres of well-improved land in Saline Township. Mr. McCray
and wife are members of the Methodist Episcopal Church, South,
and take an active part in all church work. They have been
blessed with six children: Flora, Clara, Jasper, James, Rosa
and Marvin. Mr. MCray has always taken an active part in anything which would tend to the improvement of the town and
county, both in a material, religious and moral sense."

Contributed by William Carroll

177

THE FAMILY OF HENRY McCRAY

Generation I

Henry (Henrey) McCray and ---?---	Matthew Carroll and Margaret ---?---
Lived in the 96th District of Spartenburgh County, South Carolina. Believed to be the progenitor of the McCrays of Arkansas.	Lived in York County, South Carolina. Friends and in-laws of the McCrays

Henry Newton McCray
b. Sept. 16, 1811 (calculated from
   gravestone; also said to be
   August 16, 1811
d. March 27, 1885
m. (1) Elizabeth Carroll, on Nov. 12,
   1835, in St. Clair Co., Ala.
   Dau of Matthew and Margaret Carroll
   of York County, South Carolina. 8ch
   b. Jan. 28, 1815
   d. Feb. 11, 1865

   (2) Mrs. Olivia (Donahoo) (Wills)
       McAdoo, on Jan. 29, 1867.
       b. 1813-1824, dau of Henry and
       Eda (Rowland) Donahoo
       d. May 4, 1901, buried Rose-
       mount Cemetery, Saline Co. Ark.
Henry and Elizabeth buried in Old Union
Cemetery, Saline Co., Ark.
   (3) Margaret Reid, Aug. 23, 1882

Henry McCray
and
---?---

Narcissa McCray (Not positively known
to be Henry's sister)
b. 1809 in South Carolina
d.
m. John Carroll, son of Matthew and
   Margaret Carroll of South Carolina
   b. 1807
   d. Jan. 7, 1850

Ch: Henry Carroll, b. 1832, Ark.
     Jane Carroll, b. 1832
     Ervin Carroll, b. 1839
     Thomas Carroll, b. 1842
     Mary A. Carroll, b. 1845
     James Carroll
     John Carroll, b. Ala.
                   d. 1938/1950 in TX

Generation I   Generation II

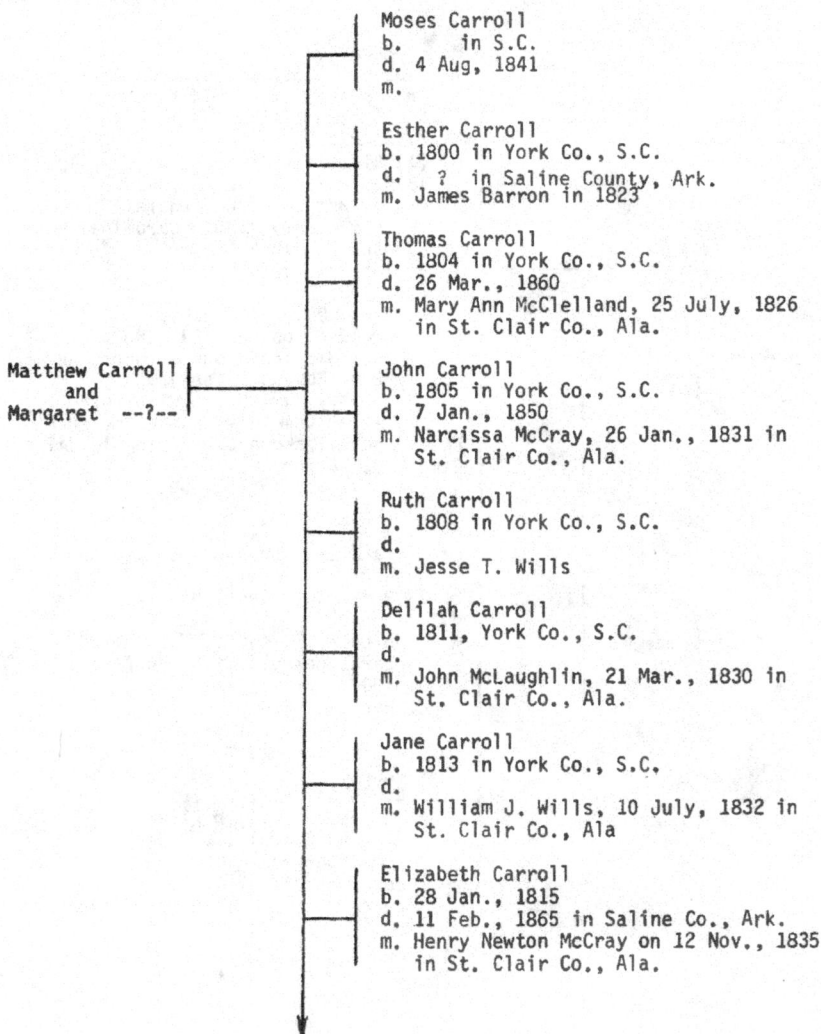

Matthew Carroll
    and
Margaret --?--

Moses Carroll
b.   in S.C.
d. 4 Aug, 1841
m.

Esther Carroll
b. 1800 in York Co., S.C.
d.   ? in Saline County, Ark.
m. James Barron in 1823

Thomas Carroll
b. 1804 in York Co., S.C.
d. 26 Mar., 1860
m. Mary Ann McClelland, 25 July, 1826
    in St. Clair Co., Ala.

John Carroll
b. 1805 in York Co., S.C.
d. 7 Jan., 1850
m. Narcissa McCray, 26 Jan., 1831 in
    St. Clair Co., Ala.

Ruth Carroll
b. 1808 in York Co., S.C.
d.
m. Jesse T. Wills

Delilah Carroll
b. 1811, York Co., S.C.
d.
m. John McLaughlin, 21 Mar., 1830 in
    St. Clair Co., Ala.

Jane Carroll
b. 1813 in York Co., S.C.
d.
m. William J. Wills, 10 July, 1832 in
    St. Clair Co., Ala

Elizabeth Carroll
b. 28 Jan., 1815
d. 11 Feb., 1865 in Saline Co., Ark.
m. Henry Newton McCray on 12 Nov., 1835
    in St. Clair Co., Ala.

180

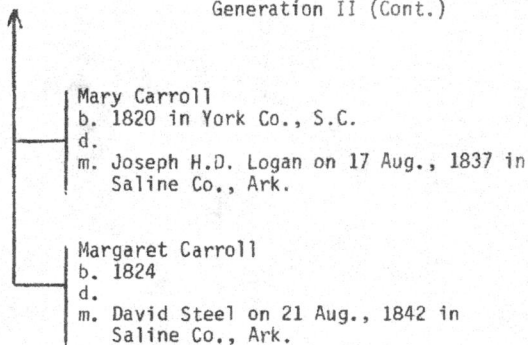

Mary Carroll
b. 1820 in York Co., S.C.
d.
m. Joseph H.D. Logan on 17 Aug., 1837 in
   Saline Co., Ark.

Margaret Carroll
b. 1824
d.
m. David Steel on 21 Aug., 1842 in
   Saline Co., Ark.

Generation I   Generation III

Henry   John Franklin McCray
   and   b. 1836 in Mississippi
---?---   d. March 27, 1886, Benton, Ark.
                                   m. (1) Mary E. Pelton, Feb. 27, 1862
                                        (2) Lou, or Lulu, J. Homan, Dec.
                                            26, 1867
                                            b. 1848-9

                                   Margaret E. McCray
   Generation II   b. 1838 in Ark.
                                   d.
Henry Newton McCray   m.
      and
(1) Elizabeth Carroll
                                   Delphia A. McCray
(2) Olivia McAdoo   b. 1841
                                   d.
                                   m. (1) Emery E. Pelton, son of John F
                                          Pelton, in 1864
                                        (2) Lauderdale Harris, on Nov. 26,
                                            1859. Son, Adison O. McCray,
                                            b. 1869

                                   Henry Newton McCray, Jr.
                                   b. 1844 in Ark
                                   d.
                                   m. Aurelia J. Pelton
                                        b. 1847 in Ark.
                                        d.
                                   Ch: Flora, 1869, Clara, 1871, Jasper,
                                        1874, James, 1876

                                   Martha (Mary?) McCray
                                   b. 1854
                                   d.
                                   m.

                                   Elizabeth McCray
                                   b. 1850
                                   d.
                                   m.

                                   182

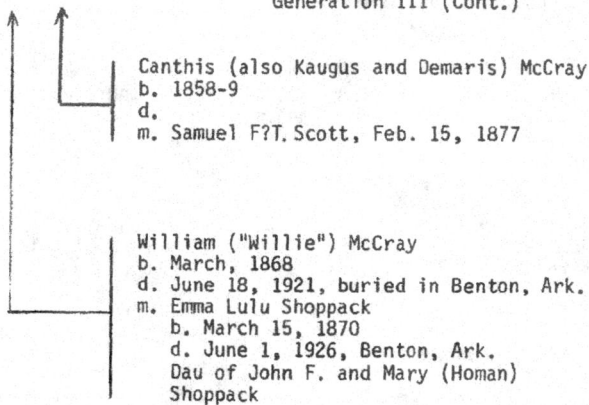

Canthis (also Kaugus and Demaris) McCray
b. 1858-9
d.
m. Samuel F?T. Scott, Feb. 15, 1877

William ("Willie") McCray
b. March, 1868
d. June 18, 1921, buried in Benton, Ark.
m. Emma Lulu Shoppack
   b. March 15, 1870
   d. June 1, 1926, Benton, Ark.
   Dau of John F. and Mary (Homan)
   Shoppack

The Enigmatic William McCray. Who Was He?

ALTHOUGH NOBODY THOUGHT TO PUT INTO RECORDS the names of the parents of a certain William McCray, and his brother, Matthew, nevertheless they really were around in Arkansas after the year 1800. Both said they were born in Tennessee. Matthew, the older of the two, carried the nickname of "Massey," and the name was carried down through the family to Mrs. Dorothy (McCray) Gray, of Granbury, Texas. As soon as she tells anyone that her great grandfather, William, was born in Tennessee, someone will always say, "Ah hah! Must have been a son of Daniel and Sarah (Nodding) McCray." Mrs. Gray agrees that they are the likely parents or grand- parents of William and Massey McCray, but no one has produced any proof other than an entry in a Bible in the Tilson family, descendants from Elisha and Rebecca(Tilson) McCray. This Bible note has it that William was a son of Charles and Betsey (Deakins) McCray. Charles was the eldest child of Daniel and Sarah.

Mrs. Gray wrote that she knows that Charles was very close to his grandfather, William Nodding, who died in Tennessee, and that he would surely have named a son William. But to date, she cannot find any McCrays who had sons named William and Matthew, although there were plenty of Williams in the family of Daniel and Sarah.

The fourth son of Daniel and Sarah (Nodding) McCray was William McCray, born in 1789, but he married four times and died in Missouri, not Arkansas. Another son of Daniel and Sarah, Henry McCray, married Mary Moore, and they had a son named William, born in 1797, but nobody knows anything about him, so he *might* be Mrs. Gray's William. Still another son of Daniel and Sarah was Elisha, who married Rebecca Tilson, and their William was born in 1813. He also died in Missouri.

William somehow wasn't about when the various decennial censuses were taken up until 1860, but Matthew, or "Massey," was enumerated in many of them. In 1850, Matthew was in Pike County, Arkansas, with a wife Lucinda, and he gave his birthplace as Tennessee, and his age, 44, mak- ing his birth year 1806.

William himself turned up ten years later in Sebastian County, Arkansas, with his wife, Martha, and five children. They put down his name as "McCree." He told the census-taker that he was born in Tennessee and that he was age 50. Martha was born in 1825. Their children were: Ann, born in 1851, Cordelia, born in 1853, Alice, born in 1856, George, born in 1857, and William, born in 1861 or 1862.

Also living in the household was John Hensley. Matthew's daughter, Leanna, married John Hensley and they had three children. There is no explanation for his living with William's family, but they both were sad- dlers, so they may have been in business together.

Martha apparently died soon after the birth of William, Junior, for by the time of the 1870 Census, William, Senior, was married to Caroline, a native of Alabama, who was about age 30 in 1870 half the age of her husband. They had six children:

Matthew, another "Massey", McCray, born 1865
James McCray, born 1867
John McCray, born 1868
Grant McCray, born 1869
Martha McCray, born, 1871
Joseph McCray, born 1873

Between the birth of Joseph in 1873 and 1880, Caroline died.

Matthew, Jr., left Arkansas and sought his fortune in Texas. Within a year he found and married Mary Frances Wylie in Bosque County, Texas. They left Bosque County for a few years to live in Grayson County, and sometime after 1900 they returned to Bosque County.

William and Martha McCray's son, Grant, married a lady named Rudy, and they had three children:

Frank McCray, born in August, 1892
May B. McCray, born in June, 1896
Martha? Zerilda (McCray) Smith, born July 1874(?)

John McCray married Martha Ferguson, and they lived on a farm in Logan County, Arkansas. They had five children: Bessie, John W., Edna Blaine and Ada.

Matthew and Mary Frances (Wylie) McCray's son, Lee Massey McCray, was born in 1863. Lee Massey was the father of Dorothy (McCray) Gray, the frustrated seeker of information about William and Matthew McCray.

Generation I

believed to be
Daniel McCray
   and
Sarah Nodding

Generation II

Believed to be
Charles McCray
   and
Betsey Deakins

Generation III

William McCray
      and
(1) Martha --?--
(2) Caroline --?--

Generation IV

Ann McCray
b. 1851, in Arkansas
d.
m.

Cordelia McCray
b. 1853 in Arkansas
d.
m.

Alice McCray,
b. 1856 in Arkansas
d.
m. --?-- Eads

George B. McCray
b. 1861-62 in Arkansas
d.
m.

William T. McCray
b. 1861-62 in Arkansas
d.
m.

Matthew ("Massey") McCray
b. June 10, 1865, in Sebasian Co. Ark.
d. June 25, 1927, in McLennan Co. TX
m. Mary Frances Wylie, May 15, Bosque
Co. TX

James A. McCray
b. 1867 in Arkansas
d.
m. Martha Ferguson, 1892 in Logan Co.
   Arkansas.

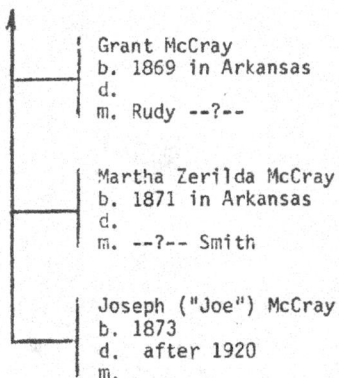

Grant McCray
b. 1869 in Arkansas
d.
m. Rudy --?--

Martha Zerilda McCray
b. 1871 in Arkansas
d.
m. --?-- Smith

Joseph ("Joe") McCray
b. 1873
d. after 1920
m.

John McCray Of Fayette County, Pennsylvania

THE SOURCE OF THIS BIOGRAPHY IS UNKNOWN. A photocopy of it turned
up in the middle of a pile of unrelated genealogical data one day, but if
it's a McCray, it belongs in this book. The title of the book from which
it was copied shows at the top of the page as *Fayette Biographies*, and
in pencil following, "Penn."

"John McCray, of Menallen (township), was born on the McCray
homestead, four miles west of Uniontown, September 18, 1824. He
is a son of Adam and Anna (Jackson) McCray.

"Adam McCray (father), was born April 12, 1780, and died
August 12, 1855. In 1807 he married Miss Anna, daughter of
Isaac Jackson of Menallen township. They had ten children:
John, Isaac, Margaret, Sarah Ann, Mary, Rebecca, Eleanor, Martha
and Emily.
"John McCray (paternal grandfather) was of Scotch-Irish
descent, born in Ireland, where he learned the trade of weaver.
He came to America, and with three of his brothers served under
Washington in the Revolutionary War. After that struggle closed
he removed to Menallen township where he died. His wife's
father made the first crown glass in Scotland. John McCray was
reared on the home farm, and educated in the subscription
schools of Menallen. He owns one hundred acres of fine land in
the township, and is engaged in farming and stock raising. He
married Mrs. Catherine Filley, widow of Dr. Horace Filley, and
daughter of John Deal of Pittsburgh, March 1854. Their union
has been blessed with four children: Maggie E.(died in infancy),
Mary, Ida (died at fifteen years of age), Anna J., born November 2, 1855, married to Alex. II Patterson, lives near Martins-
burgh, W.Va., and has five children: Sarah Louisa, born July
30, 1862, married to Oliver B. Jeffries, of Uniontown, and has
one child.

"Mr. McCray is a good business man, a good farmer, a respectable citizen, and has for many years been a follower of
"the lowly Nazarene," being a highly respected member of the
Presbyterian church at New Salem."

John McCray, undoubtedly the grandfather in the above biographical sketch
was listed in the Federal Census of 1800, living in Fayette County. This
biography adds considerable credence to the legend that four McCray
brothers came to America before the American Revolution. Were his other
brothers Samuel, William and James, according to the legend?

FRANCIS and SARAH (McGOOKIN) McRAY/ McCRAY

Ireland After The American Revolution

DURING THE PERIOD FROM 1718 until the Revolutionary War the migrations consisted of mainly Scots-Irish, but during the next century there was a steady flow of Irish, mostly Catholic Irish, who came here to escape from the British government's anti-Catholic oppressions, grinding poverty, denial of opportunity for education and employment of any consequence. Protestants, including the Scots-Irish were generally better off. They owned businesses and were given public offices, and they joined with the anti-Catholic bigotry of the government.

Catholics in Ireland had been disenfranchised since 1688, and were without any political privileges. There was an Irish Parliament in Dublin, but only Protestants held office there, although its bills were subject to veto by the King's Privy Council and the cabinet. Ireland had a thriving linen and cotton textile industry, and some ship-building and other heavy industry as well, but it was all owned by Protestants. Only Protestants were admitted to the skilled trades as apprentices, and the only jobs for Irish Catholic workers were garbage collection, janitoring cleaning sewers, ditch-digging and other low-paying and despised jobs.

As the enormity of Great Britain's loss of the American Colonies began to sink into Whitehall's mentality, Parliament ruefully counted the cost in lost empire that English arrogance had wrought. Worrisome reports drifted into London of revolutionary ideas creeping into Ireland, and security forces were dispatched thence to use any means to suppress any notions of liberty for Irish Catholics. Eruption of the French Revolution, alarmingly close to London, caused concern among British M.Ps. When, in 1791 two secret Irish societies formed to demand complete separation and freedom, and the "rabble government" of France launched several fumbled expeditionary forces to Ireland to join the "damned rebels," they harrumphed in alarm and decided that perhaps some concessions might quiet Irish dissent. The secret societies would have none of it. It was to be a free Ireland or there was going to be one hell of a fight.

Over the next hundred and twenty-five years the English Parliament reluctantly threw bone after bone to Ireland, hoping to quiet the ever-growing unrest and violence, but the snarling Irish wolfhound never stopped lunging at the English hand that offered peace for the price of submission. Parliament just didn't get it.

The Industrial Revolution came to Ireland about 1800, some fifty years behind the rest of Great Britain. Belfast was built on the swampy

188a

estuary of the Lagan River as a Protestant enclave, textile factories were built for weaving linen and cotton fabrics, and shipyards were born on Belfast Lough (Bay). Belfast was a ghastly environmental and social cancerous growth on Antrim's shores. Dreary rows of brick houses were built for factory workers in narrow streets with no sanitary facilities, and rents were kept at a level guaranteed to keep the workers in perpetual poverty. Women and children labored from dawn to dusk in dimly lighted, unheated and unventilated brick piles, operating dangerous machines and breathing lint and dust. They were paid a pittance for piece work, and when they were sick or injured there was no compensation. Most factory workers, if they survived the hazards of unguarded moving machine elements, usually died in early middle age of tuberculosis, emphysema or pneumonia. The city was a vast money machine for wealthy Protestant Ulster Scots and absentee English aristocrats, and for the poor, Protestant and Catholic, it was a hell-hole.

Overpopulation became a major problem in Ireland. Its limited arable land had been cut up into ever-smaller tracts, and by 1845 the population had leaped from a million or so to over eight million, while farms averaged a bit less than three acres. Families usually ran to eight or ten people, and small farm crops provided hardly more than subsistence living. Irish leaders and the English government agreed on one thing; Irish people should migrate to anywhere they could get to--except England, which had no land to spare, nor did the landed gentry want any dirty Irish anywhere near them. Bad enough, they thought, that they were but twenty miles away across the Irish Sea.

Some did migrate. They went to New Zealand and Australia where free land could be had, and where willing workers were welcome, and they went to America where Irish navvies were needed to lay iron rails across the wide prairies. Boston and New York nouveau riche sought young Irish women as servants and nannies and Irish men as butlers and yard workers. Canada needed strong men to help grow wheat on thousand-acre farms.

The result was that the ones who left were Ireland's best. They were the educated, disciplined and thrifty, who had jobs paying well enough to permit laying up savings for passage. These migrants would often mail back money to other family members to help them escape Ireland's poverty to a better life. But with thousands of fecund families producing more thousands of fecund young people, the population of Ireland grew exponentially, and the few who migrated made no measurable difference. While the population grew the ability of the land to produce reached saturation, and hunger was the Irishman's bedfellow and companion. The only hope was for greatly accelerated migration, an unlikely happening.

England grudgingly released Ireland from its chains at an agonizingly slow snail's pace. Finally, in 1920, following several years of a state of terrorism by British "Black and Tans" (military and civil police), during which many civilians and soldiers on both sides were shot in cold blood in street riots and ambushes, the Act of Union divided Ireland into North (Protestant) and South (Catholic) Ireland. South Ireland was given Dominion status, while Ulster voted to retain close ties to England. Catholics in Ulster vowed to fight on.

A riot in the streets of Dublin in 1921 resulted in the torching of the City Hall. Practically all existing records of marriages, deaths, police and court actions, and land transfers, were destroyed. Today it is a difficult and time-consuming task for genealogists to find true evidence of Scots or Irish who lived in Ulster before 1921.

During World War II Catholic resistance to military conscription caused much trouble in Ireland, with Irish Catholics taking the position that it was England's war, not theirs, and that resisting the draft made more trouble for England. When the war ended, South Ireland finally became the Republic of Ireland, completely separate and free. Catholic Ulster has never abandoned the fight for freedom, so the bloodshed goes on today.

The Migration Of Francis McCray and His Family

NOT ALL THE McCRAYS LEFT ULSTER in the eighteenth century. At least one family of McCrays left County Antrim about the middle of the nineteenth century, went to Canada where they stayed for twelve years, and then entered the United States and settled in Wisconsin.

In 1840 Francis McRae/McCray, Sarah, his wife, and two children, boarded a ship in an Irish port, probably Belfast, since it is known that one of the children was born in Belfast. The ship, probably a hybrid craft with steam-driven side paddle wheels, but with masts and yardarms still in place (just in case, y'know), sailed out past Whitehead, Black Head, and then rounded Ireland's north coast. They sailed past Lough Foyle, where King Billy's navy relieved the seige of Londonderry 152 years before, and as they passed Malin Head on the port side, with the green hills of County Donegal in the distance, Francis and Sarah, holding their children in their arms, silently meditated on the finality of their farewell to Ulster, and of the new life ahead in North America. Then Ireland faded in the distance.

Francis McCray was born on November 12, 1804, in County Antrim, Ireland. Antrim is Ulster's most northeast county, and its most populous. From Fair Head, near Ballycastle, Scotland can be seen on a clear day (which is seldom), lying but twenty miles away. Francis married Sarah McGookin, and sure she must have been as Irish as Paddy's pig. She was born in County Antrim on November 22, 1806.

The family settled in Canada until 1852, living probably in Smith Falls, Ontario, about forty-five miles southwest of Ottowa. Sarah had three more children while they were living in Canada. They were: John, born in 1845, Ellen, born in 1847, and Matilda, born in 1851. The next year they moved to the United States, settling first in Jefferson County, Wisconsin, and two years later in Sauk County. While they lived in Jefferson County, they had another child, George McCray.

Francis used the name, "Francis McRae" in his application for citizenship, and signed it with "X", which may or may not indicate that the clerk in the Naturalization office may have spelled it the way it sounded to him, since Francis couldn't write his name. On other and later documents the name appears as McRay, McCrea, McCrae, and finally in 1855 they settled on the McCray spelling.

Donald and Connie McCray, who supplied the information about this family, are descended from George McCray. They said that George was the youngest of nine children, but only six were included in the data given. The family lived in Sauk County until between 1963 and 1977, when they moved to Madison, Wisconsin's capital city.

Note: The material was received from Don and Connie almost at the last minute before the mansucript was completed, and has been included with this unusual page numbering.

Generation I   Generation II

                                          Mary McCray
                                    ┌───── b. 12/1/1833 in Ireland
                                    │   d. 7/9/1902 in Sauk Co. WI
                                    │   m. John Carlile

                                          Eliza McCray
                                    │   b. 19/1/1839 in Belfast Ireland
                                    ┤   d. 27/10/1902 in Sauk Co, WI
                                    │   m. Robert Hunter

                                          John McCray
                                    ┤   b. 18/3/1845 in Canada
                                    │   d. 27/6/1920 in Sauk Co., WI

                                          Ellen McCray
                                    │   b. 21/11/1847 in Smith Falls, Ontario
                                    │   d. 16/1/1907 in Sauk Co., WI
Francis McCray   │   m. Elbert Fish on 23/10/1867
b. 12/11/1804 in County   │   b. 6/5/1848 in New Baltimore, N.Y.
   Antrim, Ireland   │   d.13/5/1895
d. 12/7/1887 in Wisconsin   │   ch: Ada Fish (1887-1953); Earl Fish
                                   ┤   (1862-1879); Lizzie Fish (1869-1907);
      and   ├──   George Fish (1874-1900); Freddie Fish
                                   │   (1876-1886); Elsie Fish (1883-1903).
Sarah McGookin
b. 22/11/1806 in County   │   Matilda McCray
   Antrim, Ireland   │   b. 20/4/1851 in Canada
d. 7/9/1902 in Wisconsin   ┤   d. 27/6/1920 in Sauk Co., WI
                                   │   m. (spinster)

                                          George McCray
                                   │   b. 9/1/1853 in Milford, Jefferson Co. WI
                                   ┤   d. 19/12/1926 in Sauk Co, WI
                                   │   m. Flora Northrup, 5 ch.

                                   └─── Three other children, names unknown

                                       188e

Generation I		Generation III

Generation I

Francis McCray
and
Sarah McGookin

Generation III

Walter John McCray
b. 20-4-1886 in Winfield, Sauk Co., WI
d. 9-3-1965
m. bachelor

Sarah ("Sadie") E. McCray
b. 18-5-1890 in Winfield, Sauk Co. WI
d. 30-5-1963 in Reedsburg, Sauk Co., WI
m. (1) Norman Woodworth on 22 Oct., 1913
ch:Ruth Elizabeth Woodworth
     b. 8-12-1920 in Reedsburg, Sauk Co.WI
     (2) James A. Stone on 31-12-1929

Generation II

George McCray
and
Flora Northrup

Ralph Willis McCray
b. 15-9-1894 in Winfield, Sauk Co., WI
d. 10-10-1977 in Madison, WI
m. Grace F. Morgan   3 ch
     b. 23-12-1902 in Clyman, Jeff. Co. WI
     d. 23-12-1988 (her birthday) in
         Madison, WI

Mary McCray
b. 16-3-1897
d. 13-3-1980 in Reedsburg, WI
m. Robert Montgomery
ch; Dorothy Montgomery
      m. Lisle Wegner
      Gilbert Montgomery

188f

```
Generation I                          Generation IV

Francis McCray
   and                       ┌── Donald Harry McCray
Sarah McGookin                │   b. 6-9-1925 in Watertown, Jeff. Co, WI
                              │   d.
                              │   m. Constance A. McCray
                              │      b. 6-9-1927 in Madison, WI
  Generation II         ┌──┬──┤   ch: Catherine Jo McCray
                        │     │      b. 3-12-1949 in Madison, WI
George McCray           │     │      m. William J. Johnson
   and                  │     │      ch: Steven Michael Johnson
Flora Northrup          │     │         b. 13-9-1985
                        │     │         David Ryan Johnson
                        │     │         b. 7-8-1986
                        │     │
                        │     │
                        │     │
                        │     │
 Generation III         ├─────┤  Amy Laurel McCray
                        │     │  b. 25-7-1952
Ralph W. McCray ┐       │     │  m. Rod L. Baker    (div)
   and          ├───────┤
Grace Morgan ───┘       │     │
                        │     │
                        │     │
                        │     │  Marion Joan McCray
                        │     │  b. 8-12-1930
                        │     │  m. Ernie J. Heiman
                        │     │     b. 18-11-1930
                        │     │     d. 16-6-1981
                        │     │  ch: Beth Heiman
                        │     │      m. Maev Palmer
                        │     │      ch: Andrew C. Palmer
                        │     │         b. 22-5-1976
                        │     │         Brian O'Connor Palmer
                        │     │         b. 4-11-1988
                        │     │
                        └─────┤  Julie Heiman
                              │  b. 11-6-1955
                              │  m. David Ellis
                              │
                              │  Kathleen Heiman
                              │  b. 7-10-1958
                              │  m. Jean Louis Ratsimihah
                              │  ch: Nicholas Seta Ratsimihah
                              │      b. 6-7-1983
                              │      d. 9-12-1988
                              │
                              │  Joel Willis Heiman
                              └  b. 13-8-1962 in Portage, WI
```

188g

the

McCRAYS

of

Northwestern Pennsylvania

CHAPTER EIGHT

THE McCRAYS OF NORTHWESTERN PENNSYLVANIA

Setting The Stage

W hen the War For American Independence ended in 1783, the American Colonies, exhausted, destitute, in debt both at home and abroad, and except for France, without friends in the world, began picking up the pieces and taking stock. The only exportable commodities we had were timber, furs and tobacco. There were no exportable manufactured products and no ships in which to transport them. But we had a non-exportable commodity in abundance that everyone, everywhere, wanted, and that was *LAND*. Boy, did we have land! We had more undeveloped acreage than was in all of Europe, and it was a buyer's market.

But in order to market land we first had to establish a government. We may never fully grasp the enormity of our debt to less than a score of brilliant men, mostly landed aristocrats, who took the wreckage and skillfully molded it into a marvelous governmental instrument, based on a belief that man's natural nobility would prevail over his natural meanness. The wonder they wrought is their memorial and our precious treasure. "Never work," said much of Europe, "Can't trust common folk to run a government." And they went back to planning new and bigger wars.

Even before the new Constitution was ratified and the new nation was truly under way, the Pennsylvania Assembly did four things that profoundly affected the lives and fortunes of the McCrays of Pennsylvania.

1) In 1784, they bought from the Iroquois Nation several million acres of land, known as "The New Purchase," in Northumberland and Allegheny Counties, constituting nearly one half of today's Pennsylvania.

2) They created The Land Ordinance of 1785.

3) They bought the Erie Triangle in 1792 from the Federal Government, thus gaining a 40-mile long shoreline on Lake Erie, and access to the Atlantic Ocean via the St. Lawrence River.

4) They passed the Land Act of 1792.

The Land Ordinance of 1785 was enacted to raise money for the state treasury by selling its only asset, land, in western and northern Pennsylvania to settlers, and to pay off its obligations to veterans of the Revolution, using land as currency. Most of the land sold was in the New Purchase.

The Land Ordinance provided for four classes of land:

1) Donation Lands. Some of the best lands in northern Allegheny County that later became Erie, Crawford, Mercer, Forest, Warren, and Venango Counties, were given outright to veterans of the Pennsylvania Line, in plots of from 200 to 2000 acres, depending upon rank.

2) Depreciation Lands. Lands in Allegheny County south of the Donation Lands, later to be Butler, Beaver, Lawrence, Armstrong, and Allegheny (greatly diminished) Counties, were offered in exchange for the depreciated certificates used to pay troops during the war.

3) State Reserves. Strategically located tracts west of the Susquehanna River were set aside to become towns and cities. The cities of Erie, Pittsburgh, Warren and Waterford, were among these towns and cities that grew up on State Reserve Lands.

4) Academy Lands. They were just that. Pennsylvania is well spotted with colleges and universites that were started on Academy Lands. Dickinson and Franklin Colleges are among these.

By no means did the Donation and Depreciation Lands embrace all of Allegheny County. However, the tracts selected were the best lands in that area, reflecting the gratitude of the State to veterans of the Pennsylvania Line.

It was a truly noble plan, and it was intended that the remaining lands would be disposed of for the benefit of all the people. In 1789 the Assembly passed a law setting aside certain other lands in northwestern Pennsylvania for sale to foreign investors who were already in the new nation looking for investment opportunities for their countries. One of them was a group of Dutch bankers who formed The Holland Land Company (of which more later), which became an important factor in the shaping of Erie County.

After creating the Land Ordinance of 1785, an outline for development of Pennsylvania's wilderness, and completing the purchase of the Erie Triangle, power groups in the Assembly began work on the Land Act of 1792. Something happened then; no more nobility of purpose. Greed and chicanery ruled. The Assembly split between the Democrats, mostly poor people of the western regions, and the conservative (and rich) Federalists of the east. The Democrats wanted to open the new lands to thousands of poor families who were not eligible for Donation or Depreciation lands. They were led by Albert Gallatin, a Swiss-born farmer from Pennsylvania's backwoods, who was opposed by a cadre of Federalists bent on making the Land Act a bonanza for wealthy land speculators. (Yes, it does sound familiar!) Gallatin fought for a law to sell all the land, not otherwise set aside by the Ordinance of 1785, for six cents an acre, in tracts not to exceed 200 acres, one plot only per family, to all who would agree to move onto and clear their parcel, build a house, and occupy the land for at least two years. No down payment would be required, and loans would be granted at seven percent. There would be no wholesaling of large tracts for speculative purposes. The intent was to help the miserable poor and unemployed who were willing to better themselves by taking on the rigors of pioneering.

Federalists sneered. The plan was utopian and unworkable. The poor would go off into the wilderness and there starve to death and the state would then be stuck with a lot of land that nobody wanted. They proposed to sell the land at twenty-five cents an acre to any and all, to permit absentee ownership, and to allow anyone to buy more than one plot, in fact, to buy as much land as they wanted. The Federalists held a majority, so the outcome was predictable. Speculators stood by smiling, and sent agents off to find the best lands for them to apply for as soon as the Assembly completed its shameful business.

The final bill was called a compromise, but it could better be called a sell-out, for while it limited the sales to no more than 400 acres, it was so cleverly worded that enforcement was impossible. After its enactment into law, the Pennsylvania Land Office "interpreted" it to permit unlimited sales to anyone, even to those whose openly declared intent was to buy for speculation. A rush for land broke out, and people began streaming down roads headed west toward the wilderness.

Although Gallatin fought the good fight and lost, he won the support of the people and went on to a long and distinguished career of service in the new nation. He was a U.S. Senator, a Congressman, Secretary of the Treasury under Madison and Jefferson, and minister to France and to Great Britain. He also built a national banking system.

Had Gallatin prevailed, James McCray, his family, and other pioneer settlers in northwestern Pennsylvania could have bought a 200-acre tract for $12, directly from the State of Pennsylvania, but instead he had to buy his land from the Holland Land Company for more than six times that amount. They moved to what would become Erie County shortly after the Battle of Fallen Timbers in Ohio in 1795. The peace that followed saw a great western movement begin toward Pennsylvania's western border.

THE SCOTS-IRISH WERE A RESTLESS LOT.   They were always in the vanguard of migrants into the frontier, seeking that land of milk and honey.
They usually would stay in one place for a few years and then abandon
their claims and move on, always westward. Although James McCray, Jr.,
and his brother, Robert, did finally sink their roots into the rich soil
of Brokenstraw Township, Erie County, Pennsylvania, the others moved on.
We don't know the details of their moves, but we can be sure they didn't
just call Mayflower and charge it on their Visa cards.

It was possible to make the journey overland by following centuries-
old Indian trails that were well-known to frontiersmen. The trails didn't
necessarily follow the easiest contours of the land, but were usually
quite direct, sometimes involving steep inclines instead of taking easier
switch-back paths up and down hills. They were easy to follow because
moccasin-clad feet had worn the paths down. Entirely suitable for foot
travel by man or beasts, they were not wide enough for even the simplest
wheeled vehicle, so travellers could take on these trails only whatever
they could carry and pack onto the backs of horses, mules, or cows. Even
cows were used to carry some of the loads when families were on the move.
Although General Anthony ("Mad Anthony") Wayne had once-and-for-all defeated the Indians of western Pennsylvania and Ohio in 1794 at Fallen
Timbers in the Ohio Region, known as the Northwest Territory, there
were still a few Indians roaming the northwestern Pennsylvania forests
who white families would not like to encounter on one of the remote trails.

Of course there were no bridges on Indian trails, and during times
of flood and high water, parts of the trails were impassable. Nor were
there taverns or inns along the trails for many years, so most of their
food would have to have been packed along with them. That the Indians
knew how to find the best routes is evidenced by the fact that most of
them were later made into roads as civilization developed.

Family members seldom were able to ride horses on their migrations.
Walking the entire distance of sometimes hundreds of miles wasn't considered to be anything remarkable; walking was how one got from here to
there, and their horses and cattle were loaded with household goods and
food. A family with what Caesar called "impedimenta," might average ten
or fifteen miles a day, but there was no guarantee that every day would be
a good day, and it could slow things down when it rained.

The McCrays probably went westward on the Forbes Road to Greensburg
and then turned southwest and into Washington County. Later, when moving
to Erie County, they would have followed the Monongahela Valley to Pittsburgh, and then followed the Allegheny and French Creek to Meadville,
either by boat, or by horse via the old French military road from Presque
Isle to Fort Duquesne. One of James, Jr.'s sons said many years later
that they sold their wagon in Pittsburgh and gone on by pack horse.

194

The Forbes Road, later known as "The Pennsylvania Road," wasn't at first any great shakes as a road. It was begun as a primitive road for the sole purpose of moving cannons against Fort Duquesne during the French and Indian War (1756-1763), the outcome of which made it possible for James McCray to migrate to Erie County some three decades later. In 1793, travellers were likely to encounter other travellers, and there were a few rough taverns and inns along the way.

Up until 1750, France claimed all the land west of the Appalachian Mountains to the Mississippi River, and south nearly to the Gulf of Mexico. The territory where Erie County, Pennsylvania, was later created was well within the territory claimed by the French. British Americans had begun making incursions into the Ohio Territory, and had established several settlements, only to be driven out by the French. In 1752, two years after the Pennsylvania Assembly created Cumberland County, with western borders vaguely defined as being somewhere around where the present eastern Ohio border now lies, the Marquis of Duquesne, Canada's new governor, got orders from France to sweep the British and their Miami Indian allies out of the Ohio country, and to build three forts between Presque Isle, on Lake Erie, and the forks of the Ohio River, where the Monongahela and Allegheny Rivers merged. With 2000 French and Indian troops, he moved southward, and after they captured many British traders and their goods, and their Indian companions boiled and ate the Miami chief at Pickwillany, the British and Miamis got the message that the French really didn't want them to come and put down roots there.

Duquesne planned the largest French fort at the forks of the Ohio. In 1754, Virginia Governor Robert Dinwiddie dispatched a work crew, with an inadequately small company of militia, under a young major named G. Washington, to march to the Ohio forks and build a fort there before the French got there. They'd hardly arrived there when the 2000 French troops canoed in and ordered them to pack up and get out, which they did. Washington started northward from his headquarters at Big Meadow, engaged the French and suffered his only defeat. The French and Indian War had begun, and the Scots-Irish stopped moving into the western regions.

The Marquis of Duquesne built a fort at the Ohio forks and modestly named it "Fort Duquesne." From its vantage point in London, the British military establishment saw no problem in easily defeating the French in America, so they sent fat, debauched, untested-under-fire General Edward Braddock, with orders to take Fort Duquesne. He marched from Williamsburg, Virginia with 2500 untrained militia, with Major Washington as aide-de-camp, to within ten miles of Fort Duquesne, where the superior numbers of French fell upon them, killing 900, including Braddock. For the next two years, while London fiddled, the war went downhill in America.

The French told the Indians that the great king Louis, who sent the sun from the east across the Big Waters, was troubled in his heart by injustices done to Indians by Englishmen. He was probably far more troubled with winning the war against Britain. They told the Indians that Louis wanted to show his love to his Indian children by giving them presents of guns, hatchets, knives, and blankets, so they could drive the English back out of the Indians' sacred hunting grounds.

The Indians may not have been deceived by French protestations of affection for them, but it appeared to be a good deal for them, so they blackened their faces, painted their bodies, took up the hatchet, and enthusiastically set out on the warpath to take some English scalps.

Soon the valleys of the Alleghenies rang with war whoops, and the settlers there and in the Shenandoah Valley made a mad rush eastward, although a surprising number of the hardy Scots-Irish stayed to tough it out. They had come across the Atlantic to get a plot of land they could call their own, and no heathen savages were going to chase them off their claims. A lot of them died, but a lot more of them successfully defended their holdings throughout the war, and Pontiac's War which followed it. For those who stayed, it meant that they had to be on guard every minute of the day, listening, watching, tensely waiting. A loaded musket was always near at hand when chopping firewood, plowing, or rocking the baby. At night the pioneers slept with their muskets in their hands. To be careless, to let down one's guard for a moment, might mean death or capture; given a choice most would have chosen instant death, for capture was often followed by horrible and unimaginable torture and slow death. Many captured children were taken into the tribe and reared as Indians, and never returned to white communities.

Meanwhile, back in Philadelphia, pacifist Quakers refused to put up money for defense of the frontier. Alarmed German and Scots-Irish farmers abandoned their isolationism and got into politics, put up candidates for the Assembly, and took control of Pennsylvania politics. They immediately voted funds for defense. In 1755 a line of forts was begun, starting at Easton, and going westward past Reading, Lancaster, Columbia, and York, stopping at a point about twenty-five miles west of Bedford, on a line roughly followed much later by U.S. Highway 30. A fort was placed each twenty miles, and a blockhouse each five miles in between forts. When there was a threat of Indians, settlers would, if they were lucky and made it, dash to the nearest blockhouse. Troops regularly marched between the forts, collecting and escorting the settlers in the blockhouses to the greater safety of the forts. When the danger passed, they would return to their burned cabins, dead cattle, and destroyed crops, and then start all over.

During the next two years the French won every encounter with the British in America. In 1757, William Pitt became Prime Minister. He said to King George II; "My Lord, I know that I can save this country, and that no one else can." Impressed, the King didn't see any more likely candidates for the job, so he gave it to him. He was a man of tremendous energy, and set about to reorganize the army and navy, redirected their strategies, and the British began trashing the French in

196

Europe. They even drove the French out of India, and proclaimed: "Now the sun never sets on the British Empire." Reports that he received from the American Colonies led him to decide the French had to be removed from the Ohio Valley.

In 1758, he ordered 6000 troops, mostly Scots, under General John Forbes, to cut a road for moving cannons through the forests of western Pennsylvania to Fort Duquesne, attack and take it, and drive the French back to French Canada. Guerrilla war came easily to the Scottish troops who had for centuries conducted hit-and-run raids against the English, back home in Scotland. An army of axemen, protected by red-coated troops, armed with their Brown Bess muskets, started at Harrisburg to chop a path, or rough road, parallel to the line of forts and blockhouses. Everything up to moderately large trees were cut to a height of nine inches, but smaller ones were left at fifteen inches -- low enough for cannon axles to pass over them. The great majestic chestnuts, oaks, beeches, and maples required too much work to cut, so the road just went around them, just as they did with large boulders. Bridges that would require constant guarding weren't built; they crossed rivers at fords.

The French at Fort Duquesne were receiving daily reports from Indian scouts that thousands of British troops were approaching with many cannons. Courage of Indian warriors is legendary, but however courageous they may have been, foolhardy they were not. They would never engage an enemy when they were outnumbered, and they never got into a fight they didn't think they could win. To fight a losing battle and die was a waste of precious manpower. Seeing what was in store for them, the Indian allies of the French quietly left one night and returned home, leaving the French hopelessly outnumbered. When they awoke and looked at their clearly untenable situation, they shrugged their shoulders in Gallic fashion, set charges of gunpowder under the fort, and blew it up. They then rode off to Canada.

The French never regained the initiative, and during the year 1759, the British took the French forts on the Great Lakes, Quebec, and finally Montreal. Pitt's plans were equally successful elsewhere in the world, and in 1763, with the signing of the Treaty of Paris, Britain reigned over a great empire with lands on every continent. In North America, she now ruled all of Canada, the Ohio country, and all of the land west of the British colonies to the Mississippi River, where Spanish claims began.

General Forbes never had to use the cannons he went to so much trouble for, but the Forbes Road later became a main highway across Pennsylvania. Although they may have put French fortunes into decline, the Indians were quite a different matter. To them, the English had always been enemies. For Britain to utilize the newly acquired lands, they had to first make peace with the Indians. At a fort along the Mohawk River in New York, they sat down with the leaders of several Indian nations to work out a treaty. They promised the Indians that all white men would

197

be removed from all lands west of the Alleghenies, and that the French forts would be destroyed and the sites abandoned. This proved to be but one more of the many shameful episodes of broken promises that white men made to Indians. The British immediately went to work and rebuilt the fort at the forks of the Ohio and named it Fort Pitt, and rather than the settlers abandoning the lands west of the Alleghenies, an unprecedented land rush began, and in 1763, while the Treaty of Paris was being signed in Europe, Pontiac, chief of the Ottowas, led almost all the Indian nations in northwestern territories against the whites. They destroyed every military post in the entire area save for Fort Pitt and Detroit, and as far east as Bedford. Finally, Colonel Henry Bouquet devised a tactic (actually, he finally began listening to what frontiersmen had been saying all along) of developing highly trained men to seek out and kill Indian warriors one at a time, and to destroy Indian villages and crops. The Scots-Irish pioneers formed groups of "rangers" who fought brilliantly in campaigns of their own, moving swiftly, striking, and disappearing. Late in 1764, the fighting stopped, and relative peace returned, although it was not until well after the American Revolution that it became safe enough for families to live in isolated cabins west of the Alleghenies. In the face of superior arms and numbers of whites, Indians gave up their lands and moved westward.

If Great Britain had not so profoundly mismanaged the American Colonies we might well have remained British to this day and been proud of it. But the Brits really blew it! It took them only sixteen years after the Treaty of Paris to anger the Colonies to the point of rebellion. Even after the Declaration of Independence, it is possible that they would have been able to settle things peaceably, but Lord North and his aristocratic cronies in Parliament were unwilling to sit down and have a sensible talk with the bloody rebels. They underestimated Colonial determination, they underestimated the effect of France's involvement in the conflict, they underestimated the size of the catastrophic loss if the Colonies got away, they underestimated the amount of military effort required to put down the rebellion -- in fact, it wasn't so much that the Colonies, with the invaluable help of France, *won* the war as it was that British blundering just plain lost the war for them.

Development Of The Pennsylvania Road

THE FORBES ROAD WAS USED BY TROOPS of both sides during the Revolution, but nothing was done to improve it. The stumps left when the road was first cut were no obsacle to cannon carriages, but civilian wagons were too low slung to use it. But it still could be used by packhorses, and with peace once more, packhorse traffic between Philadelphia, Lancaster, and Pittsburgh began to boom. Slowly at first, it began to be improved. Farmers along the route worked on pulling the stumps out of the road in lieu of tax payments, and men convicted of misdemeanors such as drunkenness in public were sentenced to grub out, say, three stumps or boulders. Merchants clamored to have the road made fit for wagons, and the Pennsylvania Assembly put up some money to do it.

Probably the first person to cross the mountains and get to Pittsburgh was Dr. Johann Schoepf, who did it in a two-wheeled chaise, in 1783, a trip most people thought to be impossible. In 1795, one could make it from Philadelphia to Pittsburgh in three weeks during most of the year. Stage coach service was slower in becoming established, and by 1804, the western terminus of stage lines was Shippensburg. It was extended to Pittsburgh in 1811.

Some immigrant German wagonmakers in a little village near Lancaster began making a magnificent wagon especially to conquer primitive roads. Known as the Conestoga Wagon, after the name of the village where the new industry was born, they soon had a specially bred great, black horse to draw them over the truly awful roads. Teams of Conestoga wagon horses hitched to Conestoga wagons became the vehicle of choice for reliable delivery of the goods. The wagons were high at each end and slung low in the middle, so loads didn't shift about on steep ascents or descents. Iron parts were simple and strong. A lightweight cover of heavy linen was stretched over steam-bent ash bows that protected loads and passengers from the elements. The proper wood was used for each part -- oak, hickory, ash, poplar, and pine. Every part was strong, but no heavier than need be. They could carry about three tons when four horses were harnessed to them. And they were painted up nicely, with reds, blues, and whites. The quality of the first ones was not changed for a hundred years, until they had delivered the last settler to Oregon or California areas to which railroads had not yet been extended.

They carried both freight and passengers. When fitted for passengers, four boards were installed across the width of the wagon, and three passengers could occupy each seat. Passengers often preferred to walk beside the wagon, rather than have their spines dislocated by sitting on the pitching seat. When the wagon got stuck, which it was almost certain to do every few miles, everybody was expected to hop out and put their backs to the task of getting unstuck. Swampy stretches of the road were paved with logs laid parallel and crossways of the road, and were known as "corduroy roads," real bone breakers, they were, but at least wagons didn't get stuck in the bogs upon which the logs rested. It wasn't a mode of travel for well-dressed passengers who expected comfort.

Wherever a fort had been built inns and taverns soon sprang up beside them. By any standards, they were at their best quite primitive. Sometimes overnight stops were made at farmhouses where passengers on wagons or packhorse drivers could put up overnight, if the farmer had room and the inclination. Typically, the inns consisted of a central dining hall and two large rooms on opposite sides for sleeping -- one for men and the other for women. Smaller inns might not even have any bedrooms, in which case everyone slept on the bar-room floor in their own bedroll. Wherever beds were provided, they were likely to be shared, catch as catch can, the washed and unwashed, ill and healthy, drunk and sober, several together in a bed, but at least, of the same sex. Food could be whatever the innkeeper had on hand, served family style on a large table in the central hall, and the most aggressive and ill-mannered eaters usually getting more of the best portions than those guests with manners. In the evening, there might be a fiddler to play for dancing. In time, the inns improved, and for those who could afford it, private rooms and good dining became available.

A new breed of folk heroes came about with the cross-state road and the Conestoga wagon. He was the "muleskinner" who drove the great wagons and giant horses. They were a rough, tough lot; they drank a lot, and swore wonderfully, danced all night at inns, or until they were too drunk to stay on their feet. Some of the more colorful individuals became widely known, and were sought out and treated with admiration and respect wherever they were. It was considered an honor to be asked by the driver to sit beside him on the high seat behind the span of four horses.

The River Highways of Pennsylvania

When the French were in charge of things in western Pennsylvania and the area soon to be called the Northwest Territory, they ringed the Great Lakes' southern shores with forts to prevent incursions of the English, not Indians. They got on famously with Indians, for they were not interested in westward expansion of the lands they held in eastern Canada along the Saint Lawrence River. North America was, for them, one grand, wild, fur farm, which they exploited fully. Most of the fur they shipped to Europe was brought in by Indians, although no small number of French trappers lived in the forests, too. But these Frenchmen didn't try to take lands from the Indians; instead, they lived almost as the Indians did themselves. Indeed, they often lived with Indians, sharing their lifestyle, including their hardships in winter. In turn, the Indians taught them how to live in the forests as well as one could expect to live there, and more importantly, they taught them how to find and trap the fur-bearing animals they sought.

One of the forts the French built was at Presque Isle (really, a peninsula), where Erie now stands. Another was Fort Le Boeuf on the upper reaches of French Creek, about one day's march from Presque Isle on a primitive road that was hardly more than a trail. Waterford now is on this site. From there one could travel clear to New Orleans without leaving his canoe. At the junction of French Creek and the Allegheny River, where Franklin is today, the French extended their influence south to the junction of the Allegheny and Monongahela Rivers, where it becomes the Ohio River. Here they built Fort Duquesne to put teeth into their claim to the Ohio River and its contiguous lands. When Fort Duquesne was built and garrisoned it was necessary to build a road between it and the Great Lakes in order to move troops and supplies. The waterway route was not always very practical because the rivers were sometimes frozen or in flood.

After the French were defeated, the road was little used, and during the Revolution it was nearly reclaimed by the forest. It may have been that the McCrays used what was left of this old military road in 1796 to travel from Washington County to upper Allegheny County where the Holland Land Company had put it about that they were offering bargains in land. Everyone agrees they made the trip by horseback or shanks mare.

Once settlers had arrived in numbers, freight and passengers were carried up and down the Allegheny River and French Creek. A unique shallow draft boat known as the flatboat, for its flat bottom, was developed for this task. Flatboats were the conveyance usually used by new settlers headed for Kentucky by way of the Ohio River. Flatboats were the freight trains of Colonial America west of the Allegheny Mountains until the arrival of canals and railroads.

Flatboats were built in boatyards along the Monongahela and Allegheny Rivers, and when used for passenger traffic down the Ohio and Mississippi Rivers they usually made a one-way trip to the point of disembarkation, where they were broken up and the lumber re-used to build houses. It was thought to be too difficult and unprofitable to push an empty boat back upstream with no cargo or passengers aboard.

They were about sixty feet long, pointed at each end, with a heavy wooden keel and a rudder at the stern. An open cockpit at the bow was equipped with five thwartwise seats for a crew to sit on and row when going upstream. The remainder of the boat was decked so goods were stored below, and a cabin for shelter in foul weather was provided amidships. Planks were laid on each side of the boat parallel to the gunwales for poling. Two men, facing aft at the bow, would each set a long pole into the river bottom and start pushing, walking aft, hand over hand until reaching the end of his pole, thus propelling the boat forward. As each pusher went aft another pair of pushers would start from the bow with poles, and in shallow places three pairs of pushers could operate. Some boats were equipped with a mast and sails, so when wind and currents favored, and the river was wide enough for tacking, the crew could relax.

Another method of propulstion was "bushwhacking," whereby the craft was pulled upstream by the crew grasping overhanging tree branches and pulling the boat upstream. Going upstream was hard work by any method, and passengers were expected to do their share of rowing, poling or bushwhacking. In time, towpaths were built on riverbanks, and boats were then towed upstream by teams of horses.

201

The Conquest Of The Wilderness

It is difficult for us to imagine the grandeur and sweep of the
Pennsylvania wilderness that had never known the ring of an axe. The
forest had begun to grow more than 25,000 years ago when the Ice Age
ended, and nothing had occurred to inhibit its growth. Centuries-old
conifer and hardwoods, trunks of which often exceeded ten feet in dia-
meter soared over a hundred feet skyward, blocking sunlight to everything
below, making it a land of twilight. The forest floor was a silent,
dark, carpet of humus and tangles of fallen tree trunks. Occasional
small clearings occurred here and there where a dead giant had crash-
ed down, taking with it branches of nearby living trees, allowing sunlight
to reach the ground for a few years, and here seeds might grow and produce saplings before branches shut off the life-giving sun again.

Although it might seem to be a very quiet place to a human walking
in the forest, there was plenty of animal life there. The land was rich
in wildlife, from mice to moose (mouse, mice--moose, meese?). Rivers
were alive with fish and beavers, the latter being the marvelous natural
engineer that created ponds and an ecosystem for semi-aquatic birds and
mammals. But there were no songbirds, only raptors, vultures, and
ravens; songbirds arrived when the forests were cleared. The wilderness was a marvelously balanced life system, where each living thing was
depended upon by some other living thing.

The gloomy forests filled the superstitious settlers with dread.
They imagined that gnomes, devils and wee folk dwelt there, prepared to
work spells and do much mischief to honest Christians, just as they did
in the peat bogs of Ireland and Germany. They attacked the trees first
of all, since they were the great enemy that prevented the growth of
wheat, oats, corn, and flax. Wild animals had been put there by God for
men to dominate and to hunt for sport; besides, the larger carnivores
got into pig pens and cattle barns and killed stock, and it never occurred
to anyone that the bears and mountain lions had to eat, too, and that men
had hunted and killed their natural food, so they were forced to eat the
cattle, sheep and swine that men brought with them.

Terms like "conservation" and "balance of nature" were unheard of,
and wouldn't have made any impression on settlers anyway, because they
saw no limit to the trees, animals, or land. What we today would regard
as wanton waste was then thought to be what God had been pleased to place
men on earth to do -- to "tame the wilderness." Men have always had
trouble understanding God, and He has seemed to be pretty unreasonable
at times.

The supply of fur-bearing animals seemed inexhaustible then. A
hunter could rather easily find plenty of bear, woods bison, wolverines,
otters, deer, elk, beaver, wolves, and panthers, and although the settler
didn't exactly seek them out, there were also plenty of large rattle-
snakes and copperhead snakes. Rivers teemed with trout, bass, perch,
catfish, pike, and gigantic sturgeon, enough to bring cries of anguish
to a modern sports fisherman, for anyone could catch fish as long as he
wanted to wet a line. So many reports survive of people catching twenty-
pound perch, black bass, and trout, and catfish larger than fifty pounds,
and six-hundred-and-fifty-pound sturgeons, that we can believe they were
not just greatly exaggerated fish stories.

Eighteenth century writers have recorded in their journals witness-
ing turkeys killed weighing 30 to 40 pounds, and grouse, partridge, and
pheasants of sizes and weights double or triple those in today's wilds.
We all have read accounts of spring and fall bird migrations of geese,
swans, ducks and unimaginable numbers of carrier pigeons, when the skies
were darkened for days and days as the flocks swept overhead. Wherever
carrier pigeons roosted overnight, they left beds of droppings a foot
or more deep, and with their weight of numbers, broke off great tree
branches.

It usually took only about twenty years to destroy the wilderness
that stood between the settler and the development of his farm. He
methodically devoted himself to cutting and burning the trees and killing off the game. The great black woods bison, a relative of the smaller plains bison of the West, which was no midget, could weigh a ton, and
was once plentiful in the East, but was extinct by 1800. Venomous snakes,
deprived of their woodland homes, moved onto the farms and inhabited
houses and barns, causing many injuries and deaths. Many other species
became locally extinct.

Here and there in isolated spots around the United States, a few
acres of virgin wilderness have been preserved, where we can still go
and stand in awe at the forest that once stretched almost unbroken clear
across the continent from the Atlantic to the Pacific. All but a few
acres of the equally magnificent millions of acres of prairie grasslands
of the midwest were plowed under more than a hundred years ago, although
efforts are now being made to restore it in many localities.

There is one tract of virgin mountain woodland in the Great Smoky
Mountain National Park near Asheville, North Carolina, unchanged except
for a paved road through it, the absence of wildlife, and the occasional
intrusive sound of jet aircraft overhead.

Alice Morrison pointed out that in Warren County, Pennsylvania,
"Heart's Content," a twenty-acre tract of virgin forest exists, "with
white pines and hemlocks so tall it is hard to see the tops." She wrote:
"Another good area to see virgin forest is in the Tionesta Scenic Area,
near Marienville, Forest County, but it was partially destroyed by the

tornadoes of 1985. There is an interesting article about this in the November, 1986, issue of *Natural History*. It was almost impossible to get the Irish to work in the woods, so many Swedes came to Warren County. The Scotch-Irish were another breed of cats...they went anywhere, and were always the first on the frontiers."

North-central Pennsylvania is today's source of most of the wild cherry used in manufacture of furniture. When the first-growth pine and hemlock was cut in the nineteenth century and early in this century, the seedlings that sprang up were largely the black cherry, and they came to maturity within the last twenty years. The State of Pennsylvania leases the land for what it euphemistically calls "harvesting."

The typical pioneer arrived in early spring if at all possible at the site he had previously selected the previous year to build his farm buildings and house. He might also have done some clearing of trees. A desirable site would be at the foot of a hill, providing shelter from winds, and so "everything might come to the house down hill." He tied bells to his horse and cow and let them forage for themselves, but he rounded them up every day and led them back to the camp, so they wouldn't get too wild. He would then put up his south-facing lean-to, called a "half-faced camp," made of two pairs of forked poles with a ridge-pole between them resting on the forks. The two triangular ends were closed with sticks and brush, and the roof poles were covered with reed thatch or animal skins. A fire maintained on the ground before it, with a reflecting wall of stone, provided direct and reflected heat for warmth and cooking, as well as protection from predatory animals. A log cabin would come later, but he had more pressing things to attend to first.

It was primarily important that he work very hard and rapidly to get enough land cleared and seeds planted to grow enough corn and pumpkins for the coming winter. Pumpkins were a major crop for pioneers; the golden fruit was cut up and dried, and it was a staple of their diet, used to make bread, puddings, and a cake that may not have been very sweet, but was quite nutritious. The entire summer was devoted to getting in the winter's food and providing proper storage for it; they dried and smoked and salted meat and fish, gathered nuts and certain roots for flavoring, medicines, and making tea. Everything, even their lives, depended upon the success of the summer's work.

Once they got some land cleared and a crop growing, and had put up some rude shelters and fences for the animals, a log cabin was "raised." It was a frontier social occasion for nearby neighbors. Nobody's labor could be hired, but everyone turned out to help, knowing that they could count on reciprocal help when they needed it. Neighbors came bearing food and axes, and the host supplied a stack of cut-to-size logs and a jug of whiskey. The twelve-by-sixteen-foot cabin was usually erected in one day, without the use of nails, bricks, or mortar, and the axe was the only tool used. It wasn't de-luxe. It had a single room and fireplace and overhead was a half-loft for storage and space for children to sleep, and it was a big improvement over the half-faced camp. A wooden puncheon floor was a luxury that might later be added.

After a year or so, with the farm established and all the things done that were absolutely essential, the better class of pioneers built a three-or four-room house of logs to replace the cabin. It was made of square-hewn logs, carefully fitted with dovetail and mortise-and-tenon joints, with nicer finishing details, such as door and window frames, more and larger windows with glass even, if there was enough money at hand, interior stairways instead of climbing pegs set into the walls, and perhaps two fireplaces; one for cooking, and one for heating the rest of the house. The dirt floor of the cabin would be upgraded to a wooden puncheon floor, or even to a plank floor if there was a sawmill nearby, permitting home-made carpets to be laid. Such grand things as rugs and carpets were rare until large-scale manufacturing of cotton was common, because hand-spun and woven home-made cloth was too precious to be used to make hooked rugs, and was worn and patched until there was little left of it.

There are still standing quite a number of these 200-year-old log houses in rural areas where pioneers settled long ago. At one time it was thought to be a nice touch to apply wooden siding over the logs, but now that they have become sought-after treasures, the siding is usually removed to reveal the hand-hewn faced-off logs and corner joints. Sharp eyes can locate many log houses still in use in many rural areas today, especially in West Virginia and western North Carolina. Near Martinsville, Virginia, a score or more of loghouses stand on a short two-mile stretch of Virginia Route 647.

CHAPTER NINE

THE FIRST TEN YEARS IN AMERICA

James And Ellen (Bell) McCray

JAMES McCRAY, THE PROGENITOR OF THE McCrays of Northwestern Pennsylvania, was born about 1735, probably in Ayrshire, Scotland. Ayrshire
has recently been renamed Strathclyde. We believe he was born in Ayrshire because that county was, and still is, the home to more McCreas
than any other Scottish county. Because the spelling "McCray" is unknown,
or nearly so, in Scotland and England, and is not uncommon in Ireland, we
think James was born James McCrea, and may have changed the spelling in
Ireland, or even after arriving in America.

What do we know, and what are we to believe about James McCray, the
elder, first of four successive James McCrays? More than a half-dozen
people have written about him and his wife, Ellen Bell, but none have
told us where they obtained the facts about the pair that they set forth.
Moreover, many of them differ on major historical points, and we have no
way of knowing which chronicler got it right.

Conflicting details raise these questions:

(1) Did Old James marry, have two sons, then later re-marry and
    have six more children? Or:

(2) Did he marry but once and have eight children? Or:

(3) Did he have but six children in one marriage?

(4) Did he come to America before 1775 and fight in the Amer-
    ican Revolution? Or:

(5) Did he come to America in 1777 or 1778 and fight in the
    Revolution, or did he settle in Westmoreland County, Pennsyl-
    vania before Washington County was created? Or:

(6) Did he live in Ireland until the end of hostilities and
    arrive in America in 1784, three years after Yorktown?

(7) Did he first settle near the Susquehanna River in Cumber-
    land County, Pennsylvania, or did he first settle in Wash-
    ington County, Pennsylvania?

Two McCray histories that have come to hand state that James married
first an unknown woman, and they had two sons, John and Joseph, who remained in Ireland. The first wife died and James then remarried Ellen
(or Nellie--Ellen spelled more-or-less backward) Bell, and they had six

206

children. Doctor Fred McCray, who wrote perhaps the first McCray family history, listed eight children of James and Ellen (Bell) McCray, and did not mention an earlier marriage. Percie McCray compiled a list of several hundred descendants from Old James and Ellen, and his very first item on the list is a first marriage and birth of John and Joseph McCray, followed by a second marriage to Ellen Bell and the subsequent birth of six children. A later short history, not reproduced here, repeats the two-marriage version.

Although hostilities between British and American armies made it unlikely that Old James came to America between 1774 and 1783, the story persists that James McCray arrived in America in time to fight in the American Revolution. It is even claimed that they arrived in 1778, the year of Valley Forge, when Philadelphia, New York, Baltimore, and the entire Atlantic coast was occupied by British forces. I was assured by a military historian at the U.S. Army Library in Washington, D.C., that there was no civil travel between Great Britain and America between the years 1774 and 1783. Unless someone finds out that the McCray family went first to Canada and then crossed into Colonial New England and made their way through British lines without being stopped, it is almost certain that Old James did not come from Ireland to America during the Revolution.

Various McCray researchers have found that James McCray was in Philadelphia in 1771. In a book of German indentures for that year* is found the following entry:

"Nov. 30, 1771--McCray, James, from the port of (blank), indentured to William Reynolds, Southwark (a village s. of Philadelphia, now a suburb), Occupation, Apprentice, taught the art, trade and mystery of hatmaker, have one year evening schooling and have all necessaries, Term, seven years, Amount (blank)."

Invariably, upon running across this entry, we all suppress a cheer, for here at last is our James, even with the correct spelling! But upon recalling some facts, we realize that in 1771 *our* James would have been but five years old, not a candidate for apprenticeship to a hatmaker. Nor would it have been his father, Old James, for he would have been somewhere above age 35, also not eligible because of age. The Pennsylvania Archives list a raft of James McCrays and James McCreas in Philadelphia during Revolutionary and Post-Revolutionary times, but there is not a shred of evidence that any of them were *our* James. The National

---

Record Of Indentures in Philadelphia, 1771-1773; Mayor John Gibson, 1771-72 and Mayor William Fisher, 1773, Pennsylvania German-American Society. Genealogical Publishing Company, Inc., Baltimore, Md., 1907, p. 34.

Archives in Washington, D.C. has three muster list sheets for two James McCrays and one James McCrea, all of whom were in different companies of militia, and even if they were all the same person, just who exactly was he? All we have for evidence is the name. The first Federal Census of 1790 lists seven James McCrays in the first thirteen states.

Back to Ireland and Old James.

Ellen McCray was the mother of six children, say most accounts. They were: William, Elizabeth (usually given as "Betsey," the common nickname of that time), James, Samuel, George and Robert, in various chronological orders. The family moved to Ireland, some say to County Monaghan. One relates that they sailed from Newry on the U.S.S. Constituion, the famed "Old Ironsides," and they spent three months crossing the Atlantic. Newry was frequently a port of embarkation by the Scots-Irish, but never on the Constitution. Her keel was laid in Boston in 1792, and the tough old oaken battleship was not commissioned until 1798. It never visited Ireland, and was not used as a passenger ship at any time.

They landed at either Baltimore or Philadelphia, take your choice. Most Scots-Irish entered Delaware Bay and disembarked at Philadelphia, but some landed at Baltimore on the Chesapeake Bay. From whichever port, at least the five eldest McCrays made their way to Toboyne Township, Cumberland County, Pennsylvania. Although we've found no clear evidence that Old James and Ellen also went there, they probably did. Most family histories have it that they landed in America in 1784, the year after the signing of the Treaty of Paris that ended the American Revolution.

At that time George would have been age sixteen, Samuel twelve, and Robert just eight. We have recorded evidence that the four brothers and their sister were living in Shermans Valley until about 1793. William and James, the two eldest men of the six children, are listed in tax rolls as taxpayers, and it is uncertain if this James was Old James or his son. The younger James would have been age twenty-one in 1788, when that name appeared in Cumberland County tax records for the first time.

A church record (See next chapter for details of the McCrays as members of Centre Presbyterian Church.), undated but known to have been prepared after 1795, lists several names with the notation "Removed." Among them were; "James McCree, Elleonar, James, Will'm, Sam'l," and "Geo. McCree, Jean." One of the two Jameses would have been Old James, for his grandson, James (III), was born in Washington County, Pennsylvania, in 1796, about three years after the parents, James and Eleanor (Townsley) McCray, had left Shermans Valley, in either 1793 or 1794. The fact that Ellen McCray's name was not included in this list may indicate that she was dead by the time the family moved away from Shermans Valley.

Sometime between February 4, 1793, when Samuel, James, and George McCrea were listed as residents within the bounds of the 3rd Battalion,

Cumberland County Militia*, and June 15, 1794, when Joseph McCray was born to James and Eleanor (Townsley) McCray in Washington County, Pennsylvania, the McCrays left Shermans Valley and moved across the state to Washington County, all except for Elizabeth who was by then the bride of William Reed. The Reeds were then living in Lycoming County, Pennsylvania, but they later moved to Erie County to join the rest of the McCray family, all of whom were then living there.

More than one family history states that the McCrays lived in Westmoreland County, while others say it was Washington County. Joseph and James (III) McCray said they were born in Washington County, and George Carey repeated this same story (See Page 251). It may be that residents kept calling it Westmoreland after Washington County was created.

Old James was alive and well in 1797 or 1798, for it was reported by one of his grandsons later that he travelled at least once from Washington to Erie County, a journey of over 150 miles through wilderness trails, to help his sons, William and James, build farm buildings. Robert, the youngest of the six, may have stayed in Washington County with his parents until they died, after which he came to Erie County and bought a 200-acre tract near the tracts of James, William and Samuel, in 1801. We have no knowledge of any will left by Old James, nor do we know where he is buried, but it was undoubtedly in Washington County.

-0-

A year after he had roundly defeated the Indians in 1763 at the Battle of Bushy Run, during Pontiac's War, Col. Henry Bouquet led an expedition down the Ohio River as far as the Muskingum River. He and his men so impressed the natives that they realized the white men were coming in numbers too great for them to resist, and they sued for peace. Now southwestern Pennsylvania was opened for settlement. It became the home of more Scots-Irish than any of the other areas they migrated to and

* All able-bodied men in Pennsylvania were required to serve some time in the Pennsylvania Militia.

** It may be well to point out that there have been five Treaties of Paris, three of which involved us. They were:

1. The French and Indian War, 1763. Also called the Versailles Treaty, not to be confused with the Versailles Treaty ending WW II.

2. The American Revolution, 1783

3. The Spanish-American War, 1898

settled in. Most came from the valleys of the Juniata and the Susquehanna Rivers in Pennsylvania, others came from central Maryland, and not a few came from the Shenandoah and upper Potomac valleys of Virginia.

Even before the French and Indian War, the boundary between Pennsylvania and Virginia was in dispute, and as both colonies grew putes became more and more acrimonious. The regions along the Monongahela River became a legal no-man's land, for both colonies claimed overlapping areas there, and both colonies granted deeds sometimes for the same tracts. Even after the boundary line was established in 1768 by the Mason-Dixon Line, land disputes were in courts for many years. In spite of the Mason-Dixon settlement, conflicting claims persisted until finally, in 1779, the two states made a final agreement and the border between the states was drawn as we know it today. Two years later, Westmoreland County was broken up into Washington, Armstrong, Indiana, Allegheny, and Fayette Counties. Later, Washington, Allegheny, and Armstrong Counties were further subdivided.

It may or may not have been significant that other McCray families were already living in Washington County when Old James and his family arrived there in the 1790's. It is tempting to think that Old James went there to be near relatives he knew were there. These other McCray families came from either the Shenandoah Valley or from some other unidentified place to the east along the Atlantic Coast.

-O-

In 1991, the Church of Jesus Christ of the Latter Day Saints completed an alphabetical listing of names in the Old Parochial Register (the OPR), an official British publication listing parish records by the various parishes in random order. The new list has names in alphabetical order for each county, Scots who married or were christened, extending back into the sixteenth century. Although hundreds, perhaps thousands, of names are contained in the list, it is by no means complete. No one knows how many records have been lost.

An examination of the lists for Ayreshire and Kirkubright failed to turn up the marriage of James McCrea, McCrae, McCree or McCraith to Ellen Bell or to any other lady named Bell. However, it settled, for me, that our name was McCrea, possibly McCrae, while in Scotland, and the spelling we use today was adopted after they left Scotland. There is considerable evidence that it was changed in about 1795, after their arrival in America.

210

John McCrea

Joseph McCrea

Elizabeth McCrea
b. 1762, Scotland
d. 1848, Clarion Co., Pa
m. William E. Reed

William McCrea
b. 1764, Scotland
d. 1836, Crawford Co., Pa.
m. Nancy Miles

James McCrea*
b. c1730, Scotland
d. after 1797, Wash'n
   Co., Pa.
m. (1) Unknown ————

   (2) Ellen Bell ————————

James McCrea
b. 1765, Scotland
d. 1839, Erie Co., Pa.
m. (1) Eleanor Townsley
   (2) Nancy --?--

George McCray
b. 1768, Ireland
d. after 1850, Crawford Co., Pa.
m. Jean Murray

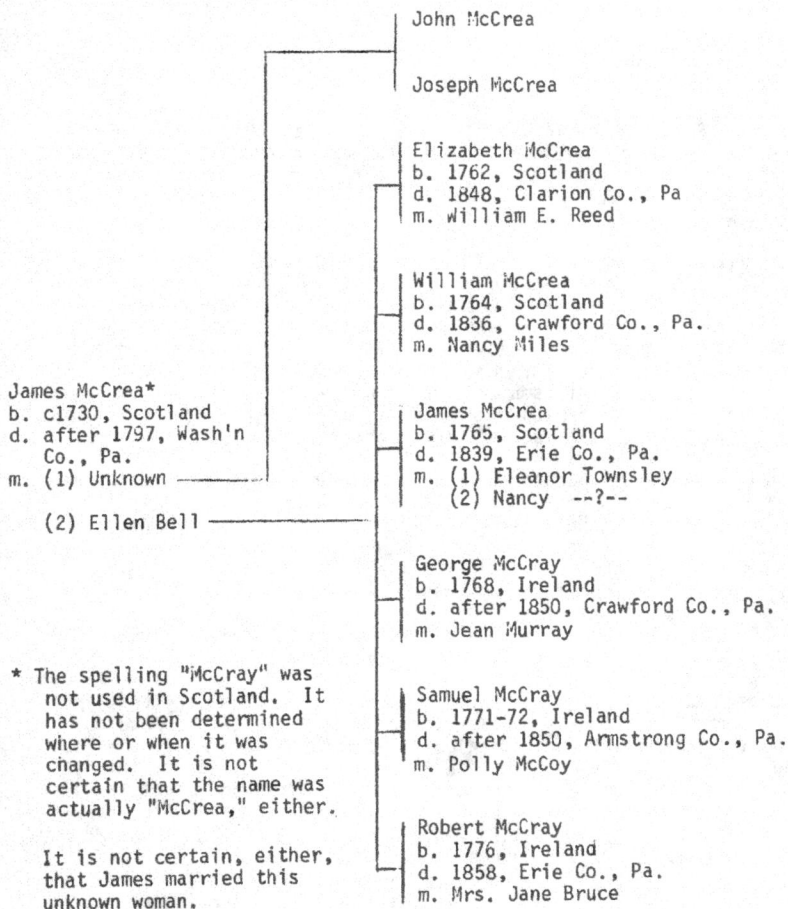

* The spelling "McCray" was
  not used in Scotland. It
  has not been determined
  where or when it was
  changed. It is not
  certain that the name was
  actually "McCrea," either.

  It is not certain, either,
  that James married this
  unknown woman.

Samuel McCray
b. 1771-72, Ireland
d. after 1850, Armstrong Co., Pa.
m. Polly McCoy

Robert McCray
b. 1776, Ireland
d. 1858, Erie Co., Pa.
m. Mrs. Jane Bruce

-THE FIRST TWO GENERATIONS-

211

James and Eleanor (Townsley) McCray

JAMES McCRAY, SON OF "OLD JAMES" and Ellen Bell McCray, was born in Scotland in 1766. The year of his birth was arrived at from gravestone inscriptions in the McCray Cemetery in Concord Township, Erie County, Pennsylvania. His grave marker stone has it that he died December 17, 1839, at age 73.

The memorial stone is fairly new, and I've not been able to learn who erected it, or how this person knew his age and the date of his death. Apparently, this person was unaware that James McCray married twice, for the stone has the name of his first wife, Eleanor, but not the name of the second wife, Nancy. Nor was the person correct in putting on the stone that he was a Revolutionary War soldier. However, the year of his birth, 1766, fits nicely between the birthyears of his brothers, William, in 1764, and George, in 1768, so I'm inclined to accept 1766 as the correct year of James's birth.

Sometime between 1766 and 1768, Old James and Ellen took their family to Ireland, never to return to Scotland. According to family legends they lived in Monaghan, but whether it was County Monaghan or Monaghan, the county town* hasn't been made clear. While the family lived in Ireland, George McCray was born in 1768, Samuel McCray was born in 1772, and the sixth child, Robert McCray, was born in 1776.

If Old James had any notion he'd like to go to America, by the time Robert was born it was too late to make the trip, for the shot heard 'round the world had been fired at Lexington the year before Robert was born, and the only way the McCray men could have taken any part in the War of American Independence would have been to have come here on a British warship, without their female family members, and wearing a redcoated British uniform and carrying a Brown Bess musket. Civil travel between Britain and the rebellious colonies was halted for eight years with the onset of hostilities. Old James had to wait until after Yorktown, and according to most family legends, he did just that. The McCray family seems to have arrived in America in 1784.

At least one family legend has it that the McCray family arrived in America at Philadelphia, while at least one other account has them landing at Baltimore. No records were kept of new arrivals to America up until about 1790, and those coming from Ireland were not seen as immigrants, but as British subjects, and therefore not immigrants at all. It is a fact, however, that most Scots-Irish arrivals debarked at Philadelphia, the port where their Presbyterianism was not sneered at.

*"County Town" in Great Britain is analogous to our "County Seat."

The route taken by pioneers westward to lands beyond the Susquehanna River was a well-travelled road through Lancaster ("Lank-str", not "Lan-caster") to Carlisle. The road later became the Lincoln Highway, and with the establishment of U.S. highways, it became U.S. 30. It was probably the first inter-city road to be paved using the technique invented by the Scottish roadbuilder, McAdam, and known as a "McAdamized Road." By standards of the time, the road was a fine road and was heavily used. Those headed for the Shenandoah Valley of Virginia and the Piedmont lands of the Carolinas went through Lancaster and continued on in a southwestern direction, crossing the Susquehanna River at Columbia. The McCrays, and others with a destination to one of the numerous valleys on the western side of the Susquehanna, turned from Lancaster to the road leading northwest through Middletown to the burgeoning town that grew beside a ferry boat operated by John Harris across the Susquehanna River. Harrisburg was destined to become Pennsylvania's capital city.

Also, the frontier was being pushed northward along the eastern bank of the Susquehanna into today's Lycoming County. William Reed, who was to become the bridegroom of Elizabeth McCray, was a settler of that region. At that time, Lycoming County had not been created out of Northumberland County. Tax records of 1787, County of Northumberland, show that William Reed was the owner of a large tract of 444 acres, and was taxed one pound, seventeen shillings and four pence for the land, plus a pound each for a horse and a cow. Compared to other taxpayers, Reed was one of the most prosperous landowners in the area.

Shermans Valley was the destination of the McCrays. Located in Cumberland County about 30 miles north of Carlisle and across a rather formidable foothill of the Allegheny Mountains, they probably entered the valley where Sherman's Creek empties into the Susquehanna almost at the same point where the Juniata River's waters join with the Susquehanna's. Cumberland County was then a vast area stretching west to the Ohio line, except for north-central and northwestern Pennsylvania (See map, P. 214). In 1784 the "Last Purchase" at Fort Stanwix and Pine Creek completed Pennsylvania's shape that we know today, except for the Erie Triangle, acquired in 1792. Births of all these new counties earned her the name, "Mother Cumberland."

Today the valley is a main feature of Perry County, and in 1790 was made up of four townships; Toboyne, Tyrone, Rye, and Greenwood, the last being the most easterly, and all of them have been many times divided and re-shuffled since then. Perry County was sliced off from Cumberland County in 1820. Shermans Creek flows briskly through the first three of the townships that lay in a long, narrow, and stony Shermans* Valley, quite isolated from the rest of Cumberland by high mountains on three sides. The creek rises from numerous springs flowing from the base of the Tuscarora Mountain near New Germantown, a few miles north of Kitta-

* Local useage is "Shermans Creek," without the apostrophe.

213

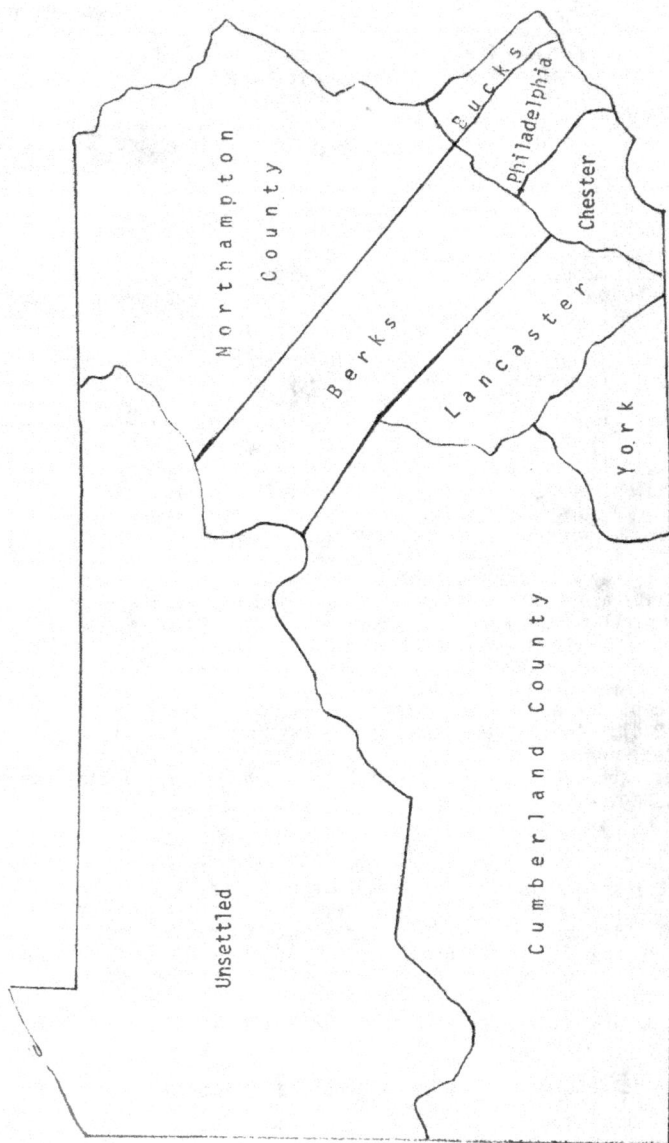

PENNSYLVANIA IN 1755

PHILIP R MCCRAY

HUNTINGDON

JUNIATA R.

WAYNE

NshBOOR

MIFFLIN

LEWISTOWN

DERRY

JUNIATA RIVER

MIFFLINTOWN

FERMANAGH

GREENWOOD

SUSQUEHANNA RIVER

JUNIATA

LACK

RYE

PERRY

LOYSVILLE

SHERMANS CREEK

TOBOYNE

SAVILLE

MCREA

NEWTON

GREENWOOD

WEST PENNSBORO

EAST PENNSBORO

CARLISLE

MONROTH

ALLEN

HOPEWELL

LURGAN

CUMBERLAND

FANNET

LETTERKENNY

HAMILTON

FRANKLIN

GUILFORD

YORK

FULTON

PETERS

ANTRIM

Philip R McCray

MARYLAND

TOWNSHIPS IN EASTERN CUMBERLAND COUNTY,
1789, WITH MODERN COUNTIES SUPERIMPOSED

——————— TOWNSHIPS ———————
━━━━━━━━ COUNTIES ━━━━━━━━

215

"M O T H E R   C U M B E R L A N D"

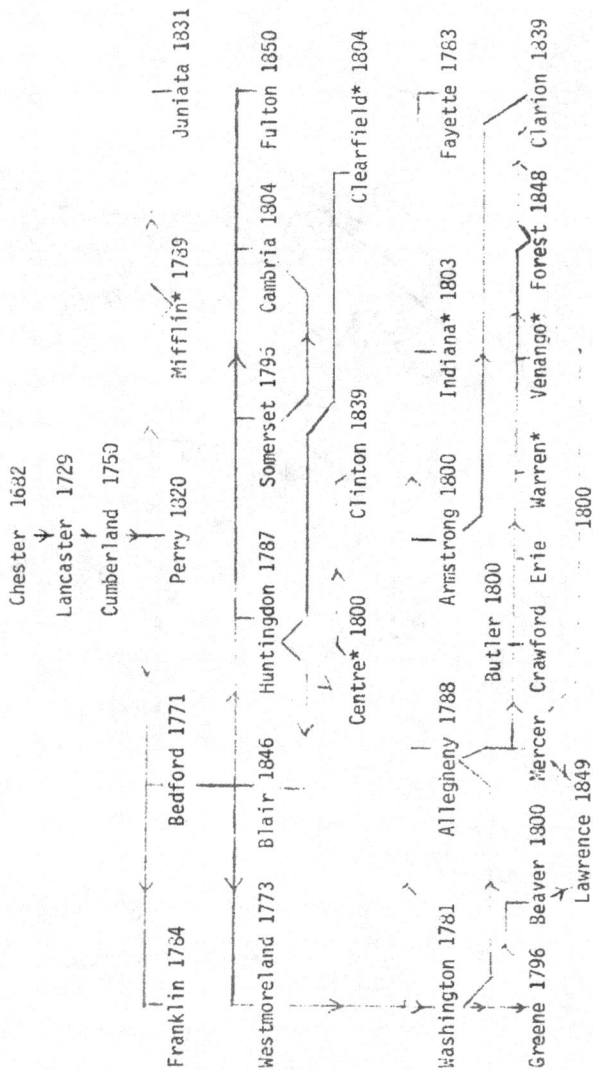

Chester 1682
Lancaster 1729
Cumberland 1750

Franklin 1784   Bedford 1771   Perry 1820   Mifflin* 1789   Juniata 1831

Westmoreland 1773   Blair 1846   Huntingdon 1787   Somerset 1795   Cambria 1804   Fulton 1850

Centre* 1800   Clinton 1839   Clearfield* 1804

Washington 1781   Allegheny 1788   Butler 1800   Armstrong 1800   Indiana* 1803   Fayette 1763

Greene 1796   Beaver 1800   Mercer   Crawford   Erie   Warren*   Venango*   Forest 1848   Clarion 1839

Lawrence 1849   1800

* Counties created partly
from other counties.

Philip R. McCray

THIRTY PENNSYLVANIA COUNTIES CREATED FROM CUMBERLAND COUNTY

216

tinny Tunnel on the Pennsylvania Turnpike, and it flows merrily along at a swift pace eastward for about thirty miles, accumulating waters of many small streams, becoming large enough to be called a river where it empties into the Susquehanna River just below Duncannon. It was, in Colonial days, navigable for riverboats for several miles upstream. In a few places the valley widens out to provide enough level land for farming, and the number of fields one sees today that are bounded by riverstone fences attests to the back-breaking work the settlers put into clearing the land more than two centuries ago.

The many springs that feed into Sherman's Creek, and into other streams in that area, must have made the first Scots-Irish settlers grin, for those limestone waters were one of the principal ingredients for the production of high-grade whiskey, made of Indian maize, rather than rye. Whiskey was a pioneer household commodity used by young and old to ease pain from broken bones or extracted teeth, as well as an aid to relaxation on social occasions. Although the Scots-Irish gained some notoriety for their legendary capacity for alcohol, drunkeness was frowned upon, and few of them were chronic alcoholics. There were no taverns on the frontier, and life there was too harsh for alcoholism. When guests arrived at a settler's cabin, the bottle was produced and passed, and if the visitor happened to be the minister, it was passed to him for the first firey drink.

Home-made whiskey was also a source of cash or barter, used by pioneers to obtain powder, lead, iron, cloth, sugar, flour and salt. They also earned money by leaching out the ashes of fires from burning trees they cleared from land for farming. The ashes were leached with water and the mess boiled in iron pots to make crude "pot-ash" (also called "black salts"). But making pot-ash was hard, hot work, and the product didn't command a very high price, whereas making whiskey was fairly easy, perhaps even fun, and, as Scots, they felt quite at home working at the still and running off a batch. When the new Government of the United States was set up, the settlers were shocked to learn that a tax had been levied upon whiskey, just as it had under the hated and lately cast-off British government. It was widely thought by unlettered folk that the war for independence had been fought to eliminate all taxes. Their anger led to the Whiskey Rebellion in western Pennsylvania in 1793 when the Scots-Irish tarred and feathered some tax collectors and Washington ordered out the militia of nearby states and arrested two insurrectionists for refusing to pay the whiskey tax. Once the new national government had showed its muscle and authority to enforce federal laws, the pioneers were released and allowed to return to their frontier homes and their stills, and presumably they thereafter paid the whiskey tax, although not very cheerfully.

Shermans Valley was well settled when the McCrays arrived there. Enough settlers had come to the lands west of the Susquehanna River by 1750 that Cumberland County was erected out of the huge and loosely bounded Lancaster County. During the French and Indian War and Pontiac's Rebellion, the settlers who remained in Shermans Valley were subjected

to raids by Indians, and not a few of them lost their lives and farm
buildings. Organized hostilities ceased in 1765, and two years later a
group of Presbyterian Scots-Irish assembled in Shermans Valley near the
creek on a little rise of ground and began cutting trees and building a
20-foot by 60-foot church building. Sections of logs were placed upended
on the dirt floor to serve as seats. The community had been served by
"supplies," circuit riders, and services were held in homes, or if a
large enough congregation assembled, in barns. The next year the Reverend John Linn, a graduate of Harvard College (then a Presbyterian school),
answered a call and became the resident pastor of Centre Presbyterian
Church. He served the church and community until his death in 1820.

One may wonder why the McCrays chose to settle there. When they got
to America all the good land within 150 miles of the coast as far west as
the Allegheny Mountains had been taken up and the new settlers usually
went south into the Carolinas, Tennessee, Kentucky, or into Ohio or Indiana. It seems safe to guess that they knew when they left Ireland they
were headed for Shermans Valley. They possibly had been in touch with
friends or relatives already in America; Benjamin Franklin had established
mail service between the Colonies and Great Britain long before the Revolution. Perhaps there is a clue in the fact that Shermans Valley was
the home of a number of families named Bell, and wasn't James's wife Ellen
Bell? And, just a few miles to the west was Newville, where a number of
McCrea families dwelt, having settled there as early as 1750, when Cumberland County was established. Many McCreas are buried in the churchyard of Big Spring Presbyterian Church in Newville, where George Washington once attended services, and the village of McCrea is just a few miles
north of Newville. At least two large families of McCreas lived just a
few miles to the south of Carlisle near the Maryland border.

Cumberland County tax records show that in 1787 James McCray paid
taxes in Toboyne Township on one horse and one cow; nine shillings and
ten pence. In 1789, "James McCree, Toboyne Township, one horse, one cow,
ten shillings." Perhaps one of the farm animals was off its feet when
the tax was lowered that year. Also, in both these years, William McCrea
paid taxes first on three cows, and then on two cows. We cannot be certain they were the brothers McCray, and they may have been father and son,
Old James and son William. In 1793 William McCray (they spelled it right
that time) paid taxes on two cows; eight shillings. In 1795, James
McCray paid taxes on 100 acres, 2 horses, 3 cows and sheep, total 21
shillings. Not only had James McCray become somewhat more wealthy, he'd
succeeded in getting his name spelled right. All of us bearing the name
McCray can testify it probably wasn't easy. Or is it possible that it
was there in Shermans valley that they changed it from "McCree" or
"McCrea" to "McCray"?

A survey of available military manpower in Shermans Valley in 1793
listed George, James, and William McCrea.

The Reverend John Linn is important to our story because he made a list of marriages performed at Centre Presbyterian Church between 1778 and 1793. We are indebted to the good reverend for having done so, and we must also thank those who preserved the record so well for us, for the list contained marriages of four of the six children of Old James and Ellen (Bell) McCray. They were:

July 9, 1790; William Reed to Elizabeth McCrea, both of Toboyne.
Nover 26, 1790; George McCrea to Jean Murray, of Tyrone.
November 17, 1791; James McCrea to Eleanor Townsley, both of Tyrone.
April 26, 1792; William McCrea to Nancy Miles, both of Tyrone.

Evidently James had moved from Toboyne Township to Tyrone Township between the marriages of George and James. We cannot be certain that the James McCrea referred to in tax lists four years earlier, along with the name of William McCrea, was Old James or his son, James. We do know that the younger James McCray married Eleanor Townsley. It is evident that the Reverend Linn, like the tax assessor and other scribes, thought he knew how to spell the name of our ancestors -- or is it possible that they *did* spell it "McCrea" at that time and later changed it? Some of William McCray's descendants used the McCrea spelling after they moved to northwestern Pennsylvania, and some still do.

Among the many names on Reverend Linn's list were names of people who were related by earlier marriages to the four McCrays above:

Robert Miles and Catherine Watt of Rye, June 27, 1781.
Margaret Miles and John Kinkead, October 31, 1782.
Jane Miles and James McClure of Limestone Ridge, Nov. 21, 1786.
Elizabeth Townsley of Centre and Hugh McCracken, Dec. 6, 1781.
John Townsley and Elizabeth (Hester) Martin, May 4, 1786.
Thomas Townsley and Sarah Patterson, January 17, 1789.
George Townsley and Rebecca Thomas, January 22, 1783.
Richard Reed and Nancy Irwin, April 6, 1789.

On Sunday, November 17, 1991, on the 200th anniversary of the marriage of James McCray and Eleanor Townsley, I came to Centre Presbyterian Church to attend services in the church that stands near the site of the original log building. As I stood under the great oak trees in the churchyard I tried to picture in my mind what the first Centre Presbyterian Church looked like two centuries ago. A cemetery is on the site today, and the Reverend John Linn and his wife are buried there.

The congregation came afoot and on horseback, and by 1791 they probably no longer posted guards outside for protection against Indians. There were two services on Sundays, with dinner between services. The meal was cold, having been prepared the night before; no work was to be done on the Sabbath. Centre Presbyterian was a log building from 1767 until 1793, when it was replaced by a stone building. The present frame building was erected in 1850.

I wondered if James proposed to Eleanor one Sunday afternoon between sermons as they sat on a log underneath one of the oak trees left standing during construction of the church. On their wedding day, did Eleanor have a pretty white dress and have flowers in her hair? And, just this once, did James put on some knee britches, white hose, powdered wig, and shoes with silver buckles borrowed for the occasion? Probably not, but I hoped they had a nice wedding, and that everyone came to it and wished them long and happy married life.

The Townsleys and the Townleys.

ELEANOR TOWNSLEY HAS BEEN TRACED BACK to the Towneley family who had an estate at Burnley, near Manchester, England. The Towneley family was granted the land by a Norman king in the 13th century,* and in about mid-fourteenth century a castle keep was erected; it was a square, two-story squat stone fort with six-foot walls, parts of which are part of Towneley Hall today. Like all such buildings that have survived the ravages of weather, wars and neglect, Towneley Hall has had many modifications and additions, and it grew into a structure of some grandeur as the Towneley fortunes improved. In 1901 the town of Burnley bought Towneley Hall, and today it is Burnley's art gallery and museum of natural history, geology and archaeology, and it is open to the public. It is located about twenty miles northwest of Manchester and a few miles south of Burnley on the A646 road.

A Townley/Townsley family history, apparently written by one of the Ohio Townsleys, with no author's name affixed thereto, tells how the Townsleys came to America:

"In the latter part of the 16th century there lived in the castle on the Townley estate located at Burnley, England, Lord Lawrence Townley, who had several sons and daughters born to him, one of whom, William, held a commission in the British Army, and was sent to Ireland by his government with a detachment of men, and settled near Dublin (if what Colonel Clarence Townsley, who was general superintendent of West Point Military Academy, found concerning his father's land to be true). This seems to be sustained by the mother of Hugh McMichael of Poceneco City (Pocomoke City) Md., wife of James Townsley whose father came to America from Dublin, Ireland.

* Not a Norman king. During the 13th century, England was ruled by Plantagenet kings.

220

"This Townsley had several sons and daughters, Robert, the eldest, and John, his brother, who are the first Townsleys who came to America. About the year 1760, it appears that near the Townley estate in Ireland there was a sheep-herder named Linsay, whose daughter, Esther, tended sheep for her father. Robert Townley met and fell in love with her, and asked his parents to consent to a marriage with her, which they refused, saying she was beneath him, as she was not of royal blood (neither were the Towneleys), and threatened to disown him if he disobeyed, but he, having a mind of his own, married the girl, and with his brother, John, sailed for America, intending to land at New Amsterdam, New York."

This history goes on to tell that when the Revolution began, John remained loyal to the Crown, but Robert threw in his lot with the Colonists. John's house was burned by local revolutionaries and he and his family fled in their night clothes, "saving nothing but the sword bearing the family coat of arms." They were then living at Valley Forge, Pennsylvania. They separated, John going to Maryland, and Robert and his wife, Esther, moving westward into the Conestoga Valley. Robert organized a company of militia and led the company to Harrisburg, signing on under the name, "Townsley," in order that no one would confuse him with his loyalist brother, John. He was in the Battle of Brandywine, and took a ball in his hip, September 11, 1777. John retained the name of Towneley, but modified it by dropping the first "e," and substituting "s." Robert Townsley had four sons and several daughters. The sons were Robert, Jr., George Henry, William Linsy, and Joseph. It has not been proven beyond doubt, but William Linsy was probably the father of Eleanor Townsley.

Eleanor Townsley was born in 1768. In 1850 her sons, Robert and Joseph, both told the census-taker that both their parents were born in Scotland. This conflicts with the Townsley chronicler in Ohio, who wrote that Thomas Townsley, Eleanor's brother, was born in Cumberland County, Pennsylvania, in 1755, and another brother, John Townsley, was also born there in 1757. It just doesn't seem likely that she would have been born in Scotland eleven years after John's birth in America, but one may find it difficult to believe that two of her sons would have some thing like that so wrong. Then, too, it has not been definitely established that John and Thomas were Eleanor's brothers, but they all lived in Toboyne Township, Cumberland County, and all went to and were married in Centre Presbyterian Church there. Circumstantial evidence rather strongly points to the three of them being siblings.

There is no doubt whatsoever that William Townsley was Eleanor's father, because in 1795 he recorded his will, naming seven daughters, one of whom was "Eleanor McCree." (Will Book E, p. 324, Carlisle, Pa. Made April 18, 1795, prob. May 28, 1795) All but Joanna Townsley were

221

listed by their married names. She probably was not the Joanna Townsley who married John Donahue, September 10, 1773. The others named were:

Janet Kincaid	Elizabeth McCracken
Agnes Innes	Margaret McMillen
Martha Kincaid	

Thomas Townsley married Sarah Patterson, January 17, 1782, and George Townsley married Rebecca Thomas, January 22, 1793.

William Townsley's will was recorded in 1795, and it appears that he didn't prepare his will because he expected to die very soon, but rather because he planned to leave the area and didn't think it likely he would return. It may be that his wife died and he didn't want to live in Toboyne Township after that. Whatever, he turned up in Kentucky with his son, Thomas in 1795, the same year that he wrote his will. He did not mention any sons in the instrument, possibly because they had for some time been on their own and were well established on their farms.

John Townsley was a soldier in the Revolutionary War, and his service is recorded in the Pennsylvania Archives, 5th Series, Volume 2, p. 241, where it was also given that he was born in May, 1753. He died in 1822 in Cedarville, Greene County, Ohio. John Townsley married Hester (also Esther) Martin on May 4, 1786, at Centre Presbyterian Church; it is an assumption that this John Townsley was the same one who died in Ohio. His children were: William, Alexander, John, Jr., Thomas, Samuel, George, Innis (his uncle's last name) and James.

Bill Townsley, of Fort Myers, Florida, whose family came from Virginia, found two items about William and Thomas Townsley in Kentucky. They were printed in the *Kentucky Gazette* (1787-1800):

"29 August, 1795--William Townsley, living with Thomas Townsley in Scott County, about seven miles from Georgetown, has a still for sale. Apply to Mr. Baxter, coppersmith, near Mjr. South's in Fayette County.

"23 Jan., 1796--Thomas Townsley, living at the head of Cherry's Run in Scott County, regarding stray mare."

With creation of the Ohio Territory in 1799, they migrated to Xenia,

Greene County, in about 1800. By coincidence, this was the same area where the McCrays who are descended from Joseph McCray of Virginia, also settled. Bill Townsley wrote that the family of John Townsley, who left a will in Cumberland County in 1791, settled in Clermont, Batavia Township, along the Ohio River in the county adjacent to Hamilton County, where Cincinnati is located. This John has not been identified, but was almost certainly a relative of the family of William Townsley.

It was Scots-Irish pioneers who settled Shermans Valley in Cumberland County, and it was Scots-Irish who mostly populated it during the eighteenth century. By 1810 Cumberland County record books show that most of the Scots-Irish names in Shermans Valley had been replaced by names of German origin. The exodus probably began in 1795, after General Anthony Wayne defeated the great Miami Indian nation at the Battle of Fallen Timbers near the Maumee River in Ohio, in December of 1794. Lieutenant William Henry Harrison was his aide at this battle. The Native Americans signed a treaty of peace forever, and unlike their white conquerors, they kept their word, and kept the peace. A great land rush ensued into Kentucky and the Northwest Territory, those lands north and west of the Ohio River.

Addendum: William Townsley was listed as a resident of West Pennsboro Township, Cumberland County, in 1751.* No other Townsley's appeared in this or any list of residents of other townships in Cumberland County.

Janet Townsley married Archibald R. Kincaid (born 1750, in Virginia) before 1782. Martha Townsley married Andrew Kincaid (born 1748 in Virginia). Both Archibald and Andrew were soldiers in the Revolution. When William Townsley, their father, left Pennsylvania for Kentucky, Archibald and Andrew and their families probably joined the exodus westward to Pittsburgh. There they boarded a longboat and headed down the Ohio River to Kentucky, the newest Promised Land to succeed the other promised lands that had lost their shine for the Scots-Irish. Archibald, Andrew and their families went ashore near today's Maysville, and settled near Old Slate Furnace in Bourbon (now Bath) County, near the end of 1795. Janet (Townsley) Kincaid died October 13, 1822, and her widower, Archibald, died four months later on February 7, 1823.**

* *History of Cumberland and Adams Counties, Pennsylvania,* Warner, Beers & Co, Chicago; 1886.

*Mrs. Leone Meyer of Marshall, Missouri, and Bill Townsley, of Fort Myers, Florida, contributed much of the Townsley information.

CHAPTER TEN

THE SETTLEMENT OF ERIE COUNTY, PENNSYLVANIA

The Holland Land Company

WITH ENACTMENT OF THE LAND ACT OF 1792, a number of companies, partnerships and individuals, invested in land in northern Pennsylvania and New York. The story of the Holland Land Company will serve to illustrate typical trials and financial perils of most of the land speculators who let greed lead them into financial traps they set for others.

Theophile Cazenove, an Italian-born Dutchman, representing the "Club Of Three," a consortium of Dutch bankers, came to America in 1789 to act as agent and to invest heavily in American funds and Federal liquidated debts. He shrewdly dealt in cash and soon was being carefully watched by American speculators, including Robert Morris, who was buying Pennsylvania lands which he planned to quickly and profitably sell.

Cazenove sent for Gerritt Boon and Jan Lincklaen to come from Holland to investigate parts of northwestern Pennsylvania and New York that were up for sale. The two had made an astonishing trip to America the year before, walking 2600 miles in the dead of winter through Pennsylvania, New York, Vermont and Connecticut, looking into the possibility of developing a major maple sugar industry large enough to divert the world's sugar trade from the West Indies to northern American colonies under Dutch management.

Acting on the report of Lincklaen and Boon, Cazenove began buying land. The Batavia Tract in western New York was a major purchase; a million and a half acres constituting the entire western part of New York. He also bought two other large tracts in central New York.

He bought and sold a half-million acres in Pennsylvania's Six Districts east of the Allegheny River, using the profits to buy the great West Allegheny Tract. He bought 400,000 acres formerly owned by John Adlum, and warrants for another 100,000 acres from Judge James Wilson, a heavy speculator. Later he bought another 499,000 acres of warranted land in the West Allegheny area from Wilson. Before he stopped buying land, Cazenove had bought up more than 5,000,000 acres of land at a cost of $222,071. He planned to find a buyer to take the whole package at once.

Cazenove failed to keep a wet finger in the wind and he fell victim to the unbounded optimism of the future of land values. Prices of land in Western Pennsylvania kept ascending, much like England's "Great South Sea Bubble," in which totally artificial land values kept going up and up, eventually plunging to worthlessness, bankrupting many English fortunes. His optimism was unbounded, but he ignored the signals that were telling him to unload his holding quickly.

On 13 February, 1796, a new organization was formed, "The Holland-esche Land Compagnie," a stock company representing 1,300,000 acres in the Genessee Tract, 499,000 acres in the West Allegheny, and 900,000 acres in the East Allegheny. Six commissioners were made managers of the land, known as "The Holland Purchase." The holdings of the company were in many tracts, by no means necessarily abutting each other, but were scattered about throughout the unsettled regions of Pennsylvania and New York.

The plan was to sell all the land in very large lots to speculators, but their timing was bad. Within a few months, Robert Morris, who had personally financed much of the Revolution, and was the largest of all the land speculators, pulled out of the market, and the big land bubble burst. All of a sudden nobody wanted to buy land. The Holland Land Company was stuck, and stuck royally, with an albatross of land on its neck for the next forty years. All they could do was to try to sell it bit by bit in small plots to poor settlers with little or no money.

Now Cazenova had to lay new plans to operate a real estate business, rather than a land speculation business. He'd hired Major Roger Alden, former aide-de-camp to General Benedict Arnold, to manage the West Allegheny lands, and he came to Mead's Settlement on French Creek in 1795, so he was in place there when the land bubble collapsed. Alden had been having his troubles there right along, however. He at first thought that the land was fast being occupied by settlers, but when he began visiting the numerous cabins and huts scattered around the Holland Land Company's tracts, he found that most were unoccupied, and indeed, had never been lived in at all. The Holland Land Company had been invaded by "improvers."

These unoccupied buildings had been put there by hordes of so-called "improvers," who seized settler's lands and then sold them. Badly worded provisions of the Land Act of 1792 were widely interpreted by some, and had found some backing in Pennsylvania courts, to mean that anyone could claim a tract of unoccupied land in the western districts by simply putting any kind of dwelling on it. The improver would then go to a State land office and file for a warrant on the land. The Land Office had decided that a dwelling of any sort, no matter how badly done, constituted an improvement which entitled the improver to claim it. Hundreds of drifters and ne'er-do-wells were in the western Pennsylvania lands to make some easy money selling lands in which they had no investment. The courts were jammed with civil actions, and the true land owners often came off second-best, due to a general dislike of wealthy land-owning individuals who happened to be judges who sided with the improvers.

Another problem centered around a clause in the Land Act that granted an exception to a requirement for a five-year occupation of land before a patent would be granted: "If a settler should, by force of arms of the enemies of the United States be prevented from making such settlement, or to be driven therefrom, and shall persist in his efforts to make such

settlement, he and his heirs are entitled to have and to hold such lands
in the same manner as if actual settlement had been made and continued."
This was a classic example of how not to write a law.

Many poor people in 1792, upon passage of the Land Act, immediately
went to the Land Office and took out warrants, packed up their families,
and headed out into the wilds, erected cabins and fences, and "improved"
the land. Native Indians, seeing their hunting grounds being taken over
and destroyed, took up the hatchet and came a'raiding. Some of the
whites stood and defended the property they deemed to rightfully be
theirs, and not a few died on their claims. The more prudent fled back
to civilization and claimed protection for their warrants under the "enemies of the United States" clause.

The Assembly overruled the Land Office's decision that Indian trouble
didn't exempt settlers from the Act's provisions, and a horde of "Improvers" dashed in, put up rude shelters, and even though nobody saw any
Indians about, came back to claim the land under the "enemies" provision.

Legislators took up the problem, talked a lot, and finally washed
their hands of it and told all concerned to settle it any way they could!
Cazenove wondered about defending his company's lands by force of arms,
thought better of it, and launched a sales blitz to get rid of the land
as fast as possible. He advertised by handbills and in newspapers in
Pennsylvania, Maryland, Delaware, New Jersey, and Virginia, and offered
land at prices from $1.40 to $2.65 an acre, entirely on credit. He also
stocked provisions and tools to sell on credit.

He directed Alden to clear Cussawaga Creek, and to begin road construction throughout their holdings. He hired a Kentuckian, Alexander
McDowell, as chief surveyor for this work.* He also hired Harm Jan
Huidekoper as land agent. A few penniless settlers began to drift in,
almost all having been attracted by the credit offered. By 1799, Alden
had accounts for $40,000 for tools and provisions, and a debit of $25,000,
most of which was never collected. Many who started for the area were
diverted by other travellers who told them tales of the marvelous lands
in Kentucky, and told them rumors of poor lands in the West Allegheny
and of bad provisions at Mead's Settlement. This resulted in many of
the pioneers changing their course in midstream, and when they got to
Pittsburgh they took a flatboat down the Ohio River for Kentucky. Some
also abandoned their Holland Land holdings after one or two winters, and
left for warmer climes. (Erie County can be very, very cold in winter.)

* Probably a descendent from Ephriam McDowell. See "Settlement of Virginia's Backwoods," Page 55.

As in all pioneer beginnings, everyone arrived at the site of his new home on equal footing with at least a rifle and powder horn, an axe, a hoe, an iron cooking pot, and perhaps a Bible. Some came with a horse and a cow. No one stood above anyone else, socially or economically. The future farm was a cooperative family enterprise founded on a married partnership. To survive, the pioneer had to be a jack of all basic trades. Everything he needed in the new home had to manufactured by family members on the site of the future farm.

The wife had to do the food preparation and preservation by salting and drying it to insure food for the coming winter. Food preparation was really from scratch--whole grain corn, wheat or oats, and meat she cut from a recently killed wild animal. Grain had to be ground in a mortar by pounding and sifting; both utensils made with an axe by the husband. Meat and fish had to be dried for winter food, and animal hides had to be scraped and stretched for clothing and bedding. There were babies to care for, household jobs to be done by children under her supervision, and clothing to be made and repaired. Cooking was done in a pot on the fireplace, with time and temperature guessed at by the wife.

Immediately and almost simultaneously, the husband had to erect a basic lean-to shelter, clear enough trees away to plant a crop for food, build a shelter and fence for his horse and cow, hunt game and fish for food, split firewood for cooking and warmth, and set aside the cleared logs selected for a cabin to be built before winter. Using only an axe he had to build rude furniture, especially a table for food preparation. Benches and chairs were almost a luxury to replace logs they sat on.

No small part of the pioneer's problems were uncertainties of titles because of the "Improvers." If a farmer should leave his holdings for a day, he might return to find an armed improver had taken over his "abandoned" property, and he must then oust the intruder, since he could not depend on help from the law. Neighbors, however, could usually be counted on to assist in such matters without due process of law. But the climate it created did nothing to encourage settlers to come, other than many who didn't have financial means to do better elsewhere.

Cazenove went back to Holland in 1798, and was replaced by Paul Busti, who seems to have been a better manager than Cazenove was. Busti had an uphill fight to keep the project solvent, as land that had been offered at $1.40 an acre couldn't be sold for 25¢ an acre in 1807.

Frustrated by the do-nothing Assembly in Philadelphia, Busti suspended operations in 1805, and served notice upon the State that he was forthwith refusing to pay any further taxes (the reader is advised to first seek legal counsel before attempting this) until the Legislature straightened out the land ownership mess. Two years later, orders came to sell out all remaining land for whatever he could get for it. In 1810, Busti found J.B. Wallace and William Griffith willing to pay $180,000 for it all, and the Holland Land Company went out of the real estate business in West Allegheny.

Griffith and Wallace bought out Holland Land at a discount of about 75%! Holland Land Company had paid over $200,000 for the land, then spent $300,000 administering and selling it, and the land they sold had outstanding mortgages of over $100,000, with little or no hope of collecting any of it, and there still were 350,000 acres of land unsold. Griffith and Wallace were unable to fulfill their contract to pay $180,000, so the loss to the Holland Land Company was eventually even greater.

The Holland Land Company still had a great deal of land in New York to sell, and they finally disposed of it in 1841. The interval was marked by lawsuits and even riots. One could say that the Dutch Club of Three lost its collective shirt on land speculation in the United States.

Harm Jan Huidekoper*had stayed on with Busti and then with Griffith and Wallace. Almost from the moment that Griffith and Wallace assumed ownership, Yankee settlers from New England began arriving, to be welcomed by Huidekoper with open arms, for these settlers promised to be a different breed. They were hard-working, debt-paying, and determined to be good farmers. The influx was hardly slowed by the War of 1812, and most of the land was sold by 1816.

These new settlers, although honest and hard-working, were wretchedly poor, and typically could not make mortgage payments in cash, for they were far from large markets and transportation was slow. The Panic of 1819 did nothing to help. Finally, in 1836, Huidekoper bought up the balance of unpaid principal that Wallace and Griffith still owed the Holland Land Company, amounting to $178,000.

- - - - - -

The story of the Dutch investment in the United States would really be incomplete if the story of the outcome of the Club of Three's original intent to corner the world market in sugar were to be left untold.

In 1793, Gerritt Boon and Jan Lincklaen returned to the two central New York tracts to experiment a bit. Lincklaen planned a complete town beside a beautiful three-mile long lake, complete with mills, shops, streets and buildings, and invited craftsmen and artisans to come and be a part of the new town. He offered many inducements to get good people, and they did come. He named the town, "Cazenovia," and his plan was socially a great success, but it wasn't so successful for him, financially.

*The Huidekoper family is still well represented in Crawford County.

Today, Cazenovia is a handsome village with a wide main street lined with grand Victorian mansions and huge trees. The Lincklaen Hotel is famous as a hospitable inn with an outstanding dining room, where parents of students at a small college come for scholastic events.

While Lincklaen tarried by his lake, planning Cazenovia, his companion, Garritt Boon,went on northeastward to the Holland Land Company's other tract to set up his maple sugar experiment. Just north of Fort Schuyler (now Utica), he selected a seventeen-acre site and set about becoming sugar king of the world, he hoped.

He hired twenty-four woodcutters to clear all the trees in the tract, leaving standing only sugar maple trees. He surveyed the cleared land and built a boiling plant at the lowest point. He bought a sawmill to saw up the largest of the felled trees into lumber, and planned a vast network of gravity-fed troughs, made of the new lumber, to go from each tree to the boiling plant. Boon knew nothing about the properties of newly milled lumber cut from green logs, and he didn't know how to buy a sawmill to do what he wanted done. The sawmill didn't work for the job, and he had to buy troughs from a distant mill. Delivering his green lumber and collecting the troughs cost him money and time, and then he found that the green lumber was causing the troughs to twist and split, so the first year's run of maple sap went mostly into the ground. He tried to nail together vee-shaped troughs, but they leaked too badly to use. He never tried the obvious and time-tested method of collecting sap in tanks on oxen-drawn sleds or carts.

He spent the entire winter and the following spring floundering in his own ineptitude, and in the summer of 1794, he went to Philadelphia to report to Cazenove and to beg for another try in the coming winter. But the bankers in Holland pulled the rug from under the maple sugar project and ordered the property, known as the "Oldenbarnveld Settlement", sold. Boon had spent 38,000 guilders to produce 800 guilders worth of maple sugar, not a promising start for even a pilot plant, and his plans were to expand the project to ten thousand acres, from the original seventeen. You can find the project's site on a map today, just north of Utica, at the villages of Barnveld and Holland Patent.

Who knows? Had Boon done his homework properly, Utica, New York might today be the sugar capital of the world.

McCray Dealings With The Holland Land Company

WHEN THE HOLLAND LAND COMPANY CLOSED out its dealings in the United States, the records were sealed in chests and shipped to Holland in 1856, where they lay in vaults, unavailable to scholars, until 1960. Custodians of the records, the van Eeghan family, had the chests opened and the contents removed. There were about 270 bundles and about 275 ledgers, and when they had been placed in acid-free folders and put on shelves at the Municipal Archives of Amsterdam, they occupied over 140 feet of shelf space.

The U.S. Library of Congress made several attempts to collaborate with various United States libraries in a project to duplicate the HLC records, and to return the duplicates to the United States, but without success. Finally, about 1980, the State University of New York (SUNY) at Fredonia, appointed Ms. Franciska Safran, Director of the Holland Land Company Project. The Gebbie Foundation, of Jamestown, New York, put up a grant to permit Ms. Safran to spend a month in Amsterdam, surveying the extent of the project, and making preparations for having the records reproduced by technicians of the Photoduplication Service, Library of Congress.

Upon her return to the United States, her encouraging report stimulated the Gebbie Foundation to offer a challenge grant that required the raising of $20,000 additional funds. Many individuals and historical societies contributed and the money was raised. The Crawford County Historical Society donated $500 to the fund.

In 1982, Ms. Safran and the photo-technical crew arrived in Amsterdam, and with a lot of excellent cooperation from the staff of the Municipal Archives, filming was soon under way. The work was completed in about fourteen months,and it consisted of 202 reels of black-and-white microfilm, plus two reels in color of scores of maps.

The records are today available in the Library of Congress, Washington, D.C., the Reed Library, SUNY, Fredonia, N.Y., and the Erie County Historical Society, Buffalo, N.Y., and probably by now in other places.

Ms. Safran generously responded to a letter of inquiry about the status of the records by recruiting two sterling lady volunteer students, who looked up the McCray names in the reels of microfilm. They copied down what they found, misspellings and all, and Ms. Safran relayed it to me. Here is what the record shows:

"Holland Land Company records. Reel #137, Item #623. Samuel Nicholson, agent.

"49   Robert McCray   June 22, 1801   Track 49
        100 acres Gratuity   50 acres at $1.50   Paid $75

"63   William McCray   July 20, 1796   Track 63
        200 acres

"80   William McCray   May 12, 1797   Track 80
        200 acres $50

"64   James McCray   June 1, 1796   Track 64
        200 acres

"65   James McCray   Feb. 6, 1802   Track 65
        100 acres Gratuity   50 acres at $1.50   Paid $75

"81   Samuel McCray   April 10, 1798   Track 81
        100 acres Gratuity   50 acres at $1.50   Paid $75

"83   James McCray   Feb. 6, 1802   Track No. N:83
        100 acres Gratuity   50 acres at $1.50   Paid $75"

None of these data had heretofore been available, and while they don't supply all the answers by any means, still, there is much here.

Of course, these records show only that James, William, Samuel, and Robert McCray bought land from District Number Six, Holland Land Company. They certainly do not support family legends that they were the first settlers in the area, nor do they prove they were not. The map shows the names of other settlers in the area* , but we don't know when the map was drawn. It doesn't show the tract numbers or the names of purchasers in the adjacent districts, such as Alexander McDowell's District Number Seven, just south of District Number Six. Having bought the land, we do not know when they actually moved upon it and occupied it. If deeds can be found, they may show this information.

It doesn't seem very likely that James and William would have moved their families onto the land that late in the year 1796. They would have needed an early spring start to get enough land cleared, and food raised, and a snug cabin completed during the summer and fall before winter struck, for Erie County was no place for living through a winter in a half-faced lean-to. After buying the land in July, 1796, they may have stayed there for the remainder of the summer, clearing trees and pos - sibly building a cabin for each of the families, which would have given them a nice leg up on the vast amount of work that had to be done the following year. They might also have put in a few hours fishing the trout streams there before returning to their families in Washington County.

*The negative-printed map is quite poor in quality, and it isn't possible to read much of the small cursive writing.

From Records Of The Holland Land Company

West Allegheny, District No. 6

Tract	Sold To	Date	Amount	Paid ($)
42	Daniel Shreves	Oct. 20, 1801	50 acres @ $1.50	75
43	John Martain	Aug. 22, 1801	50 acres @ $1.50	75
45	Daniel Prosser	May 10, 1802	50 acres @ $1.50	75
47	Daniel Prosser	May 10, 1802	50 acres @ $1.50	75
48	Daniel Prosser	May 10, 1802	50 acres @ $1.50	75
49	Robert McCray	June 22, 1801	50 acres @ $1.50	75
50	William Singer	June 22, 1801	50 acres @ $1.50	75
61	Thomas Parks	Jan. 26, 1802	50 acres @ $1.50	75
62	William Rosswell	Nov. 19, 1801	100 acres grat.	
63	William McCray	July 20, 1796	"To Acres 200 at..."	
64	James McCray	June 1, 1796	same	
65	James McCray	July 6, 1802	50 sold at 1·/2	75
66	John Cooke	Mar. 1, 1802	same	75
67	James Bruis (Bruce?)	June 28, 1801	same	75
75	Robert Richards	May 12, 1797	"To A 200 at "	50
76	Joshua Hutchin	Jun 30, 1802	100 acres grat.	
77	Samuel Hutchin	May 21, 1802	100 acres grat.	
80	William McCray	May 12, 1797	(200 A ----)	50
81	Samuel McCray	April 10, 1798	50 acres @ $1.50	75
82	Samuel Jobs	May 12, 1802	50 acres @ $1.50	75
83	James McCray	Feb. 6, 1802	50 acres @ $1.50	75
84	John Cooke	Mar. 1, 1802	50 acres @ $1.50	75
85	James Bruis (Bruce?)	June 28, 1801	50 acres @ $1.50	75
94	William Cochran	Mar. 6, 1800	50 + 100 grat.	75
95	William Miles	Aug. 31, 1801	200A ----	50

(Written in pencil below the above) "Omitter
1802 Daniel Harrington", and same terms *

All the above entries; "50 acres @ $1.50" included an additional
100 acres "gratuity", which was sometimes noted and sometimes not.

It will be noted that James McCray was the earliest land purchaser
entered in this ledger, and his brother, William, bought the adjacent
tract a month later. This may, or may not, prove that James McCray was
the first settler in what became Brokenstraw Township in the year 1800.
Their brother, Samuel, bought his land in 1798, and it was not until
William Cochran bought his tract in the spring of 1800 that the McCrays
had any neighbors. Further research is needed to determine if this
ledger is a complete record of land purchases in that area.

* See Thomas McCray, page 338.

232

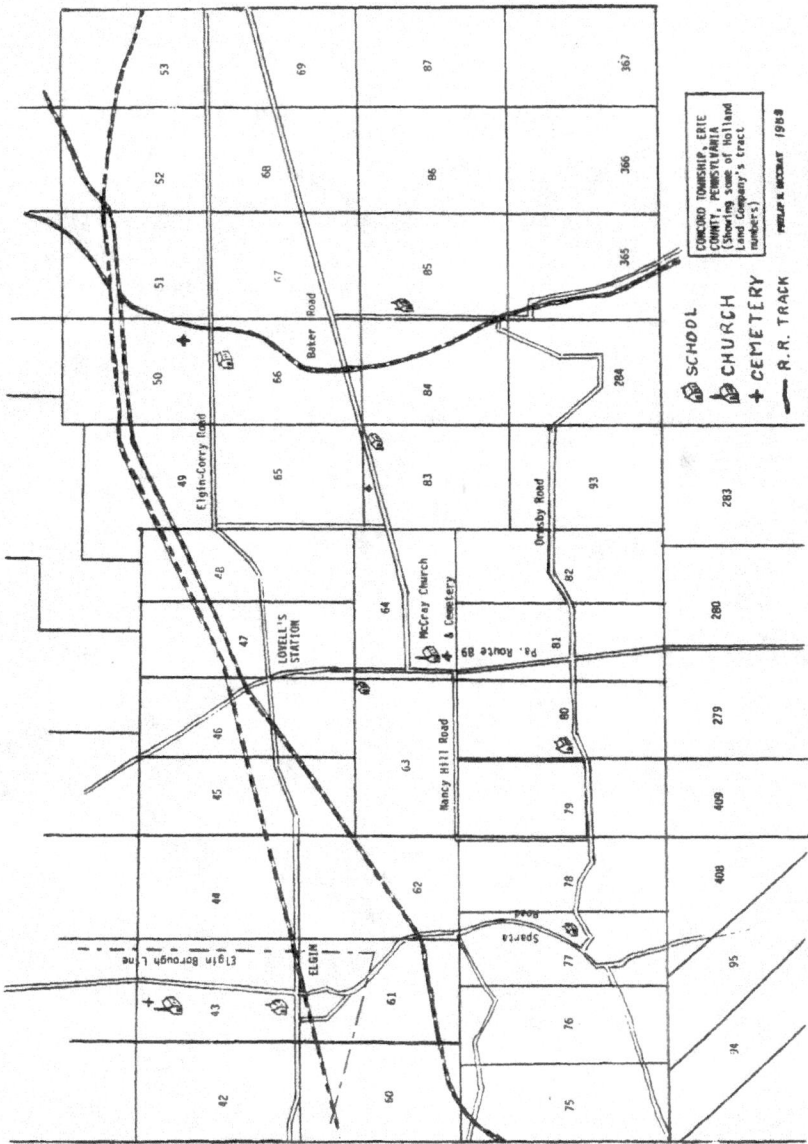

CONCORD TOWNSHIP, ERIE
COUNTY, PENNSYLVANIA
(Showing some of Holland
Land Company's tract
numbers)

PHILIP R. MCCRAY   1988

🏫 SCHOOL
⛪ CHURCH
✝ CEMETERY
━ R.R. TRACK

233

Alice Morrison wrote about the Holland Land Company in a letter:

"Quite a few of the Holland Land Company tracts were sold
with this agreement with settlers: since only a warrant could
be taken out by HLC, the patent only being secured by actual
settlement of the land, the company offered 100 acres of the
400-acre tracts to the settler free or for very little cost if
he would move on the tract and fulfill the requirements for a
patent (i.e., clear a certain area and make it into agricultural land, build a dwelling, and occupy it for five years).
The HLC would then pay the commonwealth for the 400-acre tract,
patent it in the settler's name, and the latter would, in turn,
relinquish 300 acres to the land company. In the case of a
settler with no cash it was a good deal and for the land company it was an even greater one."

Most of the tracts in District Number 6 were nominally 400 acres,
but they were laid out in different shapes, varying from long and narrow
to nearly square. Tracts 63 and 64, contracted for by William and James
respectively in July 1796, were both nominally 450 acres, and. were
nearly square. Considering the difficulties of doing surveys in the
dense forests littered with fallen logs amongst large tree trunks using
relatively low-tech surveying instruments, they managed to achieve quite
good accuracy. Tract 64, for instance, nominally 450 acres, actually
contained 443 acres, while Tract 80, bought by William in 1797, contained
398.59 acres.

The Holland Land Company's various financial difficulties are reflected in James McCray's final settlement for his Tract 64, for it was
not finally settled until 2 September, 1830*. The instrument begins with
a long introduction, full of florid legalisms and the names of various
Dutch bankers, and when boiled down to its real meaning, it establishes
John B. Wallace and William Griffith as owners of the District 6 tracts,
and empowered to sell the land to whomever they could find willing to buy.

The property sold to James, Jr., is described as follows:

"Beginning at the Southwest corner of the whole tract a post,
thence by Tract No. Sixty three North, two hundred nineteen
perches to a post, ------ Tract Nos Forty seven and Forty
eight East, one hundred fifty five perches to a Sugar (a sugar
maple tree) thence by land part of the whole Tract, South Two
hundred and nineteen perches ----- to a White Oak Thence by
Tracts Nos Eighty two and Eighty one West, one hundred and
fifty five perches to the place of beginning Containing Two
hundred acres twenty five perches of land be the Same more or

* Deed Book "L", p. 146. Erie County Courthouse, Erie, Pa., 1988.

234

less the allowance of six percent (Being part of a certain
part of a tract of land numbered in a general plan or map of
the lands of the Said William and John filed in the Recorders
office in the county of Erie No. sixty four)"

"Perches" aren't used anymore in measurement of land. A "perch"
became a "rod," equal to 16½ feet. Converting perches to feet, James's
tract measured 3613½ feet by 2557 feet, or 9,241,526¼ square feet, and
at 43,560 square feet to the acre, the tract contained 212.156 acres.
But there was a built-in allowance of 6% dedicated to public roads that
might be built through the tract, which reduced the land he could actually
call his own to 199.426 acres, not bad measuring at all.

Holland Land Company's original record of the land sale in 1796 did
not mention price, but other tracts the McCrays bought went for $75, or
$2.66 an acre. These two parcels bought by William and James, Jr., were
probably the best in that part of District Number 6, being situated on
the highest point, but with ascents to them gentle enough that land could
be plowed and cultivated with a minimum of washing and soil loss. James,
Jr., probably built his cabin near Slaughter Run, which flows through a
little valley behind the McCray Church and Cemetery.

What William did with his Tract 80 and 63 hasn't been discovered so
far, but John T. McCray, James Jr.'s son, bought the northern 100 acres
of 80 on 14.July, 1831. From the description and bounds of the property,
the east-west width of Tract 80 was 162 perches, or 2673 feet. Tracts
79, 80, 81, and 82 are all the same width, so it can be deduced that
Tract 63, lying north of Tracts 79 and 80, would be twice the width of
Tract 80, or 5346 feet, just a tad over a mile. The north-south dimen-
sion of Tracts 63 and 64 were given in the previous deed, so both Tracts
63 and 64 would each measure 5346 feet long by 3613½ feet, or 443.475
acres.

Deeds from the years 1803 to 1823 were lost in a totally destructive
fire of the Erie County Courthouse in 1824. There may be some deeds
still kept in family strong boxes and files that would help tell the
story of the development of Brokenstraw Township during those crucial
first twenty years that might be made public with a publicity campaign
by the Erie County Historical Society. Are you listening, ECHS?

- - - - - - -

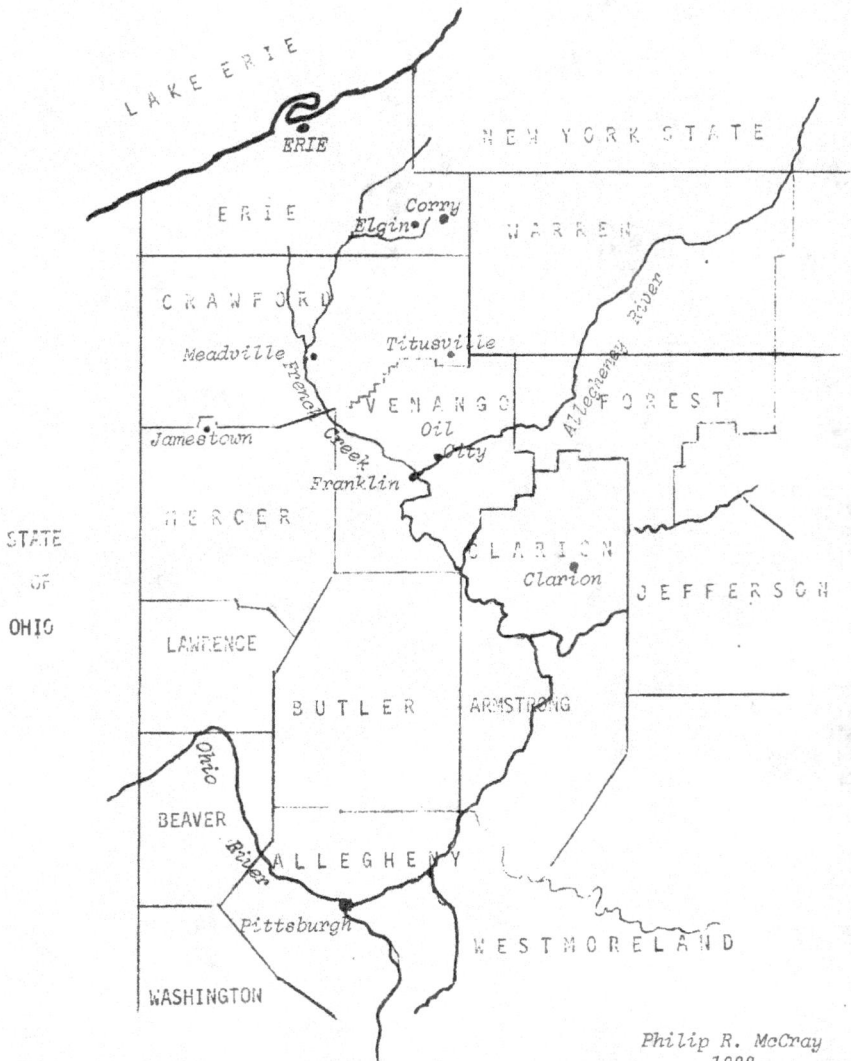

LAKE ERIE

ERIE

NEW YORK STATE

ERIE

Corry
Elgin

WARREN

CRAWFORD

Meadville

Titusville

VENANGO

FOREST

Allegheny River

Oil
City

Jamestown

French Creek

Franklin

CLARION

MERCER

Clarion

JEFFERSON

STATE
OF
OHIO

LAWRENCE

BUTLER

ARMSTRONG

Ohio

BEAVER

River

ALLEGHENY

Pittsburgh

WESTMORELAND

WASHINGTON

Philip R. McCray
1988

236

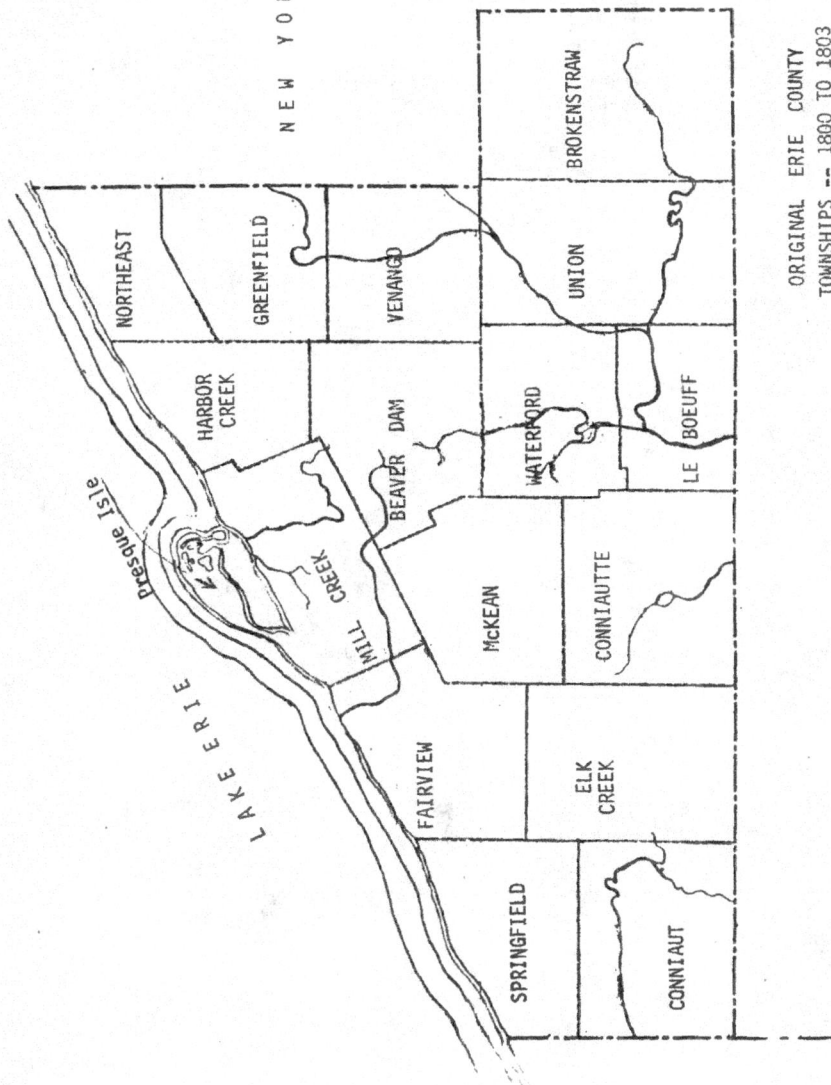

ORIGINAL ERIE COUNTY
TOWNSHIPS -- 1800 TO 1803

The Birth Of Erie County

WESTERN PENNSYLVANIA IN 1790 WAS MADE UP OF only Washington and Allegheny Counties, the latter being second in size only to Northumberland County, which made up all of north-central Pennsylvania. Tucked into the southwest corner of the state, Washington County had by then several thousand pioneer families, but most of Allegheny County was but sparsely settled. Although Britain and the United States had stopped shooting at each other, and a temporary peace existed, the Indians who had been England's allies had signed no treaty and small bands of hostile Indians still caused occasional trouble around the northern parts of Allegheny County. After their defeat in 1794 on Ohio's Miami River at the Battle of Fallen Timbers, the Indian nations in the Northwest Territory agreed never to take up the hatchet against white men. Indian promises could be relied on.

It soon became apparent that Allegheny County was not going to be able to administer the exploding population of settlers in such a vast territory, so the Pennsylvania Assembly cut it up into Erie, Crawford, Venango, Mercer, Forest, Warren and Butler Counties, effective in 1800. Erie County didn't get off and running then, and until 1803 its affairs were handled by Crawford County. By then Erie County was home to large numbers of settlers, hard at work clearing land and building homes and barns. As soon as peace settled on the land, land speculators such as the Pennsylvania Population Company and the Holland Land Company, were pushing the sale of large tracts out of the millions of acres they owned.

Although a great deal of the land was in litigation, the large speculators advertised for settlers, to whom they offered generous credit terms for both land and supplies. The response was immediate and when surveyors arrived in 1795, would-be settlers were at their heels. By 1800 many roads had been improved so they were passable under good conditions of weather, and others were under construction. Sawmills and gristmills sprang up in Erie and Crawford Counties, and farm settlements were growing into villages. The little settlement around Fort Erie soon became a village, then a town, and eventually, a city.

In 1796 the Pittsburgh Gazette announced:

"A careful person is imployed to go from this place to Presqu' Isle, once every two weeks. He will leave the Printing Office at ten o'clock. Those who wish to write to friends in that quarter will now have the opportunity."

By 1801 the Post Office Department had taken over this route and made it biweekly. *The Mirror*, Erie's first newspaper began publication in 1808.

Erie County, like all the other counties in northwestern Pennsylvania, needed roads to permit commerce between the Atlantic regions and the interior, and road construction was given the highest priority. The Industrial Revolution, long delayed in America by British laws that forbade the Colonies to manufacture anything that was being produced in England, now surged ahead, uninhibited and invigorated by "Yankee Ingenuity," and manufactories were springing up everywhere. In 1807, Robert Fulton's steam-driven ship, "Cleremont," butt of jokes and condemned in pulpits as contrary to the will of God, bravely chuffed up the Hudson River to Albany. In so doing, "Fulton's Folly" clearly announced the beginning of the end of sail-power, and the beginning of reliability in water transportation. In only eighteen more years the first railroad in the United States was in operation in New Jersey. Meanwhile, road builders were at work everywhere in the wilderness, and wherever a new road arrived in a town it was heralded with joy, for now the goods of the East could be shipped in by wagon in quantity instead of in hundred-pound packets on horseback.

When the area was occupied by the French, they had constructed a crude road between Presque Isle and Fort Duquesne that was adequate for hauling cannons and large wagons. During the Revolution it deteriorated to the point of uselessness, but with the new expansion a major effort was put into restoring it. It became the principal route for delivery of salt to southwestern Pennsylvania and adjacent Virginia and Ohio; salt was a commodity of great importance, as it was used in large quantities to preserve meat for winter consumption. It was shipped from the salt mines at Syracuse, New York, by boat to Erie, then trans-shipped by packhorse or wagon to Pittsburgh. By the time alternate salt sources had been developed along the Ohio River Erie had accumulated enough profit from the salt trade to develop roads at a fast pace without burdensome taxes on the citizens. It continued to be a major road for shipment of flour, glass, iron and whiskey. Erie became a major terminal upon completion of the Erie Canal in 1825.

Lake Erie teemed with fish, providing income for Erie fishermen, principally from sturgeons, twelve to fifteen feet long, weighing hundreds of pounds. The fishing industry stimulated boat-building, too. The ships commanded by Commodore Oliver Perry in the War of 1812 were built at Erie, and *Walk In The Water*, a strange and clumsy steamboat. Launched in 1818, it was driven by several steam-powered oars, and it produced more wonder and fascination by Indians and whites than it did revenue in runs between Detroit and Buffalo for a few years.

The War of 1812 caused a temporary slowdown in Erie's development, but the boom in land picked up at the conclusion of the war. Many new settlers arrived from New England in 1816 and 1817 who were fleeing the results of an event half-way around the world in 1815, about which the refugees knew nothing, but which led them to abandon their farms and flee. Mount Tamboro in Indonesia, a 13,000-foot high volcano similar in type

239

to Mount Vesuvius, blew up, reducing its height by four thousand feet, and spewed out millions of tons of volcanic ash that was blown by atmospheric winds around the globe, blanketing the sunlight, and when it came time to plant seeds in New England the ground was still frozen. The chill remained all summer long, and there were snowstorms in Maine in July. No crops were grown and starvation stalked the land, and many just packed up and left for other parts, some settling in Erie County. The Blakeslee family was probably one of those refugee families, coming from Upper New York near the Massachusetts border. (There have been many Blakeslee/McCray marriages.)

The Borough of Elgin in Concord Township, Erie County, had a booklet written for its centennial, celebrated in 1976, which contained a history of the area, here reproduced in part:

"Years before Elgin was founded this was a great expanse of virgin forest, consisting of oak, pine, beech, walnut, hickory, chestnut, ash, maple and many other kinds of trees and many wild animals.

"In the spring of 1783 the State Legislature directed laying out large tracts of land in northwestern portions of the Commonwealth, into districts which would be given to soldiers who served in the Revolutionary War. It sent David Watts and his brother-in-law, William Miles, to survey the 10th District, which started one mile east of Waterford, across Amity and Wayne (Townships) to the Warren County line. They finished their surveying and returned to their home in Carlisle, Pa., that fall.

"Ten years passed before any other white men came into the 10th Donation District. The Legislature made their coming possible by passing an act in 1795, which gave settlers 400 acres of land and a six percent allowance to settle the land, providing they would pay into the state treasury 7 pounds and 10 shillings for every 10 acres of land, after which they and their heirs would have clear title to the land forever.

"David Watts and William Miles again came here since they had knowledge of the land south of the 10th Donation District which included Union, Concord and half of Wayne Townships. Miles and Watts entered into partnership with a man named Scott. Scott was supposedly rich and was to furnish the money; Watts, a lawyer, would give legal advice, and Miles the surveyor, would do the ground work. Profits would be shared.

"In 1795 the first settlers recorded in Wayne Township were Michael Hare and two men named Ridue and Call. In 1797 were Joseph Hall and Josiah Prosser.

"In 1798, The Holland Land Company, composed of rich men living in Holland who had purchased large tracts of land in Western New York and Pennsylvania from Robert Morris, financier of the Revolution, laid claim to the entire 10th Donation District. The company based its claim on the contract with Morris on which they had lent money to the United States to finance the Revolution, and filed suit to eject Scott, Watts and Miles from the lands. Scott went bankrupt and Watts wasn't able to find any evidence that would enable his company to win a suit against Holland Land Company by giving up all Scott's, Watt's and Miles' claim to the land on condition that each settler was to have a clear title of 200 acres of land whenever his settlement was completed. All the deeds of today go back to that name.

"The Company hired Miles as their land agent to replace Major Alden, the first agent of the company. Miles held this position until 1805, when Harm Jan Huidekoper of Holland, an original member of the Company, assumed control over all the Company's lands in Erie, Crawford, Warren and Venango Counties.

"After the settlers laid claim to their land and built their cabins, they had to buy all their provisions until they could clear land to raise them. Clearing the land usually took about a year and a half. All their provisions had to be brought from Pittsburgh by boats pushed up the Allegheny River and then up French Creek. The cost was so high many settlers found themselves deeply in debt. As there wasn't a mill established they had to pound their corn in a mortar, and to separate the coarse from the fine, they used a sieve made from a dried deer skin punched full of small holes and stretched over a hoop. The fine corn was used to bake bread on a board in front of the fire on the hearth. The coarse was made into samp, which was a corn mush or soup. For their meat they hunted deer, bear, rabbit, raccoon and squirrel.

"The first election held in Erie County was in October, 1798. On April 8, 1799, six districts were created, one at the house of William Miles of Concord Township. In the Act of April 11, 1807, Brokenstraw and Union were constituted one election district and was called No. 10. John Taylor's house was used as the election place and at Beaverdam the house of Thomas Morton.

"Around 1800, the land east of Union and Amity was known as Brokenstraw Township. In 1821 it was changed to Concord Township. In 1826 the township was divided, the northern portion was called Wayne (Township) and the southern portion kept the name Concord. In March, 1876 about one mile square territory was taken out of the western part of Concord Township and incorp-

orated into Elgin Borough. In 1798 Joseph Hall, a Virginian,
settled on the stream of water called Beaver Run, about six
miles south of the corner of southern New York State. The current in the stream was such as to make it a good place to have
water power for a grist mill and lumber mill. A little settlement sprang up around these mills and was known as Halltown.
In 1856 a general store was started. When the Philadelphia and
Erie Railroad was built in 1859 the settlement was known as Concord Station. Then houses and businesses were built.

"In 1836 the Erie County Anti-Slavery Society was organized by Joseph Moorhead, William Gray and Rev. T.H. Burrows of
Concord Township who took in slaves and hid them. They were
hidden in attics and hollowed-out haystacks. When safe they
were taken on "cracky wagons" to North East and there boarded
boats to Canada and freedom. There was another station in the
field past the Beaver Dam Cemetery where they were also hidden."

From: *Elgin Borough, 1876-1976*,
a pamphlet prepared for Elgin's
100th anniversary.

There is a photograph in the Elgin centennial booklet of the Elgin
Mill, with the date 1887 on it in large numerals. The caption reads:

"The feed mill that Joseph Hall erected here burned and
this one was erected. The dam was directly behind it. In the
summer the kids swam there (I was one of the kids) and in the
winter they all ice skated there, being careful to dodge
stumps. The dam went out in 1932."

Ernest McCray, son of Grant and Addie (Roberts) McCray, operated it
for a number of years before he left the East for southwestern United
States, where he served first as teacher and later as superintendent of
several Apache and Navajo reservations in Arizona and New Mexico.

A map of the Holland Land Company's District No. 6 shows a tract
directly north of present-day Elgin, with the name, "J. Hall, settler,"
on it. The tract's number is undecipherable on my map, but it is adjacent to the boundary of the Donation Lands No. 10 on the north. Tract
No. 43 in District No. 6 lies just south of it.

242

The following account of life in the days of Erie County's birth expresses the flavor of the time. It was written by Mrs. Elinor Carr, and was printed in *Middlebrook Anniversary Booklet,** in a chapter, "Pioneer Presbyterians." Presbyterians were the first to be organized, and the first American church was built by Presbyterians at Middlebrook. Middlebrook was located in Venango Township. Minor deletions were made in this account:

Pioneer Presbyterians

" Northwestern Pennsylvania was opened for settlement in the latter part of the eighteenth century. The French had been driven out, the Indians were not militant, and a region rich in promise beckoned to the hardy pioneers. Venturesome Scotch and Scotch-Irish folk, with some English, crossed the Alleghenies and began to claim the territory as their own. They came afoot, or on horseback, or in dug-out canoes up the river from Ft. Duquesne.

" Meagre as was their equipment -- rifle, ax, and simple household goods -- they yet had room for the Bible and Psalm book, in order that they might continue the custom of family prayers. A few neighboring families would occasionally gather together for community worship. It was not long before itinerant preachers began going from settlement to settlement to hold services of public worship and to administer the sacraments. It would seem as though Presbyterians were in the majority in those early days, and here and there a Presbyterian Church would be organized.

" Most of the settlers came to the southern part of the Presbytery by dugout canoe up the Allegheny. Nearer the lake (Lake Erie), pioneers came overland from eastern New York and New England along crude forest trails bringing with them wives and children on horseback with a horse or two, sometimes a cow and a pig, a few chickens, an ax and rifle and a limited supply of cooking utensils. Early records indicate many of the people were of Scotch-Irish descent and brought a Bible with them and a strong desire for some organized form of religion.
"Land needed to be cleared, homes needed to be provided and fields for harvest must be cleared. Families worked together to provide these essentials for survival. Log cabins were built, perhaps no more than fifteen feet square and sometimes only with three sides to protect a family from the elements. Meager patches of corn, oats and potatoes and wheat were grown among the great stumps and roots of the partially cleared forest.

* Inventory of the County Archives of Pennsylvania, Erie County, No. 25. Collected under direction of the Works Progress Administration. Printed by direction of the Board of County Commissioners, Erie, Pa., August, 1940.

"These people speedily wrought clearings in the vast forest which
surrounded their little cabins. Immense monarchs of the forest were first
girdled, then laid low, cut into logs and piled up on great heaps and
burned up. The county was so much in the woods that one could see no
sort of landscape from any point. The tall forest shut in the little
clearings, and one could not tell how much was cleared, nor could one get
any clear idea of what the country really looked like. There were no such
vistas of fertile lands and bountiful crops as one may now see from the
site of that first church building. Those "good old days" held much that
was not thought particularly good for the pioneer who had been used to the
conveniences of civilized community life "down east"; and the actual physical conditions of the settlers were in many ways far from agreeable and
comfortable.

"Right in the Middlebrook section, as in other places in the county,
the provisions for feeding and housing the livestock were so poor that
many animals perished from exposure and hunger. Thus the term "spring
poor" held a very significant meaning in the pioneer life of the county.
"Browsing" and nibbling the young shoots of the bushes and small trees was
much resorted to by the cattle in order to eke out their scanty supply of
winter food. Grain was too scarce to feed. Even the food supplies of the
people themselves were often little more plentiful, and it was not an unusual occurrence for the head of the house to put a two-bushel bag of grain
on his shoulder, which weighed 100 or more pounds, and walk off through
the obscure woods trails for six, ten, maybe twenty miles to a mill to
have it ground for his family use. A little patch of flax grew the fibre
from which the family linens were made on the crudest of home-made implements; while later a few sheep grew the wool which, mixed with the flax
fibre, made the "linsey-woolsey, butternut colored clothing," but we must
remember that theirs was the age of home-spun. A day's work in the harvest
field was equivalent to a bushel of wheat; and a pair of shoes were worth
a cord of wood or of bark. The product of their labor and skill in the
forest or in the field was, by the force of circumstances, their substi-
tute for legal tender.

"Rev. Elisha McCurdy and Joseph Stockton were sent into the region of
the Ohio Presbytery in 1799. The settlers had been in Middlebrook a few
short years when an earnest desire for community worship was realized.
Some of the frontier missionaries were sent out by the Presbyteries of
Fieldstone and Ohio.

"A letter from William Dickson of Lower Greenfield (Northeast) was
written by Rev. Johnston Eaton as follows:

"Our house was the first place of worship erected in the county of
Erie. It was on this wise: Mr. Satterfield had been sent into our neighborhood to preach a Sabbath. We fixed a kind of pulpit for him under a
beech tree in the woods, and then notified every family in the congregation of his coming. We had a good congregation and enjoyed the meeting.

244

At the close, old Father Hunter (Mr. James Hunter) who had been an elder over the mountains, called a number of the young men together, and said: 'Boys I want you all to meet me on next Thursday morning early, at a certain land corner, and bring your axes and dinners with you.' We all knew what was wanted and at the appointed time were on the ground bright and early. The old man said in a brief speech: 'We must have a house of worship. The Lord will be with us if we serve Him. Now let us go to work,' And work we did with a will. The trees were cut down and cut into lengths, notched and laid up. Whilst some were doing this, others cut down a red oak and split a part of it for clapboards for the roof, and a part into puncheons for the floor, and so diligently did we work, that just as the sun was going down, the whole structure was complete. There was not a nail nor a bit of iron in the entire arrangement. The door was made of thin puncheons with wooden hinges and latch. Openings were cut for windows, but the windows not put in. Even the chunking and daubing was done, with seats and pulpit complete.

"Yes we found one of the nicest red oaks you ever saw to make the puncheons of. It split just like a ribbon, and when the strips of wood fell apart, they required very little dressing to fit them for their purpose. The breastwork of the pulpit was simply a narrow strip of wood pinned to two upright strips, and all was complete. The truth is, we were real proud of our meeting house.

"It would have done you good to have seen the meeting of the boys that evening, after the house was finished, around the red oak stump that had furnished the tree for the puncheons. Father Hunter made us another little speech; he said: 'Now boys, we got a meetin' house, we must have preachin'; these ministers can't come here and preach for nothin', swimming streams and sleepin' in the woods at the roots of trees, as Mr. Wood did, not long ago. We must raise a little fund to pay them for their work. Now I propose that we appoint a treasurer and raise a fund, fining twenty-five cents each.

"This was good advice, and we at once began laying down our money on the stump, mostly laying down fifty cents apiece. When it came Father Hunter's turn, he laid down a dollar. Seeing this, one of the number took up his half and laid down a dollar instead. This was the beginning of a fund that was never exhausted whilst I continued in that congregation. The blessing of the Lord seemed to rest upon it. I think too, that from that day to this, that log meeting house has been a blessing to that entire region of County. It was a kind of center of attraction to people from the east, when seeking a location. Indeed the land has all been taken up by people who wished to be within hailing distance of the meeting house. So that, from a temporal sense, that day's work was well spent, though we young people did not think much about it at the time. I think it was one of the times when we builded better than we knew."

245

James McCray, Jr., was Scottish by birth and blood, a sojourner in Ireland, an American by adoption, but wherever and forever, a Presbyterian. Most of the first pioneers in Erie County were Scots-Irish who came, as one of them remarked, "with their Bibles, their Confession Of Faith, their catechisms, and their rifles." They undoubtedly held religious services as best they could in each other's homes, or whenever a circuit-rider came by. Whenever an ordained minister rode in, no matter what his denomination, word would quickly spread, and such a large number of families would turn out that services would be held out of doors, or, if the weather was very bad, in someone's large barn. It is difficult for us, living as we do in a largely unchurched society where only about ten percent of the population regularly attend worship services, to understand the hunger of our pioneer ancestors for preaching and religious instruction. Pioneer community life centered around churches, and the better class of pioneer families all held regular family prayers and Bible readings.

The Ohio Presbytery in 1799 sent the Reverend Elisha McCurdy and a youthful assistant, Joseph Stockton, into northwestern Pennsylvania to explore the prospects for establishing Presbyterian Churches there. They recommended that a church be built at Meadville. Because there was a predominence of Scots-Irish people, several small Presbyterian churches sprang up here and there, but there was a scarcity of ordained Presbyterian pastors, and they had to depend upon itinerant preachers to drop by at irregular intervals to hold worship services and administer sacraments. Nor did they deny their pulpits to ministers of other faiths, for they had a hunger for hearing The Word that was not to be denied them just because the minister didn't happen to be Presbyterian.

The scarcity of ministers made many Presbyterians turn to other churches, most notably the Baptist and Methodist ones. Presbyterians required that candidates for ministry spend several years learning not only the Bible and church dogma and liturgy, but also Hebrew, Greek and Latin, plus history, literature, philosophy and some science. Methodists weren't so fussy, and their clergy were trained in the Bible and the teachings of John Wesley, while just about any Baptist who felt that God had called him to preach could launch a ministry in any pioneer settlement, and worry later about details with the Conference. Far too few Presbyterian divines were ordained to supply the demand on every frontier, and so Scots-Irish pioneers turned to the Methodist and Baptist Churches simply because they were there and available.

In 1801 the Lake Erie Presbytery was founded to cover seven counties of northwestern Pennsylvania and some of the adjacent parts of New York.

246

The Reverend Elisha McCurdy was one of the most active in getting the Presbytery established.

> "The first church in Brokenstraw was a Presbyterian
> Church built of hewn pine logs and located on the William
> Belknap farm at Beaverdam. Rev. Mr. Ready was the first
> Pastor."

From George Carey's
"Some Early Recollections."

Carey's "Recollections" are rather sparing in dates, however, in his anecdote of the wedding day of John T. and Sarah(Blakeslee) McCray, Carey wrote that they were on their way to Beaverdam for the ceremony. Since John McCray was brought up in a Presbyterian family there is every reason to believe that they were married in the log Presbyterian church at Beaverdam. Family records reveal that their wedding date was May 11, 1826, so we know the church was erected before 1826. We may be quite sure, too, that the family of James and Eleanor McCray were charter members of that church and attended Sunday services there.

James McCray died just two weeks before the end of the year 1839, and eleven years later the McCray Church was built on the southwestern corner of his first Holland Land tract purchase of 1796. Why was the McCray Church a Methodist and not a Presbyterian church? Who knows? We know today that whole families sometimes leave a church, and as often as not join a church of another denomination. Their reasons for leaving can be as simple as that they just don't like the minister, or it can be that their beliefs take a turn in a different direction.

There are indications that James McCray, Jr., intended that a church be built where the McCray Methodist Church stands today. The farm he bequeathed to his son, Robert, is described in his will as a 60-acre farm, but an 1865 map of Concord Township shows the tract containing the church bears a notation, "90 acres" on it. The church property on this map was not separated from the rest of the tract. A modern Erie County map shows the church property to be 28 tax-free acres, which together with the "60-acre farm" James bequeathed would be a rounded-off ninety acres. I suspect that James told his son Robert of his hopes that a church would be built there someday, and set aside approximately thirty acres for the purpose of providing a place for it.

The settlers of Concord Township began meeting in homes and conducting Methodist services. When this movement began isn't recorded, but the Crowells, Blakeslees and McCrays were among the leaders. Elders Gray and Chase were early preachers in these home worship services. A Wesleyan Society was organized in 1844.

247

Cora McCray, daughter of Josiah R. McCray and grand-daughter of James McCray, Jr., who died at age 97 in a nursing home in Meadville, on November 11, 1987, wrote that the McCray Church was organized in 1845 by the worshippers who had been meeting at a schoolhouse. The building was built in 1851, and Jonathan Broadhurst was their first preacher. An early pastor was Thomas Burrows.

The building was used for a number of years by both Methodist and Congregational congregations. They didn't always seem to get on together in true Christian fellowship, for, as Cora McCray wrote, friction developed between the two groups, and it became so virulent that when the Methodist service was concluded on Sunday mornings, they would nail the door shut. When the Congregationalists arrived later in the day for their services, they would force open the door, hold their services, and then nail the door shut once more. The door must have become rather splintered after several sessions of this nonsense.

The Reverend Herbert Boyd, of Meadville, replied in 1988 to my letter of inquiry about the early days of the McCray Church, and whatever he could tell me about this conflict between the two church bodies. He sent a reply and enclosed this item:

Erie County Court records show that the property was jointly used by the Congregational Church and the Methodist Episcopal prior to 1900. Shortly before this date a lawsuit developed between the two bodies as to who had the use and control of the property. Court costs were to be paid by the Methodists. This was not done. As a result, one Manely Crosby, a trustee, sold the interests of the Methodists at public auction. For lack of bidders, he purchased the building himself. The Methodists purchased the property from him in 1902 and have been using it ever since. The church celebrated its 100th anniversary in 1945. In 1958 the building was raised and a basement put under it to provide a fellowship hall. Many improvements have been made, including new floors and pews.

Reverend Boyd said he had no knowledge of the silly business of the two groups nailing shut the door against each other. Probably everyone concerned would just as soon forget the whole farce and get on with the business of saving souls.

The McCray Methodist Church today is a neat white frame structure that overlooks a broad valley that James McCray never saw because trees blocked his view. What we see today barely resembles the bare-bones structure built at the mid-point of the last century. A 1940's photograph shows was a spare rectangular box with an "A" roof and lapped siding and domestic-type double-hung windows. Improvements since then have greatly improved its appearance; the profile is broader and lower in appearance, with a more attractive entrance and narthex having been added.

It is questionable whether or not James McCray would be pleased with today's church. Presbyterian churches of his day didn't hold with fancy ideas of having comfortable pews, colorful altars (Presbyterian churches do not have altars), stained glass windows and pipe organs. All of one's mind was supposed to be directed solely toward the communion table and the minister in the pulpit, and nothing was permitted to distract from those things. Hymns were sung unaccompanied, but God was probably pleased anyway. Presbyterians liked to think so, and they firmly held to their spartan ideas until quite recent times, and they still have critics who regard them as stiff and unbending.

The McCray Church may have been founded as a Methodist Church for the usual reason; the area just ran out of Presbyterians. Mrs. Gertrude McCray, vice chairman of the Borough Council of Elgin, suggested this in telling what happened to the Presbyterian Church at Beaverdam:

> "When attendance at the Presbyterian Church fell to a very few, they sold it to the Elgin Charge (Methodist), which is now the Elgin Methodist Church. My grandfather helped move it. He crawled on his knees and moved the rollers ahead. It was slated to be put down on the corners in Elgin, but they broke down where it is located now, and they decided to leave it there."

Mrs. McCray provided some maps and a pamphlet, *Elgin Boro, 1876-1976, Centennial*. One of the maps was hand-copied from a map at the Erie County Historical Society in Erie, Pennsylvania, dated about 1870, and a United Presbyterian Church is shown on the Elgin-Corry Road (Pleasant Street), near the Elgin crossroads, so apparently at that time there were still some Presbyterians around. The pamphlet gave details of other churches of Elgin:

> "The Disciple Church was erected in 1867 through the efforts of Mrs. G.W.N. Yost, of Corry. Rev. Walker and Rev. Way were its first ministers. The membership soon decreased through removals and in a few years ceased as an organization. Catholic services were held in Elgin and Concord Township. They were conducted by priests from Corry who commuted by train."

CHAPTER TWELVE

McCRAY FAMILY HISTORIES

A SCHOLARLY HISTORIAN George L. Carey was not, but what he left us was good history. During the decade of the 1880's, at the suggestion of the Historical Society of Erie County, he wrote a rambling assortment of recollections that he gleaned from children of the first settlers.

As any good historian does, Carey quoted his sources; they were John Smith, Jr., and Joseph, Robert and William McCray. The trouble was that he didn't further identify them. Knowing that they would all have been adults alive in 1882 and living in Concord Township, I referred to Upton's invaluable list of McCrays and found fourteen people bearing those names. Some were too young, some were dead by 1882, and others were living elsewhere. After eliminating the ineligible, I was left with one each Joseph, Robert and William who fit the conditions.

Joseph and Robert were sons of James and Eleanor (Townsley) McCray, and William was Robert's son. Carey's writings then began to appear to be very useful. Joseph was born in Washington County two or three years before the family moved to what was soon to be Erie County, and he would have had first-hand knowledge of those early days and may even have remembered the migration from Washington County. Robert, the youngest son who inherited the family farm, would have been able to recall, together with his brother, Joseph, and his son, William, many details they themselves remembered, as well as things told to them by James and Eleanor McCray about the early beginnings of Brokenstraw Township.

Carey provided the only written evidence that Old James was not only alive in 1796 or 1797, but he was in good enough health to have travelled from Washington County to Erie County and to work very hard. It was Robert who told Carey that "On one of James McCray's trips from Washington County, James McCray, Sr., returned with him and assisted him in erecting his permanent buildings and clearing his farm." This also tells that at least two trips were made back and forth before they finally settled in Brokenstraw Township, Erie County. If Old James had also settled there it seems certain that it would have been mentioned by Carey, so it may be safe to say that Old James died in Washington County. It is a pity that no mention was made of Ellen (Bell) McCray, and we can only guess where and when she died.

Mr. Carey's sparse prose exactly fits his subject, and I found his sometimes fanciful stories made me recall listening to the yarns spun by my dad and uncles at Grandfather Grant McCray's home in Elgin when I was a boy. Our family had experiences, I learned, which if described by anyone else but members of my family, might not have been believed by some listeners with a critical ear.

Some Early Recollections

by

George L. Carey

"About the year 1872, while I was town clerk, I received a letter
from the Historical Society of Erie, Penna., asking me for information
relating to the settlement and early history of Concord Township. The
records, once within the possession of the Society, had been burned with
the court house in 1824.

"It was presumed that I could find the desired information in the
township records, but no records had been kept that were of any value
(Mr. Carey's delightful honesty!), and the following was gathered by
personal visits to the old settlers and their families, and it is presented as a statement of fact.

"John Smith, Jr., Joseph McCray, William McCray, and Robert McCray
contributed matter, and for it to them I am indebted.

"I am fortunate these old settlers were interviewed at that time,
for many are now dead, and many valuable scraps of early history would
have died with them.

"William Miles was the first settler. He came from Ireland and first
settled in eastern Pennsylvania, but just where I could not ascertain.
He was a Revolutionary War soldier, and was captured at Fort Freeland
and taken to Canada where he was kept prisoner of war until peace was
declared. After his return he was appointed surveyor of the #10 Donation Tract of land.*

"Following that vocation for about ten years, he then settled on the
Wilber Webb farm where Eugene Webb now lives, situated about 7½ miles
northwest of Spartansburg at the foot what is known as Stranahan Hill.
This was in the year 1795. He then became agent for The Holland Land
Company who then owned a large tract of land in this section.

"At that time bands of Indians roamed through the forest on hunting
and fishing expeditions. There were the Cattaraugus Indians of the Corn-
planter tribe, the remnants of which live in Warren County to this day.

* The #10 Donation Lands were adjacent to the north side of the Holland
Land Company's District #6, which included Brokenstraw Township.

251

" William Cook, a brother-in-law of William Miles settled on what is known as the Stranahan farm in 1796. James McCray settled on the Robert McCray farm in the same year.* James McCray came from Scotland to Ireland then to the United States. He came from Washington County to Pittsburgh where he sold his wagon and put his bedding and provisions upon the horses, strapped his two boys Joseph and James upon the load leading the horses and his wife leading the cow, coming through the woods following the trail made by blazed trees. He built a shelter for his family and returned to Washington Co., for more provisions, and during his absence a bear killed the cow and the wolves ate it. A short time after this, the two boys were at play near the creek when a bald eagle attacked James, the smallest one and attempted to carry him away, but Joseph beat him off with a club and saved his life but not until the eagle had badly torn James' lips and otherwise injured him.

"On one of James McCray's trips from Washington Co., James McCray, Sr., returned with him and assisted him in erecting his permanent buildings and clearing his farm.

"It is well to say here that up to this time or rather up to 1820, Concord, Amity and Wayne Townships were in one plot and were known as Brokenstraw.

"William Smith settled on the Perkins farm near the George Spencer farm in 1795. One day a Yankee pedler by the name of Sackett came along and Smith told him that he wanted to sell his farm, and Sackett told him that if he would give him (Sackett) Power of Attorney he could find a buyer and sell his farm for him. Sackett sold the farm to Seely Neal and ran away with the money.

"John Smith, son of William Smith, was born on this farm and was the first white child born in Brokenstraw. William Smith lived the last days of his life with his son John and died about 1884** having become totally blind.

"The following statement was obtained from John Smith of his pioneer life: (Carey didn't use quotation marks, so it isn't possible to tell how much of the following was obtained from John Smith) My father came from County Derry Ireland in 1775, I was born in the township of Brokenstraw, Sept. 24, 1797, near where the George Spencer farm is now, 2½ miles northwest of Corry in the present Township of Wayne. We had hard times to get a living in the old days as all the provisions were brought from Pittsburgh up the Allegheny River to the mouth of French Creek then to LeBeouf. At that time, flat boats were used on the river and pushed up

* Robert was the son of James and Eleanor (Townsley) McCray.

** This date indicates that this was written between 1884 and 1891.

252

against the current with poles, and it would take from six to ten days to make the trip. These boats would carry from two to three tons to a load.

"This business was largely carried on by William Miles, who also furnished farm tools to the settlers, such as plows, drag teeth and such implements as were needed. The plows had on iron points and a wooden mould board. The drag (harrow) was two poles fastened together in the form of a capital letter A with about seventeen teeth driven through the poles at equal distances. Our hoes were more like a grub hoe and weighed seven or eight pounds. Our axes weighed about eight pounds and in chopping down a tree, we chopped around it so needed a good runner as well as a good chopper to cut down a tree.

"They built log houses and covered them with bark or shingles about three feet long and four to twelve inches wide and they were fastened on with poles instead of nails. Nails were an expensive luxury and made by the blacksmith and cost twenty-two cents a pound.

"There were no stoves and the first stove I ever saw was when I was about 20 years old. It was shaped like a square box, and holes for kittles and cost about twenty-five dollars. Before we had stoves, all the cooking was done at the fireplace.

"Fireplaces in those days were made of stone built to the height of five feet and on top of this the chimney was made of split sticks about two feet long and two inches square, laid up squarely and plastered inside and out with clay mixed with straw. We cut the straw used for this purpose with a hoe.

"The fireplace had no sides or jambs as they were called and to build a fire in one of them a large log was laid at the back of the fireplace and was called the back log and then smaller wood placed in front resting on iron horses called andirons. The back log would last for several days and when it was burned out another one would be place as before.

"Cooking was done by placing poles across the chimney above the fireplace and kettles were suspended from large iron hooks over the fire. Kettles made with a tight iron cover were used to bake with. The kettles would be placed on the hot coals and more coals be placed over them in that manner bread or cakes were baked.

"Later there bake ovens like an open sided box made of tin and by setting this before the fire the heat would bake and food by radiation.

"Very early in the lives of these settlers there were no mills to grind the corn and wheat and sometimes it was pounded between two stones into a coarse meal. The first grist I ever saw was from a mill about one mile from what is now Wattsburg, and was owned by a Mr. Reed. It was on

East Branch of French Creek. I remember going there once with my Uncle Wm. Smith and he carried his grain on the backs of his oxen. The first wagon I ever saw was brought into the country by Mr. Kincaid.

" My uncle Robert Smith, settled on a farm near Hare Creek and I remember him telling me that when he had his log house built that the wolves got into the house one night when he was alone and he had to climb up on the poles used for joists and stay there until morning when they left.

"When I was about ten years old, I remember my mother driving up the cows. One night a young deer came up with them and began browsing on some basswood sprouts that grew around the stump of a tree. Mother caught it and called to the children to bring a knife which they did, and she cut its throat and we had venison to eat, which was acceptable. Some of the settlers suffered from hunger, but we usually had enough to eat. I often saw Indians hunting and sometimes they would camp near our house and mother gave them food.

"My uncle William was a very ingenious man. He braided straw for saddles for packing goods on horseback and he was also a carpenter. More than seventy years ago, I roamed over the land where Corry is now and heard the howling of wolves, and saw bear and deer and plenty of them.

"In 1797, William McCray settled where Jason McCray now lives and George McCray settled on the Stewart farm in 1798. A bear once took a hog out of a pen on his farm and started for the woods with it, carrying it in his arms, walking on his hind feet. George chased it and killed it with a heavy chisel.

"Other settlers that came about this time were Jeduthia Gray, Joseph Hall, James Winders and Seely Neal. The Holland Land Company allowed them to settle on 400 acres of land and after five years of occupancy would give them a deed of 200 acres. But, before the expiration of the five years, all went back to Washington County except James McCray, Joseph Hall and James Winders. Wild animals destroyed their crops and they became discouraged. Some of them returned after several years and had to pay two dollars an acre for the same land. The first settlers had to go to Franklin or Pittsburgh for their flour and meal. After a while the Holland Land Company built a grist mill one mile south of Titusville and those who took their wheat there had to turn by hand the bolt to sift the bran from the flour.

"In 1809, William Miles moved to Union* and built the next grist mill in this vicinity. Miles had three slaves and one of them was a miller named Dick Bone, and he helped attend the mill. A state law made a slave free when he became twenty-eight years old. These were the last slaves

* Now Union City.

254

owned in this county*, for in 1821, slavery was abolished in this state.

"William Miles had a store at Wattsburg and all of his goods were poled up Big French Creek and sold to most of the settlers on credit. Those who were unable to pay he compromised with by taking part or all of their land. Miles was a shrewd man and was at this time almost a king among the settlers. The voting place was at Union and the settler went there to vote, and Miles told the election board that they must empty the ballot box and begin again, which they did, and after he and his son went to Waterford and voted, it was decided that emptying the ballot box at Union made the election illegal, so all the voters lost their vote.

"Miles had some claim against the Holland Land Company which was in court about twenty years,+ when the Land Company compromised with him giving him a large tract of land. Huidekoper then became the agent of the Land Co., and finally bought their interests.

"William Cook and Miles were brother-in-laws and their wives were the first white women in this country. John Cook settled on land now owned by A.A. Hammond. James Brown settled on land now owned by A.L. Woles. Seely Neal on land now owned by George Spencer. James Winders on the Ezekial Lewis farm back of the Edwin Hammond Farm.

" There were no shoemakers and no leather to make shoes of so they made moccasins out of deer skins. Finally, a tannery was built at Beaver Dam. When the settlers could get leather, they had a shoemaker come to their house and make shoes for the whole family. Very few guns were owned and of course the ones they did have were flint locks. There were no matches made and flint and steel together with a piece of fungus called punk, gathered from the hollow of soft maple trees was the means

* The Gradual Emancipation Act of 1780 stated that no child born in Pennsylvania after date of the Act could be a slave. The twenty-eight years he referred to was the number of years since enactment of the Act, and if Dick Bone was born prior to that he would have remained a slave until slavery was abolished in 1821.

+ There were several firms selling land in northwestern Pennsylvania, and William Miles had a business in this line with David Watts. Watts had a partnership with Alexander Scott in The Population Company, which was in litigation for years with The Holland Land Company over 162 acres which both firms claimed. A settlement was reached that proved unsatisfactory for both claimants.

of making fire. By striking the steel down across the edge of the flint
a spark would throw out that would catch in the punk and could then be
blown into a flame. Another way to make a fire was to shoot a small
charge of powder into a wad of tow which would ignite the tow. The coals
were banked at night, that is covered with ashes, and would usually keep
the coals alive until morning when they could be blown into a blaze. Dr.
Perkins of Wayne Township brought the first stove into the country from
the Black River country in New York State and people came from miles
around to see that stove.*

"Michael Hare was an early settler on Hare Creek about sixty rods
above the present pumping station of the Corry Water Company. From there
he moved to Union and later moved to Waterford where he died and is
buried. He was a native of Ireland and served in the French War (The
French And Indian War), and was at Braddock's defeat at what is now
Thompson's Station on the Penna. Railroad. He lost his scalp in fighting afterward during the Revolutionary War.** He was born June 10, 1727,
and died May 3, 1843, at the age of 116 years.

"Joseph McCray went to school in Titusville for two months and then
was drafted into the army. He walked to Erie through the snow and was
assigned to Captain William Smith's company. He served forty days and
was allowed to return home.+ At one time when Joseph was returning home
from a neighbor's he saw two cubs trying to climb a tree. He caught
them and started for home, the little cubs biting and scratching him to
the best of their ability but he held them until the old mother bear
made her appearance when he thinking discretion the better part of valor
dropped the cubs and made his escape. Uncle Robert told of a bear coming to his home during the haying time and took a hog out of the pen and
started carrying it in his arms, but they attacked him so lively with
their pitchforks that he dropped the hog and made his escape. He also
told that at one time when they were living on the side hill just west
of the Heman Heath farm, they heard a cow bellowing as if in distress
down towards the tamarack swamp. The oxen broke loose and ran toward the
noise and the men followed with pitchforks. When they reached the James

* Probably a "six sheet stove," the first practical cast iron stove for
domestic use, and an instant success. Six flat cast sections were
bolted together to form the firebox.

** Seldom did anyone survive scalping.

+ This was a Pennsylvania state draft, not the U.S. Army. The Army did
not draft men into service until the Civil War, and anyone with money
could buy his exemption from service.

256

Crowell farm, they found that a bear had killed Sam Smith's cow and was eating her. Upon seeing them, he ran into the swamp. Sam Smith set a bear trap the next day and caught the bear. He also told about Sam Smith going at one time to a neighbor's where he bought a little pig and when he was carrying it home in his arms the pig became uneasy and began to squeal, which attracted the wolves and they came after the pig which Sam dropped and the last Sam saw of it the wolves were fighting for it.

"Those who tried to keep sheep at all had to keep them in a strong pen built of logs at night and in an enclosure in the daytime to keep them away from the wolves.

"Joseph Hall was among the very first settlers here. He came from Virginia and settled where Elgin now is. There were many privations and much suffering among the settlers at times and many incidents could be told of their trials. One of them is worth repeating here. Frank Stranahan tells of one time when all the neighbors collected themselves at one house with all their provisions, where they stayed except for a few of the men who went to Pittsburgh for more provisions. The food of those left behind became exhausted before the return of the men and the snow was deep and the little colony had about given up hope of living when one day a two year old steer came around the house. No one knew who owned it and they shot it and that furnished food until the return of the men from Pittsburgh.

"A Mr. Loney settled on land now owned by Samuel Stowell about the year 1798. He had a large family and several of them died and were buried on his farm. The farm was on a chestnut ridge and the wild animals were attracted there until he declared there was a squirrel under every leaf. His crops were destroyed and he became discouraged and declared he wished the devil had broken his leg before he ever came to this country. Curiously enough, shortly after that he had the misfortune to break his leg and as soon as he could be moved his neighbors put him and his family on a flat boat on French Creek and let them float down to Pittsburgh where they came from.

" The first church in Brokenstraw was a Presbyterian Church built of hewn pine logs and located on the William Belnap farm at Beaverdam. Rev. Mr. Ready was the first pastor.

" There were no carriages or roads for them if there had been any, and when the young people rode out the young lady rode behind her escort on the same horse. One of the early anecdotes related to me was as follows: John McCray* was to be married and taking his bride-to-be upon his horse behind him he started for Beaverdam, several young people going with

* John T. McCray and his bride, Sarah Blakeslee, my gr great grandparents. The date was May 11, 1826. Obviously, the church was built before 1826.

257

them. Before they arrived at their destination, while passing a tree with low branches, John's bride-to-be was brushed off the horse with a limb, John riding on for some time before he discovered the accident. When he returned and she was once more assisted to her seat, the party proceeded on their way.

" The first election in Brokenstraw was about the year 1800, and only three voters attended the election. These three voters appointed themselves on the election board and administered the oath of office to each other in all manner of ways. The object of this election was to get their share of taxes upon the unseated lands and apply it to road building.

"Seely Neal came in at an early date and located on land known as the George Spencer Farm, which was previously settled by William Smith. Neal built a saw mill in a small stream on this farm and sawed the timber and built the first frame house in Brokenstraw. Part of this house is still standing.

"Concord Township was organized in 1820 but by whom or by what authority, I do not know. It is likely that Sealy Neal was one of the men as he named the township Concord after his native town of Concord, New Hampshire. The township is bounded as follows: on the north by Wayne Township and the City of Corry, and the south by Crawford County, on the west by Union Township, and on the east by Warren County. When formed the township contained 20,590 acres. This has since been reduced to 19,623 acres by the organization of the City of Corry in 1836 and Elgin Boro in 1876.

" The first supervisors were Sealy Neal and James Stewart. The amount of tax assessed that year was $230.17. The auditors were Simeon Stewart, Eli Gray and James McCray. The constable Eliab Perkins. The first roads built were the County Line Road between Crawford and Erie Counties, and from Union to Columbus, Warren County. Simeon Stewart was one of the commissioners and ran the road from Union to Columbus past the Stewart Place.

" The first church in Concord was the McCray Church. The Weslyan Society was organized in 1844 and built the church in 1851. Jonathan Broadhead was their first preacher. The first school house was built in 1825 at Cook's Corners near the foot of Stranahan Hill. Milton Graves was the first teacher there. The first frame barn was built on Dr. Baker's place 1½ miles east of Oxbow Hill and built by Simeon Stewart. The first saw mill was on Little French Creek a short distance from where Corry now stands. This was also built by Stewart & Co., the first post office was at Cook's Corners. The population of the township in 1873 was 1438.

"Elders Gray and Chase were early preachers and held services in private houses. George McCray settled on the Stewart farm in 1798. James

Winders on the Ezekial Lewis farm and James Stewart on land now owned by Oscar Chase in 1818. Stephen and John Heath came here in 1823 and Heman Heath came in 1832. John B. Chase in 1835. Paul Hammond in 1837. William Olmstead in 1830.

"Until the year 1850, the state law required all able bodied men between the ages of 18 and 45 to meet each year for militia drill. The men from the locality assembled under those orders at Union and Wattsburg. John Bates, Sr., was the Colonel and John Lelley (Lilly?) and Charles Kennedy were the captains. Captain Josiah Brown organized a rifle company in 1839 and held drill at Stranahans.

"No fruit was to be had by the settlers until their young orchards could bear with the exceptions of wild berries. Preserves and sauce were frequently made from pumpkins and large quantities of pumpkin was dried for winter use. The first sleighs were long sleds with runners often ten or twelve feet long. These sleighs rode very easy over smooth ground but were very uncomfortable over rough ground or over obstructions. No such thing as a bob sled had been made up to this time.

"NOTE: whoever reads this gathering of material does not want to forget that it was made in 1872 but the writer has made it pretty clear by references to present owners so that only one familiar with the families mentioned should have no trouble in following the record."

-0-

Dennis Davis, of Erie, Pennsylvania, a descendant from Cyrus McCray, contributed the following article, published in *The Pennsylvania Farmer*, April 6, 1929. It was written by his great great great uncle, Henry McCray, son of James and Eleanor (Townsley) McCray. It was found among the personal effects of his grandmother, Blanche Mae Ingalls Davis (See "An Adoption", further along in this document). Henry McCray was age eighty when he wrote this article.

An Old Timer

"As we speed over the paved road from Corry, Pa., or as we fly over in the latest type airplane, we little dream of conditions as they were at the end of the eighteenth century. My great grandfather, James McCray, Sr., came to this country from Ireland in 1796 and settled in Westmoreland County, Pa., Three years later my grandfather, James McCray, and his wife came to Erie county, Pa., by way of Pittsburgh, where grandfather bought two horses. This was before the days of covered wagons, so they packed their goods on one horse and rode the other. Most of the way the trail led through the woods, as this part of Pennsylvania was practically all forest land. In 1799 they settled in Concord township, Erie County. In those days the question of railroads, paved roads, schools or churches did not enter into the selection of a homesite. The chief objective then was to locate near a spring. Concord township was dotted with springs and today one will find the homes located near clear sparkling springs. In 1820 my father, John McCray, took up 240 acres of land in Concord Township. He cut down trees near a good spring and built his log house. There were no public roads at that time.

" I do not remember the old log house where my mother reared sixteen children, teaching school in her home a part of each year. In 1836 my father built a modern frame house near a public road. I was born in that house near the old homestead, and lived there until I sold it a year ago and moved to Corry. I have lived in Concord township all my life with the exception of a few boyhood years in the oil country, at Foxburgh, 42 miles below Oil City. That was in the early seventies, and oil at that time was worth $4 a barrel and business was booming. While there I tended a toll station between Foxburgh and St. Petersburgh on a pike road. Often there were as many as seven stage coaches a day paid toll. A man by the name of Dunk Carr tended a ferry boat at Foxburgh on the Allegheny River. It was there in the oil country that I cast my first ballot, voting for U.S. Grant for president. One man challenged my vote, thinking that I was too young to vote, but I proved I was of age. Since that time I have voted for a president every four years, my last vote being for Herbert Hoover.

" I was the youngest of eight boys. Five of my brothers were in the Civil War. One died on his way home after serving his time out in the Army. Another died in Anderson Prison and is buried at the National Cemetery there. One brother, Captain of Company A, 145th Regiment, Pennsylvania Volunteers, was wounded at Gettysburgh but stayed till the close of the war. (That was Horace McCray) I had eight sisters. The oldest celebrated her 96th birthday in Corry last December. (That was Amy M. McCray, who died in 1929.)

"Last fall I visited the old oil fields where I worked in 1880 and
saw some changes. The old pike road is now a good paved highway, and
automobiles and buses have replaced the old stage coach. At Foxburgh a
nice iron bridge spans the Allegheny River, doing the work of Dunk Carr's
old ferry boat. I remember when the Erie and Sunbury railroad was built
through Concord township, now as the Erie and Philadelphia. I also remember the laying of the Atlantic and Great Western, now called the Erie.
The two railroads formed a junction where the City of Corry now is. I
came down to the junction with an older brother who hauled a load of oil
up from Titusville. (That was Wilson C. McCray.)

"Corry was nicknamed the city of stumps later. Some years ago they
had "Old Home Week" in Corry and my boy Vance, who is now in Cedar
Rapids, Iowa, was a lad. He had a yoke of steers broke and the committee
for the night parade got him to drive them. They placed an old stump on
a boat (a sled-like vehicle) and the steers led the parade drawing the
boat with a sign which read 'The last stump removed'."

Henry McCray

Note: The first paragraph of Henry's account was lifted intact from
his copy and put at the beginning of the history on page 270. The last
two sentences of Henry's account were substituted in the pirated history.
One can note other similarities in the various McCray family histories
that indicate that later writers were inspired by earlier writers. They
doubtless had no intention of plagiarizing, but they probably thought
certain passages were well written and used them again to dress up their
family account.

The Many And Varied McCray Family Histories

There are many histories of the family and descendants of James
and Ellen (Bell) McCray, and every few years someone finds another one.
Fortunately, they all relate quite similar stories, and most of them
agree on a more or less "standard" version. Comparison shows that many
of them were partly copied, sometimes word-for-word, from earlier versions, and some have been embellished with improbable details. We are
indebted to the people who wrote them, however they may differ, for they
set a stage for research, and without them we might be still floundering
and lost in the stacks and courthouse files.

Differences in detail revolve principally around (a) the time of
arrival of the McCrays in America (b) whether or not Old James and/or
his son saw service in the American Revolution, and (c) where the McCrays
lived from the time of their arrival in America to their undoubted settling in Erie County, Pennsylvania near the end of the eighteenth century. Until official records (which may not exist) are found, the differences cannot be absolutely settled, but meanwhile we should be able
to accept the version put forth in the majority of the stories, which
are pretty well substantiated by census records, newspaper items, and
biographical sketches in county histories.

The earliest identifiable family history was written by Dr. Fred
McCray about 1948, when he was seventy-three years old. He was the son
of Jason and Amanda (Cushing) McCray, and grandson of my great great
grandparents, John T. and Sarah (Blakeslee) McCray. Dr. Fred McCray
married Grace I. Gates, and they moved to Sioux City, Iowa, in 1909. He
referred in a letter to a McCray family history, but did not further
identify it, so someone did write a version earlier than his. Dr.
McCray died in Sioux City, Iowa, in 1951, and both he and his wife are
buried there.

Based on information obtained from Mrs. Daniel Blakeslee (Bessie
Crowell), a descendant from James and Eleanor (Townsley) McCray, Fred
wrote that the family arrived in America in 1777, a date Mrs. Blakeslee
said came from her grandfather, Robert McCray, son of James and Eleanor.
Fred acknowledged in 1946 in a letter to J. Duane Upton that he was
aware that other McCrays had said the arrival year was 1784, but he did
not explain why he believed the earlier date was correct. He may have
preferred that date because of several references to James McCray, a
Revolutionary War soldier, in the Pennsylvania Archives*. The Archives

* *Pennsylvania Archives*, 5th Series, Vol III, p. 507, and Vol VI, p. 137-8
and p. 537.

262

did not identify these men further. Each of these men was in different companies of militia, under different commanding officers, and were undoubtedly three different men with a common name.

In 1946 in a letter Fred wrote to Upton that his aunt Ellen (Ellen McCray McPherson), daughter of John T. and Sarah (Blakeslee) McCray, had written: 'All I know about Great Grandfather is that he was in the Revolutionary War. This statement by my aunt, together *with the fact that as far as we can learn* (Italics mine), the family was living in Cumberland County, 1778 to 1782, the Service Record in the State Archives of James McCray of that county, and the absense of claims of descent from this ancestor by other families of the name, for the basis for my claim that he was my ancestor.'

"So far as I can learn, I am the only member of the family so presumptuous as to claim the first James McCray as a Revolutionary ancestor.

"A few years ago I became interested through reading an item in a book prepared by several chapters of the D.A.R. of Erie County:'Soldiers of the American Revolution, who at some time were residents of, or whose graves are located in Erie County, Pennsylvania.'

"Under 'Names of Men Whose Services are not Clearly Established', is the item which is as follows:

'McCRAY JAMES--James McCray is said to have come to America with his parents when about 17 years of age; settling first in eastern Penna., and later of Westmorland (sic) County, still later coming to Concord Twp., Erie County, where he took up about 800 acres of land in 1796. There is no record of his birth or death, but his will is on file in Erie County probates, dated Dec. 9, 1839; reg. Jan. 10, 1840, so he probably died between those dates. His wife was Eleanor Townley, of whom no further record has been obtained.

'Service for a James McCray is found in Penna. Archives, 5th Series, Vol. 3, p. 507; as private, Captain Jacob Stake's Company, 10th Penna. Regt Sept. 10, 1778; enlisted for during the war. Also, 5th SEries, Vol. 6, p. 137-8; as private, 8th Class, Captain John Woods' 7th Company, 1st Battalion, Cumberland County Militia, in service March, 1778; James McCray.

'Owing to lack of birth and death dates of James McCray above, it is impossible to state definitely whether or not these services apply to the James McCray of Concord Twp., Erie County. His tombstone has not been found, but he may have been buried over the county line in Crawford County.'"

It's a pity that Fred didn't explain how he knew that "the family was living in Cumberland County, 1778 to 1782." The dates need proving.

"In 1941 I wrote the D.A.R. Registrar General for information as to records of James McCray as a Revolutionary War ancestor, and received the following:

' Up to the present time no member of our Society has claimed the record of this ancestor, and until a record has been examined and verified in the regular way we could not give a decision as to either lineage or service.'

"Yes, the marker on the James McCray grave in Concord Center Cemetery, I believe is a mistake.* This belief is strengthened by the evident confusing of the two James McCrays in the D.A.R. item quoted above.

"A couple of years ago, I submitted to the Society of Sons of the American Revolution a supplemental claim (I was already a member through descent from my mother's ancestors) of descent from James McCray, 1st., and my claim was approved by the Society."

In another letter to Upton, he copied this, saying: "The following is a copy of the first historical items of the McCrays that came into my hands:

'James McCray, son of James and Ellen (Bell) McCray, born in Manalian, Ireland in 1760. He came with his father's family to America in 1777, landing in Philadelphia, Penna. He lived for a time in Cumberland, also in Westmorland County, but located permanently in Erie County, being one of the first settlers of Concord Twp. He died in January 1840. He married in 1792?, Eleanor, daughter of John and Polly Townley. Firm in his beliefs and rather hot tempered. Was a Democrat and a Presbyterian. Six feet tall, weight 180 lbs., fair complection (sic) and blue eyes. Children; John, Robert, Joseph, George, James, William, Ellen, Jane and Betsy.'

"This, as I understood at the time, was supplied by Mrs. Blakeslee's grandparents. Probably it is correct as to the main facts. However, I do not take much stock in some of the details. As to "Mannalian", in my opinion, this may be a mistake; or, may have been confused with a Manallen in Pennsylvania."

With this much contradictory and just plain wrong data, it is not surprising that Dr. McCray's version of the early McCrays contained so many errors. Examination of two quite good and complete maps of Ireland did not turn up a Manalian or anything similar; I suspect that the unknown author of the above paragraph got his material by word of mouth, and misunderstood the name of the Irish county, Monaghan. The childrens'

* It is carved on this stone that he was a Revolutionary War soldier.

names are partly correct, but Ellen was the mother of the children, and if there was a Jane McCray, this is the only record of it. Samuel wasn't listed, and John and Joseph may have been half-brothers of the other six siblings. Like all the other McCray family histories, this one is almost totally devoid of mention of sources of the material, which makes it difficult to either verify or deny accuracy. One letter contained this paragraph which I think has all the earmarks of something taken from one of those numerous county histories:

"James McCray was a British soldier, but deserted, and came from Canada to the United States, where he afterward made his home. His grandson, J.W. McCray, of the firm of McCray Brothers, oil producers, Bradford, was born in Crawford County, Penna., in 1840. He started in business for himself, in 1865, at Titusville, Penna."

In another letter to Upton he mentioned having been told by Mrs. Rollo McCray (Annice Ensworth) that James McCray landed in Baltimore. He also quoted from an un-named source:

"ELEANOR TOWNLEY, born in Washington Town, Washington County, Kentucky, married James McCray in 1793. Moved to Concord Twp., Erie County, Penna., about 1798.

"Washington, Kentucky, is in Mason County. However, there is a Washington, in Washington County, Pennsylvania, where, more careful study shows, James and Eleanor were married in 1793."

Regardless of the errors in the following history of the McCray family, Dr. Fred McCray set down what seemed to him to be the best account, based on the reams of confusing data he had to work with, and for it we can be grateful. It was a good beginning and it provided a base from which other historians have slowly developed more complete and accurate histories. Let it be here said that *this* history is not the last word on the McCrays, and I am quite certain that it contains many errors that some future researchers will disclose, hopefully in a spirit of kindness, remembering that they, too, may be in error.

The references above to "Manalian" may have been to Menallen Township, in Fayette County, Pennsylvania (see p.188), where one John McCray lived in the late eighteenth century. There is no known connection between John's family and any other McCray families, but it strengthens my belief that there was a close enough relationship that each of the McCray families in America knew where the others had settled.

THE McCRAY FAMILY

by

Fred McCray

James McCray and Ellen Bell, born of Scotch parents and natives of Scotland, married and removed to Ireland, evidently making that country their home for a number of years. James and his family emigrated to America in 1777, landing at Philadelphia, Pennsylvania, and settled in Cumberland County of that state.

He was a Revolutionary War soldier. His service record as given in the Pennsylvania Archives:
5th Series, Vol. 3, p. 507
5th Series, Vol. 6, pp 137-8 and 537

Children of James and Ellen (Bell) McCray: Samuel, William, James, George, Robert, Joseph, John and Betsey. We have no further word of Samuel, John, Joseph, or Betsey.

William (James 1) married Nancy Miles of Titusville, Penna. Children: William, Robert, and James. (We understand that this James was the "Corntassel Jim" of Oil Creek fame.)

George (James 1) lived in Clarion County. One of his descendants, Rolla McCray, was, and may be at present, a county official of Erie County.

Robert (James 1.) born in 1760. Died Jan 1, 1840. Married in 1792, in Washington, Washington County, Penna., Eleanor Townley, daughter of John and Polly Townley. Children of James 2 and Eleanor (Townley) McCray: Joseph, William, James, John, George, Eleanor, Jane and Betsey. The descendants of James and Eleanor McCray make up the majority of the McCrays of Erie County.

The above covers our knowledge of the first and second generations; and aside from a few exceptions, our acquaintanceship with the history and genealogy of succeeding generations is limited to somewhat sketchy records of the descendants of my immediate ancestors, James and Eleanor McCray.

Joseph McCray (James 2, James 1), born probably in Washington Co., Pa., in 1794, died in Erie Co., in 1884. Married 1st, ...Townley? One son, George, by this marriage; married 2nd, Sara Scott. Children: Thomas, John, James, Joseia and William. Thomas, John, and James were soldiers in the Civil War. The first son, George, was born in Kentucky and spent his life in that state.

Mrs. Fred (Viva McCray) Snapp, great granddaughter of John T. McCray, wrote a history which she said came from Mrs. Minnie Stearns, granddaughter of Josiah McCray.

"James McCray born in Scotland was taken by his parents to Ireland when a child, during the time of the Persecution, and they settled in the county of Monoghan. They had two children, John and Joseph. His wife died sometime later. James married a second wife Miss Nellie Bell. The year of James immigration to Ireland is not known. James and Nellie Bell had six children, they came to America in 1784 bringing their six children namely--William, James, Betsy or Elizabeth, George, Samuel and Robert. Joseph and John the sons of the first wife never came. Robert was seven when he came to America, James 19 or 20."

She continued with names of later generations, then added:

"John and Sallie (John T. and Sally Blakeslee McCray) lived on the road running west near the McCray Church, I think the family were born there, later when Warren was married I remember my mother saying they lived where Leon Blakeslee now lives and she lived where Thayer McCray's widow now lives."

Thayer McCray died in 1933, so this was written after that year.

Rollo McCray, mentioned by Dr. Fred McCray in his history, wrote an account of the origins of our family. He was descended from George and Jean (Murray) McCray, and lived in Waterford, Pennsylvania.

McCRAY FAMILY

"1. About 1784 James McCray and his wife (maiden name, Nellie Bell) came to America with their six children -- William, James, Betsy, George, Samuel, and Robert. After a voyage of some three months they landed at Baltimore, whence they went into Pennsylvania, settling at that time in Cumberland County. William, James, Betsy, and George were born before the emigration.

" 2. William, the eldest child, married Nancy Miles, and reared a family of twelve children, most of whom live in Erie and Crawford Counties, Pa.

" James, Second, son of James First, married Eleanor Townley. They had nine children -- Joseph, James, William, Jane, George, John, Eleanor, Robert, and Betsy. This James Second is the one whose grave is near the front of the McCray Cemetery in Erie County, Pa.

" Betsy, the only daughter of James, First, married William Reed. This family is scattered around Clarion County and Crawford Counties.

"George, the third son of James, First, married Jennie Murray. They had ten children, a number of whom settled in and around Youngsville and Garland, Warren County, Pennsylvania. Their children, so far as known, are: Anna (Mrs. Fulton); Margaret (Mrs. Green); Polly (Mrs. Brown); .... (Mrs. Duncan); Alexander, George, William F. (Billy), Jim, and Joe.

"3. William F. McCray, son of George McCray and Jeannie Murray, married Mary Jackson (of Spring Creek, Warren County, Pennsylvania), December 17, 1835. Their children were:

" Eli McCray, born December 21, 1837; died May 1, 1857, Centerville, Pennsylvania.

"Mary Ann McCray, (Morton), born July 21, 1844; died November 14, 1914, at Spring Creek, Warren County, Pennsylvania.

"Alonzo Jackson McCray, born January 21, 1840; died July 5, 1881, in Arkansas.

"William Alexander McCray, born April 26, 1842; died February 8, 1914, at Spring Creek.

"Charles Edwin McCray, born December 28, 1846; died November 23, 1908, at Magnolia, Mississippi."

- - - - - - -

J. Duane Upton, author of *Genealogical Record of Heron, Kerr, McCray, Porter, Shelmadine, Snyder, Tubbs, Upton,* wrote a digest of the McCray family histories. This is by no means the extent of Mr. Upton's account. This portion is included for comparison with other versions.

"The standard version of the McCray family history reveals that the writer's great great great grandfather, James McCray, Sr., was married to Nellie (Bell) McCray, great great great grandmother to the writer of this family history. They were both Scotch, of Scotch parentage, who removed to Monaghan County, Ireland, at the time of the Persecution in Scotland. It is contested about James McCray, Sr., being a Revolutionary War soldier, several members of the clan claiming this to be untrue -- as the family did not come over to America until after the war. Several others claim the family arrived in time for James McCray, Sr., to participate in the Revolution. The writer is inclined to believe, after careful research, that the service of our James McCray, Sr., in the Revolutionary War is very doubtful, and he would not claim this without more substantial proof than he has seen."

Mrs. Daniel R. Blakeslee, in one of her letters to Upton concerning
the early history of the McCrays, said that her sister, (probably Annie
Crowell) had written a McCray history that was read by Cora McCray at a
McCray reunion. Cora was a great great granddaughter of James and Eleanor
(Townsley) McCray who lived to age 97 and died in 1987. Mrs. Blakeslee
said "My grandfather, Robert McCray, told my sister what to write."

Annie Crowell's History

" Our great great grandfather James McCray Senior was born in Scotland. His wife's name was Nellie Bell. He moved to Ireland and thence
to the U.S. in 1777. Was a member of the Presbyterian Church in Titusville. Was a Democrat. Had seven sons and one daughter. Namely: William, James, George, Robert, Joseph, John, Samuel and Betsey.

" James Junior was born in Mannahan, Ireland in 1760. Came to the
U.S. in 1777. Landed in Philadelphia. Lived in Cumberland Co. Later
settled in Concord Township, Erie Co. Was the first family to settle in
Concord. He married Nellie Townsley in 1792. He died January First,
1839, at the age of 79 years."

Cora McCray herself produced a McCray history. She got a few more
things correct, and she seems to be the first to have accepted the arrival date in America as 1784 and so wrote it. Her account has them
landing in Baltimore instead of Philadelphia.

Cora McCray's History

" About 1784 James McCray and his wife whose maiden name was Nellie
Bell came to America with their six children, William, James, Betsey,
George, Samuel and Robert. After a voyage of some three months, we are
told they landed in Baltimore, whence they went into Pennsylvania, settling at that time in Cumberland County. William married Nancy Miles and
reared a family of twelve children. Most of them lived in Erie and Crawford Counties.

"James II married Eleanor Townsley. They had nine children. This
James II is the one whose grave is near the front of the McCray Cemetery
in Concord Township. George, the third son of James I married Jennie
Morrow. They had ten children. A number of whom are located in and
around Youngsville and Garland, Pa.

"Samuel, the fourth son, married Polly McCoy and they had one son,
James, but we have no record of this branch of the family. Robert,

youngest son of James McCray I commonly was known as Old Uncle Bob. He married Mrs. Jane Bruce and they had four children. It is to Samuel McCray, son of Old Uncle Bob that we owe the most of our information."

One of the descendants of James and Eleanor (Townsley) McCray and their son, John T. McCray, and grandson, Warren McCray, wrote a history of the McCray family. The name of the author isn't given, but this person provided a bit of color and excitement to his account. The latest date given here is 1945, so it must have been written after that.

"As we speed over the paved roads or as we fly over the earth with the latest type of airplane, we little dream of conditions as they were at the end of the eighteenth century.

"Our great great great Grandfather, James McCray, Sr., was born in Scotland, moving to Ireland when small. He came from Ireland to America in 1784 then in 1796 he brought his family and settled in Westmoreland County, Pennsylvania. Three years later our great great grandfather James McCray Jr and his wife came to Erie county by way of Pittsburgh, where he bought 2 horses. This was before the days of covered wagons so they packed their goods on one horse and rode the other one. Most of the way the trail led through the woods as this part of Pennsylvania was practically all forest lands. In 1799 they settled in Concord township, Erie county. In those days the question of railroads, paved roads, schools or churches did not enter into the selection of a homesite. The chief objective was to locate near a spring. Concord township was dotted with springs and today will find homes located near clear sparkling springs. At that time the woods were full of wild game.

"One day our great grandfather John then but a boy was carrying grist hung across his horses back when he spied two cubs at the foot of an old hollow tree, he had an empty sack with him and boy-like he jumped off his horse put the cubs in the sack and started home. He rode on feeling pretty rich with his pets but he had not gone far when the scene changed. Old mother bear came home and finding her cubs gone she tracked the boy and soon overtook him. Lucky for him there were two good dogs along and they fought off the bear and our great grandfather got home but one of the dogs was bitten and torn so badly that it died the next day. One day our great great grandfather heard one of his pigs squealing and ran out to investigate, he saw a big bear walking off with a pig, not having time to load his gun he grabbed a pitchfork and attacked the bear which dropped the pig after a short fight.

"In 1820 our great grandfather John McCray took up 240 acres of land in Concord Township. He cut down trees near a good spring and built his log house. There were no public roads at that time. Our great grandmother reared sixteen children, and taught school in her home part of

270

each year. Our grandfather was born in that log house in 1827. In 1836 our great grandfather built a modern frame house near a public road and had it most cleared when he died in 1855. In 1892 his youngest son Henry McCray our great uncle built his new brick house near the old homestead. These 16 children were 8 boys and 8 girls. Our grandfather, Warren McCray, was in the Civil War with four of his brothers. One brother died on his way home after serving his time out in the army. Another one died in Andersonville Prison and is buried at the National Cemetery there and one brother Captain of Company A, 145th Regt, Pennsylvania Volunteers, was wounded at the Battle of Gettysburg but stayed until the close of the war.

"Most of them lived to be quite old. One sister, Mrs. Amy Heath, mother of Frank Heath whom we all know, lived to be 96 years old. One sister Nellie McFarson is still living. Our grandfather Warren McCray married Harriet Hollis, they settled in Concord twp, later they bought a farm of 80 acres near Britton Run on old state road, (one line of the copy obliterated) only road there, they built a log house by a good spring, later they built on to the log house, built it of pine. They had six children, some of them born at this place and some of them born in Concord, Philetus, Aretta, Phineas, Carley and Alton. Alton was the youngest and smallest so they called him Titmun for a nickname. His bed was a trundle bed on runners so as to slide back under the other bed.

"Around 1890 grandfather built the new house up by the road, this was built of pine also. Grandfather died Feb 22 1897 aged 70 years. A son Carley bought the farm and moved in with grandmother. She died in 1899. Carley lived there until his death May 14, 1911. His wife and family lived there until their son Clyde got married in 1925 and has since resided on the farm. The McCray homestead and the house is the same as when grandfather built it. Two barns have been moved together and a large basement barn made. Electricity was put in a few years ago and a paved road now passes the house. The old log house was torn down and the addition built on the log house was moved straight down the hill through the meadows to Britton Run just south of the U.B.Church and cemetery. Alton McCray lived there. Later it was sold to Weatherbee and moved across the road where it is still standing. Our grandfather helped build this church and was a devoted member, never missing services. He had a little black dog, that always followed him to church. His children would come home for Sunday dinner, which pleased him very much and he would say, "I wish my children liked to attend church as well as my little dog does." Our grandmother was a very good christian but her health prevented her from accompanying him to church."

Historical Facts Regarding The

Early Pioneer Of The McCray Family

" About 1784, James McCray and his wife, whose maiden name was Miss Nellie Bell, came to America with their six children: William, James, Betsey, George, Samuel, and Robert. After a voyage of some three months, we are told they landed in Baltimore, whence they went into Pennsylvania settling at that time in Cumberland County.

"William, the eldest child married Nancy Miles, and reared a large family of twelve children, most of whom live in Erie and Crawford Counties.

" James, the 2nd (second son of James the 1st and Nellie Bell) married Eleanor Townley. They had nine children: Joseph, James, William, George, John, Eleanor, Robert, and Betsey. This James the 2nd is the one whose grave is near front of the little McCray Cemetery.

"George, the third son of James the 1st, married Jennie Morrow. They had ten children, a number of whom are located in and around Youngsville and Garland vicinity.

" Samuel, the fourth son married Polly McCoy and they had one child, James, but we have no record whatsoever of this branch.

"Robert, the youngest son of James McCray the 1st, was commonly known as "Old Uncle Bob." He married Mrs. Jane Bruce and they had four children: Robert, David, Samuel, and Sarah. It is to Samuel McCray, son of Old Uncle Bobby, that we owe the most of our information regarding the early McCrays.

" Late in the 18th century (about 1798) James the 2nd, accompanied by his wife and two sons, Joseph and James, came from Westmoreland Co., driving a yoke of oxen and leading a cow. They were going to found a new home in what was then known as "Out West." This being the time before the time of the Lincoln Highway yes, in fact, before the days of any roads other than a meager trail through the forest, and in open places what was known as a blazed trail, where the trees were occasionally marked by an axe. After having traveled for weeks, camping out nights, James finally reached the farm now occupied by John Babcock, which is the site of the old McCray Church. He was the first settler in what is now Concord Township. His nearest neighbor, except for Indians, was a family by the name of Hare, living several miles north of the present site of Corry, and a family by the name of Miles, living somewhere to the west. James reached his destination too late to get a very large piece of land cleared, having to cut and burn the green trees, but having the great persistency of the pioneers, he "did what he could" and when at harvest time he discovered that he did not have enough to provide food for his little family and his stock during the winter, he cached his supply and returned to Westmoreland County where he spent the winter with his parents. Early the following spring he started forth again on his long perilous journey. His wife did not come with him, but came later, making the journey alone on horseback with James, the 3rd on her lap and Joseph on the horse back of her.

" When James reached his new home, he found his supplies in good shape, and with new land he could clear, together with what he had cleared the previous year, he raised enough to furnish him with food for his coming need and this time he wintered in Concord, Erie Co. Such were the hardships required to plant the McCray family here in this good old McCray settlement. James certainly had a hard time, taking into consideration his long hard trips. He also had to withstand the ravages of wolves, bears, and thieving Indians.

"We are now particularly interested in the family of James the 3rd, the babe who made the trip from Westmoreland Co. in his mother's arms. He married Sallie Blakeslee. To this union were born seven children: James (the Fourth), Lucinda, Jason, Jesse, Jacob, and Sarah.

"James married for his wife Amy Lilley. To their union were born four children: Abner, Lorenzo P., Marion B., Elmer A., and Martha Ellen.

"Jacob McCray married Matilda Nash. They had six children: Olive, Helen, Irene, Calvin, George, and Dennis. Jacob's second wife was Electa Matteson. They had no children.

"Sarah married John Bishop. They had no children.

"Lucinda married William Sturdevant."

(Author unknown)

Incidents In The Backwoods Life In Erie County

"James McCray second settled in Concord Township in Southeastern Erie County taking up about 800 acres of land in 1796. Neighbors were scarce except the Indians and numerous animals which usually inhabit the forest such as bear, deer, wolves, panther and other carnivorous kinds.

"In 1798, James McCray second came from Westmoreland County and a short time later his wife came on horseback with James Third a babe in her lap and Joseph riding back of her. They settled on the farm later owned by Robert McCray who furnished the land for the McCray Church and Cemetery. Robert's father, James, was the first McCray in Concord Township.

273

" A few years after James had settled on his land, he was away from
home in the early part of winter and his cow died while he was away probably due to lack of feed and care as there was no one home but the mother
and two or three small children. They managed to get some one to take
the hide off and the same night after the roar of the wolves had been
heard from various directions, the howling and barking of the pack increased as they drew nearer until it seemed as if the air would rend with
the noise, as they drew nearer and nearer to get a meal of the old cow.
They were seen by the mother and her terrified children like a flock of
sheep, it was almost impossible to protect them from these devouring
pests. Sometimes hogs and pigs were taken out of the pens close to the
house even in daylight by a hungry old bear and taken away in spite of
their pursuers. James was taken sick in the war of the rebellion and
came home and died. "

(Author unknown)

The McCray History (Author unknown)

" James McCray, born in Scotland, was taken by his parents to Ireland,
when a child, during the time of the Catholic Persecution, and they settled in the County of Monohan. He grew up to manhood and married a wife
whose maiden name we never learned. They had two children: John and Joseph. His wife died.

" Sometime later James married a second wife, Miss Nellie Bell. The
year of James immigration to Ireland is not known.

" James and Nellie Bell had six children: ------, William, James, Betsey, George, Samuel and Robert.

" Soon after the Revolution, when peace had been fully established between Great Britain and the Colonies, they immigrated to America in 1784,
leaving John and Joseph behind, of whom we have never learned anything
satisfactory. The youngest child was some seven years of age at this
time.

" They took passage on the American vessel called the Constitution.
Sailed from Newra. After a voyage of some three months with some three
months with some severe storms and dangers, they landed safely at Baltimore (we think).

" A terrible storm overtook them on the voyage which drove them some
thousand miles out of their course. A large whale was discovered on route,
which prudence dictated best to tack around the monster, and so escape
injury.

" Also a large school of herring at one time obstructed the ship's
course. At length, seeking another direction, they got away from their

numerous company.

"Shark had been seen following the ship for several days. Some thought it a warning that death would occur. A plan was conceived to make his sharkship a prisoner, which was accordingly done.

"A sailor, an expert, took a large hook, well baited, and with a strong line attached, and descended to the water's surface, throwing his hook to the open mouth of the creature. The signal was given, and in almost a twinkling, he found himself on board with other passengers, where a man stood with a broad ax drawn to cut his tail off to prevent his splitting the deck. This also prevented any approaches of the harm of any of the spectators who crowded around to see the prisoner.

"The death occurred according to prophecy, in that a little child who received the solomn sea funeral of being cast overboard to find a grave at the bottom of the ocean, a sad sight for parents and friends to endure.

"Our family leaving Baltimore went to Pennsylvania, where they settled in Cumberland County.

"When William, the eldest child, arrived at the proper age, he married Miss Nancy Miles. They reared a large family and resided most of his married life in Erie and Crawford Counties. William McCray and Nancy Miles had twelve children: James, Betsey, Polly, William, Eleanor, Jane, Robert, John, Nancy, Samuel, Margaret, Sarah.

"James McCray, second son of James McCray and Nellie Bell, married Miss Eleanor Townsley. James McCray and Eleanor Townsley had nine children: Joseph, James, William, Jane, George, John, Eleanor, Robert, Betsey.

"Betsey McCray, the only daughter of James McCray and Nellie Bell, married William Reed. Their children, seven in number are: Eleanor, John, Jane, Elizabeth, James, William, Margaret.

"George McCray, the third son of James McCray and Nellie Bell, married Jennie Morrow. They had ten children: Anna, Alexander, James, Polly, William, Eleanor, Jennie, George, Robert, Margaret.

"Samuel, the fourth son of James McCray and Nellie Bell, married Polly McCoy. They but one child: James.

"Robert McCray, the youngest child of James McCray and Nellie Bell, was commonly known as "Old Uncle Bobby." He married Mrs. Jane Bruce. They had four children: Robert, David, Samuel, Sarah.

"In 1798, James McCray (No. 2) came from Westmoreland County. Shortly afterwards, his wife, (Eleanor Townsley) came to Concord Township alone on horseback, with James in her lap a babe, and Joseph back of her.

They settled on the A.G. Crowell farm, and were the first McCrays in Erie County.

" William McCray, third son of James McCray and Eleanor Townsley, married Jane Bruce. They had five children: James, Josiah, Andrew, Julia Anne, Nancy Jane.

"Josiah married Sally Hammond, and was our Dad's father."

Contributed by Adele H. McCray, Corry, Pa.,

gr gr granddaughter of James and Eleanor

(Townsley) McCray.

Raise A Toast!

Special laurel wreaths are due to three people who have worked very long and well to list names and family connections of about 1800 McCrays of northwestern Pennsylvania who are descended from James McCray and Ellen Bell. They are:

Percie McCray
J. Duane Upton
George L. Carey

The order of their listing in no way reflects the value of their contribution to the story of our family. Each of them made a unique contribution of considerable value.

Had George L. Carey not written down the account which follows it is almost certain that much of the story could not be remembered today. He set it down in simple and sparse prose that exactly fits his subject, and reading it and the sometimes fanciful stories included, brought back recollections of "yarns" I used to hear from my dad and uncles at Grandfather Grant McCray's home in Elgin, Pennsylvania, when I was a boy.

Percie McCray probably began collecting McCray names sometime around the year 1900. He was born in 1879 and died in 1964, and was the son of Chapman B. and May (Crowell) McCray. He married Ethel Owen (1882-1977), and they had no children. He typed his list of McCrays onto about 120 sheets of paper with an Oliver Model 1890 typewriter, one of which is on display at the Smithsonian Institution's Museum of American History in Washington, D.C. The Oliver had a keyboard of three rows of keys, with the letters arranged in today's QWERTYUIOP standard. The shift key had three positions: lower case letters in the middle, capital letters in the *UP* shift position, and numerals and punctuation in the *DOWN* shift position. The shift key locked in whichever position it was put. Percie or whoever typed the papers didn't exactly get the hang of this shift key, for in several places in the list there are lines of numbers and punctuation and symbols intermixed instead of names and dates, giving it the appearance of having been written in a code devised by a schoolboy. It is easily straightened out by using the cipher technique of "Cipher Substitution."

Someone probably has the original copy, but the copies we encountered were duplicated by the nearly-forgotten Hektograph process sometime in the 1920s or 1930s on miserable duplicating stock that has turned brown and fragile. Hektograph was a "spirit duplicating" process. Copy was made on a typewriter using a special hectographic ribbon. The copy was then placed on a gelatin pad that had to be cooked up using animal glue, gelatin, glycerin, and bicarbonate of soda. The pad had to be kneaded like bread and spread out smooth in a pan somewhat larger than the paper to be copied. The copy was spread smoothly onto the surface of the gelatin pad, which transferred the lettering onto the surface

277

of the gelatin pad, only reversed. A sheet of paper was then laid onto the pad and quickly smoothed down, then removed. The paper now had the copy duplicated in purple on it. Up to about twelve more copies could be made this way, with the paper left in contact a bit longer for each succeeding duplicate until the transferred letters were too dim. Then the pad had to be cleaned with alcohol and the original copy could then be used to make another set of twelve copies. The best thing that could be said about it was that it was cheap and it was the only method readily available, but it was messy, slow, odorous, and a very great deal of trouble, and those who have ever used spirit duplicating can fully appreciate Xerox.

Percie's system of genealogical number identification was unique and takes some getting used to, but once you get onto it, it does have system, although it may drive you mad before you get onto it. Nevertheless, the list has been extremely valuable, and it has saved us today many hours of tedious digging, and it is likely that much of the information in it would not be now available.

J. Duane and June Upton, of Hemet, California, have done outstanding work collecting genealogical information on eight family names connected to the Upton line, which includes McCrays descended from William and Nancy(Miles) McCray. A summary of their work is contained in *Genealogical Record Of: Heron, Kerr, McCray, Porter, Shelmadine, Synder, Tubbs, Upton,* privately printed. A great deal of the material contained in this volume came from their book and from an enormous stack of their collected notes, which they generously made available.

Duane and June were married in 1942, and after the birth of a daughter in 1944, they thought it "might be fun to see what we could find out about our ancestors...it turned into quite an experience." Indeed! It is an "experience" that many others well have known. They dug into files at the courthouses of Warren, Forest, Venango, Erie and Crawford Counties. They visited cemeteries and copied monument inscriptions. They found obituaries, marriages, births and deaths in newspapers of the cities of Warren and Titusville. They found and interviewed near and remote relatives, and got material from replies to letters. June said they never got help from professional genealogists, preferring to do their own research.

They credited many people whose help they sought, among them:

James Delos Upton, Duane's father
Arthur Upton, a nephew
Seth Holmes
Edith Mandeville Carlson
Mable Rhodes Boland

Linda Waha
Isabel McCray Hamilton
Dr. Fred McCray
Mrs. Gladys Shepler

Dennis Davis
Rollo McCray
Neva Young Burt
Mrs. Jennie Wallace
Mrs. Eleanor Buchanan

Mrs. Minnie Trapani
Mrs. Fred Snapp
Mrs. D.R. Blakeslee
Mrs. Ilo Grisham
Mrs. Grant Sears

Of immeasurable help has been a list and index of McCrays and related families the Upton's compiled, beginning with Old James and Ellen
(Bell) McCray, down to today's generations. Duane sent me the list
several years ago. I bound it into a hardback book about an inch or so
thick, and it has been kept at hand and used extensively.

I had always supposed that the Uptons had built their list onto
Percie McCray's list, but June Upton cleared that up for me. She wrote:

"None of our original information came from Percie
McCray's records that we know of. In fact, we never even heard
of his records until a few years ago.."

CHAPTER TWELVE

THE McCRAY SETTLERS OF NORTHWESTERN PENNSYLVANIA

The Family of William and Elizabeth (McCray) Reed

JOHN AND EVE (McGUFFY)REED SAILED FROM IRELAND to America about
1755.* One of their children died on the voyage, something that tragically happened often to children because of the nearly inhuman living
conditions on some of the ships transporting Scots-Irish. We don't know
if the Reeds had any children with them other than this one who died.
The Reed/McGuffy marriage is a demonstration of how love has a way of
flourishing in an atmosphere of hatred, for seldom did the Scots and
Irish achieve civility with each other, much less fall in love and marry.

Once ashore in America, they made their way to Shermans Valley,
Cumberland County, Pennsylvania, and settled there to rear four sons and
two daughters, the only one we know by name being William, born in 1755.
His birthday is derived from a notation in Cumberland County tax lists
for Toboyne Township, 1776, alongside a tax record for John Reed, "William Reed, Freeman." John Reed had been enumerated three successive
years before with no mention of William, so we might conclude that William was born 21 years before, or about 1755.

Tax and other records for Shermans Valley show names of several
other Reeds, but whether or not they were members of the family of John
Reed isn't known. Samuel Reed paid taxes on 100 acres, two horses and
two cows in 1782 in Greenwood Township.+ Richard Reed married Nancy
Irwin, April 6, 1788, at Centre Presbyterian Church. The will of Alexander Murray, a prominent landowner and father-in-law of George McCray,
listed five shillings disbursed to William Reed for 1792 taxes, and
there were four items for rent and taxes paid to Murray's estate by Adam
Reed, totalling 67 pounds. If these Reeds, Samuel, Adam and Richard,
were brothers of William, we will have accounted for the four sons of
John and Eve (McGuffy) Reed.

William Reed explored the territory upstream on the Susquehanna
River, as indicated by Northumberland County tax record for the Lower
Bald Eagle Township. "Reed, Wm." paid taxes on 444 acres, one horse and
one cow, in the amount of one pound, seventeen shillings and fourpence.
A Reed family history by Judith E. King says that John Reed moved to
Lycoming County in 1795. Bald Eagle Township was included in Lycoming
County when Northumberland County split up in 1795.

+ *Cumberland County State and Supply Transcripts,* Pennsylvania archives.

* *Commemorative Biographical Record of Central Pennsylvania,* Vol. II,
p. 1478. J. H. Beers & Co., Chicago, 1898. Copy in Denver Public Library.

At the time of its birth, Lycoming County was a vast area extending from roughly the upper Susquehanna River westward over most of the northern part of Pennsylvania, as far west as roughly the northeastern border of Erie, Crawford, Venango, and Butler Counties, all of which were part then of Allegheny County. Therefore when it is recorded that a person was born in Lycoming County between 1795 and 1804, when Lycoming was divided into several new counties, we have but a hazy idea of where the birth actually occurred, unless the township is given. If a researcher uses a modern map of Pennsylvania counties to attempt research during any of the nineteenth century there will almost certainly be a lot of confusion. This is especially true for Cumberland, Northumberland, and Lycoming Counties.

William Reed wooed and won Elizabeth McCray, and on 9 July, 1790, they were married in the same log church where Richard and Nancy Irwin had wed two years before. The same minister, the Reverend John Linn, officiated at both ceremonies. Shortly afterward the couple moved from Shermans Valley a few miles up the Susquehanna River to Sunbury, Northumberland County, and set about the business of begetting a family.

Meanwhile, back in Shermans Valley, John Reed gave up farming and moved to Lycoming County, and we know this would have to have been after 1795. Exactly where he retired isn't recorded, but it seems to be a safe guess that he went to the 444 acres upon which William had paid taxes in 1787, when the farm was in Northumberland County. Why didn't William and his bride, Elizabeth, also go and live on the Bald Eagle tract? Who knows? Perhaps his brothers and sisters were running the farm.

However, William and Elizabeth did move to the Bald Eagle farm from Sunbury later. We know that two of his sons, William and James were born in Lycoming County. William, Jr., was born in either 1801 or 1802, and James was born before William, Jr., so they must have left Sunbury for Lycoming County just before the dawn of the nineteenth century.

The *Commemorative Biographical Record* lists the children of William and Elizabeth (McCray) Reed in the following chronological order:

1. Eleanor Reed
2. John Reed, b. 29 May, 1773, at Sunbury
3. Jane Reed
4. Elizabeth Reed
5. James Reed, b. "near Sunbury"
6. William Reed, Jr., b. 22 August, 1801 or 1802, in Lycoming County, Pennsylvania
7. Margaret Reed, b. 1805, in Erie County, Pennsylvania

According to the *Commemorative Biographical Record*, quoted from on the previous page, the Reeds "in 1804 moved to Erie County,...and settled on the Holland land purchase and made his home for five years." No records survive that show where on the Holland Land Company's tracts they settled, or even if they actually bought a tract there. Holland Land Company's records do not show a purchase by him, and all other Erie County land and tax records from 1800 to 1823 were destroyed in a fire.

It is probably safe to say that they lived in Brokenstraw Township and close to Elizabeth's five brothers, who lived quite close to each other near the present-day village of Elgin.

But, like a number of other settlers in Brokenstraw Township, Erie County didn't suit the Reeds, and in 1809 they struck out south about twenty miles and rented "The Holdsman Farm" near Titusville, along the Allegheny River. Erie County's winters can be devastatingly cold, and weather cycles in the latter decade of the eighteenth century were giving that area a particularly harsh drubbing, so the weather may well have been a prime reason for moving on. Reed, like most of the Scots-Irish, probably had itchy feet, as indicated by the number of moves he had already made. They stayed in Crawford County but ten years, and they then picked up and moved once more in 1819, this time further south to Richland (now Highland) Township, Clarion County, where they both died in 1848 at about age 94. Their last move was to a farm identified only as "The Joseph Farm."

George McCray, Elizabeth's brother, also left Erie County at about the same time the Reeds did. George also settled with his family near Titusville, and he didn't move again as far as we know. The two families must have lived fairly close together, as indicated by the fact that one of George's sons, Alexander, went to Clarion County with his family, to live near Uncle William and Aunt Elizabeth (McCray) Reed.

By this time his children were mature adults and began marrying. Jane Reed married Alexander Porter, who may have been living on the Porter farm when the Reeds arrived. Living nearby was the Lamb family, and there must have been some electricity between the Lambs and Reeds, for Margaret Reed married James Lamb, John Reed married Jane Lamb, and William Reed, Jr., married Nancy Agnes Lamb. Elizabeth Reed married Ephriam Mix,* of Connecticut, and they moved to Jefferson County and died there. John Reed, William's son, bought 1100 acres, part of the estate of George Harrison, in Venango County, but apparently didn't stay there if indeed he ever lived there at all.

James Reed married Mary Hulings, who had formerly lived at Bald Eagle, Lycoming County. She was a granddaughter of Marcus Hulings and Mary Boone. Mary Boone was a daughter of Benjamin and Susannah Boone; Benjamin Boone was an uncle of the frontiersman, Daniel Boone who was born near Reading, Pennsylvania, in 1734. Mary Huling's parents, William and Jane Hulings, moved to Clarion County about 1817, where Mary and James met.

Alexander McCray, son of George and Jean (Murray) McCray, who served with Commodore Peary on Lake Erie in the War of 1812, also moved from near Titusville to Clarion County and there reared his family. He and Elizabeth (McCalmont) had ten children, and two of them married Reeds. Adeline McCray married Columbus Reed, son of John and Jane (Lamb) Reed,

_____
* The screen actor, Tom Mix, is descended from this family.

and Charles Reed, Columbus's brother, married Adeline's sister, Sarah H. McCray. Most of John and Jane's children are buried in the cemetery near Miola, Clarion County.

John Reed, William and Elizabeth (McCray) Reed's son, bought a large tract of timber and set up a sawmill on Tarkill Run, and turned out lumber from the trees he was clearing on his farm, and after first working as a sawyer for some years, he turned to farming the land he had logged. He later constructed river longboats for ferrying coal down the Allegheny River to Pittsburgh. He died on his farm in 1866, and Jane, his wife, died in 1844.

William Reed, Jr., was also a sawyer and boatbuilder. His boatyard was on the banks of the Clarion River, but he and John apparently were not partners in business. He built the largest longboat (100 feet) ever built until then, which carried 100 tons of metal downstream to Pittsburgh. He retired in 1861, and died in 1875. His wife, Agnes, died a few years later. They too are buried in the Miola Cemetery.

After William Reed, Sr., died, his son, James and his wife Mary (Hulings) took over the farm and lived out their lives there. James Reed and his parents are buried in the cemetery at Helen Furnace, a village about seven miles north of the county seat, Clarion. John and Jane (Lamb) Reed, William and Nancy (Lamb) Reed, as well as many other Reeds of later generations are buried in the cemetery at Miola, halfway between Helen Furnace and Clarion.

William Reed, like his brother-in-law, James McCray, Jr., dedicated part of his farm for creation of a church and cemetery. The church was built and named Greenwood Presbyterian Church, but later was renamed Shiloh Presbyterian Church, and today it faces on Reed Road in the village of Miola. Mary Reed and Jane Hulings are listed in early church records. William and his wife, Elizabeth (McCray) Reed, both died within a few weeks of each other in 1848, and are buried in the churchyard cemetery.

Mrs. Diana Zimmermann, of Littleton, Colorado, a descendant of the Reeds, supplied most of the information about William and Elizabeth (McCray) Reed and their families. She described in a letter driving in the country up Reed Road, lined by trees, to the cemetery at the top of a hill. "It is completely surrounded by trees, with no homes in the area. Very beautiful and peaceful."

```
Generation I                              Generation III

James McCray, Sr.                         Eleanor Reed
                                          b. 1817
                                          d. 28-4-1851
                                          m. Uriah (Urial) Fletcher


                                          John Reed
      Generation II                       b. 29-5-1793
                                          d. 19-12-1866
   Elizabeth McCray                       m. Jane Lamb , d. 1844

          &

   William Reed, Sr.                      Jane Reed
                                          b.
                                          d. age 44
                                          m. Alexander Porter


                                          Elizabeth Reed
                                          b.
                                          d.
                                          m. Ephriam Mix*


                                          James Reed
                                          b. 1798. in Sunbury, Northumberland
                                          d.                        Co., Pa.
                                          m. Mary Hulings


                                          William Reed
                                          b. 22-8-1801/02
                                          d. 25-7-1879
                                          m. Nancy (Agnes?) Lamb


                                          Margaret Reed
                                          b. 1805
                                          d.
*Tom Mix, movie star, descended           m. James Lamb
 from the family of Ephriam Mix.
```

284

Generation I	Generation IV

Generation I

James McCray, Sr.

Generation II

Elizabeth McCray
&
William Reed, Sr.

Generation III

James Reed

&

Mary Hulings

Generation IV

Elizabeth J. (Betsy) Reed
b. 1829
d.
m. John Walters

Harriet Reed
b. 1832
d.
m. Isaac Smathers

William Reed
b. 6-10-1832
d. 10-6-1869
m.

Julia Reed
b. 1835
d.
m. William McClelland   12 ch

Emeline Reed
b. ca 1837
d.
m. < (1) George Beatty 3 ch
    (2) Louis Franz/Frantz 1 ch

Robert Reed
b. 1838
d. 24-9-1864 of starvation, Andersonville, Ga., prison
unmarried

John Reed
b. 1840
d. 1913
m.
Civil War soldier; 5'6" tall, grey
eyes, light hair

Malinda Reed
b. 16-8-1842
d. 6-8-1919
m. James Craig Benner

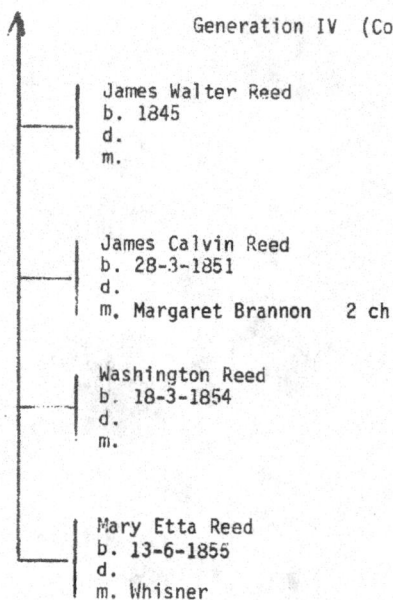

James Walter Reed
b. 1845
d.
m.

James Calvin Reed
b. 28-3-1851
d.
m. Margaret Brannon   2 ch

Washington Reed
b. 18-3-1854
d.
m.

Mary Etta Reed
b. 13-6-1855
d.
m. Whisner

Generation I   Generation V

James McCray, Sr.   John Benner
                                            b. 2-1872
                                            d.
                                            m.

Generation II

Elizabeth McCray
        &   Mary Elizabeth Benner
William Reed, Sr.   b. 5-1873
                                            d. 28-8-1949, in Los Angeles, CA
                                            m (1) William Parks Henry
                                               (2) Mead E. Wells

Generation III

James Reed
                                            James Horn Benner
                                            b. 4-1876
                                            d.
Generation IV   m.

Malinda Reed

      &

James C. Benner

287

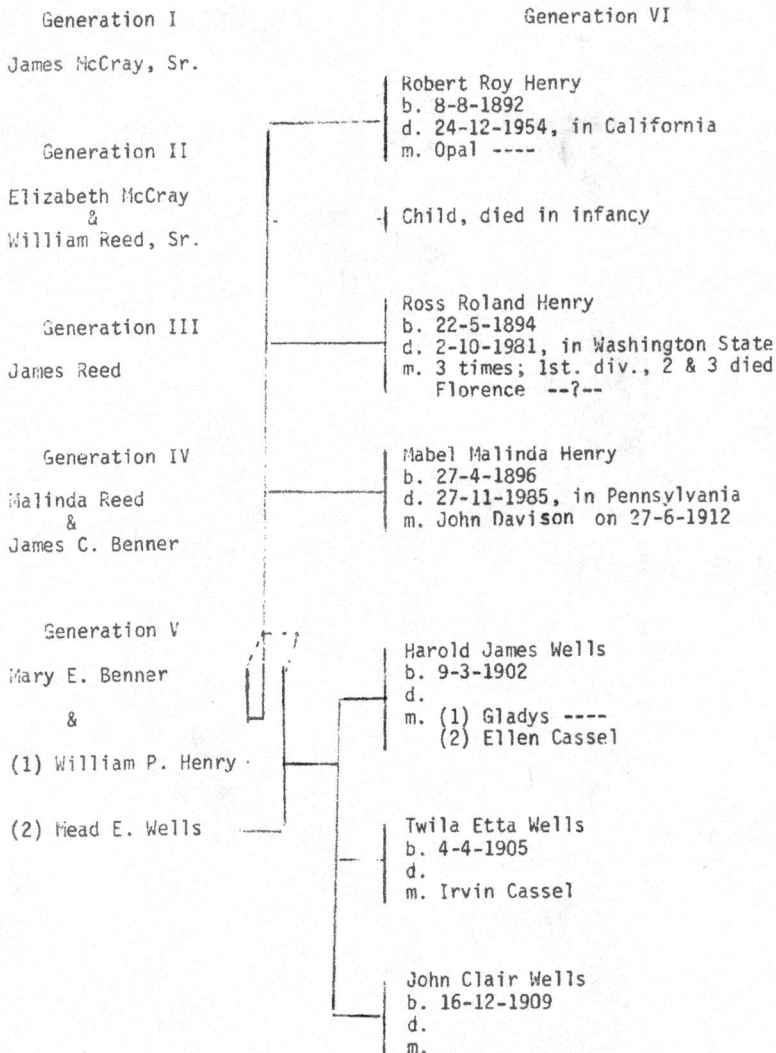

Generation I

James McCray, Sr.

Generation II

Elizabeth McCray
&
William Reed, Sr.

Generation III

James Reed

Generation IV

Malinda Reed
&
James C. Benner

Generation V

Mary E. Benner

&

(1) William P. Henry

(2) Mead E. Wells

Generation VI

Robert Roy Henry
b. 8-8-1892
d. 24-12-1954, in California
m. Opal ----

Child, died in infancy

Ross Roland Henry
b. 22-5-1894
d. 2-10-1981, in Washington State
m. 3 times; 1st. div., 2 & 3 died
   Florence --?--

Mabel Malinda Henry
b. 27-4-1896
d. 27-11-1985, in Pennsylvania
m. John Davison on 27-6-1912

Harold James Wells
b. 9-3-1902
d.
m. (1) Gladys ----
   (2) Ellen Cassel

Twila Etta Wells
b. 4-4-1905
d.
m. Irvin Cassel

John Clair Wells
b. 16-12-1909
d.
m.

288

Generation I   Generation VII

James McCray, Sr.   Ronald Henry Davison
                                      b. 6-4-1932
                                      d.
Generation II   m. Mary June Hupp

Elizabeth McCray
    &
William Reed, Sr.   Janet Davison
                                      b. 18-2-1935
                                      d.
Generation III   m. Leonard Orange

James Reed
                                      Mary Evelyn Davison
                                      b. 6-7-1915
Generation IV   d.
                                      m. William James Neadeau
Malinda Reed
    &
James C. Benner   Irvin Aldridge Davison
                                      b. 22-6-1917
                                      d. 12-9-1975
Generation V   m. (1) Myrtle Reese
                                          (2) Esther Hipsley
Mary E. Benner
    &
William P. Henry   Inez Christine Davison
                                      b. 2-8-1919
                                      d. 1986
Generation VI   m. Harry Samuel Paul

Mabel Milinda Henry
                                      Irene Davison
    &   b. 16-7-1922
                                      d.
John Davison   m. (1) Joseph Gongloff
                                          (2) Albert C. Williams

                                      Imogene Olive Davison
                                      b. 19-11-1925
                                      d.
                                      m. Charles Frederick Singer

                        289

Twiletta Iverna Davison
b. 19-8-1927
d.
m. (1) Thomas Gorney
    (2) Edward Marshall

John Robert (Jackie) Davison
b. 18-4-1930
d.
m. (1) Margaret Falsey
    (2) Betty Lau'ree

Generation I

James McCray, Sr.

Generation II

Elizabeth McCray
&
William Reed, Sr.

Generation III

James Reed
&
Mary Hulings

Generation IV

Malinda Reed
&
James C. Benner

Generation V

Mary E. Bonner
&
William P. Henry

Generation VI

Mabel Malinda Henry
&
John Davison

Generation VII

Mary Evelyn Davison
&
William James Neadeau

Generation VIII

Arlene Ann Neadeau
b. 2-9-1935
d. 19-2-1940

Marjune Joan Neadeau
b. 3-1-1939
d.
m. Osmer James Brooks

Carol Evelyn Neadeau
b. 11-3-1940
d.
m. Osmer James Brooks

William Eugene Neadeau
b. 21-11-1943
d.
m. Christie Lee Millsom

twins

Diana Jean Neadeau
b. 21-11-43
d.
m. Robert Menno Zimmermann
   Ch. Scott Jason Zimmermann
      b. 23-9-1968
      d.
      m.

      Jason Robert Zimmermann
      b. 1-3-1970
      d.
      m.

THE FAMILY OF

WILLIAM AND NANCY (MILES) McCRAY

William McCray, the second child and first son of James and Ellen (Bell) McCray, was born, probably in Ayreshire, Scotland, in 1764, and the family's surname was then "McCrea." Some believe that James had two sons in an earlier marriage. When William was about three years old the family moved from Scotland to County Monaghan, Ireland. They lived there until the American War for Independence ended, and in 1784 they came to America, landing at either Philadelphia or Baltimore. By then the family had grown to eight children: John, Joseph, Elizabeth, William, James, Jr., George, Samuel and Robert. John and Joseph are believed to have remained in Ireland.

The family settled on a farm, probably rented, in Toboyne Township, Cumberland County, Pennsylvania. Cumberland County tax records show that in 1787 both William and James McCrea paid taxes on a few animals, but not on any land. We cannot be certain if these two McCrays were father and son or brothers. Since William was the eldest, aged 23 years, and Old James was still young enough to work and manage a farm, the pair was probably father and son.

Within a few years they moved to another farm in adjacent Tyrone Township, and in 1790 they were taxpayers on a farm in that township. It was here that they were members of Centre Presbyterian Church and became neighbors with several families in the growing community that was to become the village of Loysville. The community was predominantly populated by Scots- Irish, but within twenty years there were but few Scottish or Irish names in Shermans Valley, having been replaced by mostly German names. As could be expected, as the McCray siblings grew to maturity they began casting about for mates, and it wasn't long before the names Reed, Townsley, Miles and Murray were in-lawed with the McCrays, and by 1793, Old James and Ellen were grandparents.

One of William's neighbors, Nancy Miles, became the object of his special interest, and they were married at Centre Presbyterian Church on April 26, 1792, when William was twenty-eight years old.

John Miles came from Ireland in 1771 with his children, Nancy, James, Robert and William. He was a revolutionary War soldier, killed in action in Northumberland County. Nancy's brother, William ("Billy") Miles was mentioned in the 1793 will of Alexander Murray that was witnessed by James and Elonar McCree and John Nelson. William Miles migrated to Broken-straw Township, Erie County, Pennsylvania, and bought a tract, Number 95, in District No. 6, from the Holland Land Company, a quarter of a mile

south of the tracts bought by William and James McCray five years after
the McCray brothers bought theirs. Before that he had been an agent for
the Holland Land Company, replacing Roger Alden, and before that he had
been surveyor of the Tenth District of the Holland Land Company's holdings. He left Holland Land Company and went into the land business with
David Watts, and became involved in years of litigation with Holland Land
Company, some of which have yet to be clearly resolved.

"William Miles was during the summer of 1797 going on with
actual settlement in opposition to warrant holders but I think
compromised that fall with the population company (The Pennsylvania Population Co.) as he had previously done with the Holland Land Company.* "

William Miles laid out the town of Miles Mills in Union Township,
Erie County, and built and operated a mill there. The town was later
renamed Union City. He also laid out and founded Wattsburg, named for
his partner's father, and then built and operated a mill there. He lived
to a fine old age, dying at age 100. Billy Miles was without any doubt
one of Erie County's important early men. I feel sure that William Miles,
after returning from his survey of District Number Ten in 1793, brought
back reports that ultimately brought William, James, Samuel, Robert, and
Elizabeth Reed to Erie County.

On July 20, 1796, William McCray bought 200 acres of Tract 63,
District 6, in Brokenstraw Township (later Concord Township), upon which
he built a log house. By 1820 he had moved to Crawford County, and was
no longer owner of Tract 63; John T. McCray built a log house there in
that year (according to Henry McCray). Deed number D444 in the Erie
County Courthouse, February 16, 1831; "Deed The Holand Land Company to
James T. McCray." James T. McCray was my great great uncle and was a
son of James and Eleanor (Townsley) McCray. In this instrument, five
Dutch gentlemen of Amsterdam, with names similar in length to that of one
of them, Jerrit Schimmelpeninck, conveyed, through their American attorney, Harm Jan Huidekoper, 100 acres of Tract 63 to James T. McCray. This
may or may not be when the family moved away from Erie County. It should
be recalled that Tract 63 was nominally a 400-acre tract, and under the
terms of original sale, William agreed to develop the land according to
set conditions, and upon final settlement, be given title to half the tract,
with the other half reverting to the Holland Land Company, all this with
no exchange of money. The land sold here may have been for part of the
Holland Land Company's half, or it is also possible that William never
fulfilled the terms of sale and the entire tract was reclaimed by Holland
Land Company.

* *Inventory Of The County Archives of Pennsylvania -- Erie County,
No. 25.*

293

The year before, William bought a tract of land in Crawford County:*

> "James McCray, of Erie County, to William McCray, of Craw-
> ford County, 403 acres and 102 perches in Oil Creek Twp.,
> bounded on the east by John Sloan, on the south by Patrick
> Sloan, on the west by "land claimed by Joseph McCray" (James's
> son) and on the north by Robert Kerr. Consideration: $200.
> Dated Sept. 17, 1830; recorded June 15, 1831. Witnesses: Wil-
> liam and James Curry."

William Curry, witness to this transaction, was administrator of
the estate of William McCray five years later. We don't know how or
when James acquired this land, but the fact that William is referred to
as a resident of Crawford County would seem to indicate that he had
come to Crawford County sometime before that. Upton in his *Genealogical
Record*** wrote that William and Nancy (Miles) McCray settled on a farm
identified as "Watson's Flats," but this has been challenged as being
incorrect. This may have happened before William bought the 403 acres
from James.

William and Nancy had eleven children:

Elizabeth, b. before 1797	Samuel, b. ca 1807
James, b. bet. 1793-1797	Sarah, b. ca 1811
Mary, b. ca 1792-1796	Nancy
William, Jr., b. 1797-99	Jane
Robert ("Deacon Bob"), b. 1804	Eleanor ("Ellen"), b. 1799
John, b. 1806	Margaret

It isn't known when or where exactly William and Nancy died or where
they are buried. William must have had some serious financial difficulties, as he sold off all but fifty acres of the land he bought in 1830,
and died intestate leaving debts that required the liquidation of the
remaining fifty acres. The estate was administered by William Curry
for whom letters of administration were granted on July 22, 1836. Two
years later Curry petitioned the Orphan's Court for permission to sell
the fifty acres north of Titusville to settle debts of William McCray.*

William McCray, Jr., lived in the Titusville area; part of his life
was spent in nearby Plumer, Venango County, where he married Elizabeth
Story. They had eight children (see family chart of William and Nancy

* *Crawford County Deed book N-1*, pp. 384. Supplied by Alice Morrison.

** *Genealogical Record of: Heron, Kerr, McCray, Porter, Shelmadine,
Snyder, Tubbs, Upton.* By J. Duane Upton, privately printed, 1967.

(Miles) McCray). William, Jr., and his wife, Elizabeth, are buried in the cemetery of the United Presbyterian Church of Plumer.

John McCray moved to Warren County and settled in Brokenstraw Township near Garland, where he married Mary ("Polly") White, and they had fourteen children. They are buried in the Garland Methodist Cemetery there.

James McCray, son of William and Nancy (Miles) McCray, also moved to the Garland Area, and he too married a White--Jane White. The Whites were pioneer settlers of the area that became Warren County's Brokenstraw Township. (Not to be confused with Brokenstraw Township, Erie County.)

Samuel McCray married Elizabeth Shelmadine of Shelmadine Springs, a village in Crawford County a few miles northeast of Titusville. He evidently later moved to Venango County and then to Forest County where he died, as reported in *The Forest Republican* of Tionesta.*

Aug. 6, 1873. Samuel McCray, aged 66, 3 mo., 16 day, died July 23, near Mill Village. He was formerly a resident of Venango County, where he raised a large family, but moved to Erie County in 1864 and settled near LeBoeuf Twp., operating a farm while his sons were in the Civil War. Mrs. McCray died 21 June, 1872.

Two other clippings from *The Forest Republican** probably concern sons of Samuel and Elizabeth (Shelmadine) McCray. Upton, a descendent of William McCray, wrote in his *Genealogical Record* that he had no knowledge of any of the children of Samuel and Elizabeth.

"Oct. 23, 1878 - We learn of the sudden and violent death of Joseph McCray, formerly of this section, which occurred near Clear Lake, Polk Co., Wisconsin, on the 19th inst. Joseph and two brothers, Chauncey and Wesley, were clearing a camp...(Joseph went hunting and accidentally shot himself.) He was 24 years of age and was a son of Samuel McCray who settled and cleared the farm now owned by the Fitzgeralds, 2 miles above this place."

"July 20; 1881 - Jack McCray, brother of Charles McCray, who resided in this section some 12 or 15 years ago, was shot and killed at Othello, Mississippi, by a negro...was married to a daughter of Mr. J.F. Connelly, of Harmony Twp., Forest Co."

* Alice Morrison, Genealogist, of Titusville, supplied this.

Sarah McCray married George McCray, (Jr.), son of George and Jean (Murray) McCray and her first cousin. George McCray lived quite nearby. Sarah and George had eleven children. He died in 1864 at age 58, while she lived to age 75, and died in 1886 in East Titusville, Oil Creek Township. A newspaper obituary of Sarah said that "her mother's brother was Billy Miles of Girard," and this would confirm that William Miles and Nancy Miles were indeed brother and sister. Their familial relationship has been for some time in question, but this obituary seems to settle the matter.

Margaret McCray married Jacob Young in 1829, and they had ten children. Jacob Young and five of his sons served in Pennsylvania regiments in the Civil War, and Robert Young was killed at Gettysburg.

Mary McCray also moved to the Garland Area of Warren County, where she married St phen Hosmer. Mary died in 1832(or 1837), and Stephen died in 1859, aged 62 years.

Eleanor McCray married Benjamin Upton, great grandfather of J. Duane Upton, whose family research has been of inestimable value in preparation of this document. They were married in 1823 at Oil Creek, now known as Hydetown, a few miles northwest of Titusville. They had seven children. They also later lived in Warren County, near Garland.

All that is known of two other daughters is that Jane McCray married Samuel Moore, and Nancy McCray married David Sims. Both the Moore and Sims families were of the Garland area of Warren County.

The Luck Of Corntassel Jim McCray

Some men spend entire lifetimes hunting gold, gems, or buried treasure, and sometimes they never get a farthing for their trouble and work. But to a very few, with no planning, or risk of limb or pocketbook, fortune comes to them, simply because they happened to be in the right place at the right time. One of the chosen few was "Corntassel Jim" McCray. He bought a farm near the Crawford-Venango County line for $2000 and a few years later, when it was no longer even a farm, he refused an offer of a half-million dollars for it. Not bad for a lucky country boy! Corntassel Jim was James McCray, the last son of William, Jr., and Elizabeth (Story) McCray. People seem to have forgotten how he got the name of Corntassel Jim.

There was this fellow, Edwin Drake, whom we all remember from our school days in history class, who had a piece of land similar to that of Corntassel Jim, but a few miles to the south. But black, sticky petroleum oozed from the ground on Drake's land. Indians came there to collect

296

the oil by soaking blankets in it and then wringing out the oil. They made certain medicines with it, and there was a quite limited market for it among white people. Drake thought that maybe if he drilled a hole into the ground he might be able to get the oil more efficiently, and maybe even make some money, too. So he set up a springpole drill* of the type used by farmers to drill for water, and set to work, jogging the pole up and down and watching the drill slowly disappear into the ground. One August day in 1859 his well suddenly had no bottom as the drill broke through into a cavity. Oil gushed out and spurted high in the air, and then and there the world's oil industry was born.

Over two thousand barrels of oil were pumped that first year, but by 1863, with many wells pumping twenty-four hours a day, more than three million barrels of oil were brought to the surface. Oil City was founded, and it and Titusville became populated by hundreds of land speculators who poured in clutching greenbacks. Land appreciated exponentially as speculators bid against each other for any space large enough to set up a drilling operation. Oil City could have just as well have been named "Mud City." There were two or three bars on every block in town, and there were probably as many bordellos as there were saloons. But with the boom in the center of a state that had long ago been settled, rather than on a frontier as were most boom towns, there was little violence in the streets and saloons. Besides, people were too busy making money on oil to waste time gambling with cards and getting drunk.

But Oil City and Titusville weren't pretty places. The air stank of oil, and the landscape was unending dreariness with hundreds of oil derricks jammed together as far as one could see. Mud in the streets, mixed with spilled oil, was more than many horses could wade through and pull wagons loaded with oil barrels. Should a person step off one of the wooden sidewalks to cross a street, he was likely to sink to his knees, and then leave his boots as the price of escape. Near Oil City a factory was set up to produce sulfuric acid used in oil refineries to process oil, and although the factory functioned but a few years, the land it occupied is still to this day barren, with no plant or animal life in or on it. When it rains the soil emits a biting smell of acid. Oil Creek ran black and thick from Titusville to Oil City, polluted

---

* Springpole drilling is done by alternately hoisting and dropping a heavy steel bit that is suspended on the end of an inclined springy tree trunk with the butt anchored solidly to the ground. The bit pounds a hole through the ground and rock. It was used by ancient Chinese, and they drilled as deep as a thousand feet, and cased the well with bamboo. Springpole drilling for oil has been replaced by large diesel-powered rotary drilling rigs, but some water wells are still drilled by the springpole method.

seemingly by almost as much oil as water, continuing sluggishly on to
the Allegheny River where it created an environmental disaster for which
no remedy then existed.

Within ten years after Drake's first well. Oil City and Titusville
settled down and began cleaning up, and soon lost their chaotic ways.
In the name of simple efficiency the oil companies got the streets repaired, drove out the gamblers and whores, and implemented orderly
growth.

Jim McCray's farm was close enough to Drake's strike that it was not
very long before speculators were beating on his door, leases in one
hand and the other hand full of impressively large-denomination greenbacks. But the term, "canny Scot" fit Jim's philosophy of life, and he
wasn't going to be stampeded into selling, leasing, or otherwise letting
go of control of his land. Seeing how the wind was blowing, he joined
with several men to lease two acres on the Buchanan Farm near Oil City,
sat back and watched prices soar. When prices got high enough for him,
he sold out his interest in the lease at a nice profit and went over
next door to the Blood Farm, and leased a piece of land there. He
brought in a drilling crew and the "Maple Shade Well" was started. The
drill was some distance down, but no oil had been found, and anxiety
crept in as days went by and costs accumulated.

Jim McCray and his family were awakened in the middle of a night by
shouts outside. The well had burst forth of its own accord, and oil was
spurting high above the drilling derrick. Once the drillers got a cap
on the well and a pump installed it flowed 800 barrels a day for months,
and McCray's share was a fourth of the oil. In no time his shares netted
him more than $25,000 in oil sales, and he then sold his interest for
$50,000. Although $75,000 is now no spectacular sum, in those days it
was a great deal of money, and tax free to boot!

Corntassel Jim was now a rich man. In 1863 the "Coquette Well" came
in very near the property line of the McCray farm, and he sold several
leases on his land. Within a year there were eight wells on McCray Flats,
each averaging 300 barrels a day. He refused an offer of a half-million
dollars for this two-thousand-dollar farm, and continued selling leases
at terms considered to be near-extortion rates, but he was never without
takers. With each lease went a stipulation that he got half the oil.
The McCray farm netted more revenue than any comparable holding in the
Pennsylvania oil fields. Corntassel Jim built a large mansion in the
center of Franklin, and lived out his life there, dying October 14, 1889.

As oil fever spread, the drilling proceeded in an ever-widening
circle around the center at Titusville and Oil City. Before long the
circle included Concord Township in Erie County, and a map of Concord
Township of 1865 shows several oil wells there. My great grandfather,

298

Wilson McCray, and my grandfather, Grant McCray, drilled wells on their land, but neither of them found very much oil, and eventually all the low-producing small wells were capped and abandoned, and Grand-dad went back to farming. As it was everywhere else, only the big investors made money in a big way. Wilson McCray drove tank wagons for a while between Oil City and Corry, where the oil was trans-shipped by rail. After the railroads ran lines into the Venango County oil fields, there was no more need for tank wagons.

The children and grandchildren of William, Sr., and Nancy (Miles) McCray found their lives strongly influenced by the new technology of oil, and not only Corntassel Jim McCray, but "Deacon Bob's" son, Absolom, turned from the McCray tradition of farming and went into the oil business. Absolom was one of the four children born to Bob's first wife, Matilda Carson. He took up a career in oil production somewhere around Corry, Pennsylvania. He married a second time to Salinda Huntington, and they had four boys, about whose birth we have but little information, except that one of the sons, Edward Ivor McCray, was born in Corry, Pennsylvania, on March 26, 1864. Absolom taught his four sons everything he knew about oil drilling, and when Edward was age twenty-two he decided to seek his fortune out west in California, not in the gold fields, but in the newly discovered oil fields just north of Los Angeles. Edward did indeed make -- and lose -- a fortune there. His father and his brothers later followed him to California, and they never returned to Pennsylvania.

John Woodward McCray, of Costa Mesa, California, grandson of Edward Ivor McCray, has been researching his family, and he sent the following article that tells about the adventures and travels of his grandfather. The article appeared in *The Union Oil Bulletin*, Vol. XI, Bulletin No. 11, November, 1930, and is reproduced below:

-Edward Ivor McCray, Oilman-

Mr. McCray came to California in 1884 in response to the request of his brother-in-law, Dave Swartz, at the time drilling foreman for the Hardison and Stewart Oil Company, that he join him. He was then twenty-two years of age and already had had six years of drilling experience in the Pennsylvania oil fields. With him came his older brother, M.L. (Morris Lynn) McCray, who died a few years ago. Both were hired by the Company. The following year the two brothers were joined by the two remaining McCray boys, L.A. "Lou", who now lives at 9950 Toluca Lake Avenue, North Hollywood, and Bert, who makes his home at Santa Paula, and their father A.M. McCray (Absolom McCready McCray), who had witnessed the drilling of the Drake well at Titusville, Pennsylvania, and himself manned the spring pole with which the early Pennsylvania wells had been drilled. They also became members of the Hardison and Stewart drilling crews.

Over a period of about ten years the names of the McCrays appear
frequently on the drilling reports of the Hardison and Stewart Oil Company, and its successor,the Union Oil Company, along with the names of
T.A. O'Donnell and the late Max Whittier, both of whom later became dominant figures in the industry of California. Of the brothers, Edward
Ivor, or "Ed", as his friends called him, spent the least time with the
company. After two years with Hardison and Stewart he ventured forth
for himself and drilled a well on contract on Ortega Hill, near what is
now the Summerland Field. The well failed to get production, though
within the last year deeper wells drilled on the same hill within a
short distance of it have tapped small producing sand. It was at lease
near Santa Paula which all but made him one of the principal stockholders
and member of the Hardison and Stewart Oil Company.

That lease marked the turning point in his career. In later years
he enjoyed reminiscing over the incidents surrounding its acquisition
and the competitors, the Hardison and Stewart Oil Company. After he had
closed the deal for it he was approached by Lyman Stewart with an offer
of $12,000 for the property. Convinced that he would make more money if
he drilled it himself, he declined the offer. Mr. Stewart admired the
spirit of the young man and told him that the Hardison and Stewart Oil
Company needed men like him in the organization and offered him a substantial block of stock if he would join the company and turn his lease
over to it. The offer was tempting, but again he declined. Shortly
afterward he received sufficient backing to drill the lease. He succeeded in getting only a few small shallow producers. The return from the
wells was far less than what he had put into the lease, and he left
the United States heavily in debt to go to the Hawaiian Islands to drill
water wells. After arriving there he induced his brother, Lou, to join
him. What appeared at first a successful undertaking turned into a
failure, when a large, rich competing firm underbid him on most of the
jobs, forcing him to quit. His brother returned in steerage to the
United States, and he left as a steerage passenger for Australia where
he learned the government was drilling for water to launch a number of
colonization projects.

When he arrived in Australia he found the drillers were using a
Canadian pole-drilling device that was slow and cumbersome. He introduced the standard method of drilling and within a few years was operating a dozen or so strings of tools, had his own supply house and machine shops, and his own site in Sydney Harbor for unloading incoming
equipment. He remained in Australia twenty years, amassed a good-sized
fortune, paid back the debts he had contracted in drilling his 12,000--
acre lease, and married an Australian girl, Elizabeth ("Narn") Annie King.

At the end of twenty years he returned to the United States and
joined his brothers and T.A. O'Donnell in forming Cousin's Oil Company
which obtained holdings in the Midway and Coalinga fields. The company
was later sold to E.L. Doheny. About that time Mr. McCray and his

brothers formed the El Segundo Land Company and acquired the land, with the exception of the site of the Standard Oil Company refinery, on which the town of El Segundo now stands. From that point on he dealt in southern California properties, but the memories he cherished most were of the old days when he was drilling in the Santa Paula and tramped over the areas where he had drilled more than forty years before. He also sought out the old timers who had worked with him to reminisce over the early days. About a year ago he visited George W. Fleisher on his ranch near Santa Paula and discovered that they were the last two survivors of the first Hardison and Stewart drilling crews. They arranged to have their photographs taken together at Santa Paula the following day. When the time arrived to go to the city Mr. Fleisher was too ill to make the trip. He died a few months later, leaving Mr. McCray the sole survivor. Three weeks before his death Mr. McCray paid a last visit to the old haunts in the vicinity of Santa Paula.

-0-

John W. McCray also sent a few notes from his files about his grandfather, Edward I. McCray:

"E.I. McCray, being first duly sworn, deposes and says: I am now residing at 2151 Hollyridge Drive, Hollywood, California; that I was born in Corry Pennsylvania, March 24, 1864, and that I first went to Australia in January 1891. I returned to America in 1904 on a short trip only, returning to Australia the same year and came back to America again in 1906 and resided there until 1922. While in Australia I was engaged in business as a merchant, importing goods from America. I have still an interest in this business and desire to make a trip to Australia with a view of closing out my business interests there. During my residence in Australia I did not become a citizen of the country and have never become a citizen of any other country excepting America. "

Affidavit before a Notary Public, 12 April, 1927

On September 26, 1890, Edward I. McCray arrived in Honolulu aboard *Forest Queen*, its only passenger.

" Marriage Certificate Number 1152:

"'Married 19 February 1898 according to the rites of the Congregational Church, at the residence of Rev. John Marshall Sands, Alexandra Street, Huntress Hill, South Wales, Australia. "

301

From and undated newspaper clipping:

Mr. Ed McCray leaves for San Francisco on Monday next, where he will make preparations to go to the Sandwich Islands in the employ of the Ewa Sugar Plantation Co. It is the object of this company, which is operating in an artesian district, to develop enough water to use for irrigating purposes and Mr. McCray is to put down wells for them. *The Chronicle* wishes him success and will keep him posted on Santa Paula news.

Will Of Robert ("Deacon Bob") McCrea/McCray

THE WILL OF ROBERT McCREA, who died in Erie County October 6, 1865, is found in the Erie County Will Book D, page 89. It reads:

"Will of Robt. McCrea   Registered October 12, 1865

"In the name of God Amen, I, Robert McCrea 4th, of Concord Township, Erie County and State of Pennsylvania, being sick and weak in body, but of sound mind, memory and understanding (Praised be God for it), considering the certainty of Death and the uncertainty of Time thereof, And to the end that I may be the better prepared to leave this world whenever it shall please God to call me hence, do therefore make and declare this, my last will and testament, in manner following (that is to say).

"First and principally, I commend my soul unto the hands of the Almighty God, my Creator.

"Second, I order that all my just debts, funeral expenses and charges of proving this, my will, be in the first place fully paid and satisfied. And after payment thereof and every part thereof, I give and bequeath unto my beloved daughter, Susan Matilda McCrea, all the rest, residue and remainder of any goods, chattels, debts, ready money, effects and other of my estate, whatsoever and weresoever, both real and personal. I give and bequeath the same and every part and parcel thereof unto the said Susan Matilda McCrea, my son and $5 to Absalom McCrea, my son. The residue to be paid to my daughter, Susan Matilda on her arriving at the age of 18 years except what it shall take to support her in an equimoncal (sic) manner in the meantime.

"And I do hereby nominate, constitute and appoint William Lamb, of Cherytree Twp., Venango County, and Absalom McCrea, my son, of Concord Twp., Erie Co., State aforesaid, executors of this my will hereby revoking and making void all former wills at any time heretofore made and declare this only to be my last will and testament.

"In witness whereof I, the said testor, Robert McCrea 4, have to this my last will and testament, set my hand and seal the 30th day of September, A.C. 1865." Witnesses: D.K. Baker and Benjamin Grant.

Generation I   Generation III

James McCray, Sr.   Elizabeth McCray
                                      b. after Jan. 1793; before 1797
                                      d.
                                      m. James Felton, 10 ch

                                      James McCray
                                      b. bet. 1793 & 1797
                                      d.
                                      m. Jane White, 4 ch
                                         b.
                                         d. Oct, 1851

Generation II

William McCray, Sr.   Mary McCray
                                      b. 1792-1797
         &   d. 18-2-1832/37
                                      m. Stephen Hosmer, 5 ch
Nancy Miles   b. abt 1797
                                         d. 11-9-1859

                                      William McCray, Jr.
                                      b. 1797/99/1805@
                                      d. 28-6-1861, in Cornplanter Twp.
                                         Venango Co., Pa.
                                      m. (1) Elizabeth ("Betsy") Story, 9 ch
                                            b. 1802?
                                            d. 10-9-1841
                                         (2) (2) Mary ("Polly") Prather, 0 ch.
                                               b. 1810
                                               d. 1867

@ 1850 census gives his age   Ellen/Eleanor McCray
as 45, and wife (Mary   b. 27/28-3-1798/99
Prather) as 40   d. 27-3-1857
                                      m. Benjamin Upton, on 12-9-1823,
                                         at Hydetown (Oil Creek), Pa. 7 ch
                                         b. 1793/95, in Maryland
                                         d. 3/4-3-1877, in Garland, Pa.

                                   303

Jane McCray
b.
d.
m. Samuel Moore, 8 ch
 b.
 d. 3-9-1869

Robert ("Deacon Bob") McCray/ McCrea*
b. 16-5-1804
d. 6-10-1865† buried in McCray Cem.,
 Concord Twp. Erie Co., Pa.
m (1) Matilda Carson, 5 ch
 (2) Sarah McCune, 0 ch
 (3) Nancy Ross, 1 ch
 b. 1827?
 d. 12-4-1855; buried with Robt.

John McCray
b. 4-4-1806
d. 8-3-1865, in Garland, Pa.
m. Mary ("Polly") White, 14 ch
 b. 12-3-1815
 d. 7-2-1896, age 81

Nancy McCray
b.
d. 22-4-1841/42
m. David/Jesse Simms/Sims 5 ch

Samuel McCray
b. 1807
d. 22-7-1873
m. Elizabeth Shelmadine, 9/11 ch.
 b. 1813
 d. 21-7-1872 or 21-6-1873 (Upton)

* Robert McCray almost
always used the McCrea
spelling, and even his
will was signed "Robert
McCrea IV," probably to
avoid confusion with
many other Robert McCrays
in the area.

304

Sarah A. McCray
b. 1811?
d. 6-2-1886/87, East Titusville, Pa.
m. George McCray, Jr., son of George
& Jean (Murray) McCray, in Aug.
1831.   11 ch.
b. 1806/10
d. 11/5/1863/64

Margaret McCray
b.
d.
m. Jacob Young on 10-22-1829
b. 12-4-1802
d. 11-16-1873

Generation I

James McCray, Sr.

Generation II

William McCray, Sr.

Generation III

William McCray

&

(1) Elizabeth Story McCray

(2) Mary Prather

Generation IV

Nancy Ann McCray
b. ca 1829
d.
m. Joseph McCaslin

Margaret McCray
b. ca 1836
d.
m. John Wilson

Robert McCray
("Died while young")

Rachel H. McCray
b. ca 1841
d.
m. (1) Robert Eakin
   (2) C.M. Garner

Isobella McCray
b. ca 1840
d.
m. Gilson Eakin

Mary Elnor McCray
b. ca 1832
d.
m. J.M. Goudy

Jane (Elizabeth?) McCray
b. ca 1828
d.
m. Henry Sedoris

Y

306

William Jackson McCray
b. 6-6-1834
d. 17/26-11-1907
m. Nancy Ann McCray, dau. John and
   Mary (White) McCray, on 17-10-1867,
   at Erie, Pa.
   b. 1843/47
d d. 12-1-1927

James Story ("Corntassel Jim") McCray
b. 16-11-1824/30
d. 14-10-1889
m. Martha Crooks, ca 1852
   b.
   d. 4-3-1889

Generation I	Generation IV

Generation I

James McCray, Sr.

Generation II

William McCray, Sr.

Generation III

Elenor McCray

&

Benjamin Upton

Generation IV

James Upton
b. 20-9-1834
d. 11-5-1905
m. Alice Iantha (Blanchard) Porter
   on 3-1-1872
   b. 17-3-1844
   d. 27-4-1922, age 78

Nancy Upton
b. 11-8-1824
d.
m. Lucius M. Van Arnam
b. 2-12-1826

Samuel Upton
b. 20-11-1825
d. 1/4-9-1847
   bachelor

Robert Upton
b. 11-3-1827
d. 7-2-1877
m. (1) Oliva Ann Osborne
   (2) Nancy Boyd

Eva Ann Upton
b. 21-8-1829
d. 25/26-4-1856
m. E.W. Vermilyea

Elizabeth (Eliza) Jane Upton
b. 7-3-1833/34
d. 10-10-1898
m. Thomas Lyons McGuire, Jr.
   b. 2-2-1834
   d. 30-3-1908

V

Generation IV

John McCray Upton
b. 1-3-1837
d. 21-11-1900
m. Mary Ann Blodgett, on 25-12-1860
   b. 1-4-1842

Generation I

James McCray, Sr.

Generation II

William McCray, Sr.

Generation III

Eleanor McCray

Generation IV

James Upton

&

Alice Porter

Generation V

James Delos Upton
b. 25-7-1873
d. 3-6-1960
m. Eva Delilah (Heron) Hayes; div.
2 ch.   1936.

Abram/Abraham Van Gorder Upton
b. 28-4-1875
d. 5-7-1956
m. Bertha A Holden, on 25/7-6-1900,
5 ch.

Isadore (Dora Belle) Upton
b. 26-2-1878
d. 1917
m. William Raddatz, on 22-8-1910, no
ch.

Robert De Forest Upton
b. 6-10-1879
d. 13-12-1953
m. Helen Rice on 23-8-1936, no ch.

Walter Eugene Upton
b. 3-3-1885
d. 10-7-1953
m. Lulu Mae Heron, sister-in-law of
James Delos Upton, on 7-1/6-1907
2 ch.

Generation I

James McCray, Sr.

Generation II

William McCray, Sr.

Generation III

Eleanor McCray

Generation IV

James Upton

Generation V

James Delos Upton

&

Eva Delilah Hayes

Generation VI

J. Duane Upton
b. 29-6-1917
now living in Hemet CA
m. June Elvetta Haller, on 16-9-1942
   b. 23-6-1918, dau of Richard R.
      Haller, of Garland, Pa. 2 ch

Mary Heron Upton
b. 15-10-1913
d. 1-3-1916

311

Generation I

James McCray, Sr.

Generation IV

William C. McCray
b. 1833/1838
d. 22/23-1-1903
m. Amelia McCray (dau John T. McCray)
   b. 23-4-1836   5 ch
   d. 13-4-1891/93

Generation II

William McCray, Sr.

Generation III

Robert ("Deacon Bob") McCray

        &

(1) Matilda Carson

(2) Sarah McCune

(3) Nancy Ross

Source: Upton's list
of McCrays. Mothers of
these five of Generation
IV not given.

Absolom McCready McCray
b.   1838
d.   1923
m Salina Huntington Parsons, 7 ch.
   b. 1844
   d. 1918

Margaret McCray
b. 6-6-1832
d. 3- -1915
m. Alexander Campbell Cordner, on
   5-4-1859, at Jefferson, OH. 9 ch.
   b. 25-7-1830/31
   d. 1910

John McCray (some uncertainty exists
b.   about his having lived.)
d.
m.

Susan Matilda McCray
b. 2-4-1852/55
d. 11-7-1924
m. Warren Trimm, 6 ch
   b. 9-1/9- 1852
   d.25-1-1937

Jane and Mary McCray; unknown if
they were children of Wife #1,
#2, or #3.

312

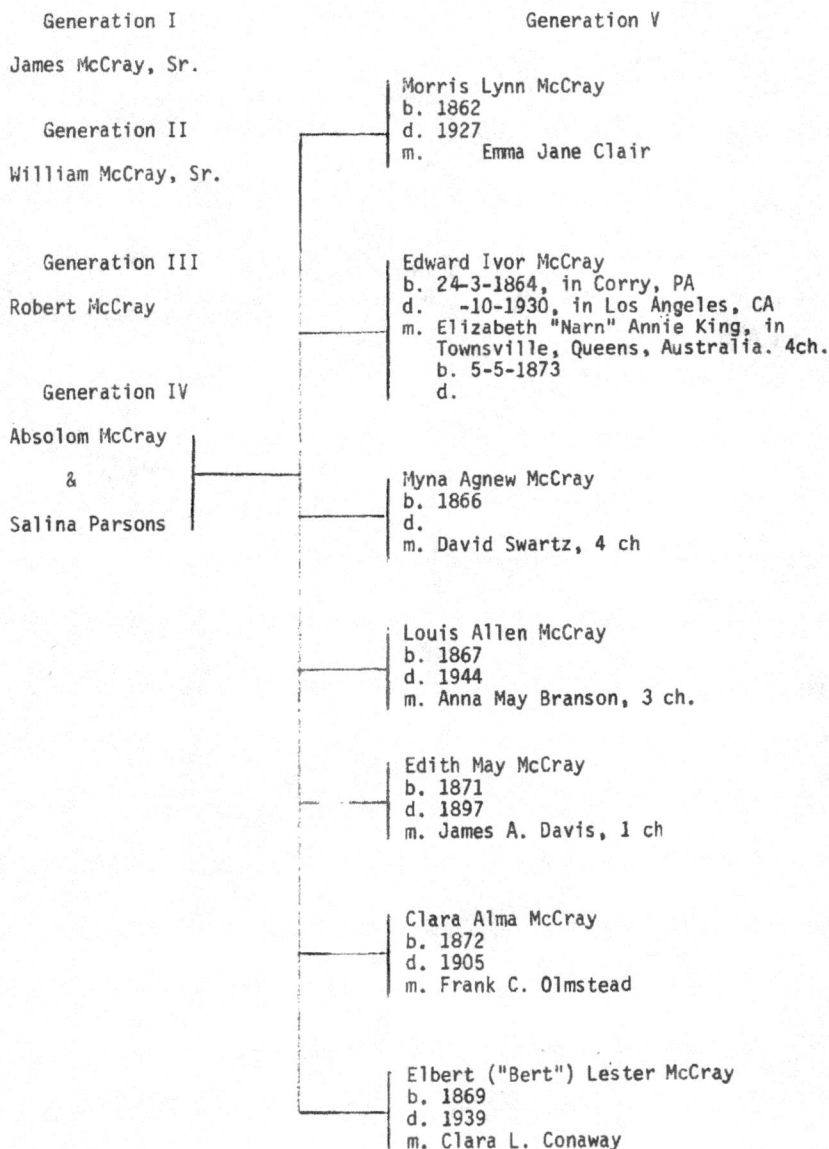

Generation I

James McCray, Sr.

Generation II

William McCray, Sr.

Generation III

Robert McCray

Generation IV

Absolom McCray

&

Salina Parsons

Generation V

Morris Lynn McCray
b. 1862
d. 1927
m.   Emma Jane Clair

Edward Ivor McCray
b. 24-3-1864, in Corry, PA
d.   -10-1930, in Los Angeles, CA
m. Elizabeth "Narn" Annie King, in
   Townsville, Queens, Australia. 4ch.
   b. 5-5-1873
   d.

Myna Agnew McCray
b. 1866
d.
m. David Swartz, 4 ch

Louis Allen McCray
b. 1867
d. 1944
m. Anna May Branson, 3 ch.

Edith May McCray
b. 1871
d. 1897
m. James A. Davis, 1 ch

Clara Alma McCray
b. 1872
d. 1905
m. Frank C. Olmstead

Elbert ("Bert") Lester McCray
b. 1869
d. 1939
m. Clara L. Conaway

313

Generation I

James McCray, Sr.

Generation II

William McCray, Sr.

Generation III

Robert McCray

Generation IV

Absolom McCray

Generation V

Edward Ivor McCray

&

Elizabeth Annie King

Generation VI

Edward Richard Ivor McCray
b. 14-11-1899, in Australia
d.
m. (1) Rosalie ----
   (2) Myna Paul, 2 ch

Robert James McCray
b. 18-5-1902, in Australia
d.   in Newport Beach, CA
m. Helen Mary Keating, 1 ch
   b. 1906

Maurice Coyle McCray
b. 14-6-1904, in Los Angeles, CA
d.
m. (1) Elsie Wagner , 1 ch
   (2) Gloria Camille Dodd, 6 ch.

Alan Archer McCray
b. 24-3-1906, in Sydney, Australia
d. 8-12-1967, in Newport Beach, CA
m. Ruth Alexander Woodworth, 4 ch.
   b. 1909
   d.

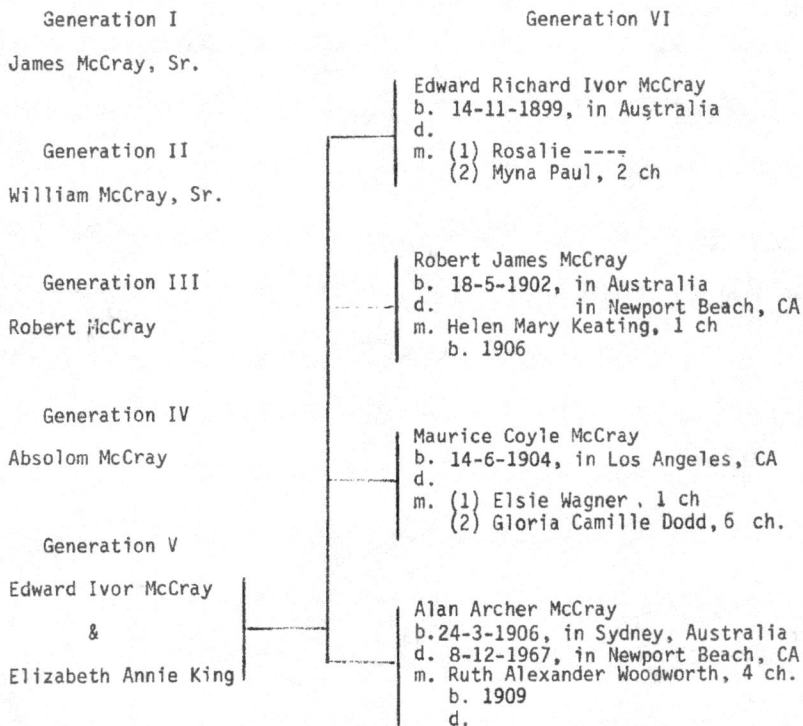

314

Generation I

James McCray, Sr.

Generation II

William McCray, Sr.

Generation III

Robert McCray

Generation IV

Absolom McCray

Generation V

Edward Ivor McCray

Generation VI

Alan Archer McCray

&

Ruth Alexander Woodworth

Generation VII

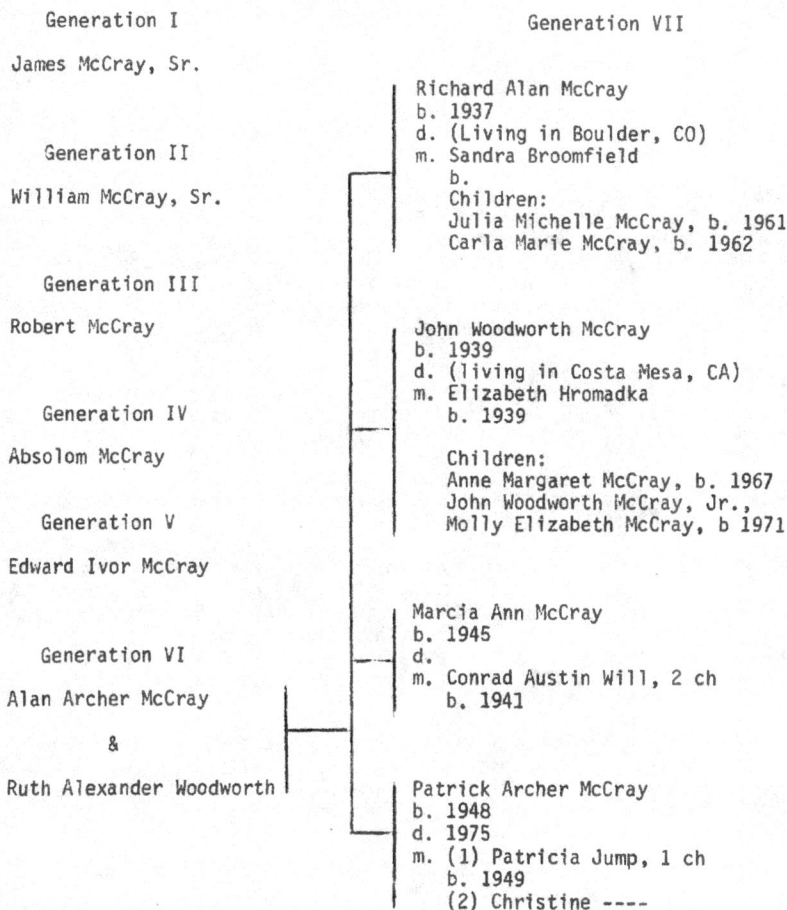

Richard Alan McCray
b. 1937
d. (Living in Boulder, CO)
m. Sandra Broomfield
   b.
   Children:
   Julia Michelle McCray, b. 1961
   Carla Marie McCray, b. 1962

John Woodworth McCray
b. 1939
d. (living in Costa Mesa, CA)
m. Elizabeth Hromadka
   b. 1939

   Children:
   Anne Margaret McCray, b. 1967
   John Woodworth McCray, Jr.,
   Molly Elizabeth McCray, b 1971

Marcia Ann McCray
b. 1945
d.
m. Conrad Austin Will, 2 ch
   b. 1941

Patrick Archer McCray
b. 1948
d. 1975
m. (1) Patricia Jump, 1 ch
      b. 1949
   (2) Christine ----

315

The Family Of

Samuel And Polly (McCoy) McCray

Samuel McCray was born in 1772 in County Monaghan, Ireland, the fifth child of James and Ellen (Bell) McCray. Family histories that mention the family having lived in Ireland say they lived in Monaghan, but none clarify whether it was County Monaghan or the town, Monaghan. Samuel was twelve years old when James and Ellen McCray brought their family of six children to America. The six were: Elizabeth, William, and James, all born in Scotland, and George, Samuel and Robert, born in Ireland.

When the family arrived in America they made their way to Toboyne Township, Cumberland County, which is located a few miles west of the Susquehanna River in Shermans Valley, and took up farming there on a farm which they probably rented for a few years before moving eastward into adjacent Tyrone Township. In about 1793 the family, except for Elizabeth and her husband, William Reed, moved westward to the opposite end of Pennsylvania to Washington County.

Polly McCoy, Samuel's wife, was born in 1782, of unknown parents. We don't know when they married, although she would have been eighteen years old in 1800. The McCray family was then living in Brokenstraw Township, Erie County, Pennsylvania, so they probably married there. Samuel bought a 150-acre tract of land there in 1798. Since their first and only son was born in 1820, when Polly was 38 years old, they probably had been married for several years before the birth of James McCray.

Samuel, and two of his brothers, James, Jr., and George, were listed as members of a company of militia in Erie County in 1813, so they may have been veterans of the War of 1812. However, militia service during the time of that war does not indicate necessarily that they saw service in the war. All men were required to join the state militia.

Samuel McCray left Concord Township after the birth of his son, and the family moved southward. They lost touch with the rest of the McCray family after that. It was only quite recently that it was found he had moved to Armstrong County, Pennsylvania.

It was because of the thorough and systematic approach to genealogical research adopted by Ilo McCray Grisham, of Pueblo, Colorado, that we learned where Samuel went after leaving Erie County. She had learned that her grandfather, Samuel McCray (not this Samuel McCray), had lived in Pennsylvania. Next she learned there had been perhaps a half-dozen Samuel McCrays in Pennsylvania in the early 1800's. Turning to the

316

Federal Census Index, she collected every census record of Samuel McCrays in Pennsylvania, and found her Samuel McCray had lived in Erie County. She then wrote to me, having obtained my name from John T. McCrea, of Miami, Florida, and asked if I could supply her with more information about her Samuel. I could, and I shared it with her. She sent me a copy from the Federal Census for 1850 listing a Samuel McCray in Plumcreek Township, Armstrong County, with a note that the data was of no value to her, but perhaps I could use it. Indeed I could.

There were only three lines on the census-taker's enumeration sheet, dated October 19, 1850:

> Samuel McCray, age 78, male, occupation not given, his land valued at $200, place of birth, Ireland.
> Polly McCray, age 68, female, born in Pennsylvania.
> James McCray, age 30, male, laborer.

These three lines yielded this heretofore unknown information:

1. Samuel McCray had moved to Plumcreek Township, Armstrong County, Pennsylvania, after leaving Erie County.

2. He was age 78, and he probably died there.

3. He was born in 1772 (1850 - 78 = 1772).

4. He was born in Ireland; therefore the McCrays were still in Ireland in 1772.
5. Polly McCoy was a native American, born in 1782.

6. Their son, James, was born in 1820, and as far the census information revealed, was a bachelor, so the line probably ended with him.

7 James was born when Polly was age 38, and was therefore probably their only child.

Rather a nice lot of information to get at one time. I had been trying for about ten years to pin down some documented information about when the McCrays lived in Ireland, as well as the birth years of some of Old James's children.

The Samuel McCray sought by Mrs. Grisham was descended from Robert and Jane (Bruce) McCray, the subject of the next section.

Samuel McCray's 329 acres was located at the junction of the Allegheny River and Limestone Run, three miles below the county line.*

*History of Armstrong County, Pennsylvania, Robert Walter Smith, Chicago, Waterman, Watkins & Co., 1883.

THE FAMILY OF

GEORGE AND JEAN (MURRAY) McCRAY

George McCray, James and Ellen (Bell) McCray's fourth child, was born in Ireland in 1768, in either County Monaghan or its county town, Monaghan--family legends don't make this clear. He came to America as a teenage lad, and came to manhood in Shermans Valley, Cumberland County, Pennsylvania. At age 22, he married Jean* Murray on November 26, 1790, at Centre Presbyterian Church in Toboyne Township, with the Reverend John Linn officiating.

Jean Murray was one of the four daughters of Alexander Murray. If there were any brothers they were not mentioned in her father's will, although there was an Alexander Murray in Shermans Valley who married Mary Blain on May 30, 1793. There were apparently at least two families of Murrays in Shermans Valley at this time. Her sisters were Margaret Neisbet (Nesbet), Mary Fisher, and Isabella Murray. Her father seems to have been a man of some substance and importance in Toboyne Township, and his daughters married into families of local importance. The names of Fishers and Nesbets can be seen today on gravestones in Centre Church's graveyard.

That Alexander Murray held a high patriarchal position in the Murray clan is indicated by the names given to his first three grandsons, for every one of them was named "Alexander;" Alexander Neisbet, Alexander Fisher, and Alexander McCray.

That the McCrays of Toboyne Township were esteemed by Alexander Murray is indicated not only by George McCray's marriage to his daughter, but also by his asking James and Eleanor (Townsley) McCray to serve, along with John Nelson, as witnesses to his will. The will, in which he describes himself as "weak in body, but of sound and perfect mind and memory blessed be God for all his mercies...", was dated April 11, 1793, and proved May 31, 1793, indicating his death occurred between those dates. James "McCree" and John Nelson signed their own names, while "Elonar McCree" made her mark on the document.

This was not the only time that the McCray name appeared with this spelling, although the will upon which it appeared is not the original, but is certified as being a true copy, so we don't know if the clerk of the court, John Morrison, made a true, literal word-for-word copy, or if he may have "corrected" the spelling of James's name.

* There is reason to wonder just what her name really was. Her father wrote her name "Jean" in his will, but her mother used "Jane" in *her* will. The Reverend Linn wrote "Jean" on the wedding register. She herself named one of her children "Matilda Jane," possibly for herself.

318

Accompanying the will was an inventory of Alexander Murray's estate*
which shows that he both owed and had lent money to many of his neighbors.
Among the debtors were William Miles and William McCray (spelled right
this time). Money was owed to the Reverend John Linn, William Reed
"collect for taxes 1792 as per do," Thomas --?-- as per do for making a
coffin," William McCree , George McCree, to "John Nelson for Samuel
Reed's taxes 1.2.6," Balance, in consideration of assets and liabilities,
£1390.6.7½. a nice healthy fortune at that time.

George and Jean (Murray) McCray left Shermans Valley and migrated to
Brokenstraw Township, Erie County in 1798,° but so far we don't know
whereabouts they lived in Brokenstraw Township. Evidence of their residence there was provided by Harry A Focht@, who said the Historians had
found in Cumberland County records:

""Deed Book BB, p. 69, dated July 4, 1808 (July 4 wasn't yet a
holiday then) -- George McCray and wife Jane of Brokenstraw
Twp., Erie Co., sold the property inherited by Jane from her
father Alexander Murray to William Anderson Esq., of Toboyne
Township". (This was Tract 223, 400 acres, warranted to Murray.)

There was no mention of such a bequest in Murray's will, but he may
have given them the land as a gift. It seems to have been surplus for
them, for they didn't move away immediately. George, Samuel, and James
McCray were listed in the Pennsylvania Archives as members of a company
of militia in Erie County in that year. It is thought they moved to the
area of Titusville about 1817, and they were listed as residents of Oil
Creek Township, Crawford County, in the Census of 1820[+].

George McCray was again enumerated in the 1850 Census. age 82, still
in Oil Creek Township, but now living in the household of his son,
George, Jr. The elder McCray was apparently a widower, since the enumeration didn't mention Jean, and family legends say she died in about
1848. An important bit of information was disclosed in this datum;
George McCray told the census-taker he was born in Ireland. It confirmed
that the family did live in Ireland before coming to America, and that
at age 82, George would have been born in 1768. About the only information we have about George McCray, Jr., is that he married his cousin,
Sarah McCray, daughter of William and Nancy (Miles) McCray, which may
have raised some eyebrows.

°° George Carey, see page 254.

@ Chairman, research Committee, Perry Historians, 1982

*Both sets of documents were provided by Myles Murray, of Chagrin Falls,
Ohio, a descendant of these Murrays.

[+] Information supplied by Alice Morrison.

A biography* of George McCray, son of Alexander McCray, and grandson of George and Jean (Murray) McCray, says "the family" (without stating exactly how many or who "the family's" head was) moved to Clarion County in 1858, and "soon returned to Venango County." The biography neglected to say who exactly returned to Venango County, but Alexander McCray stayed there, somewhere near the family of William and Elizabeth (McCray) Reed. Alexander is buried in the churchyard of Shiloh Presbyterian Church near Miola, Clarion County. The gravestone says he was a veteran of the War of 1812, and was born in 1790 and his death was in 1882. One hopes the birth year is in error, since his parents were married in November of that year. We believe the gravestone inscription is in error.

Alexander's son, George, was one of those who returned to Venango County, and later moved to President, Crawford County, where he operated a hotel-boarding house. He apparently had a son whom he named George, and he continued to operate the hotel, as shown by a newspaper clipping that Alice Morrison sent:

"Monday last (Feb. 19, 1877) being the 10th anniversary of the marriage of Mr. and Mrs. George McCray, of President, a pleasant little party gathered at their place on that evening."
From *The Forest Republican* of Tionesta, Forest County, February 21, 1877.

A son of George and Jean (Murray) McCray also lived near Titusville in Oil Creek Township. A notice in a Meadville newspaper, April 17, 1840, informed the public that Robert McCray bought a tract of land in that township. Also, on April 17, 1838, Robert McCray was listed as a member of a Democratic-Republican Party.

I have been unable to contact any descendants from George and Jean (Murray) McCray, so much material concerning them is missing.

In a history of Concord Township, Erie County, Pennsylvania, written between 1884 and 1891, George Carey wrote that "George McCray settled on the Stewart Farm in 1798. It would have been clearer if he'd said, "...settled where the Stewart Farm is today," for there was no Stewart Farm there in 1798. In 1865 there was a Stewart Hotel on the Holland Land tract designated as No. 83, which James McCray, Jr., contracted for in 1802. Erie County deed books probably contain the information needed to locate the Stewart Farm.

---

* *History of Venango County, Pennsylvania*; excerpt provided by Alice Morrison, who also provided the news item from the Tionesta newspaper.

320

Dennis Davis, of Erie, Pennsylvania, has supplied several items in this volume. One concerns a grandson of George and Jean (Murray) McCray. Andrew Jackson McCray was a son of George, Jr., and Sarah (McCray) McCray. He was born April 24, 1830, in Titusville, Pennsylvania, and was apparently still alive when this biography was written. Mr. Davis found and bought a book of biographies* in a yard sale, and in it was this biography of Judge Andrew Jackson McCray.

"No man in Forest County is better known that the subject of this sketch. He is a man whose life's experience is a shining example of what may be accomplished by persistent effort when the outlook is gloomy and forbidding. For with a will power and perseverance that attracts the admiration of all, he has fought his way gradually to the front, until to-day he holds one of the most responsible positions in Forest County, Pennsylvania. Being a man of strong characteristics, with most decided views, Judge McCray is a man whom it is a real pleasure to meet as he is most courtous and obliging and good natured. He was born at Titusville, Crawford County, Pa., April 24, 1830. He is a son of George, Jr., and Sarah (McCray) McCray (daughter of William and Nancy (Miles) McCray), and grandson of George McCray, Sr.

"George McCray, Sr., was a native of the north of Ireland, when he came to America, settling two miles from Titusville, Pennsylvania. There he purchased a tract of land, and from a perfect wilderness cleared a fine farm, and became a peaceful tiller of the soil. He died in 1851, upon a portion of this farm, which had previously been purchased by George McCray, Jr. In his political convictions, he was a believer in the Jeffersonian principles of Democracy.

"George McCray, Jr., first saw the light of day on his father's farm near Titusville. During his youth he remained at home and received a common school education. When manhood's state was reached, he purchased two farms of 100 acres each, one of which was a portion of the homestead tract. But farming was not his chosen calling, and leaving that to the management of others, he followed lumbering, but always as a jobber. He also was a pilot on the Allegeny River, being considered by many to be the most expert pilot in that section. In politics he was a Democrat up to Lincoln's time, when he changed his views and died a strong Republican, having held many township offices. His marriage to Sarah McCray resulted in the birth of eleven children, namely: Andrew Jackson, subject of this sketch; Martha, wife of John Scott, residing near Elmira,

* Book Of Biographies, Biographical Sketches Of Leading Citizens of the Thirty-Seventh Judicial District Pennsylvania, Biographical Publishing Company, Buffalo & Chicago, 1899. pp 592-594.

N.Y.; Mary W., widow of Miles Fulton, -- she resides with our subject; Rebecca, wife of Charles Whaley of Grand Valley, Warren County, Pa.; Elizabeth, a maiden lady who also resides in Grand Valley; Nancy Jane, wife of Thomas Houge, living near McCray, Pa.*; Deborah, who was twice married -- her first husband was a Mr. Hill (she is now the wife of John Young of Gray Valley, Warren County, Pa.); Melissa, wife of Daniel D. Green of Grandinn, Mo; John W.., of Bradford, Pa.; Leman of Forest County, Pa.; and one more who died in infancy. Our subject's father died in 1864, aged fifty-four years; his mother survived her husband twenty-two years, her death occurring in 1886, at the age of seventy-five years. She was a most devout Christian, and each of her seven daughters was given a name selected from the Holy Bible.

"Judge McCray, the eldest of the family, remained at home attending school until he attained the age of seventeen years. Then as was the custom in those early days, he started out to make his own way of life. His first employers were Brewer, Watson & Co., of Titusville, Pa. with whom he remained for seven years, working most of the time in the mill as a sawyer. During that time he saved considerable money, with which he purchased 400 acres of land around and near East Titusville. After renting a small mill, he began cutting and sawing the timber from his land, and shipping his products down the river to the Pittsburgh markets. He was engaged in this line until 1862, and made considerable money in it.

"In 1862, oil was discovered on his land and he was enabled to sell the property at a handsome advance on the price paid. After selling, he went to Garland, Pa., purchased 200 acres of timber land and erected two saw mills, one operated by water power and one by steam, the former of which was afterwards destroyed by fire. Here Judge McCray remained for two years, actively engaged in cutting and sawing his timber, for which he obtained a good price. At the close of that time he sold out. In the meantime he had been dealing to some extent in oil, and after selling his lumbering interests, he was engaged in the oil business for three years. In 1880 Judge McCray went to Forest County and again busied himself in lumbering. In company with Frank Williams, he owned and operated a saw mill near Marienville for a period of four years, when he again returned to Titusville, a well-to-do man.

"This was in 1884, when the oil excitement was sweeping the country. The subject of this sketch went into the Exchange, and for two years was a power in the oil market. But in 1886 he "bucked the tiger" once too often and lost his last dollar. Here he was at the age of fifty-six, without a dollar in the world, but although discouraged, he did not give up. His motto was "Never say die," and during the same year he again

* In Forest County, no longer an active postoffice.

returned to Forest County. He soon found employment with W.H. Frost of
Pigeon, as lumber inspector, remaining one year. The following Spring
he was offered the superintendency of the Baker-Hammond Lumber Company,
which is now called the Hammond-Crosby Lumber Company. This was in 1887,
and our subject has remained there ever since. This is one of the most
extensive plants in that section, and the members of the firm leave
everything to their superintendent, including the sale of lumber. In
1861 Judge McCray built the McCray House at Titusville, and conducted a
hotel for five years. In 1884 Judge McCray was united in marriage with
Isabelle Bryan, nee McCullen of Titusville.

"In 1896 the subject hereof was elected by the Republicans, of
whose party he is a strong supporter, one of the associate judges of
Forest County. This is his first office, as never before could his
friends prevail upon him to accept public office, as he preferred working hard for the success of others. Judge McCray stands deservedly high
in his community, and is exceedingly popular; it was in honor of him
that both McCray station and postoffice were named."

```
Generation I                              Generation III

James McCray, Sr.                         Anna McCray
                                          m. Robert Fulton   3 ch


                                          Margaret McCray
                                          m. Isaac Greene   13 ch


                                          Matilda Jane (Jennie) McCray
     Generation II                        b.
                                          d. 4-3-1870
George McCray                             m. John Brown in 1812, in Titusville,
                                             b. 1793/4    7 ch            Pa.
     &                                       d. 1871/80
Jean Murray
                                          Ellen ( Eleanor) McCray
                                          b. --5-1803
                                          d. 1-4-1829
                                          m. William Duncan (Dunkin)

                                          George McCray, Jr.
                                          b. 1806/10
                                          d. 11-5-1863/64  11 ch
                                          m. Sarah McCray, dau William & Nancy
                                             (Miles) McCray
                                          Alexander McCray, vet. War of 1812
                                          b. 1790--probably wrong, more like
                                             1791 or 1792.
                                          d. 1882; buried Shiloh Presbyterian
                                             Church nr. Miola, Clarion Co., Pa.
                                          m. Elizabeth (Betsy) McCalmont
                                             b. 1798
                                             d.


                                          William F (T?) McCray
                                          b. ca 1795
                                          d. 17-3-1854
                                          m. Mary Jackson, 17-12-1835   5 ch
                                             b. 5-7-1807
                                             d. 22-7-1876

 Polly McCray                             James McCray
 b.                                       m. Salinda Ritter   3 ch
 d.
 m. Simeon Burgess  1 ch
There may also have been                  Robert McCray, bachelor
a Joseph McCray.


                          324
```

THE FAMILY OF

ROBERT AND JANE (BRUCE) McCRAY

ROBERT McCRAY, THE LAST OF THE SIX CHILDREN of Old James and Ellen (Bell) McCray, was born on August 17, 1776. Although some McCray family histories say he was the only one of the six to have been born in America, two of his sons, Robert, Jr., and George, both told a census-taker in 1880 that their father was born in Ireland. Census records are known to contain errors, but this is the only official record extant and should probably be accepted.

He came to America at the end of the American Revolution when he was age eight, and lived in Toboyne Township, Cumberland County, Pennsylvania, for several years before he moved with his parents and brothers to Washington County, Pennsylvania.

According to local histories of Brokenstraw/Concord Township, Erie County, as well as family histories, William, Samuel, and James, Jr., moved to Erie County. Those mentioning the place from whence they came give it variously as Westmoreland or Washington County, with one claiming it was Northumberland County. Washington County was given as the place by James McCray, Jr.'s son and grandson, and it seems best to accept their word for it. By about the year 1800 all six of the siblings except Robert were living there. I would speculate that Robert stayed in Washington County until the death of his parents, after which he moved to Erie County.

In 1801 Robert, at age 25, bought tract No. 49 from the Holland Land Company. The tract abutted Tract 65, purchased by his brother, James, and today it lies just east of Lovell's Station. He married a widow, Mrs. Jane Bruce, who had a daughter, also named Jane Bruce, who was born about the middle of 1812. Their first child, Robert, Jr., was born in March of 1813, followed by three more children. Their family was:

> Robert ("Wicker") McCray
> b. March 2, 1813; d. March 23, 1890
>
> David McCray
> b. July 16, 1815; d. 1822 (age 7)
>
> Samuel McCray
> b. September 23, 1817; d. 1885
>
> Sarah ("Sally") McCray
> b. April 19, 1820

325

Beyond this we have little information about the life of Robert McCray. He died on either March 23, 1858, according to Percie McCray, or April 4, 1858, according to the carving on his gravestone in the McCray Cemetery. The fact that he and his wife Jane, are both buried there would indicate they both lived out their lives in Concord Township, Erie County. Jane died on March 22, 1855.

There isn't much information available about their firstborn son, Robert, Jr., or how he got the nickname "Wicker." Sarah, their daughter, married Samuel Hayes, and that's all we know about them, other than that they had three children. There are several Hayes gravestones in the McCray Cemetery, but not Samuel's nor Sally's.

Through a series of remarkably timed coincidences, I learned a good deal about third--born Samuel and his descendants from one of them, Mrs. Ilo McCray Grisham, of Pueblo, Colorado. Mrs. Grisham has been looking for information on the McCrays of Erie County, and her letter of inquiry came to my hands almost by accident, when George W. Page, of Bryans Road, Maryland, and I were trading McCray information, and he said, "Oh, by the way...", and then produced a letter from her that he'd received that morning. After reading it, we agreed that I should answer it, so I sent her the information that I had, and she, in return, sent me several sheets of family charts that trace the descendants of Samuel McCray down to her. This Samuel was a son of Robert and Jane (Bruce) McCray.

Samuel became a much-married itinerant preacher. We don't know where he was trained in divinity subjects, or if he was ordained as a pastor, but he preached his way across a good part of the United States as it looked in those days. He said he was born in Westmoreland County, Pennsylvania, but it seems more likely that he was born in Erie County; by the time of his birth Robert and Jane Bruce were firmly rooted in the soil of Concord Township.

At age 23, he married Eliza Jane Perkins, on New Years Day, 1840. She was 22 years old, having been born January 6, 1818. A daughter, Pamela McCray, was born March 13, 1841. Eight months later, on November 2, 1841, Eliza Jane died and was buried in the McCray Cemetery. She must have been one of the very first to be buried there, as this was but fifteen months after the death of James McCray, Jr., who died in 1839.

Pamela McCray lived only thirteen years. Superstitious people may make of it whatever they wish, but she was born on the thirteenth of March, 1841.

Eight years later, Samuel wooed and won Mary Dodd in McHenry County, Illinois. Mary may have been so dazzled by Samuel's courtship that she didn't notice that the courthouse scribe recorded it was "Mary Dunn," not once but twice. But then, maybe he got the name from the Reverend M. Dicker, who joined the couple together.

Samuel and Mary and three children, all believed to have been born in Erie County; Augusta O. McCray, Augustus S. McCray, and Elizabeth

Mary Jane McCray, the last an obvious combination of the names of his first two wives. A little over two and a half months later, on June 3, 1858, Mary died and was buried in the McCray Cemetery.

Once more Samuel was a widower -- but not for long. He spent little time in mourning, for within four months (to the day), on October 3, 1853, ne sought comfort in a new marriage to Betsy Ann Price, in her hometown of Braceville, Trumbull County, Ohio, and took her back to his home in Erie County, Pennsylvania. Edwin McCray was born to them there in 1854, and two years later, Ellen was born in Crawford County.

In about 1858 they moved from Pennsylvania back to Wisconsin. Mrs. Grisham wrote:

"Grandpa (Augustus) used to tell me how he walked all the way from Pennsylvania to Wisconsin when he was seven years old and led the horse. Betsy rode the wagon and was pregnant as usual. Betsy was the woman whom Grandpa thought of as "Mother."

Mrs. Grisham believes that Samuel's sister, Sarah, and her husband, Samuel Hayes, may have accompanied them in the move, as there were some Hayes families nearby when Mrs. Grisham was a child, and her father referred to them as 'shirt-tail relatives." She continued:

"They settled in Green Lake County, Wisconsin. Samuel cleared a farm and rode a preaching circuit. Betsy ran the farm while Samuel was riding the circuit and also produced Julia, Norman, Matthew and Willie. There is also a small white stone on the family burial plot that says simply "Lucy." She may have been another child in the family.

"When my dad was a laddie he used to hang around the hardware store in Green Lake (it was called Dartford then) and listen to the old-timers tell stories. They told him that his grandfather, Samuel, had red hair and red whiskers and was very strong. He had powerful arms and shoulders and could 'sink an axe into a log further than any man alive.'

"Augustus married Frances Lillian Luckey in 1875. They had nine children, all born in Green Lake County, Wisconsin. I am the daughter of William, who was the eldest son. I was also born and raised in Green Lake, Wisconsin and moved to Colorado in 1949."

According to J. Duane Upton, in his family list of McCrays, Samuel and Betsy Ann Price had a daughter, Elmina ("Mina") McCray, born December 6, 1858. She died July 6, 1944; married Willis Laverne McCray. He was born November 1, 1857; died April 6, 1926. Upton doesn't mention a Julia, but he lists all the other children born to Betsy. Mr. Upton and Mrs. Grisham list other names that they don't both agree upon.

Samuel and Betsy seemed to have had an agreeable marriage; at least they had six children during the next nineteen years; Edwin C., Ellen M., Julia E., Norman S., Matthew Eugene, and Willie. Still, something went wrong, and they separated on January 12, 1872, only a bit less than three months after Willie's birth. Mrs. Grisham wrote of the separation:

"Maybe Samuel didn't take Betsy all the way back to Erie County, Pa. Maybe he dumped her off in Trumbull County, Ohio, where he said he married her and then went on to Erie County and married Sally McCray."

"Sally" was Mrs. Sarah Hammond McCray, widow of Josiah McCray, son of William S. McCray, and grandson of James, Jr., and Eleanor (Townsley) McCray. Josiah's mother was Samuel's father's step-daughter, Jane Bruce. Sound complicated? That's why they invented charts like this:

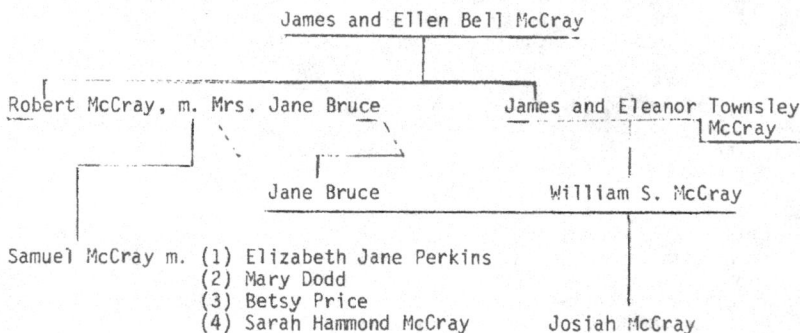

```
                       James and Ellen Bell McCray
                         ┌───────────┴───────────┐
Robert McCray, m. Mrs. Jane Bruce          James and Eleanor Townsley
  ┌───────────┐     \       \                          │  McCray
  │           │    ┌──────┐                            │
  │        Jane Bruce                        William S. McCray
  │                                                    │
Samuel McCray m. (1) Elizabeth Jane Perkins            │
                (2) Mary Dodd                          │
                (3) Betsy Price                        │
                (4) Sarah Hammond McCray      Josiah McCray
```

Mrs. Grisham didn't mention a divorce or Betsy's death, but we assume and hope that things were properly taken care of in time, for in less than two months after the separation, in a haste that must have raised a few eyebrows around Concord Township, he married Sally McCray in Corry, Pa.

Samuel and Sarah had one daughter, Minnie B. McCray, born 21 March, 1875. Minnie married Lewis J. Stearns. Upton gives his dates: b. 1-9-1870, d. 10-15?- 1920/24, and added, "monument shows 1920." The monument is in the McCray Cemetery. Minnie died somewhere in eastern Washington, in Walla Walla or Yakima, according to Mrs. Grisham. Upton lists four children of the marriage of Minnie and Lewis:

Glenn Stearns; b. 6-28-1899; m. Sarah Roberts. No children.
Elton Stearns; b. 8-16-1902; m. Marjorie Dye.
Paul Stearns; b. 6-6-1904; m. 1st Inez Bush, 2nd Mable Jones
                                     or James.
Edith Stearns; b. 2-10-1910; or 5-10-1910; m. Russel Livenspire.

Mrs. Grisham added a note to one of the family sheets: "I used to write to Aunt Minnie for Grandpa (Augustus) but I can't remember her name to save my neck." Upton's information that Minnie married Lewis Stearns may well have saved Mrs. Grisham's neck. We hope so.

Another cryptic note she added to the family sheet for Samuel McCray goes:

"I don't know whatever became of these people (children of Samuel and Betsy Price) after they went back east. There was a Sim McCray who was a lawyer in the Chicago area during the '20's. He may have been a son of one of them. There was also a James McCray who was an artist and exhibited in Oshkosh, WI, museum. My Uncle Jesse claimed James was a relative, too, but you have to be kind of careful of Uncle Jesse's information. If he didn't know for sure, he'd make up something."

I've found many people in the world who follow Jesse's philosophy, and I've gotten lost sometimes when I sought directions from them.

-0-

The exact location of the graves of Samuel's first two wives may not be known today because their gravestones were found beside the cemetery's utility shed in 1983 by Alice Morrison, and in 1986 they were still there, broken, with parts of their legends missing. Neither grave was listed in a compilation of the graves in the McCray Cemetery done by a Mrs. Durham in 1952.

Generation I

James McCray, Sr.

Generation III

Robert ("Wicker") McCray
b. 2-3-1813
d.   1890
m. Roda Tozer Bogardus, 1 ch
   b. 1818
   d. 1891

Samuel McCray
b. 23-9-1817
d.   1885; buried in Tom Hill
   Cemetery, Green Lake Co., WI
m. (1) Eliza Jane Perkins, on 1-1-1840
       in Concord Twp. Erie Co., Pa.
       b. 6-1-1818   1 ch
       d. 12-11-1841[+]
   (2) Mary Dodd, on 2-5-1818, in
       Woodstock, IL   3 ch.
   (3) Mrs. Betsy A. Price, on 3-10-
       1853, in Braceville, OH. 5 ch.
    (4) Mrs. Sarah ("Sally") McCray,
       on 26-3-1872, in Corry, Pa.
       Widow of Josiah McCray. 1 ch.
       b. 1830
       d. 1910, buried in Tom Hill
          Cemetery, Green Lake Co. WI

Generation II

Robert McCray

&

Mrs. Jane Bruce

Sarah ("Sally") McCray
b. 19-4-1820
d.
m. Samuel Hayes, 3 ch. (The Hayes may
   have gone to Green Lake Co., WI
   with Samuel and Sally, above.)

[+] Buried in McCray Cemetery,
Concord Twp, Erie Co., Pa.
(My own assessment; Mrs. Ilo
Grisham, a descendant, says
the memorial stone is for some
other woman.

David McCray
b. 16-7-1815
d. 1822

Generation I

James McCray, Sr.

Generation II

Robert McCray

Generation III

Samuel McCray ──────────

&

(1) Eliza Jane Perkins ──

(2) Mary Dodd ──────────

(3) Mrs. Betsy A. Price

(4) Mrs. Sarah McCray ──

Bracketed numbers (3),
indicate one of the four
wives of Samuel.

Generation IV

(1) Pamelia (Pamela) McCray
    b. 14-3-1841
    d. 10-10-1854

(2) Augustus Samuel McCray
    b. 14-1-1851, in Erie Co., Pa.
    d. 29-4-1941, age 90
    m. Frances L. Luckey
        b. 10-10-1854 (the same day Pamelia
           died.)
        d. 22-5-1922, in Fond du Lac Co. WI
           Buried in Mt. Tom Cemetery,
           Green Lake Co., WI.

(2) Augusta McCray
    b. 24-5-1849, in Erie Co., Pa.
    d. 23-5-1925
    m. unmarried

(2) Elizabeth Mary Jane McCray
    b. 25-3-1853, in Erie Co., Pa.
    d.
    m. Mark (Roy?) Woodside

(3) Edwin C. McCray
    b. 9-9-1854 in Erie Co., Pa.
    d.
    m.

(3) Ella M. McCray
    b. 23-7-1856, in Crawford Co., Pa.
    d.
    m.

(3) Julia E. McCray
    b. 6-12-1856, in Green Lake Co., WI

331

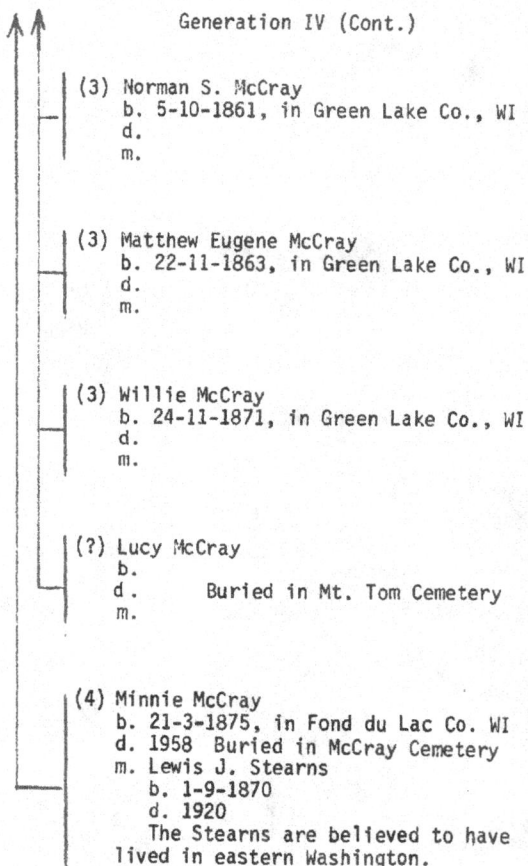

(3) Norman S. McCray
   b. 5-10-1861, in Green Lake Co., WI
   d.
   m.

(3) Matthew Eugene McCray
   b. 22-11-1863, in Green Lake Co., WI
   d.
   m.

(3) Willie McCray
   b. 24-11-1871, in Green Lake Co., WI
   d.
   m.

(?) Lucy McCray
   b.
   d.   Buried in Mt. Tom Cemetery
   m.

(4) Minnie McCray
   b. 21-3-1875, in Fond du Lac Co. WI
   d. 1958 Buried in McCray Cemetery
   m. Lewis J. Stearns
      b. 1-9-1870
      d. 1920
      The Stearns are believed to have
lived in eastern Washington.

Generation I

James McCray, Sr.

Generation II

Robert McCray

Generation III

Samuel McCray

Generation IV

Augustus Samuel McCray

&

Frances Lillian Luckey

Generation V

Maud Lilly McCray
b. 14-6-1876
d. 9-11-1882, in Green Lake Co., WI
   buried in Mt. Tom Cemetery, Green
   Lake Co., WI

Bertha May McCray
b. 20-2-1878
d. 1-4-1882 in Green Lake Co., WI
   Buried in Mt. Tom Cem.

William Ray McCray
b. 20-9-1883, in St. Marie, Green
   Lake Co., WI
d. 10-8-1952, in Green Lake Co. WI
m. Mable Hannah Spenser, on 28-3-1905
   in Kit Carson Co., Colo.   3 ch.

Marian Sophia McCray
b. 28-5-1885, in St. Marie
d. 19-7-1946, in Dubuque, IO; buried
   in Plattville, WI
m. Obediah Gibson   no ch

Francis Augustus McCray
b. 28-8-1888, in Green Lake, WI
d. 14-9-1960, in Huntsville, TX
m. Aytchie -------   no ch

Jesse Gorman McCray
b. 23-4-1890, in Green Lake, WI
d. 20-4-1967, in Oshkosh, WI
   Buried in Oshkosh

333

Generation V (Cont.)

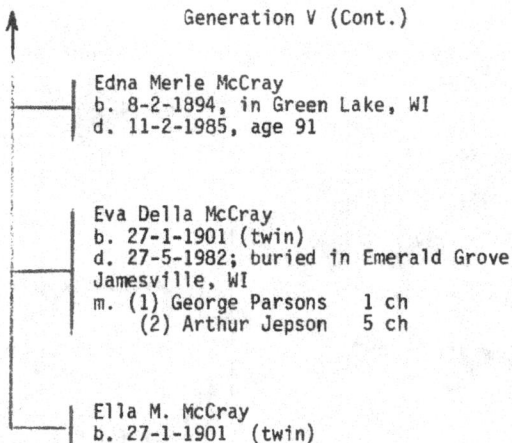

Edna Merle McCray
b. 8-2-1894, in Green Lake, WI
d. 11-2-1985, age 91

Eva Della McCray
b. 27-1-1901 (twin)
d. 27-5-1982; buried in Emerald Grove
Jamesville, WI
m. (1) George Parsons   1 ch
   (2) Arthur Jepson   5 ch

Ella M. McCray
b. 27-1-1901 (twin)

334

Generation I	Generation VI
James McCray, Sr.	
	Floy Ruby McCray
	b. 28-7-1908, in Green Lake, WI
Generation II	d. 25-8-1908, in Green Lake; burial
Robert McCray	in Green Lake
	Audrey Mabel McCray, teacher
	b. 1-5-1911, in Beloit Rock, WI
Generation III	d.
Samuel McCray	m. John Winters, on 19-5-1935, in
	Ripon, WI
Generation IV	Ilo June McCray, teacher
	b. 18-6-1925, in Green Lake, WI
Augustus Samuel McCray	Living in Pueblo, CO
	m. Lee Edward Grisham, on 7-6-1953
	Div. 1974 3 ch
Generation V	Their Children:
William Ray McCray	William Edward Grisham
&	b. 5-9-1954, in Pueblo, CO
Mable Hannah Spencer	
	Anne Marie Grisham
	b. 17-10-1957, in Pueblo, CO
	David Scott Grisham
	b. 14-6-1962, in Pueblo, CO

335

Concerning Those Blakeslees

When we look at the third generation of McCrays in Erie County, we are struck by the number of marriages between them and the Blakeslees. The first five of the nine children of James and Elanor (Townsley) McCray all married Blakeslees! Was it circumstance, or some magic attraction?

Probably a large part of the magnetism that drew them together was simply proximity. Because the number of settlers was not great until sometime around 1815 or so, there may not have been many prospective spouses about. Look at maps of Concord Township in later years, and wherever there are McCray farms there are also Blakeslee farms nearby.

We'd like to think, of course, that the extraordinary and traditional good looks of the McCray family was a factor, and if the Blakeslees would agree to that, we can say that it was the equally good looks of the Blakeslees that brought them together. Both families have benefitted by the mixture of genes that have produced some pretty remarkable people.

David Blakeslee, Sr., always referred to as "Captain David Blakeslee," was born in New Haven, Connecticut, on April 30, 1741, but seems to have lived much of his life in Granville, New York, which sits nearly astride the New York-Vermont border, prior to coming to Pennsylvania. He was a Revolutionary War soldier, having served with the Charlotte County (now Washington County), New York Militia, and was commissioned a captain in 1782, after the Revolution. He brought his family to Meadville, Pennsylvania, in 1817, and then moved to Sparta Township, Crawford County the following year, and settled just a few miles from the McCrays, about ten miles to the north in Brokenstraw Township, Erie County. It was a distance easily covered by horseback in an hour or so. Pheromones of some species of animal life are detected over similar distances.

The reasons for the Blakeslee's move from Granville, in Upper New York, hasn't come down to us, but it may be surmised that "the year without a summer," as 1816 is remembered today by meteorologists, motivated the shift to northwestern Pennsylvania in the spring of 1817.* One can easily imagine the terror that gripped the populace in the most affected areas when the soil remained frozen in the spring of 1816, and snows kept returning during the summer, and starvation stalked the land. Knowing nothing of high-altitude winds and the nature of major volcanic actions half-way around the world, they would probably have said the land was accursed and was being punished by a wrathful God for the undoubted sins to which man is prone. They should, therefore, go forth like the wandering Israelites, in penance, to find a new place to live, and hopefully to sin somewhat less. Holland Land Company's records show a dramatic spurt in sales for the years 1816, 1817 and 1818.

Only a few miles separated the farms of the two families, and it probably didn't take the young people very long to find each other.

* See p. 239, Mt. Tamboro.

The five McCray/Blakeslee marriages of the children of James and Eleanor (Townsley) McCray constitute a confusing tangle of circumstance that's guaranteed to confuse any but the most careful readers. They were:

1. James T. McCray married Sarah Blakeslee, daughter of Captain David Blakeslee.

2. George McCray married Polly Blakeslee, daughter of David Blakeslee, Jr.

3. John T. McCray married Sarah Blakeslee. Note carefully that she was not the above Sarah Blakeslee, but was Polly's sister, and technically, her sister-in-law, sort-of.

4. Robert McCray (not to be confused with his uncle, Robert McCray) married Betsey (Elizabeth?) Blakeslee, who was also a sister of Polly (Blakeslee) McCray.

5. Betsey (Elizabeth?) McCray married Jesse A. Blakeslee, son of Captain David Blakeslee, and sister of Sarah (Blakeslee) McCray.

Confusing, isn't it? But that's not all.

Confused About Mrs. Jane Bruce and Jane Bruce?

Mrs. Jane Bruce, who married Robert McCray, youngest son of James and Eleanor (Townsley) McCray, had a daughter by her first husband, and she named the daughter Jane Bruce. Jane Bruce married William S. McCray, son of James and Eleanor. They were two different ladies, mother and daughter, and I suppose you could say, aunt and niece, perhaps.

Mrs. Jane Bruce may have been Mrs. James Bruce in her first marriage. Evidence of this is sketchy at best, but on June 28, 1801, "James Bruis" bought two fifty-acre pieces of land from the Holland Land Company. They probably abutted each other to form a one-hundred acre tract, as one of the pieces was in Tract 67 and the other in Tract 85, both with a common border. Isn't it likely that "James Bruis" was a mis-spelling of "James Bruce"? We have no other clues on this matter.

Other McCrays of Northwestern Pennsylvania

The six children of Old James and Ellen (Bell) McCray were not the only McCrays to settle in northwestern Pennsylvania around the beginning of the nineteenth century. Thomas, John and James McCray also settled in western Crawford County at about the same time that Old James' five sons and a daughter were clearing land in eastern Erie County. Both of these McCray families moved tnere from the Susquehanna region of Pennsylvania, and there is some reason to believe that they may have been related.

Thomas McCray was born January 4, 1756. His wife's name was Elizabeth, but that is all we know about her. The only child of theirs known with certainty was Mary, who married Daniel Herrington in Lycoming County in 1793. Thomas McCray's name is in the 1790 Census as head of a household in Northumberland County, and in nearby Mifflin County, James McCray was listed. Although Lycoming, Mifflin and Northumberland Counties lie close to each other, we can only speculate whether these McCrays were related. Thomas McCray was listed as a taxpayer in 1789 in Armagh Township, Mifflin County, which bordered Northumberland/Lycoming Counties, with today's Williamsport, Lycoming's county seat, lying just across the West Branch of the Susquehanna River, which divides Mifflin and Northumberland Counties. One could speculate that since Lycoming County was taken from Northumberland County in 1795, and there was no Lycoming County until then, Daniel and Mary may have married in Williamsport, a strategically located and rapidly growing town and that the Thomas and James McCray families managed to meet at each other's homes, attend worhip services together and shop.

M. Ben Hodges, of Bellingham, Washington, who is a descendant from Daniel Herrington, found a paper, "Ancestors and Descendants of James Herrington (1763-1842) of Union Township, Crawford County, PA," in the library of the Crawford County Historical Society in Meadville, county seat of Crawford County.* Daniel Herrington, a son of Jacob and Hanna Herrington, of York County, Pennsylvania, was a Revolutionary War soldier, serving in militia companies of both Pennsylvania and Maryland. York County shares its border with Baltimore County, Maryland, and many of York County's settlers came from Baltimore, and newly arrived Scots-Irish and Germans who landed at Baltimore went to Pennsylvania on the old York Road.

Herrington bought land in 1785 in Ohio County, Virginia, and later returned there with his bride, where in 1814, he acknowledged a deed. In 1825 they moved west to Illinois, where he died August 13, 1836, in Danville, Vermillion County. His widow, Mary, applied for a widow's pension in Hamilton County, Ohio. It's county seat is Cincinnati. Later

---

* *Crawford County Genealogy*, Vol XII, No. 2, 1989, p. 102

she moved to Sadsbury Township, Crawford County, Pennsylvania, probably to live with a McCray brother or sister. She died there July 3, 1951.

Alice Morrison, Titusville genealogist, sent an enigmatic entry from Survey Book No. 1, Allegheny County, Pennsylvania, located in the courthouse of either Meadville or Erie. Keep in mind that Crawford County was created in the year 1800 out of Allegheny County.

"Situate on the waters of Beaver Creek in Allegheny County containing 401 acres, 150 perches and allowance of 6% for roads, etc. Surveyed the 26th day of October, 1794 in persuance of a warrant of 400 acres granted to James McCree bearing date of May, 1792."

A sketch of the plot accompanied the entry, and on its center was the name, "James McCrea." The adjacent tract to the south bore the name "John McCree." The tract to the west bore the name "Robert McGee," and north and east respectively were "Matthew McConnel" and "Benjamin Loxley."

Within the bounds of Allegheny County as it was in 1794 were two "Beaver" watercourses; Beaver River is formed at New Castle by the confluence of the Shenango and Mahoning Rivers. It flows south into the Ohio River at Beaver Falls. Beaver Run is a small stream that flows south through Elgin Borough, Erie County, and proceeds through Holland Land Company Tracts 43 and 61, and empties into the South Fork of French Creek.

Of the two of these streams, Beaver River seems to be the one referred to in the above warrant. The consortium of Dutch bankers had been awarded all of District Six by 1794, which included Beaver Run. Furthermore, the warrant of "Thos. McKray of Sadsbury, Crawford County" was granted on February 27, 1818. The warrant had been applied for by "Thos. and James McKray." State Archives land records* show six other tracts for which warrants were applied in Allegheny County before 1800, and they were later finalized to John, James and Thomas McCray/McCrea/McCree (variously spelled) of Crawford County.

The Federal Census of 1800 does little to clear up the relationship of the McCrays of Crawford County and those still living to the east along the Susquehanna River. Thomas McCray is listed as head of the household with two males under age 10, one male between 10 and 16, one male over 45, one female between 10 and 16, and one female between 26 and 45.

---

* *Land Records, Allegheny, North and West of the Ohio River;* State Archives, Harrisburg.

However, listed in Mifflin County, Thomas McCray, age between 26 and 45 and a female, undoubtedly his wife, also age somewhere between 26 and 45. As in the 1790 Census in Northumberland County James McCray and a woman, probably his wife, were also listed. Anyone who cares to is free to guess what relationship there was between them.

Thomas McCray's name appears several times in the ubiquitous Beers books of county history*. On page 665, Vol I: "Summit Township, Conneaut Lake...the first saw mill was built by Alexander Power. George Dickson built an early log grist and saw mill about a half-mile south of Harmonsburg, but soon after sold it to Henry Broadt. He then sold it to Thomas McCray, by whom the present grist mill, owned by George Dean was built." On page 664, Vol. I: "Other pioneers were Silas Chidester... James McCray..."

On page 661: "Dicksonburg is a little village located in the southern part of the (Summit) township, and contained about 15 dwellings, a store, school, blacksmith shop, Methodist Church, and a large gristmill owned by J.B. McDowell**. The place on the old Beaver and Erie Canal, and in early times was known as McDowell's Postoffice. John Thompson and Silas Proctor were early merchants. George Dickson built the first gristmill. Joseph McCray erected the present one."

On page 666, Vol. I: "A Union Church, the first in the village was erected on the lot immediately north of the present schoolhouse in 1821 or 1822...The Church was free to all Christian denominations and the Methodists worshipped in it until the erection of their building. Among the earliest members of the church were John Smith, Watson Smith, and Thomas McCray."

County newspapers mentioned from time to time John, Hiram, Joseph, and James McCray, after the death of Thomas McCray on September 22, 1813. Some of them, or perhaps all of them, may have been sons of Thomas McCray. John McCray was a schoolteacher, whose daughter, Emma, taught school and was a member of the Methodist Episcopal Church. She married H.M. Proctor in January of 1871 (one of the very few dates supplied by Beers), and they had three children: Roy, Guy and Paul Proctor. Beers reported on page 881, "Emma, daughter of James McMillan, who settled Summerhill Township, married Hiram McCray."

* *History Of Crawford County, Pennsylvania,* Vols. I and II; Warner Beer & Co., Chicago, 1885.

** Probably John B. McDowell (1778-1858), great great uncle of my mother, Marion Louise McDowell. The blacksmith shop mentioned may have been where my great grandfather, George Nelson McDowell, plied his trade of "Buggy Ironer," a fabricator of metal parts for buggies.

New material on the McCrays of Crawford County was recently received from Mrs. Della Upshaw of Arizona. She is descended from Thomas McCray II and his son, Jesse McCray. Jesse married Mary --?-- in 1838, and they had three children:

> James McCray, born in 1840
> Almon McCray, born in 1842
> Mary McCray, born in 1844

Jesse McCray was a carpenter who, by 1850 had moved his family to Mercer County, the next county south of Crawford County. Jesse had four brothers and at least three sisters. John F. McCray was one of them. Jesse's name wasn't listed in the 1860 Census in the household of Mary McCray, although it listed James, Almon and Mary McCray. This may indicate that Jesse McCray died between 1850 and 1860.

Jesse's son, James McCray, also a carpenter as well as a farmer, married Emaline Struble in 1865 in Mercer County. Mrs. Upshaw's letter related that Emaline's father disowned her and cut her out of his will for marrying James McCray against his wishes. Although there may have been bad feelings between Emaline's father and the young couple, apparently not all of the Strubles were so upset, for James and Emaline, together with James' brother, Almon McCray, and Emaline's uncles, Levi and Adam Struble, all sold their Mercer County holdings and left the East forever, and went to Girad, county seat of Crawford County in the southeast corner of Kansas. James later moved on into Oklahoma and there lived out his life in Brammon, Key County, Oklahoma, where he died in 1900 at age 60. Emaline died the next year at age 54. They had six children:

> Luther McCray, born in 1867 in Mercer County, Pennsylvania
> Bertha B. McCray, born in 1869 in Mercer County.
> Leonard Elton McCray, born September 1, 1871, in Girad, Kansas
> Etta Belle McCray, born in 1874 in Girad
> James McCray, born in 1877 in Girad
> Jessie McCray, born in February, 1880

Leonard McCray, Mrs. Upshaw's grandfather, became everyone's idea of a drifting cowboy on Oklahoma's frontier. She wrote:

"After Leonard's father, James, died, he drifted away from home and, being a young cowboy on the wild frontier of Oklahoma he sometimes found himself on the wrong side of the law, but he soon found that side didn't pay, and he learned what life could be like. He grew to be loved and respected by family and friends, but he never returned home. It was not until after my mother had grown up that his two sisters, Bertha and Belle and their brother Luther, found him in Sallisaw, Oklahoma. Mother sad it was one happy day in their lives when grand-dad Leonard was reunited with his family, but he never forgave himself for not coming back to see his mother before she died. I think of him when I hear some of the cowboy songs of today."

Leonard, the lonesome cowboy, during one of his rambles encountered a widow, Maggie Holt, mother of three children, Barton, Jack and Sallie Holt. Maggie's maiden name was Holt, but John Holt, the man she married was not related to her. Maggie captured his heart and before he knew it he was roped, tied and branded, and on December 14, 1907, they married at McKey, Oklahoma. Leonard adopted Maggie's three children and gave them a new last name of McCray. Marriage changed Leonard so much that he abandoned the unsteady life of punching cattle and turned to farming and ranching. Many a country-western ballad has been wrought and mournfully sung about roving cowboys who became entangled in the web of matrimony, never more to roam.

Leonard and Maggie had six children to add to Maggie's first three. The first of these six was Mrs. Upshaw's mother. The children were:

Edith Belle McCray, born December 8, 1909

Alva Woodus McCray, born March 30, 1913

Jessie McCray, born January 2, 1915

Archie Lee McCray, born March 20, 1916

Cora Inez McCray, born April 3, 1918

Imogine McCray, born March 1, 1924

Archie McCray served in World War II, and Mrs. Upshaw told of his narrow escape from death:

"He was captured in France by the Germans. They were holding somewhere around 80 to 100 Americans and Frenchmen in a clearing in a forest, and there were two large trucks with machine guns mounted on the cabs of these trucks. It was quite obvious what the Germans had in mind, and a friend of Uncle Archie's asked him what he was going to do. Archie said that if shooting started he was going to make a break for it. They were in the back row, and when the shooting started Archie and three others headed for the forest. Only Uncle Archie made it, and he was seriously wounded. He carried a piece of shrapnel near his heart, and the doctors said it was too close to risk surgery, but if it ever dislodged it would probably cause a heart attack, and on 28 October, 1977, it happened. He had a massive heart attack and died before they could get him to a hospital in Stillwater, Oklahoma."

Edith Belle McCray married Walter Edward Avants on September 26, 1925, in Sallisaw, Oklahoma. Their nine children were:

Thomas E. Avants, born August 4, 1926

Gladys L. Avants, born December 3, 1927

Della M. Avants, born April 10, 1930

Jessie M. Avants, born April 5, 1932

Leona Avants, born July 13, 1934

Thelma Lee Avants, born March 27, 1937

Walter Edward Avants, born March 27, 1939

Ernestine Avants, born April 22, 1943

Orvil Leon Avants, born October 9, 1946

Della Avants had a brief and unfortunate marriage in 1947 to J.H. Buckins that lasted only long enough to be annulled. Della bore a daughter, Linda, later that same year. In 1949 she married Berl F. Upshaw, who adopted Linda. They had two more daughters, Cheryl E. Upshaw and Christine Beryl Upshaw.

Cheryl Upshaw became a police officer on the Phoenix, Arizona, force, and served twelve years. She suffered two near-fatal injuries in line of duty, and after seriously damaging her spine in an automobile crash she left the police force and now lives in the quiet of the mountains of Montana. She married Gary Huish, but they were divorced.

Mrs. Upshaw is retired and she and her husband "enjoy the great outdoors. Every now and then we see an eagle circling in the sky over our place in a green valley nestled in the mountains with the Verde River meandering through it."

* * * *

ADDENDUM: There is recently discovered evidence of a possible familial connection between Thomas McCray and the six McCray families in Brokenstraw Township, Erie County. Daniel Herrington, who married Mary, Thomas' daughter, turned up in Brokenstraw in 1801, as indicated by an entry in Holland Land Company records (see p. 232). It is unclear what his dealings were, but he was in some way involved with William Miles concerning Tract 95. Did Daniel and Mary come to Erie County to visit relatives there, and met Miles there? It's difficult to think of a scenario that doesn't involve Daniel, Mary, William Miles and the McCrays, all together.

DESCENDANTS FROM THOMAS AND ELIZABETH McCRAY

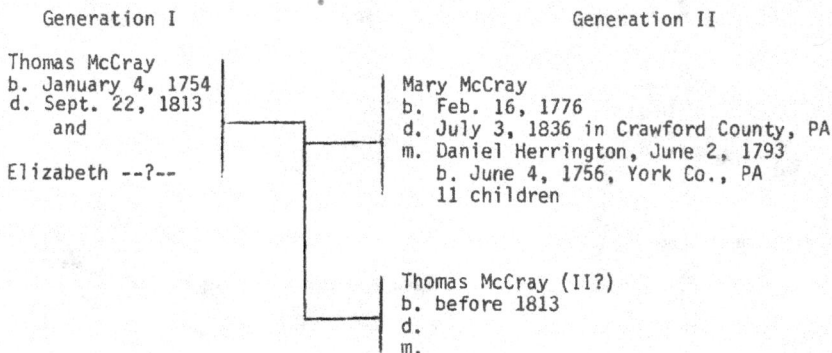

Generation I   Generation II

Thomas McCray
b. January 4, 1754
d. Sept. 22, 1813   Mary McCray
    and   b. Feb. 16, 1776
                            d. July 3, 1836 in Crawford County, PA
Elizabeth --?--   m. Daniel Herrington, June 2, 1793
                                b. June 4, 1756, York Co., PA
                                11 children

                            Thomas McCray (II?)
                            b. before 1813
                            d.
                            m.

Thomas and Elizabeth McCray may have had other children, but if they
did their names have been lost. Thomas may have had brothers James
McCray and John McCray

```
Generation I                                    Generation III

Thomas McCray                        Jesse McCray
    and                              b.
Elizabeth --?--                      d. after 1842
                                     m. Mary --?--
                                        2 children



   Generation II

Thomas McCray (II?)                  John F. McCray
    and                              b.
     ?                               d.
                                     m.
```

There were four other males and at least
three female children, names unknown.

Generation I   Generation IV

Thomas McCray   James McCray
    and   b. 1840
Elizabeth --?--   d. 1900 in Brammon, OK
                                       m. Emaline Struble in 1865
                                          six children

    Generation II

Thomas McCray (II?)   Almon McCray
    and   b. 1842
     ?   d. 1901 in Brammon, OK
                                       m.

    Generation III

Jesse McCray   Mary McCray
    and   b. 1844
Mary --?--   d.
                                       m.

Generation I   Generation V

Thomas McCray   Luther McCray
    and   b. 1867 in Mercer Co, PA
Elizabeth --?--   d.
                                      m.

Generation II   Bertha B. McCray
                                      b. 1869 in Mercer Co., PA
Thomas McCray (II?)   d.
    and   m.
     ?

                                      Leonard Elton McCray
                                      b. Sept. 1, 1871 in Girad, KS
                                      d.
Generation III   m. Maggie (Holt) Holt, on Dec. 14,
                                          1907. (Widow of John Holt, 3 ch.)
Jesse McCray   6 children with Leonard McCray
    and
Mary --?--

                                      Etta Belle McCray
                                      b. Dec. 25, 1874 in Girad KS
                                      d.
                                      m.
Generation IV

James McCray
    and   James McCray, Jr.
Emaline Struble   b. 1877 in Girad KS
                                      d.
                                      m.

                                      Jessie McCray (fem)
                                      b. Feb. 1880 in Girad KS
                                      d.
                                      m.

347

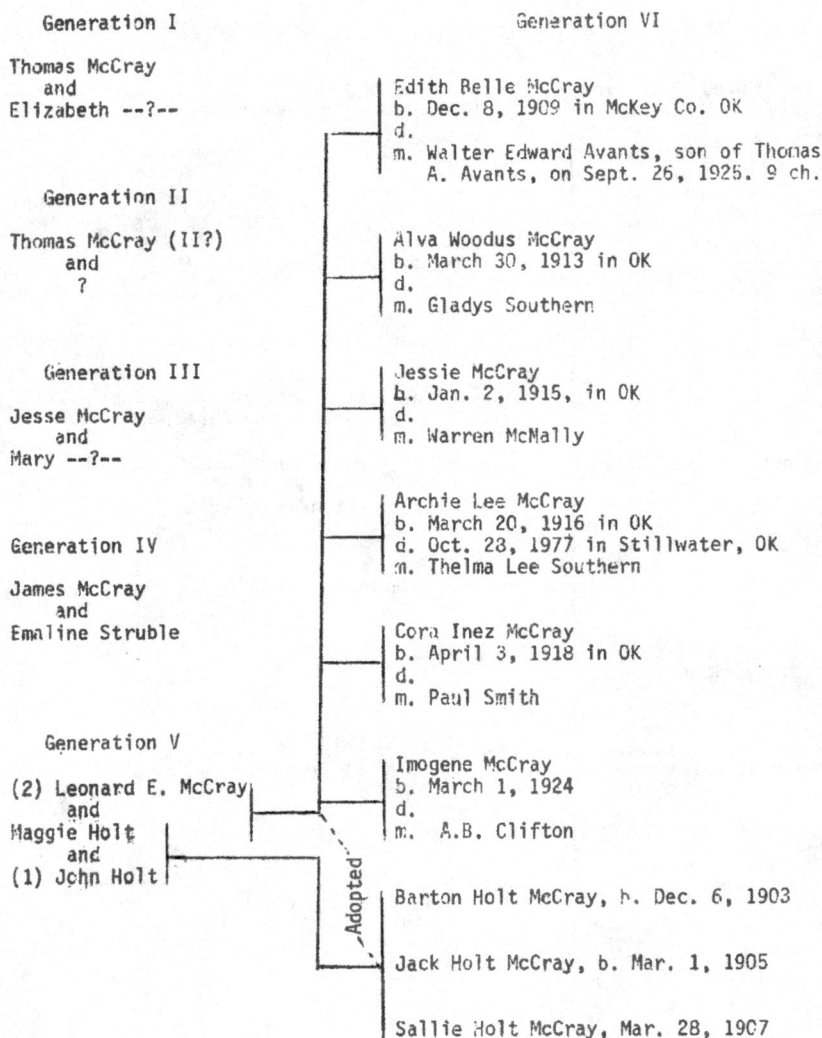

```
     Generation I                          Generation VI

Thomas McCray
    and                        Edith Belle McCray
Elizabeth --?--                b. Dec. 8, 1909 in McKey Co. OK
                               d.
                               m. Walter Edward Avants, son of Thomas
                                  A. Avants, on Sept. 26, 1925. 9 ch.
     Generation II

Thomas McCray (II?)            Alva Woodus McCray
    and                        b. March 30, 1913 in OK
     ?                         d.
                               m. Gladys Southern


     Generation III           Jessie McCray
                               b. Jan. 2, 1915, in OK
Jesse McCray                   d.
   and                         m. Warren McNally
Mary --?--

                               Archie Lee McCray
                               b. March 20, 1916 in OK
     Generation IV             d. Oct. 23, 1977 in Stillwater, OK
                               m. Thelma Lee Southern
James McCray
   and
Emaline Struble               Cora Inez McCray
                              b. April 3, 1918 in OK
                              d.
                              m. Paul Smith

     Generation V
                              Imogene McCray
(2) Leonard E. McCray         b. March 1, 1924
      and                     d.
Maggie Holt                   m. A.B. Clifton
    and
(1) John Holt
                              Barton Holt McCray, b. Dec. 6, 1903

                              Jack Holt McCray, b. Mar. 1, 1905

                              Sallie Holt McCray, Mar. 28, 1907
```

Adopted

348

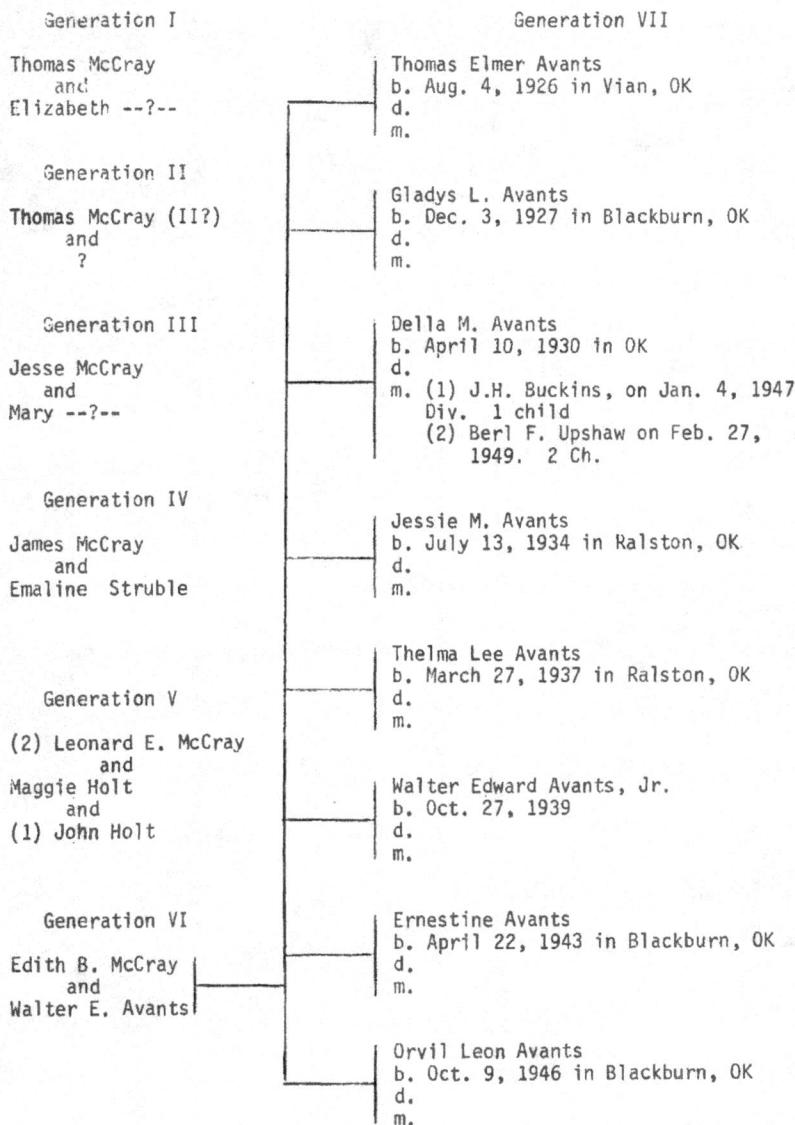

Generation I	Generation VII
Thomas McCray and Elizabeth --?--	Thomas Elmer Avants b. Aug. 4, 1926 in Vian, OK d. m.
Generation II Thomas McCray (II?) and ?	Gladys L. Avants b. Dec. 3, 1927 in Blackburn, OK d. m.
Generation III Jesse McCray and Mary --?--	Della M. Avants b. April 10, 1930 in OK d. m. (1) J.H. Buckins, on Jan. 4, 1947 Div. 1 child (2) Berl F. Upshaw on Feb. 27, 1949. 2 Ch.
Generation IV James McCray and Emaline Struble	Jessie M. Avants b. July 13, 1934 in Ralston, OK d. m.
Generation V (2) Leonard E. McCray and Maggie Holt and (1) John Holt	Thelma Lee Avants b. March 27, 1937 in Ralston, OK d. m. Walter Edward Avants, Jr. b. Oct. 27, 1939 d. m.
Generation VI Edith B. McCray and Walter E. Avants	Ernestine Avants b. April 22, 1943 in Blackburn, OK d. m. Orvil Leon Avants b. Oct. 9, 1946 in Blackburn, OK d. m.

349

Generation I	Generation VIII & IX

Generation I

Thomas McCray
   and
Elizabeth --?--

Generation II

Thomas McCray (II?)
   and
   ?

Generation III

Jesse McCray
   and
Mary --?--

Generation IV

James McCray
   and
Emaline Struble

Generation V

(2) Leonard E. McCray
      and
   Maggie Hold
      and
(1) John Holt

Generation VI

Edith B. McCray
   and
Walter E. Avants

Generation VII

Della M. Avants
   and
(1) J.H. Buckins

(2) Berl F. Upshaw

Generation VIII & IX

Linda Buckins Upshaw
b. Nov. 21, 1947, in Pawnee, OK.
   Adopted by Berl Upshaw
d.
m. John Leroy Mack, Jan. 22, 1967. 3 ch.

Cheryl E. Upshaw
b. Feb. 3, 1950 in Hominy, OK
d.
m. Gary Huish, Div. No ch.

Christine Beryl Upshaw
b. May 3, 1954 in Denver, CO
d.
m. (1) Dennis McBrayer, March 2, 1969
      One ch., Heather McBrayer. Div. 1973
   (2) Larry Zufelt, aug. 25, 1976 in
         Sedona, AZ. Div. 1984
   (3) Dale Fox, Oct. 1986. One Ch
         Des'Ra Edwards Fox,
         b. Dec. 11, 1991
   Des'Ra Edwards Fox adopted by Dale Fox

Generation I	Generation IX & X

Generation I

Thomas McCray
  and
Elizabeth --?--

Generation II

Thomas McCray (II?)
  and
  ?

Generation III

Jesse McCray
  and
Mary --?--

Generation IV

James McCray
  and
Emaline Struble

Generation V

(2) Leonard E. McCray
  and
Maggie Holt
  and
(1) John Holt

Generation VI

Edith B. McCray
  and
Walter E. Avants

Generation VII

Della M. Avants
  and
(1) J.H. Buckins
(2) Berl F. Upshaw

Generation VIII

Linda B. Upshaw
  and
John L. Mack

Generation IX & X

Tina C. Mack
b. Sept. 27, 1967 in Pond Creek, OK
d.
m. Timothy Hardy, Oct. 26, 1984 at
     Camp Verde, AZ
Ch: Timothy Leroy Hardy
     b. May 17, 1986, Cottonwood, AZ
     Danielle Hardy
     b. March 27, 1988, cottonwood, AZ

John Leroy Mack
b. Jan. 8, 1969
d.
m. Brittany
CH: Brittany J. Mack
     b. Feb. 18, 1988

Feleena Marie Mack
b. Sept. 5, 1969, Tucson, AZ
d.
m. Wayne Brown, May 9, 1991, in OK
CH: Amber Brown
     b. Nov. 18, 1984 in OK
     Angeleena Brown
     b. June 15, 1989 in CA

351

CHAPTER THIRTEEN

THE FAMILY OF JAMES AND ELEANOR (TOWNSLEY) McCRAY

IT WAS A SCOTS-IRISH TRAIT to move on from wherever they were to whatever was around the next bend in the road. James and Ellen (Bell) McCray left Scotland for Ireland, seeking a better life they dreamed of. After several years there, their dream failed to materialize, and they looked westward to America. There they settled for a few years on a farm on the upper reaches of Sherman's Creek in Cumberland County, in central Pennsylvania. There, their son, James, Junior, found and wed a lass named Eleanor Townsley, and they dreamed of their Shangri-La, somewhere down the road, perhaps just around the next bend.

When stories drifted in about Washington County, at the opposite end of the state, James and Eleanor thought that there to the west might be *The Place* they sought, so they loaded a wagon with their things and journeyed to Washington County--where they stayed a short while. Washington County, well, it really wasn't just what they'd been looking for, either. Then they heard about a vast wilderness area to the north that was going to soon open for settlement. James and his brother, William, rode off north to have a look, and in a month they returned with word that they had found *The Place*, and that they had begun a settlement upon two tracts there. They returned the next spring and built cabins and barns and planted crops, staying until they could harvest, dry, and store the crops for the next year's use. Then, the next spring they again loaded their wagons and abandoned Washington County, stopped in Pittsburgh to sell the wagon and buy an extra horse, and followed the blazed trail through the woods to the northern extreme of Allegheny County. This, they declared, was *The Place*, and there they stayed. They reared a family, and the wilderness became a community called Brokenstraw Township, Erie County.

They were a determined and hard-working family that strove mightily to make a working farm out of their piece of the wilderness. Many of the other settlers didn't find contentment there, and moved southward to areas more to their liking, perhaps where the winters were a bit milder and predatory animals had all been killed off. James and Eleanor stayed.

They left us no pictures or letters, but Upton wrote of James:

"We are fortunate in having a description of James McCray, Jr., progenitor of the Concord Township McCrays. He was described by relatives as rather hot-tempered and firm in his beliefs. He was a Democrat and a Presbyterian, and was six feet tall, and weighed 180 pounds. He had fair complexion and blue eyes."

One should remember that the Democratic Party of 1800 was more nearly like today's Republican Party--conservative politically, and firm in the rightness of the dominance of political power for property owners.

Eleanor died in 1818 and was buried on the highest spot of the first tract of land bought by James in 1796. Her grave is now in the cemetery next to the McCray Church, and therefore it can be stated that hers was the first grave in the cemetery.

Now a widower, James re-married. There is no record of this second marriage, and all that is known about the second wife was that her name was Nancy. She is named twice in James's will. No trace of her has come to light and no one today knows who she was or where she is buried.

With the onset of winter in 1839, James was gravely ill, and on December 9, he called in two neighbors, Robert Heath and Hiram Cook, and one of them wrote while James dictated his will. He was too ill to sign it, and he made his mark at the end of the paper. Eight days later he died and was buried next to Eleanor.

Today there is a quite handsome gravestone on the grave, inscribed with the names of James and Eleanor. It declares that he was a soldier in the Revolutionary War. I have been unable to find out who placed the monument there. Mrs. Daniel Blakeslee, in a letter to Upton of December 1945, told what she knew about the gravestone:

"I really do not know who put the D.A.R. marker on James McCray's grave. I had always supposed it was Jennie McCray. She is Cass (Cassius) McCray's daughter and she has said he was a captain in the Revolutionary War, but my grandfather, son of James McCray (John T. McCray), never said that, and his two sons, Charles and Lee (Luther Lee) McCray say James and two brothers came after the war. Jennie said there were five brothers came also."

The Last Will And Testament Of James McCray

(Copied as written)

In the name of God, Amen, I James McCray of the Township of Concord, Erie County, State of Pennsylvania, being sick and weak in body but of sound mind, memory, and understanding (Praise be God for it) and considering the certainty of death and the uncertainty of the time thereof and to the end that I may be better prepared to leave this world whenever it shall please God to call me hense, do therefore make and declare this my last will and testament in manner following that is to say first and principally, I commend my soul into the hands of almighty God, my Creator, hoping for free pardon and remission of all my sins and to enjoy everlasting happiness in the Heavenly Kingdom, through Jesus Christ, my Savior.

My body I commit to the earth at the discretion of my executors herein after named, and as to my earthly possessions, first I do will and bequeath unto my wife Nancy, one bed, bedstead, and bedding, one stand, one table, one chest, and two hundred dollars good and lawful money, which I deposit in the hands of my son, Robert, for her to call for and receive lawful interest on the same annually, and also call for and receive the amount of two hundred dollars in case it should be kneeded for her support in sickness or otherwise, the sum of twelve dollars interest above mentioned yearly to her own proper use and benefit and the two hundred dollars above mentioned, if kneeded for sickness or otherwise. The above provisions to remain for her while she remains my widow. If the s,d two hundred dollars should not be expended fully or any part thereof at her decease or marriage then the remainder to remain with my son Robert to his own proper use and benefit and she, my wife, Nancy, is to live with my son Robert if she chooses, free from all expense, except that of sickness, and further do I will and bequeath unto my daughters, Eleanor Gleath (Heath), and Betsy Blakeslee, fifty dollars each to be paid by the executors of this my last will and testament.

In two years from the execution of this instrument and unto the children of my son, James, deceased, the sum of one dollar each and to the children of my son William, deceased, one dollar each, and unto Mary McCray I do will and bequeath one three-year old cow, one bedstead, and bedclothing suitable for s,d bed, and unto my son, Robert, I do will and bequeath my farm on which I now live, containing sixty acres of land, be the same more or less together with appurtenances thereunto belonging, to have and to hold the same forever, provided that the said Robert shall pay or cause to be paid to my sons, Joseph, John, and George, the sum of three hundred dollars in manner following, viz: in six annual payments at fifty dollars each, the first payment to be made one year from the commencement of the execution of this presents, and fifty dollars yearly

354

at the expiration of every year untill the sum of three hundred dollars
shall be paid, and the remainder of my property after paying debts and
expenses, I do will and bequeath unto my sons Joseph, George, and John,
to be equally divided between the three .

This is my last will and testament, and further I do constitute and
appoint my sons, George McCray, and John McCray, executors of this, my
last will and testament, and further, I do will and bequeath unto the
children of my daughter, Jane, deceased, one dollar each.

In witness wherof I have hereunto set my hand and seal this nintty
day of December, in the year of our Lord, one thousand eight hundred,
and thirty nine.

James McCray

L.S.

+

mark

Signed and sealed   Rob't Heath
in the presence of
                           Hiram Cook

- - - - - - -

Nearly a month later, George and John McCray, along with Robert
Heath and Hiram Cook, rode across Erie County to the growing city of
Erie, and presented themselves before the Register of Erie County, one
Thomas Moorhead, Jr., George and John McCray declared themselves to be
the administrators of the estate of their father, James McCray, and
Robert Heath and Hiram Jones, certified that they had witnessed the
drawing up and signing of James's will. When they left to ride back
home, they left the papers below in the Register's office.

Registers Office
Erie County Pa.   Before me Thomas Moorhead, Jr., Register
                         for the Probate of Wills and granting
Letters of Administration in and for said county personally
appeared Robert Heath and Hiram Cook the subscribing witnesses
to the foregoing will of James McCray who being duly sworn according to law deposeth and saith that they were present and
heard and saw the same James McCray publish pronounce and declare the within and foregoing instrument of writing to be his
last will and testament and at the time of his doing so he the
said James McCray was of sound mind and memory and discretion to
the best of their knowledge observation and belief and that we
saw the said James McCray make his mark. He being so ill as to

be unable to write his own name and that we signed the same in our proper hand writing as witnesses in the presence of the said James McCray and at his request.

Sworn and subscribed before   Robert Heath
me this 10th day of January AD 1840   Hiram Cook

Thomas Moorhead, Jr., (signature)

Registers Office   George McCray and John McCray being duly
Erie County Pa   sworn according to law doth depose and say
                        that as executors of the last will and
                        testament of James McCray deceased they
will well and truly administer the goods and chattels rights
and credits of said deceased according to law and diligently
and faithfully regard and will and truly comply with the provisions of the law relating to collateral inheritances.

Thomas Moorhead, Jr. Register   George McCray
      (signature)   John McCray

From *The Erie Gazette*, January 2, 1840, (Vol. II, p 1581), "James McCray died December 17, 1839, aged 73 years."

James bequeathed to Mary McCray a cow, a bedstead and bedclothes, items of considerable value in those days. Beds, bedding, and clothing were prized items in most pioneer households, and a cow was an animal second only to a horse in value. Children usually slept on pallets, and beds were usually rough, hard shelves built into the log walls. When a household had several free-standing beds, several chairs, and a table or two, it made a statement that they were a prosperous family.

James's son, Robert, had a daughter, Mary Ann McCray, who was eight years old at the time of James's death. She may have been the apple of his eye, and the Mary McCray of his will. She was the only Mary I could find who was near at hand and might have been a beneficiary in the will. It seems likely that Robert and his family may have lived with, or close by, his father and stepmother, Nancy. Robert was charged in his father's will to take Nancy, James's widow, into his household, "if she chooses."

356

The hard work that James bestowed upon his land paid off well for him, for he left an estate of a 60-acre farm and at least $1000 in cash, no mean sum in those times. He may have realized his fortune by selling some of the land he bought at the turn of the century, as evidenced by his owning only sixty acres at his death out of at least six hundred acres he had bought from the Holland Land Company in three tracts.

We know that James McCray was educated enough that he could write at least his name, as evidenced by the statement of Robert Heath and Hiram Cook that he was too ill to write his own signature. Also, he had signed his name to the will of Alexander Murray, his brother George's father-in-law, some forty-seven years before, using the name "McCree." At least, that was how the courthouse scribe wrote it.

Glimpses Into The Lives Of Descendants From James And Eleanor McCray

IT IS UNFORTUNATE THAT ALTHOUGH we have rather complete lists of the names of descendants from James McCray, Sr.,we know very little about their lives. If they wrote diaries or letters, they either haven't survived or they haven't yet been made available to McCray researchers. We may hope that someday we may have access to family letters that will help us to know something more about the lives of the hardy pioneers who came to America more than two hundred years ago than just the dates of their vital statistics.

The places where they lived and the way they lived shaped their personalities, and certainly their early Presbyterianism molded their thoughts. Each generation worked very hard, but not as hard as the previous generation, and as the years passed, each generation enjoyed more good times and pleasures, had more access to education, and developed an expanding outlook on the shrinking world. Later generations probably smiled more, had more picnics and family feasts, eating a greater variety of foods at holiday get-togethers.

It would be nice to get to know them better.

Thanks to some enterprising souls who wrote histories of counties in most of the well-settled states toward the end of the last century, we do know some of our ancestors a bit better. Knowing how everyone hopes for some measure of immortality here on earth, and how we all like to see our names in print, these "historians" interviewed rural men, and then wrote biographical sketches that extolled the many virtues of the prospects, knowing it was almost a certainty that everyone whose life was so glowingly preserved in print would contract to buy several books. Many of these books are in local libraries today, for which we may be very thankful.

Joseph And Thomas B. McCray

" Distinguished not only for his life record of honesty and integrity,
but for his valiant services as a soldier during the Civil War, Thomas
B. McCray, of Corry, is especially deserving of more than passing mention
in a work of this character. A son of Joseph McCray, he was born in Concord township, Erie County, February 25, 1841. He comes of excellent
Scotch ancestry, his grandfather, James McCray, having been a native of
Scotland.

" Emigrating to America, the land of great promise, James McCray was
one of the pioneer settlers of Washington County, Pennsylvania, where he
lived a number of years, taking while there an active part in developing
the agricultural resources of that part of the state. From there he
came overland to Erie County, his wife bringing one of the children on
horseback. Locating in what is now Concord Township, he purchased a tract
of timber from the Holland Land Company, cleared a space, and there built
a log house for himself and family. There were then neither railways nor
canals in the country, and there being no convenient markets, all supplies
for the household and farm were brought from Pittsburgh by teams. The
pioneers of those days used to burn timber, and with the ashes make black
salts, the only product that could be sold for cash. In after years, when
they began raising cattle in large numbers, all of the stock had to be
driven either to Philadelphia or New York to be sold. On the farm that
he improved from the wilderness, James McCray spent his later years of
life, contented and happy. To him and his wife, six children were born,
as follows: Joseph, George William, James, John, and Ellen.

"Born in 1794, in Washington County, Joseph McCray was reared among
pioneer scenes, as a boy doing much pioneer labor on the parental homestead. While yet in his teens, he enlisted as a soldier in the War of
1812, and afterwards served for a time in the regular army, being stationed on the western frontier. On receiving his discharge from the
Army he returned home, and engaged in farming and lumbering, rafting the
logs down the rivers. On one of his river trips, he stopped awhile in
Kentucky, and there married. Settling in Bracken County, that state, he
continued his agricultural labors. A few years later his wife died of
cholera, leaving an infant son, George McCray, who was reared by a Mr.
and Mrs. Parks, and is still a resident of Kentucky. Returning to Pennsylvania after the death of his wife, Joseph McCray lived for awhile near
Titusville, from there coming back to Erie County. Buying timber land in
Concord Township, he erected good buildings, cleared and improved a valuable farm, and there resided until his death at the age of ninety years.
He married for his second wife, Sarah J. Scott, a native of Ireland. Her
father, Thomas Scott was born in the north of Ireland of Scotch ancestry.
Coming with his family to this country he settled as a pioneer in Crawford County, where he redeemed a farm from the wilderness as a tiller of
the soil, becoming quite successful. Mrs. Sarah J. (Scott) McCray died
on the farm at the good old age of four score and four years. She reared
five sons, James, Thomas B., John, Josiah, and William.

"Receiving a good common school education, Thomas B. McCray also acquired a substantial knowledge of the various branches of agriculture, he enlisted in Company F., Pennsylvania Volunteer Infantry, and served for three months under Captain Morgan, being on duty at Pittsburgh. Being then honorably discharged from the Army, he returned home, and on August 13, 1862, enlisted in Company A, One Hundred and Forty-fifth Pennsylvania Volunteer Infantry. Going south with his regiment, he arrived at Antietam just at the close of the memorable battle there fought. Subsequently, with the exception of the time that he was confined in the hospital, Mr. McCray continued with his regiment, taking part in many important engagements, among them being the battles of Gettysburg, Fredricksburg, Chancellorsville, those of the Wilderness, and the battle of Spotsylvania, where his lower jaw was shattered, and his tongue badly cut. The greater part of the jaw had to be removed, and it was a long time before he could talk, In October, 1864, he received his honorable discharge from the service and returned home. As soon as he was able to do anything, Mr. McCray was elected constable and collector, and served two years. Turning then his attention to agriculture, he bought the interest of his brothers in the old home farm, in Concord township, and there carried on farming and stock raising until 1902. In that year he erected a house on Center street, Corry, where he has since lived retired from active pursuits.

"Mr. McCray married, in May 1866, Carrie G. Parsons, a native of Concord township. Her father, Henry Parsons was born June 11, 1842, on the Atlantic Ocean, while his parents, James and Ann (Roberts) Parsons, were en route to this country. Mr. Parsons was born in England, and his wife in Wales, and both died in Concord township, Erie county, on the farm which they cleared and improved when he had an acute attack of the gold fever. With a companion, he started on foot for California. His companion died while on the way, but he pushed on across the dreary plains, at the end of several months arriving at his point of destination. Not meeting with the anticipated success in his mining operations, he returned to Erie county, and until his death was engaged in farming in Concord township. In July 1861, offering his services to his country, Henry Parsons enlisted in Company A, One Hundred and Eleventh Pennsylvania Infantry, and with his comrades participated in several engagements, one of the more prominent having been that of Cedar Mountain. In 1862 he was honorably discharged on account of disability, returned home, and soon began to learn the carpenter's trade. He followed his trade awhile after which he engaged in farming for a number of seasons. Locating in Corry in 1895, he resumed his trade, working as a carpenter until failing health compelled him to give up active labor, and he is now living in this city, retired from business pursuits. The maiden name of his wife was Martha McCray. Of the union of Mr. and Mrs. McCray six children have been born, namely: Parke, Webb, Reed, Scott, Miles, and Evelyn, who died, December 4, 1906, aged four years, two months and eleven days."

From *A Twentieth Century History of Erie County Pennsylvania* by John Miller, 1909, Vol. II., The Lewis Publishing Co., Chicago.

The biography on the preceding pages contains another testament that James McCray, Jr., was "a native of Scotland." It probably was Thomas McCray, Joseph's son, who told the biographer that his father was born in 1794 in Washington County (not Westmoreland), proving that James and Eleanor (Townsley) McCray had moved from Shermans Valley to Washington County by then. There is no reason to doubt the biography in this matter.

The lady who married Joseph McCray in Kentucky isn't named in the biography, but several family chroniclers have stated that she was Joanne "Townley," using the spelling they assigned to Eleanor Townsley. William and Thomas Townsley are known to have lived in Scott County, Kentucky, in the last decade of the eighteenth century. Scott County is separated from Bracken County, where Joseph and Joanne lived, by no more than thirty-five miles. Bill Townsley, of Fort Myers, Florida, wrote that Joanna Townsley married on January 25, 1814, but he didn't name the groom, nor did he identify Joanna. Joseph McCray would have been age twenty then, and according to the biography had already done a heap of living, having soldiered in the War of 1812, and afterward "engaged in farming and lumbering, rafting the logs down the rivers." The War of 1812 ended in 1815, so perhaps Joseph's time of service was brief. William Townsley, Eleanor's father, named a Joanna Townsley as his daughter, but one would prefer to think that Joseph didn't marry his mother's sister. Bill Townsley suggested that Joseph's bride may have been a daughter of Thomas and Sarah (Patterson) Townsley.

Accounts of the life of Joseph McCray differ in certain important details. Cora McCray, daughter of Josiah and Carrie (Wade) McCray, who was born in 1888, and died in 1987 at age 99, wrote in 1983 that Joseph married his first wife, Joanne Townley, in Kentucky, and that she died there in childbirth. In a letter to Richard N. McCray of Hendersonville, North Carolina, she wrote:

"Joseph came back to Pa., leaving the baby to be brought up by the mother's family. He did keep in contact with his son, who came to Pa. several times to visit his father. George, his son, married Rebecca --?-- and had a large family. I don't know their names. If I remember correctly there was an Orval McCray who died young leaving two boys, Eddie and Walter. Walter came to live with his grandfather (Joseph), and later he lived with my father and mother. The last I knew of him he lived with a son who travelled around a lot.

"Ed died young, leaving young children. I corresponded for a long time with his daughter, Della, who visited me. She died a few years ago."

John Miller's biography, quoted on pages 258 and 259, gives some details of Joseph McCray's life that differ not only with Cora McCray's account, but also differ with information supplied by Percie McCray in his McCray list. Percie didn't give his sources either, and it is quite possible he got his information from Miller's biography in this instance.

The available data on Joseph's later marital life gets confusing. While the Miller biography doesn't mention it, three historians claim that Joseph remarried after Joanne's death. J. Duane Upton lists this lady of his second marriage as Joanne McMillish, Pollock* names her to have been --?-- McMullische, and Percie McCray called her Joane McMillish, and added that she bore five children to Joseph. Upton found the date, November 12, 1837, when Joseph married for the third time, this time to Sarah J. Scott, when Joseph would have been age 43. Nobody seems to have noted what happened to the second wife.

Joseph and Sarah had six sons in the first thirteen years of their marriage, and they both lived long lives; Joseph died at age ninety, according to his gravestone, but others say he lived to be age ninety-seven. Sarah lived eighty-four years, and died in 1892.

* *Blakeslee History*, by Nina Pollock, privately printed, 1983.

John T. McCray

John T. McCray, my gr gr grandfather, was the sixth of the nine
children of James and Eleanor (Townsley) McCray. He was born February
15, 1805, in Brokenstraw Township, Erie County, Pennsylvania. When he
was age twenty-one, on May 11, 1826, he married Sarah ("Sally") Blakeslee, the first-born daughter of Captain David, Jr., and Betsey (Burch)
Blakeslee. She was born in Granville, Washington County, New York.

George Carey related (p. 257) how John rode to Beaverdam, with his
sweetheart mounted behind him on a horse, for the wedding. Carey wrote:
"The first church in Brokenstraw was a Presbyterian Church...on the Belnap farm at Beaverdam." Since John was of a Presbyterian family, it is
a safe guess that the McCray families were among its first members.

John bought part, or part of, Tract 63 that his uncle, William
McCray, bought in 1796 from the Holland Land Company. William moved to
Crawford County in 1809, and we haven't been able to learn anything about
how he disposed of his tract. Maps of Concord Township, drawn about 1865,
show "J. McCray," and "no. McCray Hrs" on Tract 63, described as "a piece
of wild land."*

"John McCray began life for himself as a farmer, living
first in a log cabin which he erected on a piece of wild land
that he purchased. He was very successful in his undertakings,
at the time of his death, when but fifty years old, owning a
well improved farm of 300 acres."

John's farm consisted of:

1) 100 acres on Tract 63, bought in 1833 from the Holland Land
Company. This tract was first bought by William McCray, his uncle, in
1796, at the same time that James McCray, Jr. bought the adjacent tract.

2) Another hundred acres abutting the first tract on the north,
bought from the Holland Land Company in 1843.

3) Sixty-five acres on the northwest corner of Tract 63, abutting
Tract 45, bought from Huidekoper in 1847, and

4) Thirty-five additional acres, bought in an unrecorded transaction, would have to be included to total 300 acres mentioned above.

* *A Twentieth Century History Of Erie County Pennsylvania,* by John
Miller, 1909; The Lewis Publishing Co., Chicago. pps 320, 321.

John probably knew in 1854 that his time on earth was going to end soon, for he wrote his will on July 24, 1855, and in less than a month he was dead. Before his death, however, he gave a portion of his land to his son (and my great grandfather) Wilson C., and another tract to another son, John Wesley. After John's death John W. and Wilson C. swapped their two portions of land with no more concern for required legalities than they would if they were swapping guns, horses or jack-knives; they did not go to Erie and record the land transfers.

Such verbal deals, known in legalese as "Parol Agreements" ("word-of-mouth" to you and me), are fine as long as the land remains in the family and both parties are alive, after which the legal niceties must be taken care of. Governments get quite sticky about these things; has to do with taxes and preserving order.

Things were all right until 1851, when the United States found it couldn't agree over dominance of the Federal or the State Governments, and the American Civil War broke out with all its horrors. John Wesley, Wilson, Warren, William, Jason and Horace McCray all went off to fight, and William and John Wesley died in service.

Lieutenant Horace McCray was wounded in the Battle of Fredricks-burg, and after hospitalization, had no more returned to his unit at Petersburg than Lee's forces captured him and held him prisoner for eight months. William was wounded, treated at a military hospital in Pittsburgh, pronounced unfit for military service, and discharged. On his journey back to Brokenstraw Township, he died.

Sergeant John Wesley was captured and had the misfortune of being sent to the notorious Andersonville Prison, where he, like 13,000 other Union prisoners, died of disease and/or starvation. John died of starvation.

In early stages of the Civil War there were several exchanges of prisoners of war, but Union strategists pointed out that the Confederate Army needed every returned soldier, and they were obliged to feed, house and guard Union prisoners, putting a drain on the South's very limited resources. Prisoner exchanges stopped, and prisons were built in the south to hold Union soldiers, Andersonville among them. It was a very cruel strategy that the Union adopted.

There Union prisoners were penned behind a high stockade which they had been forced to erect on a gentle slope near the village of Anderson-ville, Georgia. Within a year it was overcrowded, understaffed, and undersupplied. The prison's sole source of water was a tiny stream through the lower end of the prison area, and it was used for drinking, cooking and sewerage flushing. Dysentery, the great scourge of the Civil War, was rampant, exacerbated by lack of proper food, sanitation, and medicines, and none but the strongest and luckiest survived. The first order of business every morning was collection and burial of corpses in a temporary graveyard outside the stockade.

The people of Andersonville often brought and shared their miserable supplies of food with the hapless Union soldiers, but they had little enough for themselves. The prison had no doctors and could obtain none, but the guards did what they could to alleviate the suffering. The only thing the South had in abundance was courage, and understandably it sent most of what it had to the Confederate Army, leaving little or nothing for the home front and the C.S.A.'s prisoners of war. When the war ended the Union revenged itself almost mindlessly against the beaten South; the prison's commandant was tried before a military court and hanged.

On a recent visit to my son, John McCray, in Macon, Georgia, we took a sightseeing trip south of Macon, admiring the beautiful and well cared-for farms in a community of Amish farmers, who had migrated to Georgia from near Norfolk, Virginia, when things got too worldly for them there. The Amish farms were near the site of the Andersonville Prison. The Union dead lie in a national cemetery there maintained by the U.S. National Park Service. Inside the gatehouse is a tiny museum of Andersonville Prison, and there is also a file of the names of the buried soldiers and location of their graves. Cely, my wife (nobody calls her "Cecelia") found in the file the name of "Sgt. Corporal John W. McCray, died on November 14, 1864."

Sarah had to endure alone the grief of losing two of the six sons who enlisted in the Army, for she had by then been a widow for nearly ten years. John T. McCray died August 17, 1855, at age fifty. Most of the McCrays who survived childhood and its ravages of typhoid, diphtheria, scarlet fever, or smallpox, went on to live the three score and ten years allotted to them in Psalms 90:10. Sarah, however, lived 88 years, dying August 20, 1891. She probably passed on to the children her gift of Blakeslee longevity. The mixture of genes of John McCray and Sarah Blakeslee proved to be a happy union, for nine of their sixteen children lived longer than 72 years, and three exceeded a life of 92 years. One of the latter three, Amy McCray, was age 97 when she died.

John's will was registered at the Erie County Courthouse on September 25, 1855, a little more than a month after his death. From the dates on the papers it appears that Robert McCray and John Bates, witnesses to the will, went to Erie to register the will, and there they learned that the men who had agreed to inventory John's assets would also have to come to Erie and to be sworn into their offices. They were by then able to make the trip to Erie and back in one day by using the P & E Railroad, whereas going on horseback would probably have meant a two-day journey.

So the next day Sarah and her son, William, appeared before William P. Trimble, Deputy Register, at the Erie County Courthouse, and on September 26, 1855, swore they would, as executors, "truly administer the goods, chattels, rights and credits, of the said deceased, according to

364

law, and diligently and faithfully regard, and well and truly comply with the provisions of the law relating to collateral inheritance."

On the same day Robert McCray, John T.'s uncle, and his son, Robert ("Wicker") McCray, Jr., similarly swore they would diligently appraise John's personal property. The inventory they filed on November 5, 1855, had a total appraised value of $4531.77, and it included:

13 cows	@ $20 each	$260
27 sheep	@ $1	27
7 calves	@ $3 each	21
1 yoke of 3-yr. old steers		75
28 horses		504
7 hogs & 7 pigs	@ $48	672

Also included were "One two hors waggon, One two hors Buggy, a Single Buggy, a two hors Slay, Saddle harness whiffletrees necyoke (neck yoke), plows, drags, sleds, horse boat, forks, rakes and shovels, etc."--it was quite a list of goods and chattels. John T. McCray was a very prosperous and successful farmer, and his estate had no debts; indeed, in the inventory was, "Amounts of notes & accounts Standing out, $1806.77." Value of the real estate was not included in the inventory, but the extent of the inventory demonstrated that it would have included several barns, sheds and a house, and some 300 acres of prime farmland.

John's children, those age 21 or older, were bequeathed:

Wilson	$450
Amy	350
Emelia (Amelia)	350
Warren	250
Elizabeth	250
William P.	250
Franklin	100
Total	$2000

As for his eight minor children, John W., Orris (Horace), Jason, Henry, Percilla, Martha Emma, Loren, and Eleanor Jane, John directed that they should get "the rest residue and remainder of my real and personal estate...to be divided when the youngest (Ellen was then two years old) is eighteen years of adge to share and share a like reserving the use of one third of said real and personal Estate to my beloved wife Sarah then to be equally divided betwixt said eight youngest children after her death."

After having written his will, John got to thinking one day in July of the following year about how kids can fool you. You *THINK* they will do this or that, all in good order and decency, but you turn your back for a time and blamed if they won't up and do something that's against God and common sense. So he sat down and wrote a codicil to his will, dating it July 24, 1855, and called in his neighbors, William Gray, young Robert McCray, Jr., and John Baits (Bates) to witness his signature. Parts of the codicil are undecipherable because it was written with non-drying ink that bled through several thicknesses of the paper, but enough is still readable to get his intention.

> "...will if they stay at home....in helping support the family until they respectively become of age but in case any of said eight youngest should be negligent or leave home before becoming of age then and in that (event) my executors shall have full power...(distri_bute the shares of said children as they think they are deserving both real and personal property shall be divided by my executors and their division shall be final and conclusive and said executors shall have power to chose one or two disinterested persons to a...him them said division and lastly it is my desire that this codicil be annexed to and made a part of my last will and testament..."

Quite clearly, John was in charge of things around the house, and he saw his role as head of the family to be firm and dictatorial, brooking no nonsense from any of his children. He laid a burden upon both his widow and his son, William, for he made them judge, jury and executioner over the eight youngest children of the family during their minority years. It is to be hoped that they all got along together nicely and that no showdowns occurred during the years following John's death.

John Bates, the witness to the codicil, had his farm south of and across the road from John's farm. It was the northern 200 acres of Tract 79. "W. Gray'," had a 143-acre farm south of and adjacent to Bates's farm, lying on Tract 409, which was the same size and shape as Tract 79. Robert McCray, son of James and Eleanor (Townsley) McCray, was living on the 90-acre tract he inherited, which lay to the east and across the road that is now State Road 89.

One of the stories my father, Lou McCray, frequently told about the Bates family, happened on their opening school day in the first grade. The teacher went from pupil to pupil, asking their names and writing them upon the blackboard. She couldn't understand the muttering of Ben Bates, who had gone to school under threats from his father, and asked him to repeat it. He did, but still with an unrecognizable murmur. "Speak up, boy!" she commanded. He eyed her with a scowl and shouted, "Ben Bates, B-en, BEN; B-ates, BATES!" The teacher then understood a good deal more than the lad's name.

An Unusual Adoption

MOST ADOPTIONS TAKE PLACE when the adoptee is an infant or a child. Seldom, and then under unusual circumstances, is anyone adopted after he or she has reached adulthood.

Cyrus McCray was descended from John T. and Sarah (Blakeslee) McCray, his grandfather, through his parents Warren and Harriet (Hollis) McCray. Cyrus was born in Concord Township, Erie County, in 1849. On January 30, 1881, he married Alice Bailey. They had five children: Charlie, born in 1881, Grace, born in 1883, Mable, born in 1888, Ellsworth, born in 1889, and Arthur Leo, born in 1891.

Dennis Davis, a descendant from John and Sarah, remarked that their marriage was a stormy relationship. During their marriage they drank from a bitter and poisoned cup that took away the joy of parenthood, and two weeks after Arthur's birth they separated and gave away their new baby! Arthur was given to Weldon and Alice Davis. What happened to the other four children isn't known.

Cyrus and Alice remained separated for several years, and sometime before 1903 they reunited for several years and gave their marriage another try. In 1903 Leon McCray was born to them, and in 1908 Sarah McCray was born, although there is some uncertainty about whether or not Sarah was born of this marriage. But the old animosity again emerged, and this time the marriage was dissolved, and shortly afterward, Alice married David Chase of Titusville. It is believed that Alice was blind and possibly deaf as well. She walked onto a railroad track near Titusville and was killed by a train. She was buried in an unmarked grave in Centerville Cemetery in Titusville. Cyrus died at age 73, and was buried in the Britton Run Cemetery, Crawford County, Pennsylvania.

Baby Arthur was cared for by Weldon and Alice Davis, and although it seems to have been a loving relationship, they did not adopt him. When he was seven years old he was given to a Mr. and Mrs. Crowell, who cared for the boy for a few years and then turned him over to Charlie Ainsworth of Union City, Erie County. When Arthur was sixteen years old he went to Kansas to live with a relative of Weldon Davis, where he worked in the wheat fields long enough to decide that wheat farming wasn't for him, and he then returned to Spartensburg, Crawford County, adjacent to Concord Township, Erie County, where he lived with the Marty Miller family for a year or two. Finally he found a loving and lasting relationship when he married Blanche Ingalls on December 23, 1915. He was then age 25. A year later he was adopted by Weldon and Alice Davis; one may wonder why it took them so long to decide this. It is easy to understand why Arthur would have bitter feelings toward his parents. Perhaps the Weldon Davises had no one to inherit their estate and so decided on this course to make Arthur their heir. Who knows?

367

Arthur Leo McCray was, from that moment, Arthur Leo Davis. Arthur and Blanche (Ingalls) Davis had five children: Weldon Arthur Davis, Russel Gerald Davis, Ralph Edward Davis, Dorothy June Davis and Robert Arden Davis.

Blanche Ingalls was a daughter of William and Nellie (Slye) Ingalls. William Ingalls' mother was Martha McCray, daughter of Robert McCray and granddaughter of James and Eleanor (Townsley) McCray. Arthur and Blanche's first child, Weldon, was one of those many young victims of poliomeylitis who died before Jonas Salk's wonderful development of a vaccine with which to combat the dreaded crippler/killer. Russell Davis was killed in action in France during World War II. He married Evelyn Barton, of Corry, Erie County. Ralph Davis married Dallas Hutto and they had three children.

Robert Arden Davis married Anne Marie Moravek, of Sparta Township, Crawford County, and they had three children: Kathleen Marie Davis, Dennis Russell Davis and Robert Arden Davis, Jr. Robert Davis, Sr., and Anne were divorced in 1978. She has remarried and Robert lives in Edinboro, Pennsylvania where he is president of RADSR, Inc., a distributor of Agway products.

Dorothy June Davis married the Reverend Robert E. Roden, a widower with three children. This was her third marriage, and had no children in any of the marriages. Dorothy died in 1936, and Reverend Roden then married Anne (Moravek) Davis, her brother's divorced wife. They live in Corry.

Dennis, or "Rusty," Russell Davis, a son of Robert A. and Ann (Moravek) Davis, was born in Corry on August 4, 1959, and he now lives in Erie with his wife, Kimberley Ann (Latimer) Davis, and their two children, Ethan McCray Davis and Taylor James Davis. Dennis said he named his son, Ethan McCray Davis so as to "insure that future generations would not forget our true heritage." Taylor James McCray's middle name is derived from our earliest known ancestor, James McCray, Sr.

The Family And Descendants
of
Warren and Harriet (Hollis) McCray

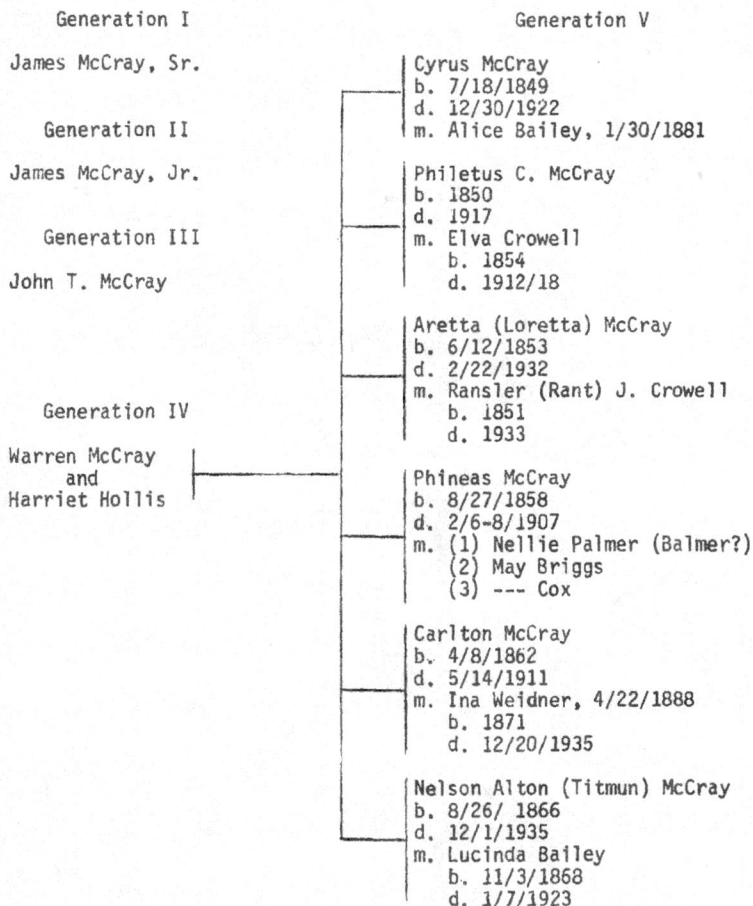

Generation I

James McCray, Sr.

Generation II

James McCray, Jr.

Generation III

John T. McCray

Generation IV

Warren McCray
and
Harriet Hollis

Generation V

Cyrus McCray
b. 7/18/1849
d. 12/30/1922
m. Alice Bailey, 1/30/1881

Philetus C. McCray
b. 1850
d. 1917
m. Elva Crowell
   b. 1854
   d. 1912/18

Aretta (Loretta) McCray
b. 6/12/1853
d. 2/22/1932
m. Ransler (Rant) J. Crowell
   b. 1851
   d. 1933

Phineas McCray
b. 8/27/1858
d. 2/6-8/1907
m. (1) Nellie Palmer (Balmer?)
   (2) May Briggs
   (3) --- Cox

Carlton McCray
b. 4/8/1862
d. 5/14/1911
m. Ina Weidner, 4/22/1888
   b. 1871
   d. 12/20/1935

Nelson Alton (Titmun) McCray
b. 8/26/ 1866
d. 12/1/1935
m. Lucinda Bailey
   b. 11/3/1868
   d. 1/7/1923

```
Generation I                          Generation VI

James McCray, Sr.                     Charlie McCray
                                      b. 10/22-23/1881
    Generation II                     d. 1/19/1907
                                      m. Jennie Buckley
James McCray, Jr.

                                      Ellsworth McCray
    Generation III                    b. 4/1/1889
                                      d. 8/21/1927
John T. McCray                        m. Flossie Bailey


                                      Leon McCray
                                      b. 6/9/1903
    Generation IV                     d. 1918
                                      m. Naomi Babcock
Warren McCray

                                      Arthur Leo McCray/Davis*
    Generation V                      b. 5/18/1891
                                      d. 5/15/1977
Cyrus McCray                          m. Blanche Mae Ingalls
    and                                   b. 2/19/1898
Alice Bailey                              d. 11/4/1974


                                      May McCray
                                      b. 7/29/1883
                                      d. 2/9/1972
                                      m. Newbern Babcock


                                      Mable McCray
                                      b. 4/25/1888
                                      d. 4/25/1888
```

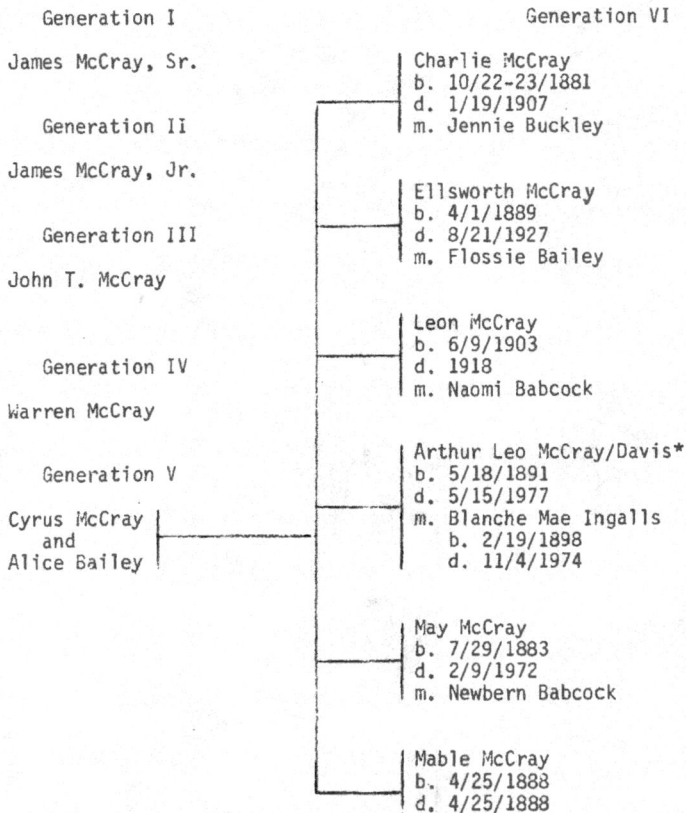

* Arthur McCray was adopted by Weldon A. and Alice Davis, August 7, 1916, and changed his name from then on to Davis.

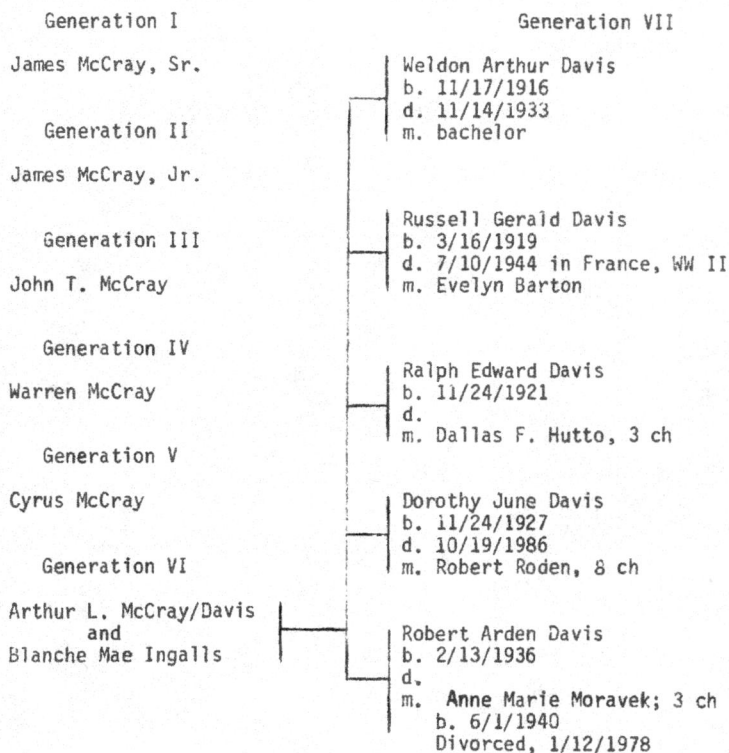

Generation I

James McCray, Sr.

Generation II

James McCray, Jr.

Generation III

John T. McCray

Generation IV

Warren McCray

Generation V

Cyrus McCray

Generation VI

Arthur L. McCray/Davis
     and
Blanche Mae Ingalls

Generation VII

Weldon Arthur Davis
b. 11/17/1916
d. 11/14/1933
m. bachelor

Russell Gerald Davis
b. 3/16/1919
d. 7/10/1944 in France, WW II
m. Evelyn Barton

Ralph Edward Davis
b. 11/24/1921
d.
m. Dallas F. Hutto, 3 ch

Dorothy June Davis
b. 11/24/1927
d. 10/19/1986
m. Robert Roden, 8 ch

Robert Arden Davis
b. 2/13/1936
d.
m. **Anne** Marie Moravek; 3 ch
   b. 6/1/1940
   Divorced, 1/12/1978

Generation I	Generation VIII

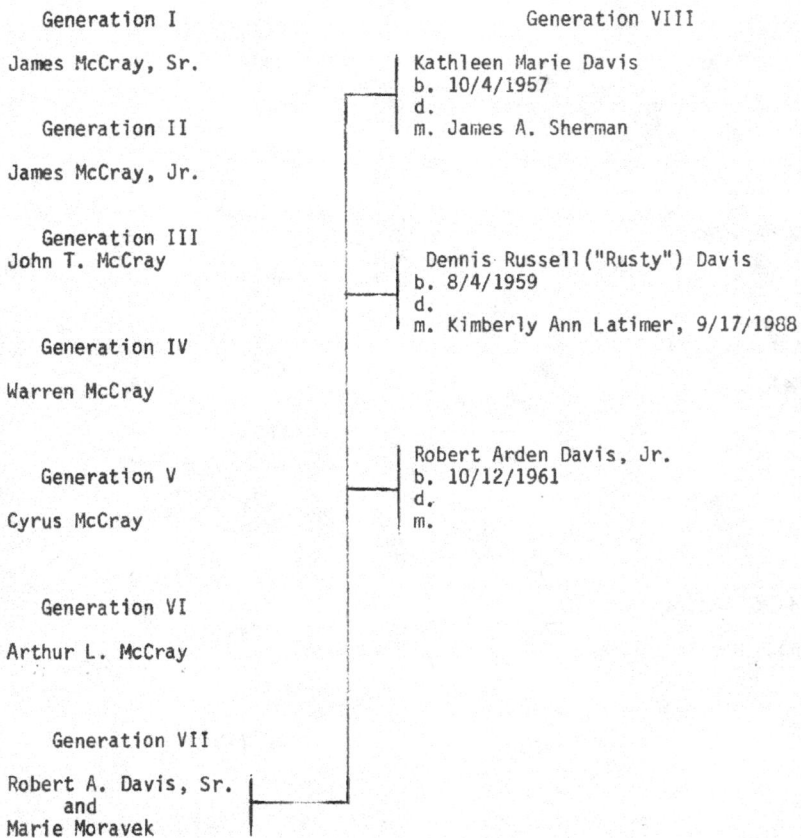

Generation I

James McCray, Sr.

Generation II

James McCray, Jr.

Generation III
John T. McCray

Generation IV

Warren McCray

Generation V

Cyrus McCray

Generation VI

Arthur L. McCray

Generation VII

Robert A. Davis, Sr.
and
Marie Moravek

Generation VIII

Kathleen Marie Davis
b. 10/4/1957
d.
m. James A. Sherman

Dennis Russell ("Rusty") Davis
b. 8/4/1959
d.
m. Kimberly Ann Latimer, 9/17/1988

Robert Arden Davis, Jr.
b. 10/12/1961
d.
m.

Generation I

James McCray, Sr.

Generation II

James McCray, Jr.

Generation III

John T. McCray

Generation IV

Warren McCray

Generation V

Cyrus McCray

Generation VI

Arthur McCray

Generation VII

Robert A. Davis, Sr.

Generation VIII

Dennis R. Davis
and
Kimberly A. Latimer

Generation IX

Ethan McCray Davis
b. Feb. 8, 1990
d.
m.

Taylor James Davis
b. 13 Feb., 1992
d.
m.

373

Chapman B. McCray

Chapman B. McCray, farmer and hay dealer, Elgin, Concord township, Erie County, Pa., was born February 1, 1858, and is a son of Josiah and Salley A. (Hammon) McCray, natives of Concord township. Chapman is the fourth in a family of eight children, was reared and educated in the public schools of his birthplace, and after leaving school, went to work by the month (??), and then engaged in the hay pressing business, but has not followed it extensively. In 1893 he purchased a farm, near Elgin, of 112 acres, and at this writing is building a fine residence on it. He is also one of the firm of Smith & McCray. Mrs. McCray is a progressive, public-spirited, prosperous citizen, and is always found at the head of enterprises that will further the interests of the community. He was married, May 26, 1878, to Miss May, daughter of David and Emily* (McCray) Crowell, natives of Concord township, Pa. Five children have been born to this union: Percy†, Emily, Bert, Roy and Dell. In political matters, Mr. McCray is independent, feeling it a duty to always vote for the best man. Willard McCray is the third in this family, and was born February 2, 1856, on the old McCray homestead, on which his grandfather settled many years ago, when the county was new. He was reared at his birth-place, and educated in the public schools of Concord township and the Edinboro State Normal School. He taught school for two years, after finishing his education, and then engaged in farming, and has followed it ever since. He is a man of more than ordinary intelligence and education, and is one of Concord's most enterprising citizens. He was united in marriage, May 12, 1881, to Elva, daughter of Zus Woodin, of Concord township. One child has been born to this union, Thayer. Mr. McCray is a Republican.**

Chapman McCray's father, Josiah McCray, was a son of William S. and Jane (Bruce) McCray, and a grandson of James and Eleanor (Townsley) McCray.

* Daughters of Robert and Betsey (Blakeslee) McCray

+ Percie McCray, the compiler of the first list of Erie County McCrays.

** *Nelson's Biographical Dictionary*, by Benjamin Whitman, S.B. Nilson, Erie, Pa., 1896. Page 764

Wilson C. and Grant McCray

"Wilson C. McCray, retired farmer, Concord township, Erie county, Pa., was born in Concord township, January 26, 1835, and is a son of John and Sarah (Blakeslee) McCray, natives of Pennsylvania. James McCray, grandfather of Wilson, came to America from Scotland about the year of 1786, settling in Erie county when it was a vast wilderness. Wilson McCray, the sixth in a family of sixteen children, was reared and educated in his birthplace, and has until recently been an extensive farmer and land owner. He has, during his farming experience, owned and operated sixteen different farms. He was united in marriage December 2, 1855, to Miss Cynthia, daughter of Abner H. and Lorence (Porter) Lilley, natives of New York State. Nine children have been born to this union: Celia, Phineas, Leon, Grant, Clement, Josephine, John, Ray and Mary. In politics Mr. McCray has always been a staunch Republican. Grant McCray, fourth in order of birth of Wilson's children, was born May 10, 1862, was reared in Concord township and educated in the public schools, and has always followed farming, in 1889, purchasing his present property at Concord Station, which consists of sixty-six acres of first-class farming land. He has since bought twenty acres, making in all eighty-seven acres. Besides this farm Mr. McCray owns a valuable pasture farm of fifty acres. He was married March 29, 1884, to Miss Addie, daughter of Harvey and Sarah (Roberts) Roberts, natives of Wales. This union has been blessed by three children: Lou, Ernest and Dorr. In politics Mr. McCray is a Republican, and at present holds the offices of school director and road commissioner. He is one of Concord's most thriving and energetic citizens."

Nelson's Biographical Dictionary and Historical Reference Book of Erie County, Pennsylvania 1896, S.B. Nelson, Publisher, Erie, Pa.   Page 763.

(Supplied by Dennis R. Davis, of Erie, Pa.)

At the time this was written, Grant's fourth son, Clifford Brink McCray had not been born. He was born in 1896.

From an unidentified newspaper clipping:

CONCORD

"Jan. 10. -- Mrs. Cynthia McCray, a resident of Concord township for more than fifty years, died on Tuesday, January 3d, 1905. She was in her sixty-sixth year and her illness extended over a period of a year.

"Cynthia Lilley was born in Oswego county, N.Y., in 1839. She was married to Wilson McCray forty-nine years ago, with whom she lived always happily. To this union were born six sons: J.P., Lee and Grant S. McCray, of Concord township; J.C. and Raphael McCray, of Geneva, Ind.; Clement McCray of Corning, Ohio; and three daughters: Mrs. Celiza Delavan, Mrs. Josephine McCray (now deceased), and Mrs. Mae Kaufman, of Geneva, Ind. The deceased is survived by her husband, eight children, and five brothers: William, "Al." Maurice, Abner and Fred Lilley, and one sister, Mrs. Smith.

"Mrs. McCray was one of the most charitable and kindest of women. Of quiet and unassuming manners, the spirit of her daily life seemed to breath with 'malice toward none and charity for all,' and each day was lived as though it might be the last she would spend on earth and she wished to leave none by pleasant impressions and kind deeds. In all her sickness, to the inquiry of children, friend or neighbor as to her condition, so mindful was she of the feeling of others that she would invariably answer, 'quite well.'

"Kind hands and loving hearts faithfully ministered to her in all of her sickness. Those who knew her best and loved her most speak of her as one of the most gentle of women, who had naught but a smile and a cheery word for friend and neighbor, and enemies were unknown to her.

"The pure, softly falling snow, gently drifting in among the flowers on her casket, was synonymous of the life she lived, and, as a friend expressed it, as the casket was forever closed on the loved face, 'What a beautiful life she lived.'

"But we sorrow not without hope, believing as we do that she has fallen asleep in Jesus. She heard the voice of the Master, 'Come unto me, all ye that labor and are heavy laden and I will give you rest.'"

The funeral services were held at the McCray church. Rev. Frank S. Heath reading the burial service for the dead, and Miss Florence Heath presiding at the organ. The six sons acted as pall bearers. Interment in the McCray cemetery."

M M

Grant Spinola McCray, His Children and His Children's Children

DURING ITS FIRST SIXTY YEARS, Brokenstraw Township developed from a heavily forested wilderness with a few primitive roads to a prosperous community of farms, villages and towns, and had been renamed Concord Township. Most of the stumps had been cleared from the fields, log houses were either replaced by substantial wood-frame houses or exterior of log houses had been hidden by white painted lap siding. Roads connected the scores of villages and towns of Erie County, railroads brought in the nation's goods and hauled out the county's agricultural output, and businesses throve. The people, mostly second- or third-generation Britons and some Germans, spoke American English, with a dash of local phrases that echoed the nearly forgotten homelands across the sea.

Tragically, the American Civil War had been raging for more than a year when Grant Spinola McCray was born on October 5, 1862, the fourth of nine children born to Wilson C. and Cynthia (Lilley) McCray, in Concord Township. The name, "Grant," may have been selected because it was a fine Scottish name, but Spinola? Ambrogio Di Spinola, a Genoese general, is remembered today only by history majors studying the wars between Spain and The Netherlands at the beginning of the seventeenth century.

People of northwestern Pennsylvania were, like people everywhere, talking of little else but the war, and of the fortunes being made at Titusville, a few miles south of Concord, where oil had been discovered three years before. It was apparent to all that the war was not going to end soon, and five of Grant's uncles were off with Union forces, as were scores of other men of Erie County. The men still on the farms were beginning to wonder if oil might not lie under the fields of wheat and oats in Concord, and soon derricks were erected here and there. These were times of unease and challenge, the old ways were changing, and the horizons seemed to have moved closer as more news came in from the world outside, and people spoke of hitherto unknown places, such as Manassas, Vicksburg, Spottsylvania and Chickamauga.

By the time Grant was eight or nine years old he had become a sturdy farm boy, with several duties to be carried out each day, shared in by his brothers and sisters. They had to arise early, feed and water the cattle, milk cows, fetch pails of water and stacks of firewood for the kitchen, and if needed, shovel paths in the snow from house to barn to the latrine and to the pump. Although he was a bit smaller than other boys his age he held his own with all of them, for he early on developed remarkable strength in a day shen manly strength was commonplace. After demonstrating his ability to handily lick the neighborhood bullies, he was able to about unencumbered by the baggage of conflict that was a part of every boy's growing up.

No records have survived to tell of Grant's education, but he may have attended school at Hemlock School on the Spartensburg Road, although it may not have been built that early. His grandmother, Sarah (Blakeslee) McCray, who had taught school in her log home, may have helped the lad with his studies. He learned at least the basic subjects, Readin', Writin' and 'Rithmetic, which prepared most people of the day for the few tasks involving paperwork, and being bright and curious, he took it all in stride, and he developed a life-long love for reading.

Although his father, Wilson McCray, owned sixteen farms at one time or another, he didn't give all his time to farming. He picked up what was probably pretty good cash pay driving tank wagons filled with crude oil from the oil fields of Titusville and rapidly-growing Oil City to the rail terminals in Corry, and it is likely that occasionally Grant and some of his other sons accompanied him on these journeys. The thousands of gallons of oil being pumped from the wells had to be moved out as fast as they surfaced. The capacities of tank wagons probably did not exceed a thousand gallons, which with the wagon itself, and the driver, would have weighed about four tons, requiring four horses to breast the primitive road. That road is today's State Road 89, and long lines of tank wagons overcrowded the road's ability to handle the traffic; the road was intended to handle only farm wagons and buggies. It didn't take long for the railroads to run tracks into the oil fields, and when the first locomotive chuffed in with a long string of empty tank cars thirsting for oil, the day of the tank wagon ended abruptly.

Exposure to the excitement of the oil boom must have shattered Grant's immune system, for he carried the germ of oilomania in his system all his life. It eventually was to lure him from the unexciting annual cycle of plowing, sowing, cultivating and harvesting, to live with the hard, dirty work, the glamour, the noise, and if lucky, the wealth, of oil.

A pretty, round-faced girl named Addie Roberts lived at the nearby farm of an immigrant Welshman, Harvey Roberts. At birth she had been named Minerva Adelaide Roberts, but in those days girls often did not use their real names during their entire lives, but went by affectionate nicknames--"Betsey," "Polly," or "Sally." Harvey and Sarah (Roberts) Roberts' daughter's name was abbreviated to "Addie," and so it remained all her life.

When Addie put up her hair and began wearing long dresses, the local swains came a'calling, and she flirted and giggled with them all, but it was jolly Grant McCray who won her heart and hand for life. They were married on March 3, 1884.

A year later, on June 30, 1885, their first son was born. Where she got the name, "Von Lucienne," to hang on the helpless baby has not been explained. Some family members think that Von Lucienne may have been the hero of one of the romantic novels to which Addie was addicted. By the time the next son, Ernest Ross McCray, was born in 1888, the name Von Lucienne had been shortened to just "Lou." Dorr Robert McCray joined

378

the family in 1891, and the group was completed in 1896 with the arrival of Clifford Brink McCray, always known as "Brink." Addie later said she had a difficult delivery with Brink, and believed she might have died had it not been for the ministrations of a midwife, a Mrs. Brink, and she expressed her thanks to her by using her name in the baby's middle name. The other unusual name, Dorr, is as much a puzzle as Von Lucienne.

Although Grant worked primarily as a farmer, thoughts about oil were never far back in his mind. Several neighbors had drilled wells on their farms, and some of them hit some oil, but none found anything approaching an El Dorado. Because the yield from these wells was so low, they were only seriously pumped when the price of oil went up, and afterward they remained dormant. Wilson McCray and his sons probably had a go at the oil business in Concord Township, and from it Grant learned the basics of well drilling, casing, blowing-in of wells, and pumping.

He may have had more financial success in real estate than in oil. He made several purchases and sales of lands in Concord Township, a number of which involved Addie's family, the Roberts. Several of the tracts he bargained for were annexed to his farm just south of Elgin on the Spartensburg Road. But oil was mixed with the blood in his veins. His younger brother, John McCray, not surprisingly known as "Jack," had gone to Geneva, Indiana, where Grant's brother, Raphael, lived, and there he drilled for oil. He invited Grant to come and join them, and that was all he needed. He and his two older sons, Lou and Ernest, lit out for the Indiana oil fields, located about thirty miles southeast of Indianapolis. It is supposed that Addie stayed on the farm with the rest of the family, but details of these times are few. Lou, Ernest and Dorr went to school while they were in Geneva, and they may have gone back to Concord township soon afterward, for there is a photograph in the family, made at Hemlock School about 1797, that includes all three of Grant's sons. Lou said he completed twelve years of school at Hemlock School, and would have finished in about 1903. We know that in 1903 he was a switchman on what was to be later known as the Pennsylvania Railroad.

It seems likely that there was a good bit of to-ing and fro-ing between Concord and the oil fields of Indiana and Ohio. Ernest lived in Concord Township for some time before 1908, for in that year he married Mary Pearl Hall, of the Hall family who were among the first settlers of Brokenstraw Township. The wedding in Corry was reported in a Corry newspaper, and the guest list did not include Grant, Addie, Dorr or Brink--only Lou, so the rest of the family was probably in Indiana at that time. Among the guests in attendance were:

> Mrs. W.C. Smith of Falconer, N.Y. (Addie's sister, Alma)
> Mr. and Mrs. Richard Roberts (Addie's nephew)
> Mrs. Benjamin Roberts (Addie's sister-in-law)
> Mr. and Mrs. Raymond H. McCray (Grant's brother)

Mary Pearl Hall was another of those who went by her middle name, and Ernest nicknamed her "Paley." They had a son, Lionel, who was the first grandchild for Grant and Addie. He finished high school in about 1926 and undertook engineering studies at Carnegie Technical Institute in Pittsburgh. At about this time Ernest and Pearl left Pennsylvania to accept appointments as teachers at a Navajo school on the Navajo Indian Reservation in New Mexico. They both loved the West, and never returned to the East to live. Ernest went up through the Indian Service system, and soon reached Superintendent level, heading several Apache and Navajo reservations in New Mexico and Arizona before his death in 1945. He was buried in Phoenix.

Dorr inherited his father's fascination with oil and the glamour, danger, hard work and sometimes, the big money that went with it. He may have left school before completing high school in order to chase his rainbow. He married Ursa Bugbee, who lived with her parents on a farm in Concord Township, about 1910. In 1911 a son, Frank Jerald, was born to them, and as might be expected, he never used his given name but all his life went by the name of John McCray, except on official papers. As soon as they could travel, they went to Oklahoma where John found work in the oil fields that had been discovered on a Cherokee Indian Reservation, much to the chagrin of the whites responsible for placing them on what they thought was worthless land. After living in a tent for a year, they made their way to join his father and his brothers in Geneva, Indiana.

Shortly thereafter, Indiana lost its charms, and Grant led his family, plus some of Addie's kin, into the oil fields in Ohio, a few miles south of Toledo at Mungen ("Mun-jen"). By then Grant had accumulated enough capital to buy a few wells there, and the McCray family went to work to earn more. Part of the family clan now had been swelled by the addition of Willis and Abram ("Ab") Roberts, uncles of Addie. Dorr and Ursa had two more sons, Ivan Wallace, born in 1913, and Stanley Wilson, born in 1915. Grant also bought a large farmhouse on Bays Road, near Mungen, where the household consisted of Grant's father, Wilson, Grant and Addie, Dorr, Ursa and their three sturdy sons, and Brink.

Meanwhile, back in Pennsylvania, Lou had assiduously courted and eventually won Marion Louise McDowell, of Jamestown, Mercer County, and they were wed in 1911. This wedding was also not attended by any of the family who were then living in Indiana, except for Ernest and possibly Pearl, although her name wasn't listed in the newspaper story of the wedding. The next year, on June 22, 1912, Richard Nelson was born to them, and in 1914, born with his mother's very red hair, was Philip Roger McCray, the author of this publication.

Addie lived in Concord Township, alone with Brink, from about 1910 until 1912, while Brink completed high school in Corry. After his graduation, they joined the rest of the family in Geneva. Addie's father,

Harvey Roberts, died in 1912.

Grant assembled a sizeable crew to operate the oil wells in Mungen.
He hired a Mungen native, James Walker, to be general foreman, and a son
of James and Saverna Walker, Clayton, or "Clete," was also hired as
roustabout*. Clete had an energetic little sister, Ethel, who at age
eighteen was noticed with considerable interest by young Brink McCray.
Ethel, although scarcely five feet tall, was a vigorous and peppery
little lady, and Brink came a'courting. One cold day, January 29, 1916,
they ran off to Monroe, Michigan, a few miles north of Toledo, and got
married. In time, they had three children:

>Roger Mason McCray, born in Mungen in 1918
>Douglas James McCray, "Jim," born in Corry in 1924
>Cynthia Elizabeth McCray, born in Elgin in 1928. She was the
only female grandchild of the generation.

Brink was one of those happy-go-lucky individuals who never quite
seem to find contentment, not too different from his oldest brother, Lou.
They both went from one job to another like butterflies in wildflowers,
anticipating the next blossom would have sweeter nectar than the last.
A year or two after he and Ethel were married they move to East Conneaut,
Ohio, where Lou was employed in the railroad terminal at the Lake Erie
docks there. Lou enlisted in the Army in 1917 and was sent shortly
afterward to France as an airplane mechanic in the newly formed aviation
arm, The Army Air Corps. He was injured in an accident and spent about
two years in various Army hospitals where Army doctors may have done
their best to repair his injured hip, but the break caused him considerable misery for the rest of his life.

Brink, Ethel and Roger moved to Corry, where he tried several jobs
in both Corry and Elgin, one being with Ernest at the Elgin Mill. Brink
found a job he liked with a large hardware firm in Corry, but in 1931 he
took a better job with the Pickett Hardware Company in Warren, Pennsylvania, where he had responsibilities for fulfilling contracts with con-
tractors on large building projects. He spent much of his time driving
between construction jobs, and he made a big hit with clients with his
pet raccoon on a leash. In his office the raccoon entertained himself
with a large steel ball bearing that Brink would drop into an otherwise
unused brass spittoon. The 'coon would reach in and stir the ball faster
and faster, then sit up straight, listening intently to the spinning
ball as it spun around inside the cuspidor, and after it stopped he'd
set it spinning again and again until Brink got tired of the noise.

* "Roustabout" has several meanings, mostly derogatory, but around oil
wells a roustabout did whatever was required to drill, case, and pump
the wells. He was a skilled laborer and mechanic of special skills and
strengths, and a respected member of the operating crew.

Something went wrong between Brink and Ethel in 1932, and they separated, ultimately to end the marriage in divorce. Ethel, Jim and
Cynthia moved to Elgin and stayed with Addie and Grant for a short time,
and then moved to Bowling Green, Ohio, near Mungen, to live with her
father, James Walker, who died in 1937. She and Brink were divorced in
1936, and she remarried the following year. Roger stayed with his grandmother Addie in Elgin until he finished school in Corry, and in 1933 he
enrolled in the General Electric Apprentice School in Erie, and joined
his father who was living with Lou and his family in Lawrence Park, a
suburb of Erie. The Lou McCray family had lived in Birmingham, Alabama,
for the previous eleven years, and had come to Erie where Lou was working
as plumber and steamfitter. His son, Richard, had been enrolled in the
General Electric apprentice program for two years.

Brink left the East in 1935 and went to New Mexico to work near his
brother, Ernest, doing plumbing installations in Indian housing projects.
His son, Jim, joined him there after completing his high school in
Bowling Green. Brink remarried to Hattie Simpson in New Mexico, and
shortly afterward they transferred to the Rosebud Sioux Reservation in
South Dakota. Brink died in 1976 and was buried in Seneca, South Carolina, home of his second wife.

Lou secured a position in Washington, D.C., with the General Account-
ing Office of the United States Government, and he, Marion and Philip
lived in the Washington area thereafter. Lou died in 1945, and Marion
died in 1979. Both were buried at Arlington National Cemetery in Arlington, Virginia. Philip enrolled at American University and later at
George Washington University, both in Washington. He married Cecelia,
or "Cely", Spear in 1940 when World War II was on the horizon. While
working for The Washington Post as a photographer, he joined the Navy in
1942 and served until the end of the war. They both worked for the
Naval Research Laboratory, and both retired from there. They live in
Prince Georges County, Maryland. They have three children: Meredith,
Thomas and John, and seven grandchildren.

Lou's other son, Richard, married Hazel Lang in 1941, while both
were employed at General Electric in Erie. They have two sons, Louis
and Norman. In 1947 they went to Sao Paulo, Brazil, where General Electric had just built a large electric appliance manufacturing facility,
and stayed there two years. When they returned to the States, Richard
sought employment in a place with higher altitude than Erie to alleviate
a breathing problem, and they located in Bluefield, West Virginia. He
worked there for firms that manufactured and repaired mine locomotives.
He and Hazel live in retirement in Hendersonville, North Carolina.

Sooner or later all oil wells run dry, and when the yield from the
wells in Mungen became unprofitable, they were capped and abandoned, and
the families separated and went their ways. Mungen faded away as a town
and is no longer on Ohio maps. Dorr and Ursa settled in Findlay with

their three boys, and Dorr became a mechanic on large trucks, and as his sons grew up they joined him in keeping the big rigs on the road. Stanley died in 1964. Abram Roberts set up a business repairing sewing machines in North Baltimore, a few miles from Mungen, and later, he established a larger sewing machine repair business in Findlay. Grant, Addie and Wilson moved to a house near Lou and his family in East Baltimore, but they didn't stay there very long. Grant wasn't happy with a life of retirement. He'd always worked hard and had always faced each day with more work than he could accomplish. He had satisfied his quest for oil, and had earned enough in oil and land to secure the remainder of his days, and he came back to Pennsylvania and the quiet and stability of life in Elgin.

He bought a small unpainted, run-down bungalow on the Corry Road just outside Elgin Borough as a temporary residence while he supervised construction of a large bungalow on a four-acre tract near the crossroads in Elgin on the Corry Road. Included in the project was a small two-story barn. Wilson McCray died while they still lived in the temporary house. The new house was up to date, the latest and best for a rural residence. It had an indoor bathroom, a huge central furnace in the basement that would burn either coal or wood, several stained glass and bevelled glass windows and doors, and floors and interior trim were chestnut. An underground pipe from the well brought water into the basement pump and pressurized storage tank, and a coil in the furnace heated water that was stored in a tank. A small coal stove with a built-in water coil provided hot water in summertime. The pump was driven by a gasoline engine, but it was later replaced by an electric motor when electric power came to Elgin. A septic tank and drain field took care of the waste from the kitchen and bathroom.

Grant was happy in his new life. He raised enough hay, oats, wheat and corn to feed a horse, a cow and a few swine, and some chickens, and a vegetable garden he planted and cared for would be a full-time project for most of us. For him it was "just something to do." He needed the horse for plowing, cultivating, and power for the buggy, and the other animals were raised to provide eggs, bacon and some fresh meat for the table. He would sometimes lend a hand at the mill where he would, at age sixty, pick up eighty-pound sacks of grain and easily toss them onto a polished sheet-steel trough that angled downward outside to a loading dock. The bags would slide down the chute to waiting wagons, where Ernest and sometimes, Brink, would each grasp two corners of the bags and sling them into a stack on the wagons.

There was a story around Elgin that Grant and one of his boys were hauling perhaps a ton or so of bagged grain on a wagon drawn by a team of horses, and somehow a rear wheel of the wagon slipped off the edge of the muddy road, and the entire load teetered on the bank above a ditch full of water. Grant climbed down from the wagon, put his shoulder under the hub of the wheel, and as he lifted his son whipped up the horses and the load of grain was saved.

He engaged in civic affairs and was elected mayor of Elgin from 1918 to 1921, and later he served as head of the school board. Surprisingly, he didn't go to church. It wasn't that he refused to go to church -- he just didn't go, and people just avoided discussing it in his presence, although as a general thing those who didn't go to church on Sunday were held in low esteem. He didn't discuss his religious philosophy, so no one knew the depth of his beliefs, whatever they may have been. His views on religion could probably be summed up in an oft-heard remark: "Everyone's free to go to hell in his own particular way."

Addie usually went to church, and sometimes her pastor would join them for dinner at the McCray home, and their relationship was respectful and even cordial because neither would judge the other for his views. He wasn't profane in speech, but would swear when it was necessary, such as when his Model "T" Ford wouldn't start even on the fourth or fifth spin of the crank, and he might then use "damn" as a modifier as he talked to the machine. He was tolerant of views contrary to his own and, while he would engage in partisan political discussion (he was a Republican), he would not become angry enough to spoil a good argument, but would find a way before long to get everyone laughing about it.

As the years went by he gradually eased up. He bought a Model "T" Ford, which he would describe as being "not much for looks but hell for strong." He sold his horse and buggy and the wagon, and the car took up residence in the barn. Without a horse, he no longer needed to raise hay, and he cut back on his plantings of corn and wheat. He hired a nearby farmer to do the heavy work in the field which was now reduced to about an acre or less. He found it wasn't economical to raise only one or two hogs, he could buy eggs and chickens cheaper than he could raise them, and fresh milk and cream was readily available from neighbors, so when his livestock was gone he didn't replace them. He still kept the vegetable garden, something he could do with little exertion. He took more time to join other elderly men at Walter McCray's general store by the railroad tracks, or to play cribbage with Addie and sit on the front porch and pass the time of day with passers-by.

He liked summer because it was then that his four sons and their children got together in Elgin. He enjoyed all the noise and confusion the children created around the place. He revelled in the title, "Granddad," and maintained a cordial dignity with all the little ones. He treated his grandchildren with grave respect, and he could tease them without belittling, laugh with them, but not at them. Cynthia, the youngest and only girl, had a special spot in his heart.

In 1928 he suffered a cerebral hemorrhage, died, and was buried in Corry at age sixty-nine.

The Roberts Family Of Concord Township

ADDIE ROBERTS, WHO MARRIED GRANT McCRAY, was the daughter of Harvey and Sarah Roberts. They were born in Wales and came to the United States sometime before the Civil War, apparently with other members of the Roberts family. Harvey's parents are not known by anyone interviewed to date. However, there are two Roberts graves in Concord Cemetery, just north of Elgin in Concord Township.

One of the memorial stones is on the grave of David and Louisa Roberts. Carvings on the stone tell us that David was born March 15, 1818, and that Louisa was born March 31, 1820. David's death is recorded there to have been on December 19,1887, but Louisa's death wasn't noted.

The other stone bears the inscription: "Avery Roberts, Co. I 45 Pa. Inf.," and underneath it, "1850-1921." Below that is "Nancy Roberts." Avery's birth year is about right for him to have been a son of David and Louisa Roberts, but exactly who his family or descendants were isn't known. However, since the grave is in Concord Township, where many other Roberts lived at that time, it seems almost certain that he would have been closely related to David and Louisa.

An 1865 map of Concord Township, Erie County, shows that "D. Roberts" owned sixty-five acres in the northern section of Tract 77 (see Page 233). There is no reason to believe that D. Roberts wasn't David Roberts, and such a supposition is well supported by a deed of sale of a farm found in the Erie County Courthouse in Erie:

> "Deed between W.C. Bradford and wife Eva M. Bradford to Grant McCray for $1000.00. Land from the centerline of road leading from Concord Station (now Elgin) to Spartenburg at the four corners of Thomas Burrows west line along north line of land *of heirs of David Roberts, Deceased* (italics mine)...along lands owned by Mr. J.P. Roberts. 21 acres more or less. Sealed 29 November, 1893.   J.H. Dean, J.P."

Another deed from this same source refers to a land deal between Grant McCray and his father-in-law, Harvey D. Roberts and wife, with Grant McCray as the purchaser (recorded in Vol. 163, Page 254):

> "Parcel of land in the north half of a part of Tract 77 of the Holland Land Company. Bordered by Syracuse Oil Co., land of Thomas Burrows, Syracuse Oil Company, to Tract 76 and lands of Thomas Burrows, Joseph Hall, Seth Pond. 25 acres more or less. $500.00. Signed by Harvey D. Roberts and Eva M. Roberts, 27 March, 1906.   P.W. Ewing, Clerk of Common Pleas Court, Hancock County, Ohio." (Findlay is the county seat.)

From this deed it is apparent that Harvey D. Roberts was an heir of at least part of the "D. Roberts" parcel of sixty-five acres on Tract 77, and that David Roberts was indeed this "D. Roberts." Just what his relationship to Harvey was isn't clear. No evidence has been turned up that there were another families of Roberts in Concord Township, so it is quite likely that anyone of that name in that area was related to David Roberts.

Harvey D. Roberts was born in Wales in 1844 or 1845, and died in Elgin on September 11, 1912. One of his brothers was Abram L. Roberts who married Florence Bell McCray, daughter of James (IV) and his second wife, Pamelia (Powell) McCray. Florence's sister, Theresa Emma McCray, married Raphael ("Ray") McCray, Grant's brother.

Another possible link to David and Louisa Roberts is in the biography of Thomas B. McCray, reproduced on Page 359, in which is the following:

"Mr. McCray married on May 1886, Carrie G. Parsons, a native of Concord Township. Her father, Henry Parsons was born June 11, 1842, on the Atlantic Ocean, while his parents, James and Ann (Roberts) Parsons, were en route to this country. Mr. Parsons was born in England and his wife in Wales..."

We probably will never know if Ann Roberts was closely related to David Roberts, or if they were travelling together on the same ship. The Parsons and the Roberts would have been about the same ages.

Among the Roberts found in the Erie County files of deeds was one Willis Roberts. His name was recorded on a deed as "Willie W. Roberts of Findlay, Ohio," which certainly makes a good case for his having been a son or brother of Abram Roberts, who also lived in Findlay at the time of this deed. It reads in part:

"Deed made 18.. between Phidelia Roberts of Concord Township and Willie W. Roberts of Findlay Ohio and Grant McCray bounded by...and adjacent to lands deeded to Grant S. McCray by W.C. Bradford and wife Eva M. Bradford sealed 29 November 1893... 12 acres...$600.00."

It was signed by Willis W. Roberts, Victoria Roberts and Phidelia Roberts. Wording in the deed suggests that Willis' wife was Phidelia, and because of their different places of residence, they were separated. Still to be identified are John P. and Victoria Roberts, who are both named in this instrument.

Harvey Robert's wife was Sarah --?--, born February 22, 1845 in Wales, and who died in 1874. Harvey then married Eva M. Bradford, widow of the W.C. Bradford mentioned in the deed of sale of Bradford's land to Grant McCray, above, after the death of his wife, Sarah. Harvey and Eva had no children. Harvey Roberts was a dentist, as was his brother, Richard Robert Roberts. Children of Harvey and Sarah were:

Alma Roberts: married Dr. W.C. Smith. They lived in Falconer New York, and had a son, Murray Smith.

Addie Roberts, born July 16, 1864,; died February 19, 1948. She married Grant S. McCray on March 29, 1884, and they had four sons: Lou, Ernest Ross, Dorr Robert and Clifford Brink.

Ada, or Adah, Roberts: she was the youngest child. She married Ernest M. Blakeslee on July 8, 1891. She was born May 4, 1871, and died November 22, 1951. The Blakeslees lived at Conneaut, O.

Richard Robert Roberts, dentist, lived and practiced in Erie. He had two sons, Richard Robert Roberts, Jr., and James F. Roberts, who was also an Erie dentist. Dr. James Roberts said that his father was born in Rasselas, Warren County, Pennsylvania. Richard Robert Roberts married Nancy, daughter of Franklin and Cynthia (Brown) McCray.

Wionna Roberts: she married Benjamin Greene, and they lived just across the state line in Sherman and Findlay Lake, New York.

Benjamin Roberts: farmer who lived near Waterford, Erie County, married Margaret --?--, and they had eight children:

Allen Roberts

David Roberts, perhaps named for his grandfather

Sarah Roberts married Glenn Stearns, who was a business partner with Grant McCray in a grocery store in Corry.

Delia Roberts

Fisk Roberts

Kelsey Roberts. He died May 19, 1976 in Arizona.

Raymond Roberts. He had a twin brother who died in infancy. His parents obtained a foster boy, Clifford Woods, to be a companion for Raymond, who mourned his dead twin brother.

During her last illness, Addie (Roberts) McCray, Ona (Roberts) Greene her younger sister, cared for her until it became necessary to transfer her to a hospital in Corry, where she died. She is buried beside her husband, Grant, in Greenwood Cemetery in Corry.

When Harvey's wife, Sarah, died in 1874, leaving a large family, some of whom were quite young, Harvey found himself quite unable to care for his children, and he found foster parents for most of them, so the family was scattered. Some of the children's foster parents treated the children entrusted to them badly and forced them to work very hard in payment for their keep. Alma was one who said she was treated especially harshly, was probably the smallest of the siblings for her age. Addie (Roberts) McCray told her grandson, Douglas James McCray, that Alma, Ona and Richard were also badly treated by their foster parents.

Sarah Roberts married Glenn Stearns, son of Lewis and Minnie B. (McCray) Stearns. See Page 328 for details of this connection.

Nancy McCray, born in 1857, a daughter of Franklin McCray and his second wife, Cynthia Peterson, married Ralph Foote, and they had four children: Pearle Foote, Frank Foote, Lulu Foote and Charles Foote. Sometime after that Nancy married Robert R. Roberts, and they had three more children who were:

Daniel Roberts	Children: Ethel Nan Roberts, m. Frank S. Backer
b. 18-5-1889	Max Robert Roberts, m. Thelma Emerick
d. 29-3-1927	Munson Roberts, m. Elaine A. Beauchaut
m. Faith Walker	Ella M. Roberts, m. Virgil Leroy Jana
b. 8-6?-1900	Robert Richard Roberts, Jr., m.
d. 17-11-1931	Phyllis Schaff

Hattie Roberts	Frank File/Lyle died seven months after their
b. 8-5-1892	marriage. They adopted two boys.
d.	(J. Duane Upton, Percie McCray and Nina
m. Frank Lyle or Files	Pollock all are uncertain if Frank's name
b. 9-4-1883	was "Files" or "Lyle.")
d. 1-9-1906	

Cynthia Roberts	Children: Nan Parlee Hardee, Gilbert E. Hardee
b. 24-1-1899	Robert D. Hardee, Harriet E. Hardee, Cora J.
d.	Hardee, James E. Hardee and William D. Hardee
m. Gilbert H. Hardee on	
17-4-1920. He was	
b. 27-12-1886	

Robert R. McCray, son of Luther Lee and Aphrenia (Warner) McCray, married Essie Roberts. They had six children.

STORIES OF THE EARLY McCRAY FAMILY, AS TOLD BY LOU
McCRAY, and REMEMBERED BY HIS SON, RICHARD McCRAY

Some of the McCray family men became involved in the oil production
industry in the late 1800's and early 1900's. The earliest I can remember hearing about was my uncle, Dorr McCray, who lived in Tiffin, Ohio,
and my grandfather Grant McCray's brother, John, (known as "Jack") who
lived near Geneva, Indiana. Most of my life I wondered how they could
have become acquainted with the intricacies of this business, pumping
low producing wells,storing the oil in tanks and selling it to oil refineries, servicing and maintaining the equipment such as the pumping engines
and draw works, pulling and cleaning the pumps and rods in the wells and
keeping the pumps running the clock around in all kinds of weather.
Other members of the family were farmers, so it was quite a departure
from the usual occupations for them to be in the oil business. The
answer to my questions became quite clear upon examination of an 1865
map of Concord Township in Erie County, Pennsylvania, showing numerous
oil well sites and several oil companies, some of them owned by in-laws
of the McCrays. Apparently, this nephew and uncle were fascinated by
the mechanics of the industry and decided to make it their life's work.
It must have been a love of the work, for it was hot or cold, heavy,
dirty work, requiring constant attention,with little monetary return
for their effort. Out of this came several stories that Lou McCray told
at various times, and they are here recorded for preservation.

Lou visited his uncle Jack in Indiana on several occasions, and on
these occasions involved himself in the everyday occupations of the family, such as watching over the large stationary pumping engines, fueled
by natural gas from the oil wells that powered the nodding pumping jacks
spread over the fields and countryside of rural Indiana. Drilling new
wells and cleaning the ones already in service required the use of heavy
steel churn drills that pounded up and down in the holes and worried
their way through the rock strata to the oil pools and domes hundreds of
feet below the surface. The drills were twenty-foot lengths of solid
steel, armed on the lower end with a detachable bit,which was removed
when it became dull and was sharpened in the forge shop, one of the buildings grouped around the main pumping engine house. The coal-fired forge
and its hand-powered bellows, the huge anvil, and a supply of sledges,
cutting and trimming hammers, and a drill press powered from an auxil-
iary shaft, driven by the pumping engine -- these were the main tools of
the shop. Too hot to be comfortable in the summer with its tin roof, it
was a warm gathering place for the men of the family during the cold
weather.

Tall tales, stories of the early days of the family, and contests to
determine who could tell the biggest lies, helped to pass the time
between checking the rigs and equipment. Arm and Indian wrestling,
weight-lifting, and other exhibitions of physical prowess, worked off
their excess energy. But sometimes these things were just not exciting
enough, so they turned to their old standby of pitting their strength
against nitroglycerine.

This powerful explosive was a necessary but dangerous part of com-
petitive oil well production. A clear syrupy liquid, it required extreme
care and a generous measure of luck in handling, because the least
physical shock could cause it to explode. It was delivered to the well
sites in five-gallon square tin cans that had to be hauled in special
wagons with very soft springs and loose running gear, to lessen the shock
of traveling over the rough fields and muddy roads. Only men with
experience handled the nitro, and they were often blown to bits because
of an accidental shock to the oily liquid. Impurities in the explosive,
due to the manufacturer's inability to obtain chemicals of high purity,
was responsible for most of these accidents.

When the driller began bringing up oily cuttings in the mud from the
well, he stopped his drilling and called in the well "shooter," the man
with the nitro. The shooter would bring in long sheet-metal cans, or
tubes, resembling ten-foot lengths of downspouting, which he filled very
carefully with the nitroglycerine as it hung suspended at the top of the
well. Then he lowered the tube slowly and carefully to the bottom of the
well, hoping that it didn't catch on any roughness along the wall of the
drilled hole. When he had put as many tubes of nitro down the well as it
would take to bring in the well, he cleared out an escape path around the
drilling rig so he could make a fast get-away. Then he carried the
"Go-Devil," an igniter, which was a heavy, elongated piece of steel, to
the well casing, and let it drop down the well. As the go-devil gathered
speed, it hit the top of the nitro tube at a rate of several hundred
miles an hour, setting off the entire nitro charge, and blowing off the
top of the oil dome. This released a pocket of gas in the dome and let
oil into the bottom of the well.

As soon as the shooter had dropped the go-devil, he took off for
other parts, and stood well off to the side of the drilling rig to watch
the well come in. First, there was a low rumble and shaking of the
ground as the explosion did its work. Then came a whoosh, a hiss, a
rattle, as the go-devil cleared the casing and sailed end over end into
the air, and then followed a roar as the oil gushed over the top of the
casing, gradually rising higher and higher, until it hit the top of the
oil derrick, spraying oil over the surrounding area.

Nitroglycerine was an everyday part of the life of an oil well
pumper, and it was only natural that it was included in their contests of
physical prowess, pitting their frail, human strength against the mighty
explosive power of the innocent-looking liquid. To demonstrate the
extent of thir manhood they would put a single drop of nitro on the big
anvil, and then, selecting their favorite sledge from the shop's collection, the braggarts would raise the sledge over their heads and bring it
down on the drop of nitro with all their force. The explosion would
rattle the sides of the forge shop and bring down a rain of dust and soot
from the roof beams, and the sledge would bound upward with great force.
Only the strongest of the men could hold onto the handle and prevent it
from flying up against the roof. Those who could not hang onto the
hammer had to be quick on their feet to keep from being hit by the falling sledge. Laughter or praise was accorded every test, depending upon
where the sledge came to rest.

Lou and Uncle Jack's sons would sometimes go hunting for small game in the woods and fields of the countryside. On one of these occasions, as they were returning home, they noticed in the middle of a field a pile of the square tin cans that had once contained nitroglycerine. The cans always had a small amount of nitroglycerine in them, so they had to be disposed of in a safe manner, and the shooters intended to return later to burn the pile. Nitroglycerine burns like an oil and does not explode when burned as it will when jarred or shocked. Of course, the boys knew how the cans were to be disposed of, but one of them suggested they have some fun. They withdrew to the woods around the edge of the field and lay down in the grass and brush so as to have a low profile. They drew straws, and the one with the short straw aimed his rifle at the pile of cans and fired. The bullet hit one of the cans and the whole pile went up with a mighty roar. It was, Lou said later, a good thing they were all lying down, for the force of the explosion knocked down some trees at the edge of the field, sent their hats flying, and blew a big hole in the earth. Pieces of nitro cans sailed over the whole area.

People came running from their homes for miles around, thinking that there had been a dreadful accident in the oil fields. It didn't take long for them to figure out what had happened when they noticed all the pieces of nitro cans all around the countryside, but they didn't know who had set off the pile of cans. But that night, Lou's father, Grant McCray, looked up from his chair and looked Lou straight in the eye and asked him if he'd been in on the prank. He knew the jig was up and admitted to his part in the episode. All the boys were assembled and got a severe dressing down, but not the licking they expected. They were lectured on the dangers of fooling around with nitroglycerine, but Lou later heard his father tell his mother that it really was one hell of an explosion, and he'd like to have seen it go.

The Pudding's Proof

Principal elements of the McCray family legends have been quite firmly proven by official records, such as those in courthouses and libraries of several Pennsylvania counties, various historical societies, The Pennsylvania Archives in Harrisburg, and in Washington, D.C., the Library of Congress, The National Archives with its military and census records, and the National Genealogical Society.

Not official but usually believable were several biographies in an assortment of county "histories", typically those put together by J.H. Beers, Warner, Beers & Co., and others using a similar format. The bulk of these biographical collections were obvious pot-boilers, written primarily to market to families of personages written up in the books. The biographical material was supplied by the prospective customer who was not likely to tell the writer anything but facts that brought credit to him. He was no doubt also restrained from embellishing his life story with fanciful untruths, for everyone in his neighborhood already knew the essential facts of everybody's life in the farm community, having lived nearby since birth. In those days before daily newspapers, anchormen and women, and Newsweek and Time, there was not a great deal for people to talk about besides weather, crops, and each other, so everyone's life went through the local gossip mill frequently.

Regrettably, these vanity chroniclers almost never attempted any research or verification of their data in places such as police, court, and church records, so most of them sadly lack many firm dates and exact locations. To their credit, they do provide much valuable data to supplement solid genealogical data from verified sources.

U.S. Census records can provide far more than just proof that those enumerated each ten years were alive when the census-taker came calling. For example, one might not think that a census record as late as 1880 would contain information about immigrants of the eighteenth century, but it was a census record of 1880 that gave us the earliest and most-sought-after facts. Two of James, Jr.'s sons, Joseph and Robert McCray, both told the Concord Township census-taker in 1880 that their parents, James and Eleanor(Townsley) McCray, were born in Scotland, information which had not been collected by census-takers before, and which was only given in family legends, and not all of them at that. Since James, Jr., was the third of the children of Old James and Ellen (Bell) McCray, we can deduce that both Elizabeth and William, his older sister and brother, were also born in Scotland. The fourth child, George, told the census man in 1850 that he had been born in Ireland and that he was age 82 at that time. This told us to within two years of when the family migrated to Ireland. In the same 1880 Census, Samuel, then living in Armstrong County, Pennsylvania, gave his birthplace as Ireland, and his age as 78. And in Concord Township, Pennsylvania, the youngest of the children of Old James, also said he had been born in 1776 in Ireland. None of these facts had been picked up before and plugged into the McCray family's story.

392

An Erie newspaper noted that James McCray died on December 16, 1839, at age 74. Unless his birthday fell between December 17 and December 31, he would have to have been born in 1766, otherwise in 1765. Odds are that he was born in 1766. The newspaper account agrees with the information on his gravestone.

Elizabeth (McCray) Reed's gravestone in the cemetery at Helen Furnace, Clarion County, Pennsylvania, has carved on it that she died in 1848 at the age of 86, from which we can decude she was born in 1762.

A newspaper of Athens Township, Crawford County, Pennsylvania, referred to "Wm. McCray, a native of Ireland." (Although William came to America from Ireland, he was a native of Scotland.) The date and place of William's death are not known, but letters of administration were granted on July 22, 1836 to William Curry. Another court paper two years later filed by William Curry described William McCray as "deceased, late of Oil Creek Township." Other newspaper accounts of the day indicate that he also lived at one time in Cherrytree Township, Crawford County.

Records of the Holland Land Company show that James, William, Samuel, and Robert McCray, all bought adjacent tracts of land in District 6, located in Brokenstraw Township, Erie County, Pennsylvania.

Cumberland County, Pennsylvania, tax records, on file at the Cumberland County Historical Society, in Carlisle, provide evidence of the McCrays, Townsleys, and Reeds, living in Toboyne and Tyrone Townships.

George Carey, a resident of Concord Township, formerly in Brokenstraw Township, Erie County, in 1872 undertook to write down as many facts as he could find about the early days of the township. Two sons and a grandson of James and Eleanor (Townsley) McCray provided information about the family's arrival and early days in Erie County.

These data were not collected in one afternoon, you may be certain. A majority of the information for the entire book was supplied by many people, mostly McCrays or in-laws of McCrays, who generously shared their findings, and without their help this history would not have been possible.

-0-

GENEALOGICAL   CHARTS

of

Nine Generations

of

The Author's Line

Descended From

James McCrea

and

Ellen Bell

James McCrea, Sr.
b. ca 1730 (estimated), in Scotland
d. after 1797, probably in Washington
County, Pennsylvania
m. (1) (unknown)   2 ch
   (2) Ellen ("Nellie") Bell, in
        Scotland. 6 ch.

There are differences in opinion about the
existence of the first wife.

There is considerable evidence to indicate
that the family name was "McCrea" while
living in Scotland.

NOTE: Names marked with (+) indicates they were buried in
      the McCray Cemetery in Concord Township, Erie County.

Generation I   Generation II

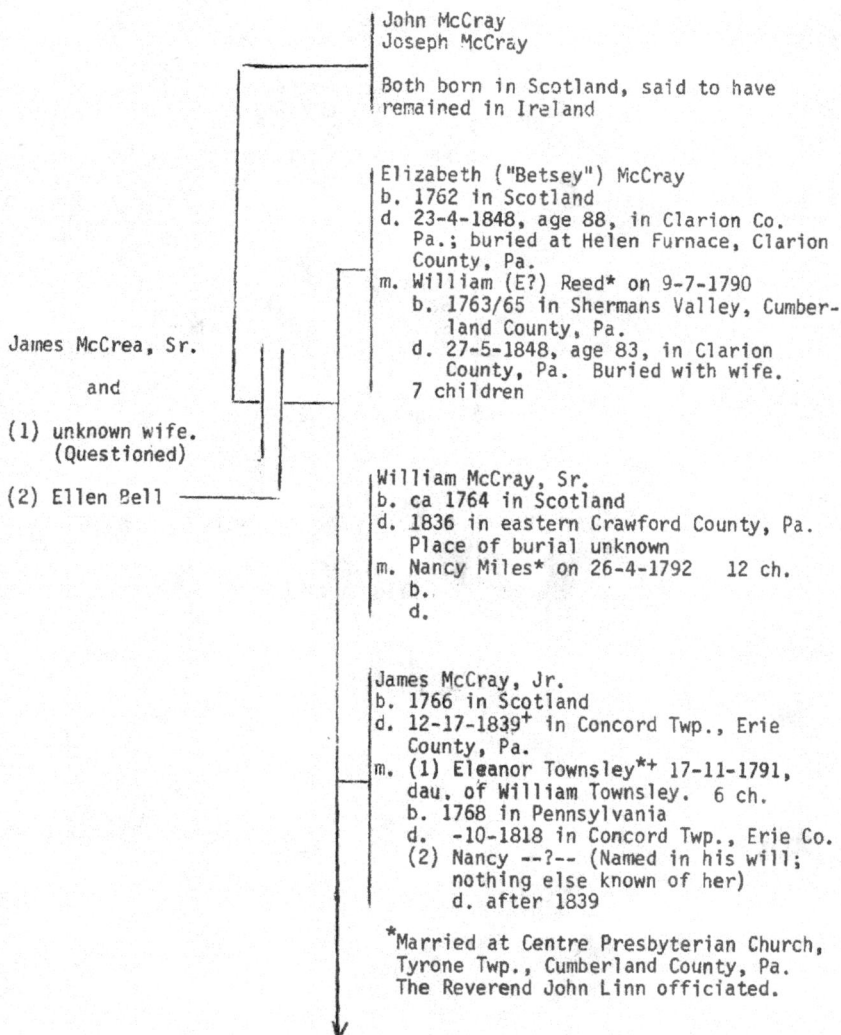

John McCray
Joseph McCray

Both born in Scotland, said to have
remained in Ireland

Elizabeth ("Betsey") McCray
b. 1762 in Scotland
d. 23-4-1848, age 88, in Clarion Co.
   Pa.; buried at Helen Furnace, Clarion
   County, Pa.
m. William (E?) Reed* on 9-7-1790
   b. 1763/65 in Shermans Valley, Cumber-
      land County, Pa.
   d. 27-5-1848, age 83, in Clarion
      County, Pa. Buried with wife.
   7 children

James McCrea, Sr.

and

(1) unknown wife.
    (Questioned)

(2) Ellen Bell ───────

William McCray, Sr.
b. ca 1764 in Scotland
d. 1836 in eastern Crawford County, Pa.
   Place of burial unknown
m. Nancy Miles* on 26-4-1792   12 ch.
   b.
   d.

James McCray, Jr.
b. 1766 in Scotland
d. 12-17-1839[+] in Concord Twp., Erie
   County, Pa.
m. (1) Eleanor Townsley*[+] 17-11-1791,
      dau. of William Townsley. 6 ch.
      b. 1768 in Pennsylvania
      d. -10-1818 in Concord Twp., Erie Co.
   (2) Nancy --?-- (Named in his will;
       nothing else known of her)
       d. after 1839

*Married at Centre Presbyterian Church,
Tyrone Twp., Cumberland County, Pa.
The Reverend John Linn officiated.

397

Generation II

George McCray
b. 1768, in Ireland
d. after 1850 (then age 82), prob.
   in eastern Crawford Co., Pa.
m. Jean ("Jennie") Murray*,26-11-1790
   b. ? , dau of Alexander   9 ch
      Murray of Shermans Valley,
      Cumberland Co., Pa.
   d. ?

Samuel McCray
b. 1771/72, in Ireland
d. After 1850 (age 78 then), prob.
   in Plumcreek Twp., Armstrong Co. Pa.
m. Polly McCoy   1 ch.
   b. 1782
   d. after 1850 (age 68 then)

Robert McCray
b. 17-8-1776, in Ireland

d. 23-4-1858† age 82, in Concord Twp.
   Erie Co., Pa.
m. Mrs. Jane Bruce, 4 ch
   b. 5-2-1776, in Scotland
   d. 22-3-1855+, age 79, in Concord
      Twp., Erie Co., Pa.

Generation I

James McCray, Sr.

Generation III

Joseph McCray
b. 15-6-1794, in Washington, Co., Pa.
d. 15-9-1884, age 90
m.(1) Joanne Townsley   1 ch.
   (2) Joanne McMillish 5 ch
   (3) Sarah J. Scott   5 ch
       b. 7-23-1807, in Ireland
       d. 11-13-1892+, in Concord Twp,
          Erie County, Pa.
       dau of James T. Scott, Civ. War
       veteran, d. 1863.

Generation II

James McCray, Jr.

&

(1) Eleanor Townsley

(2) Nancy -----
    (No known issue)

James T. McCray
b. 1796
d. 10/16-9-1833+
m. Sarah Blakeslee, dau. Capt. David
   Blakeslee, Sr.   5 ch
b. b. 1796
d. 1833+

William S. McCray
b. 11-4-1799
d. 6-9-1835+, in Concord Twp. Erie Co.
m. Jane Bruce, dau of Mrs. Jane Bruce
   b. 17-6-1810, in Scotland
   d. 28-9-1895+ in Concord Twp. Erie
      County, Pa.

George McCray
b. 29-5-1802
d. 1877, age 75
m. Polly Blakeslee, in 1831, 8 ch.
   b. 1807
   d. 1882
   dau. of David Blakeslee, Jr.

Jane McCray
b. 1803
d. before 1839
m. James Gray, 3 ch.

399

John T. McCray
b. 15-2-1805
d. 17-8-1855[+] in Concord Twp., Erie Co.
                                   Pa.
m. Sarah Blakeslee, on 11-5-1826, 16 ch.
  b. 26-7-1807
  d. 20-8-1891[+] in Concord Twp.
  dau. David Blakeslee, Jr.

Eleanor McCray
b. 18-8-1806/07
d. 12-5-1876[+]
m. Samuel Heath, 9 ch
b b. 20/22-10-1798
  d. 28-5-1882[+]

Robert McCray
b. 29-5-1808
d. 22-1-1892
m. Betsey Blakeslee on 3-1830, 8 ch.
  b. 29-7-1811
  d. 31-12-1905
  Dau. of David Blakeslee, Jr.

Betsey McCray
b. 6-12-1810
d. 18-6/7-1850/59[+]
m. Jesse A.Blakeslee in 1829, 8 ch.
  b. 1800
  d. 12-22/23-1872/73[+]
  Son of Capt. David Blakeslee, Sr.

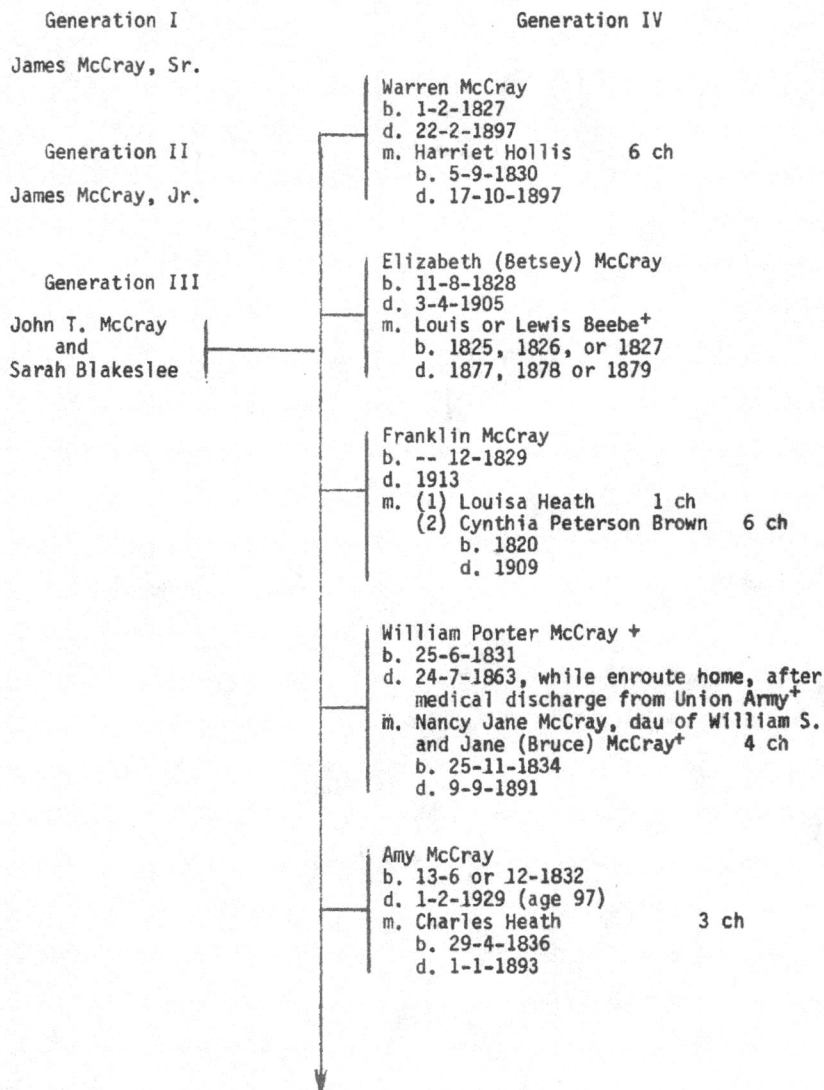

Generation I   Generation IV

James McCray, Sr.
                                    Warren McCray
                                    b. 1-2-1827
                                    d. 22-2-1897
    Generation II   m. Harriet Hollis   6 ch
                                       b. 5-9-1830
James McCray, Jr.   d. 17-10-1897

                                    Elizabeth (Betsey) McCray
    Generation III   b. 11-8-1828
                                    d. 3-4-1905
John T. McCray   m. Louis or Lewis Beebe+
    and   b. 1825, 1826, or 1827
Sarah Blakeslee   d. 1877, 1878 or 1879

                                    Franklin McCray
                                    b. -- 12-1829
                                    d. 1913
                                    m. (1) Louisa Heath   1 ch
                                       (2) Cynthia Peterson Brown   6 ch
                                           b. 1820
                                           d. 1909

                                    William Porter McCray +
                                    b. 25-6-1831
                                    d. 24-7-1863, while enroute home, after
                                       medical discharge from Union Army+
                                    m. Nancy Jane McCray, dau of William S.
                                       and Jane (Bruce) McCray+   4 ch
                                       b. 25-11-1834
                                       d. 9-9-1891

                                    Amy McCray
                                    b. 13-6 or 12-1832
                                    d. 1-2-1929 (age 97)
                                    m. Charles Heath   3 ch
                                       b. 29-4-1836
                                       d. 1-1-1893

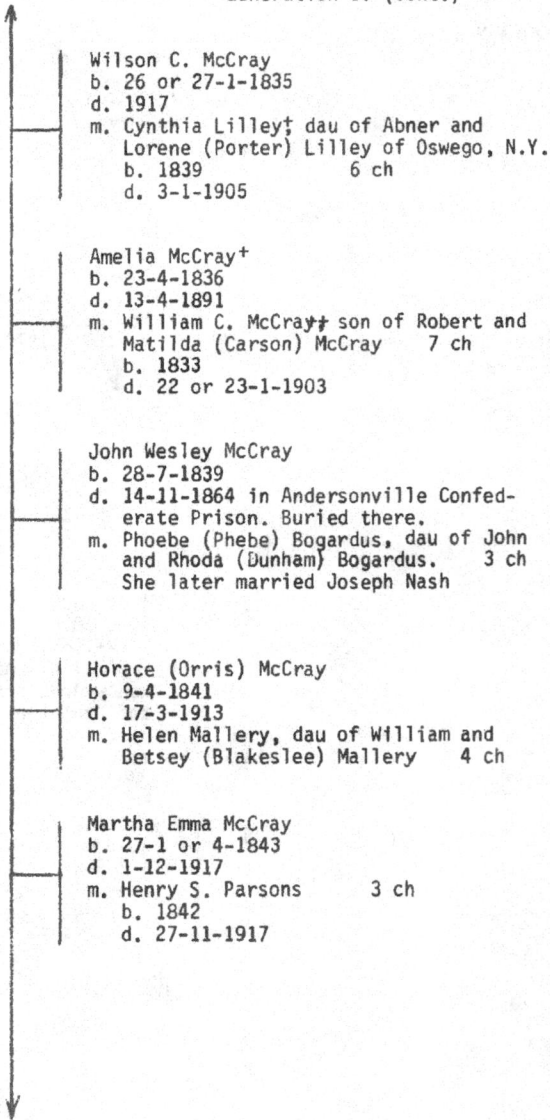

Wilson C. McCray
b. 26 or 27-1-1835
d. 1917
m. Cynthia Lilley† dau of Abner and
   Lorene (Porter) Lilley of Oswego, N.Y.
   b. 1839   6 ch
   d. 3-1-1905

Amelia McCray[+]
b. 23-4-1836
d. 13-4-1891
m. William C. McCray‡ son of Robert and
   Matilda (Carson) McCray   7 ch
   b. 1833
   d. 22 or 23-1-1903

John Wesley McCray
b. 28-7-1839
d. 14-11-1864 in Andersonville Confederate Prison. Buried there.
m. Phoebe (Phebe) Bogardus, dau of John
   and Rhoda (Dunham) Bogardus.   3 ch
   She later married Joseph Nash

Horace (Orris) McCray
b. 9-4-1841
d. 17-3-1913
m. Helen Mallery, dau of William and
   Betsey (Blakeslee) Mallery   4 ch

Martha Emma McCray
b. 27-1 or 4-1843
d. 1-12-1917
m. Henry S. Parsons   3 ch
   b. 1842
   d. 27-11-1917

Jason McCray +
b. 15-8-1844
d. 1 or 2-5-1932
m. (1) Amanda Cushing +   4 ch.
          b. 22-1 or 12-1848 in Wisconsin
          d. 20 or 30-3-1881
      (2) Lucy E. or S. Page   0 ch.
          b.1847
          d. 1922
          She was somehow related to Amanda

Loren/ Lorena ("Rena") McCray
b. 4-2-1846
d. 3-8-1888
   unmarried

Sarah McCray
b. ?= 12-1847
d. 17-5-1848

Henry McCray
b. 23-5 or 12- 1850
d. 17-8-1936
m. Jennie Hardy   4 ch
      b. 28-6-1866
      d. 24-9-1934

Eleanor Jane ("Ellen," "Nellie") McCray
b. 21-1-1852
11-?-1944
m. Lynn McPherson
      b. 1850
      d. 1919

403

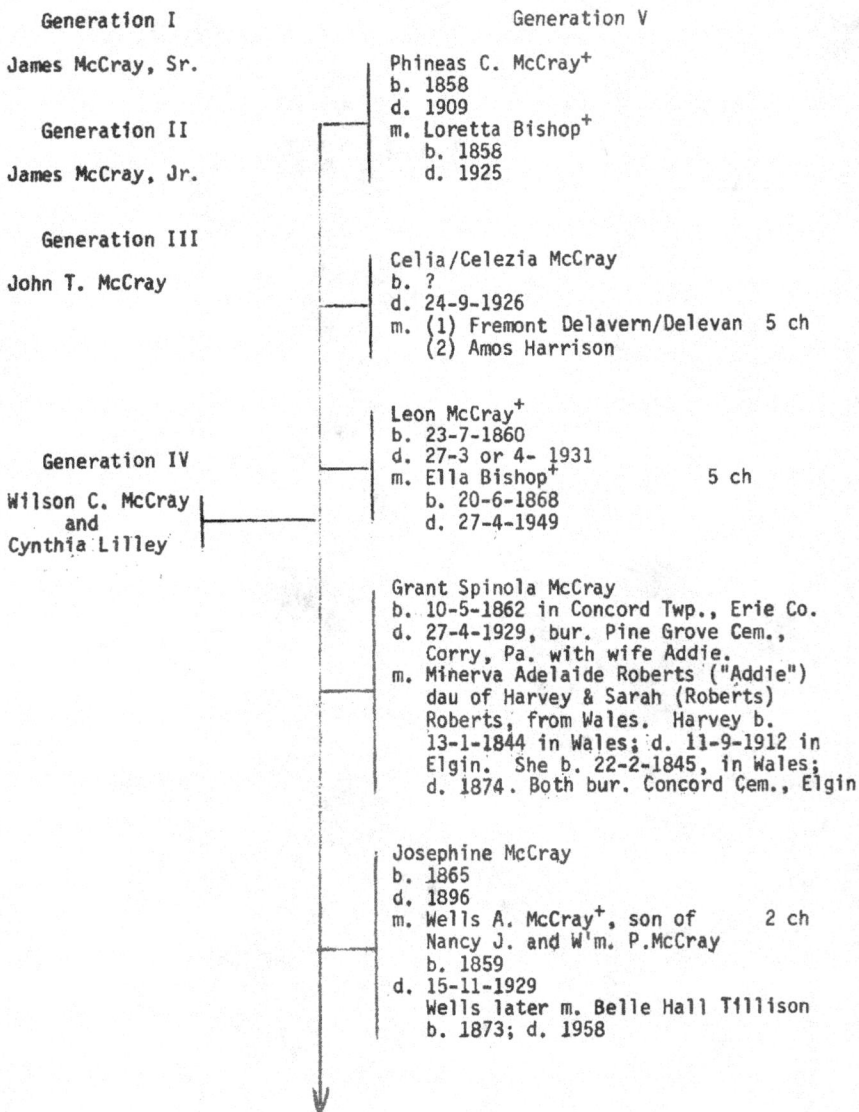

Generation I	Generation V

Generation I

James McCray, Sr.

Generation II

James McCray, Jr.

Generation III

John T. McCray

Generation IV

Wilson C. McCray
and
Cynthia Lilley

Generation V

Phineas C. McCray[+]
b. 1858
d. 1909
m. Loretta Bishop[+]
   b. 1858
   d. 1925

Celia/Celezia McCray
b. ?
d. 24-9-1926
m. (1) Fremont Delavern/Delevan 5 ch
   (2) Amos Harrison

Leon McCray[+]
b. 23-7-1860
d. 27-3 or 4- 1931
m. Ella Bishop[+]   5 ch
   b. 20-6-1868
   d. 27-4-1949

Grant Spinola McCray
b. 10-5-1862 in Concord Twp., Erie Co.
d. 27-4-1929, bur. Pine Grove Cem.,
   Corry, Pa. with wife Addie.
m. Minerva Adelaide Roberts ("Addie")
   dau of Harvey & Sarah (Roberts)
   Roberts, from Wales. Harvey b.
   13-1-1844 in Wales; d. 11-9-1912 in
   Elgin. She b. 22-2-1845, in Wales;
   d. 1874. Both bur. Concord Cem., Elgin

Josephine McCray
b. 1865
d. 1896
m. Wells A. McCray[+], son of   2 ch
   Nancy J. and W'm. P.McCray
   b. 1859
d. 15-11-1929
   Wells later m. Belle Hall Tillison
   b. 1873; d. 1958

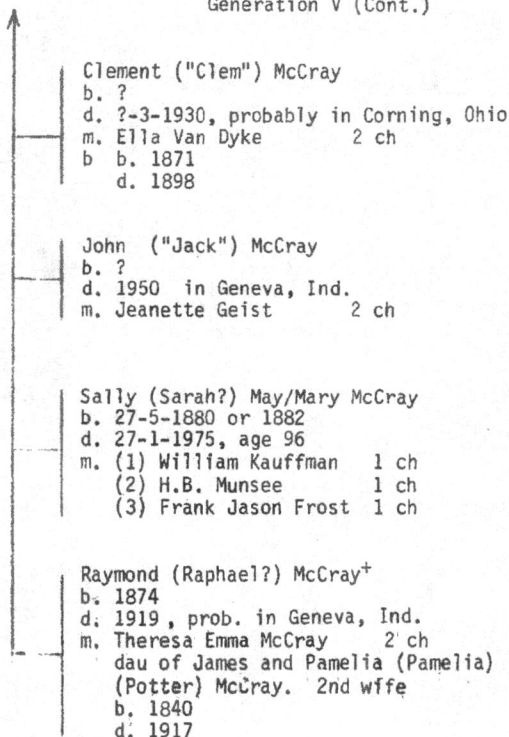

Clement ("Clem") McCray
b. ?
d. ?-3-1930, probably in Corning, Ohio
m. Ella Van Dyke   2 ch
b   b. 1871
    d. 1898

John ("Jack") McCray
b. ?
d. 1950 in Geneva, Ind.
m. Jeanette Geist   2 ch

Sally (Sarah?) May/Mary McCray
b. 27-5-1880 or 1882
d. 27-1-1975, age 96
m. (1) William Kauffman   1 ch
   (2) H.B. Munsee   1 ch
   (3) Frank Jason Frost 1 ch

Raymond (Raphael?) McCray[+]
b. 1874
d. 1919 , prob. in Geneva, Ind.
m. Theresa Emma McCray   2 ch
   dau of James and Pamelia (Pamelia)
   (Potter) McCray. 2nd wife
   b. 1840
   d. 1917

Generation I	Generation VI

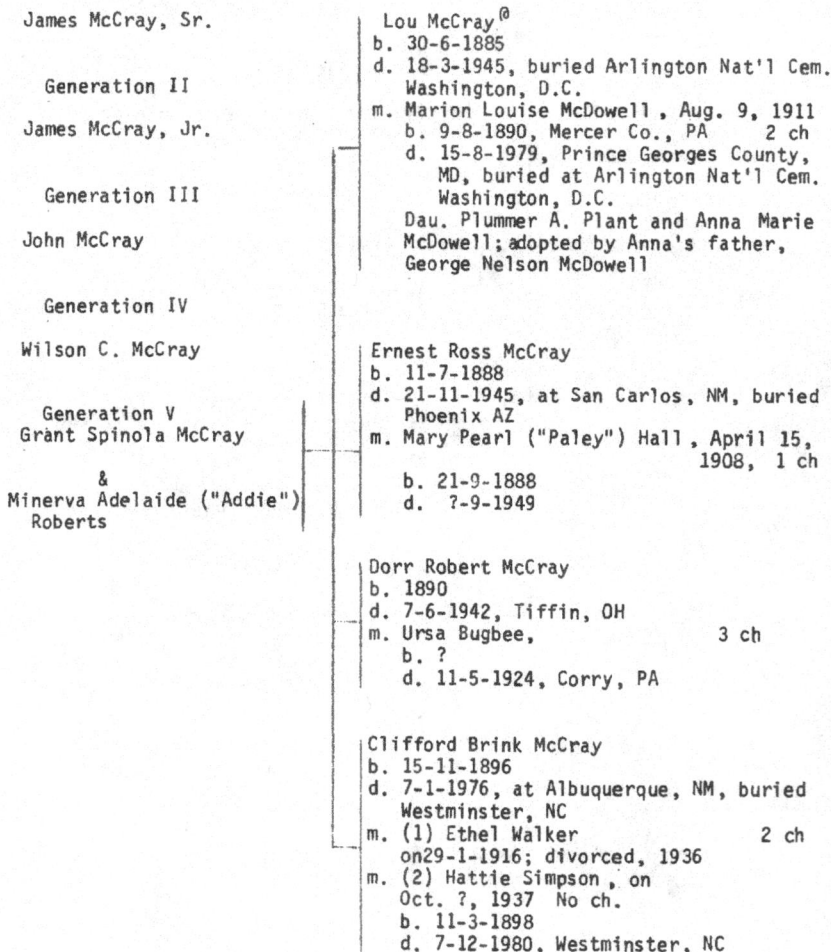

Generation I

James McCray, Sr.

Generation II

James McCray, Jr.

Generation III

John McCray

Generation IV

Wilson C. McCray

Generation V

Grant Spinola McCray

&

Minerva Adelaide ("Addie") Roberts

Generation VI

Lou McCray[@]
b. 30-6-1885
d. 18-3-1945, buried Arlington Nat'l Cem.
    Washington, D.C.
m. Marion Louise McDowell , Aug. 9, 1911
    b. 9-8-1890, Mercer Co., PA   2 ch
    d. 15-8-1979, Prince Georges County,
       MD, buried at Arlington Nat'l Cem.
       Washington, D.C.
    Dau. Plummer A. Plant and Anna Marie
    McDowell; adopted by Anna's father,
    George Nelson McDowell

Ernest Ross McCray
b. 11-7-1888
d. 21-11-1945, at San Carlos, NM, buried
    Phoenix AZ
m. Mary Pearl ("Paley") Hall , April 15,
                           1908, 1 ch
    b. 21-9-1888
    d. ?-9-1949

Dorr Robert McCray
b. 1890
d. 7-6-1942, Tiffin, OH
m. Ursa Bugbee,   3 ch
    b. ?
    d. 11-5-1924, Corry, PA

Clifford Brink McCray
b. 15-11-1896
d. 7-1-1976, at Albuquerque, NM, buried
    Westminster, NC
m. (1) Ethel Walker   2 ch
    on 29-1-1916; divorced, 1936
m. (2) Hattie Simpson , on
    Oct. ?, 1937 No ch.
    b. 11-3-1898
    d. 7-12-1980, Westminster, NC

[@] His Christian name at birth, "Von Luciene
McCray", which he never used, but the name
change was not formalized by court
action. "Von Luciene" should not be used to
identify him; use only "Lou."

406

Generation I	Generation VII

Generation I

James McCray, Sr.

Generation II

James McCray, Jr.

Generation III

John McCray

Generation IV

Wilson C. McCray

Generation V

Grant Spinola McCray

Generation VI

Lou McCray
   and
Marion Louise McDowell

Generation VII

Richard Nelson McCray
b. 22-6-1912, Jamestwon, Mercer Co., PA
Living in Hendersonville, N.C.
m. Hazel Shaw Lang on 19-6-1941 at St.
   Stephen's Lutheran Ch., Erie, PA
   b. 22-9-1909 in St. Louis, MO, dau of
      John Lewis and Sarah Alice Lang. He
      b. 2-9-1880 in Butler Co., PA; d.
         22-1-1964 in Erie. She b. 18-3-
         1880 in Bridgefoot, Workington,
         Cumbria, England; d. 25-8-1974 in
         Erie.

Philip Roger McCray
b. 26-2-1914 in Jamestown, Mercer Co., PA
Living in Ft. Washington, MD
m. Cecelia Belle Spear on 29-6-1940 in Washington, D.C.
   b. 25-11-1915 in Miles City, Mont., dau
      of William Delmont and Mattie (Mor-
      seth)Spear.* He b. 3-21-1860 in
      Hustisford, WI; d. 28-4-1929 in Miles
      City. She b.27-7-1873 in Trondheim,
      Norway. They m. 1-25-1898 in Fulda,
      Minnesota.
Living in Fort Washington, Maryland.

* *The Speare Family From 1642*, Charles Leon Speare, Tuttle Publishing
  Co., Rutland, Vermont, 1938. p. 76.

Generation I	Generation VII

Generation I

James McCray, Sr.

Generation II

James McCray, Jr.

Generation III

John T. McCray

Generation IV

Wilson C. McCray

Generation V

Grant S. McCray

Generation VI

Ernest Ross McCray
        and
Mary Pearl (Hall) McCray

Generation VII

Lionel Grant McCray
b. 19-12-1909
d. 26-5-1948
m. Frances Elizabeth Frazer on
   14-6-1957
   b.3-9-1908 at Clinton, MO
   Now living in Tucson, AZ, and is
   married to Robert Nicholas

Generations VIII & IX

Ernest Grant McCray
b. 6-6-1932 at Ganado, AZ
m. (1) Margaret Sickle; div. 28-4-1969
        Ch Penny Lynn Sickle McCray
          b. 23-7-1953, adopted by Ernest
    (2) Ruth Mantilla, dau of Dr. Marino
        Mattos Mantilla and Berta
        Galvis Escobar, of Bogota Col-
        umbia.
        b. 12-18-1950 in Bogota
        Ch Lionel Robert McCray
          b. 24-6-1959 in Texas City,
          m. Judy --?--   TX
          Adopted dau, Jackie McCray

        Dorothy Frances McCray
        b. 10-8-1956 in Houston, TX
        m. Tim Hamm
        Ch Seth McCray
           Heidi McCray
        Living in Troy, Montana

Mary Frances McCray
b. 8-10-1936
m. Virgil Larry Seal
   b. 29-4-1936
CH Lawrence Grant Seal
   b. 16-5-1963
   Robert Davis Seal
   b. 24-2-1965
   Andrew Thomas Seal
   b. 15-12-1968

Generation I

James McCray, Sr.

Generation II

James McCray, Jr.

Generation III

John McCray

Generation IV

Wilson C. McCray

Generation V

Grant Spinola McCray

Generation VI

Dorr Robert McCray

&

Ursa Bugbee

Generation VII

Frank Jerald (John) McCray
b. 17-1-1911
d.
m. Pearl ----   no children

Ivan Wallace McCray
b. 8-9-1913
d.
m. Hazel -----   no children

Stanley Wilson McCray
b. 22-5-1915
d. 7-2-1964
m. Louisa Greenwald
ch.
   Gene   McCray
   Shirley McCray
   Richard McCray
   Loretta McCray
   Danny McCray

409

Generation I

James McCray, Sr.

Generation II

James McCray, Jr.

Generation III

John T. McCray

Generation IV

Wilson C. McCray

Generation V

Grant Spinola McCray

Generation V

Clifford Brink McCray
       and
Ethel Walker

Generation VII

Roger Mason McCray
b. 18-10-1917 in Ohio
d.
m. Frances Marie McCray
   b. 16-7-
   d.

Douglas James McCray
b. 30-1-1924, at Corry, Pa.
d.
m. Lucille Ulrey on 21-10-1945 at
   Kalida, Ohio. Dau of Ralph (1888-
   1963) and Gladys (Smith)(1896-1970)
   Ulrey of Kalida, Ohio
   b. 19-7-1924 at Lima, Ohio   2 ch

Cynthia Elizabeth McCray
b. 4-11-1927 at Elgin, Pa.
d.
m. Stanley Fletcher on 13-3-1946 at
   Napoleon, Ohio

   b. 6-2-1908, Bowling Green, Ohio
   3 ch.

410

Generation I

James McCray, Sr.

Generation II

James McCray, Jr.

Generation III

John T. McCray

Generation IV

Wilson McCray

Generation V

Grant Spinola McCray

Generation VI

Lou McCray

Generation VII

Philip Roger McCray
          and
Cecelia Belle Spear

Generation VIII

Meredith Lucy McCray
b. 15-6-1944 in Washington, D.C.
m. James McMurray Blizzard in Washing-
    ton D.C., on 2-6-1965   2 ch
    b. 10-6-1943, son of Samuel and
        Hattie Blizzard of Princeton, N.J.
    Div., 26-8-1985
Meredith lives in Manlius, N.Y., and
has resumed the name, Meredith McCray.

Thomas Grant McCray
b. 11-12-1945 in Washington D.C.
m. Linda Lea Harucki,20-6-1970,   2 ch.
    dau of Chester and Margaret (Gouge)
    Harucki of Ft. Washington, MD
    b. 2-20-1946
Now living in Columbia, MD

John Douglas McCray
b. 26-4-1949 in Washington, D.C.
m. Katherine Elizabeth Lentz on 21-8-1971
    in Hyattsville, MD. Dau of Harry
    and Elizabeth (Armstrong) Lentz of
    Wheaton, MD   4 ch
    b. 1-7-1947 in Washington, D.C.
Now living in Macon, GA

411

Generation	Generation VIII

James McCray, Sr.

Daughter, un-named, stillborn
b. 2-5-1943

Generation II

James McCray, Jr.

Louis Nelson McCray
b. 6-7-1944 in Erie PA
Living in Louisville, KY

Generation III

James T. McCray

m. (1) Sue Kimberly Bock, 8-5-1972;
   Div. 17-6-1974
   (2) Donna Marguerite Sexton on 18-3-1975
       b. 21-3-1952
       d. 11-5-1980 (auto. collision)
       Dau of Don Columbus and Vera
       (Heidel) Sexton of Wartburg, TN
   (3) Deborah Joan Kress on 21-2-1981
       in Cleveland, TN. Dau of James
       Leroy and Ruth Phyllis (Crough)
       Kress.
       b. 26-12-1953

Generation IV

Wilson C. McCray

Generation V

Grant S. McCray

Generation VI

Lou McCray

Generation VII

Richard Nelson McCray
and
Hazel Shaw Lang

Norman Richard McCray
b. 2-7-1946 in Erie, PA
Living in Martinsburg, WV
m. Grace Marie Graves on 5-4-1975 near
   Flag Pond, TN. Dau of Emmett and
   Emma L. Graves.
   Div. 1987

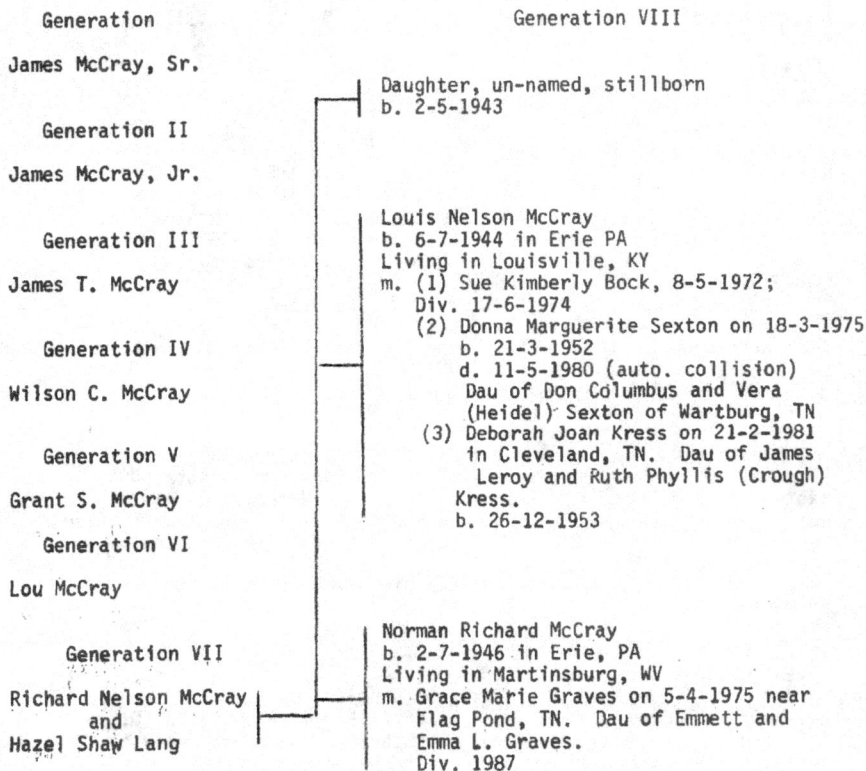

Generation I

James McCray, Sr.

Generation II

James McCray, Jr.

Generation III

John T. McCray

Generation IV

Wilson C. McCray

Generation V

Grant Spinola McCray

Generation VI

Clifford Brink McCray

Generation VII

Roger Mason McCray
and
Frances Marie McCray

Generation VIII

David Michael McCray
b. 26-5-1939
d.
m. Eileen Frances Kiely
   b. 25-11-1938
d.

Linda Ann McCray
b. 17-11-1941
d.
m. James M. Shulmeyer
   b. 1-12-1938

Generation I

James McCray, Sr.

Generation II

James McCray, Jr.

Generation III

John T. McCray

Generation IV

Wilson C. McCray

Generation V

Grant Spinola McCray

Generation VI

Clifford Brink McCray

Generation VII

Douglas James McCray
and
Lucille Ulrey

Generation VIII

Sue Ellen McCray
b. 6-7-1953 at Bowling Green, Ohio
Lives in Ithica, N.Y.

Ruth Ann McCray
b. 31-10-1958 at Bowling Green, Ohio
m. Jefferson Shetzer June 16, 1979
Live in Bowling Green, Ohio

414

Generation I	Generation VIII

Generation I

James McCray, Sr.

Generation II

James McCray, Jr.

Generation III

John T. McCray

Generation IV

Wilson C. McCray

Generation V

Grant Spinola McCray

Generation VI

Clifford Brink McCray

Generation VII

Cynthia Elizabeth McCray
and
Stanley Fletcher

Generation VIII

James Albert Fletcher
b. 28-7-1947 at Findlay, Ohio
d.
m.(1) Judy Osterhaut, Feb. 11, 1966 in
    Swanton, Ohio. Div. 1973
Ch: Todd Fletcher, b. July 26, 1967
    in Toledo, Ohio
    James Fletcher, b. March 28, 1970
    in Toledo, Ohio *
(2) Carlene Hunley in Weston, Ohio
    Ch: Mary Beth Fletcher, b. Mar.
        31, 1984

Coleen Fletcher
b. Oct. 17, 1949 in Bowling Green, O.
d.
m. Fred Bobel Aug. 22, 1970 in B.G.
Ch: Philip R. Bobel
    b. 16-6- 1974 in Bowling Green
    Heather Bobel
    b. 8-2-1978 in Bowling Green

Perry Fletcher
b. Feb. 10, 1955 in B.G. Ohio
d.
m. Anita Dauer March 22, 1973 in Water-
    ville, Ohio
Ch: Keri Fletcher, b. Sept. 26, 1974
    Kimberly Fletcher, b. Apr. 20, 1976
    Cory Fletcher, b. Apr. 7, 1978
    All born in Bowling Green, Ohio

* Late bulletin: James Fletcher married Terri Kissinger,
27-6-1992 in Swanton, Ohio.

415

Generation I

James McCray, Sr.

Generation II

James McCray, Jr.

Generation III

John T. McCray

Generation IV

Wilson C. McCray

Generation V

Grant Spinola McCray

Generation VI

Lou McCray

Generation VII

Philip Roger McCray

Generation VIII

Meredith L. McCray
and
James McMurray Blizzard

Generation IX

Jason Samuel Blizzard
stillborn 1-6-1971 in Syracuse, N.Y.
buried in Syracuse, N.Y.

Christopher David Blizzard
b. 19-12-1945 in Syracuse, N.Y.
Living in Manlius, N.Y.

Joel Samuel Blizzard
b. 16-3-1976 in Syracuse, N.Y.
Living in Manlius, N.Y.

416

Generation I

James McCray, Sr.

Generation II

James McCray, Jr.

Generation III

John T. McCray

Generation IV

Wilson C. McCray

Generation V

Grant Spinola McCray

Generation VI

Lou McCray

Generation VII

Philip R. McCray

Generation VIII

Thomas Grant McCray
and
Linda Lea Harucki

Generation IX

Megan Ann McCray
b. 6-8-1974 in Washington, D.C.
Living in Columbia, MD

Lauren Lea McCray
b. 12-2-1978
Living in Columbia, MD

417

Generation I	Generation XI
James McCray, Sr.	

Generation I

James McCray, Sr.

Generation II

James McCray, Jr.

Generation III

John T. McCray

Generation IV

Wilson C. McCray

Generation V

Grant Spinola McCray

Generation VI

Lou McCray

Generation VII

Philip Roger McCray

Generation VIII

John Douglas McCray
        and
Katherine Elizabeth Lentz

Generation XI

Shannon Elizabeth McCray
b. 15-3-1979 in Oklahoma
Living in Macon, GA

Ian Michael McCray
b. 12-10-1981 in Washington, D.C.
Living in Macon, GA

Andrew Scott McCray
stillborn, 26-10-1983, in Macon, GA
buried in Macon, GA

Erin Elizabeth Amy McCray
b. 14-6-1985 in Macon, GA
Living in Macon, GA

Generation I	Generation IX
James McCray, Sr.	

Generation II

James McCray, Jr.

Generation III
John T. McCray

Generation IV

Wilson C. McCray

Grant S. McCray

Generation VI

Lou McCray

GenerationVII

Richar N. McCray

Generation VIII

Louis N. McCray
and
Donna M. Sexton ─────────── Anne Katherine McCray
b. 17-9-1977 in Cleveland, TN

Generation I   Generation IX
James McCray, Sr.

Generation II
James McCray, Jr.

Generation III   ┌─── Grant Graves McCray
John T. McCray   │   b. 4-8-1979

Generation IV
Wilson C. McCray

Generation V   ┌─── Sarah Grace McCray
Grant Spinola McCray   │   b. 3-1-1982

Generation VI
Lou McCray

Generation VII
Richard Nelson McCray

Generation VIII
Norman Richard McCray   ┌──────┘
        and   │
Grace Marie Graves   │

420

About Those Great, Grand and Removed Relatives

A first cousin is a child of your uncle or aunt.

Your first cousin's child is your first cousin once removed.

Your first cousin once removed's child is your first cousin twice removed.

A second cousin is your grandparent's brother's or sister's grandchild.

Your second cousin is your grandparent's brother's or sister's grandchild.

Your second cousin's child is your second cousin once removed.

Your second cousin once removed's child is your second cousin once removed.

Your great-grandparent's brother's or sister's great-grandchild is
    your third cousin.

This should enable you to go on to identify your relationship to your
    remotest cousins.

Your grandparent's brother or sister is your great-uncle or great-aunt,
    not your grand-uncle or grand-aunt.

The brother or sister of your great-grandparent is your great-grand-uncle
    or your great-grand-aunt.

The grandchild of your brother or sister is your grandnephew or your
    grandneice (one word).

You, too, can be great!

-- BIBLIOGRAPHY --

Biographical Annals of Cumberland County, Pennsylvania; Genealogical
Publishing Company, Baltimore, MD, 1950

Bolton, Charles K; *Scotch-Irish Pioneers in Ulster and America*

Brumbaugh, Gaius M.; *Maryland Records; Colonial, Revolutionary, County
And Church*, 2 vol.

Buck, Solon J. and Elizabeth: *The Planting of Civilization in Western
Pennsylvania*, Pittsburgh, 1939.

Butcher, Bernard L.: *Upper Monangahela Valley, West Virginia*, 2 vols.

Center Presbyterian Church, 1766-1966; bicentennial booklet.

Clarke & Scott: *Abstracts From The Pennsylvania Gazette*, Genealogy
Publishing Company, Baltimore, Md..

Chalkley, Lyman: *Virginia: Extracted From The Original Court Records of
Augusta County, 1745-1800*, 3 Vols.

Crozier: *Early Virginia Records*

Dinsmore, J.W.: *The Scotch-Irish in America*, Chicago, 1906

Dunaway, Wayland F.: *A History of Pennsylvania*, New York, 1905

> *The Scotch-Irish of Colonial Pennsylvania*, 1944,
> The University of North Carolina Press, Chapel Hill,
> North Carolina.

Eckard, Allen W.: *The Frontiersman;* 1967

> *Wilderness Empire*, 1969
>
> *The Conquorers,*   1970
>
> *The Wilderness War*, 1978
>
> *Gateway to Empire*, 1983
>
> Little, Brown & Company.   Also by Bantam Books.

(Although these books by Eckard are classed as "Historical Novels,"
they tell true stories of events in Colonial and Revolutionary
America, with only people/ characters who are known to have lived
and participated in the events he describes. Very well written,
and very good history.)

Egle: *Cumberland County State and Supply Transcripts, 1778-85*, State Printer of Pennsylvania, Lancaster City, Pa., 1846.

Evans, Paul Demund: *The Holland Land Company*, Buffalo Historical Society, Buffalo, New York, 1934.

Fendrick, Virginia S.: *American Revolutionary War Soldiers of Franklin County, Pennsylvania*, the Franklin County Chapter, Daughters of the American Revolution, Chambersburg, Pennsylvania, 1944.

Fiske, Wilson: *Appleton's Cyclopedia of American Biography*, D. Appleton & Company, New York, 1888.

Gipson, Lawrence A.: *The British Isles And The American Colonies, 1738-1754*, Alfred A. Knopf, New York, 1958.

Glasgow, Maude: *The Scotch-Irish In Northern Ireland and in the American Colonies*, New York, 1936.

Hanna, Charles A.: *The Scotch-Irish, or The Scot In North Britain, North Ireland, and North America*, 2 volumes, New York & London, 1902.

Hunt, George T.: *The Wars of The Iroquois, A study in inter-tribal Relations*, Madison, Wisconsin, 1940.

Illick, Joseph E.: *Colonial Pennsylvania, A History*, Charles Scribner, 1976.

Klein, Philip S., and Hoogenboom, Ari: *A History of Pennsylvania*, McGraw-Hill, 1973.

Journal of The Department of History of The Presbyterian Church of the U.S.A.

Leyburn, James G.:*The Scotch-Irish, a Social History*, The University of North Carolina Press, 1962.

Lockyer, Roger: *Tudor And Stuart Britain, 1471-1714*, St. Martin's Press, New York, 1964.

Maryland Marriages, 1778-1800, Genealogy Publishing Company, Baltimore, Maryland, 1978.

McCray, Fred. W.: *David Blakeslee, His Ancestors and Descendants*, Privately printed, 1947.

Moore, Frank: *Diary Of The American Revolution*, Square Press, New York 1967.

Naval Documents of the American Revolution, U.S. Government Printing Office, Washington, D.C.. 1966.

New England Historic And Genealogy Register, 146 volumes.

Parkman, Francis, *History of The Conspiracy of Pontiac,* New York,1929.

Pennsylvania In The War Of The Revolution, Battalions and Line, Vol. 1, Lane Hart, State Printer, Harrisburg, Pennsylvania, 1880.

Pennsylvania Magazine of History and Biography, Vol. XVIII, Historical Society of Pennsylvania.

The Pennsylvania Archives, 9 Series, many volumes. Philadelphia, Harrisburg, Pennsylvania, 1852-1931.

Record of Indentures in Philadelphia, 1771-1773, Pennsylvania German Society, Genealogical Publishing Company, Baltimore, Maryland, 1907

Rupp, I. Daniel: *History and Topography of Dauphin, Cumberland, Franklin, Adams, and Perry Counties.*

Somerset County (New Jersey) Historical Society Quarterly, 10 Vols. 1918.

Smith, Abbott E.: *Colonists In Bondage,* 1947.

Stemmons, John & Diane: *Pennsylvania In 1780,* National Geographic Society.

Stewart, David; *The Scots In Ulster,* Belfast, 1952.

Stroup, John & Bell, Martha: *Pioneers Of Mifflin County, Pennsylvania,* 1942.

Swope, Gilbert E.: *History Of Big Spring Presbyterian Church, 1737-1898,* Times Steam Printing House, Newville, Pennsylvania, 1898.

Tepper, Michael: *Emmigrants To Pennsylvania, 1641-1819,* Genealogical Publishing Company, Baltimore, Maryland, 1977.

Titus, Irene McDaniel: *History of The McCray Family,* privately printed, 1954.

Tocqueville, Alexis de: *Democracy In America,* many translations avail.

Upton, J. Duane: *Genealogical Record of Heron, Kerr, McCray, Shelmadine, Snyder, Tubbs, Upton,* privately printed, Santa Ana, California, 1967.

Wallace, Paul W.: *Indian Paths of Pennsylvania.*

-- I N D E X --

Jackson, Andrew 148
Jackson, Adam 188
Jackson, Isaac 188
Jackson, Mary 268, 324
James I (VI) 1, 5, 12
James II 22, 24, 40
James, Henry 175
Jamestown, PA 380
Jana, Virgil 388
Jenkins, Achsa 136, 161
Jenkins, Charles 135, 136, 161
Jenkins, Emma 163
Jenkins, Elijah 134, 136, 159, 161
Jenkins, George 135-138, 161, 163
Jenkins, Joseph 136, 161, 163
Jenkins, Nancy 136, 146, 161, 162
Jenkins, Sally 136, 161
Jenkins, Sally, 136, 161
Johnson, David 188g
Johnson, Steven 188g
Johnson, William 188g
Jones, Clint 107, 118
Jones, Elam 62, 72
Jones, Emily 175

Kaufman, Mae 376
Kauffman, William 405
Kearney, Iowa 64
Keating, Helen 314
Keily, Eileen 413
Kerr, Robert 294
Killingsworth, Rebecca 93
King, Benjamin 142, 152
King, Elizabeth 300, 313, 314
King, Joshua H 142, 151
Kinkead, John 219
Kirk, beginning of 5
Knox, John 4
Koontz, Mariah 149
Kress, Deborah 412

Lamb, Agnes 282-284
Lamb, James 282-284
Lamb, Jane 282-284
Land Act of 1792 191
Land Ordinance of 1785 191
Lang, John 407
Lang, Hazel 382, 407, 412

Lang, Sarah A. 407
Latimer, Kimberly 368, 372
Laud, Archbishop William 16-18
Leach, Elizabeth 80, 85
Leach, John 80
Lebanon, OH, Courthouse 106
Leith, Treaty of 4
Lentz, Elizabeth 411
Lentz, Harry 411
Lentz, Katherine 411, 418
Lewis, Ezekial 255, 259
Lewis, John 55
Lilley, Abner 375, 376, 402
Lilley, Amy 272
Lilley, Cynthia 375, 376, 402
Lilley, John 259
Limerick, Treaty of 26
Lincklaen, Jan 224, 228
Linn, Rev. John 218, 219, 281, 318, 319
Lipp, Francis 99, 114
Liverspire, Russell 328
Log College 40
Log Buildings, erection of 204, 218, 245, 253
Lopier, Dr. James 52
Loney, M. 257
Londonderry, seige of 25
Longman, Albertus 122
Longman, Cecil (fem) M. 122, 123
Longstreth, Elizabeth 115
Louisiana Purchase 130, 171
Love, Jeremiah D. 153
Low, Zachariah 52
Luckey, Francis 327, 331, 333

Mack, Feleena 351
Mack, John L. 350, 351
Mack, Tina 351
Macrea, Allen 47
Madden, Adeline 125
Madden, Christy 125
Madden, Clinton 125
Madden, Douglas 125
Madden, George 112
Madden, Mary 116, 125
Madden, Nancy 125

McPherson, Lynn 403

McSpadden, Charlotte 140, 154, 155

M C C R A Y S

Northwestern Pennsylvania McCrays Follow

-- *I N D E X* --

433

THE
NORTHWESTERN PENNSYLVANIA

McCRAYS

M^c C R E A S

New Purchase   191
Nicholas, Frances   408
Nicholas, Robert   408
Nickleson, Joseph   107
Nickleson, Lydia   104, 125
Nixon, Ellet McC.   83
Nixon, George   83
Nodding, Elizabeth   132
Nodding, Mary   132
Nodding, Sarah 131, 132, 141
Nodding, William   128, 131, 132
Norman, James E.   91, 92
Norman, Pattie Lee   92
Norman, Sharon L. 92
Northrup, Flora   188e, 188f
Norwood, Margaret E.   39

O'Donnell, T.A.   300
Oil in Pennsylvania   296-299
Oil well drilling 297, 390
Old Swede's Church   39
Oldenbarnveldt Settlement   229
Olmstead, Frederick L. 131
Olmstedd, Frank   313
Olmstead, William   259
Orange, Leonard   289
Orcutt, Catherine B.   162
Osborne, Emily   113
Osborne, Mary E.   113

Page, George 326
Page, Lucy 403
Palmer, Andrew   188g
Palmer, Brian   188g
Panic of 1819 131, 172, 228
Parks, Thomas   232
Parsons, Ann 359, 386
Parsons, Carrie   359,386
Parsons, Henry   359, 386, 402
Parsons, James   359, 386
Parsons, Salina   312, 313
Patrick, John F.   154
Patterson, Sarah   219
Paul, Harry   289
Paul, Myna   314
Paxton, Hugh   60
Pelton, James 176
Pelton, Mary   175, 182

perch, defined   235
Perkins, Eliab   258
Perkins, Eliza   326, 328
Perry County, Pa   213
Peters, Sarah   101
Phillips, Charles   95
Pickwillany   195
Plant, Plummer   406
Pinckney, Gen. Thomas   144
Piper, Benjamin 164, 162, 164
Piper, Homer L.   164, 165
Piper, Julia Ann 146, 162
Piper, Ralph 134, 146, 165
Piper, Ross P.   165
Pitt, William   196
Plimouth Plantation   6
Pontiac, Chief   198
Port Tobacco, MD 51, 53, 132
Porter, Alexander   282
Porter, Alice   308
Porter, Ann 108, 117
Porter, Jane 107, 114, 117, 118, 127
Power, Alexander   340
pot ash   217
pototo in Ireland   13
Presbyterian Church, early 10,11
Presbyterian Church, Erie County, PA,
   243, 246, 257
Presque Isle   200
Price, Betsy 327, 328, 330
Price, Hermon   78
Prince George's County, MD   52
Proctor, H.M.   340
Proctor, Hiram   340
Proctor, Guy   340
Proctor, Thomas   340
Prosser, Daniel   232
Puritans 6, 11, 16, 48

Rack renting 29, 34
Railroads in Erie County, PA 261
Ralston, Mark   96
Ralston, Michael   96
Ralston, Steve   96
Ralston, Robert   96
Ratsimihah, Jean L.   188g
Ratsimihah, Nicholas   188g
Reed, Adam   280

437

www.ingramcontent.com/pod-product-compliance
Lightning Source LLC
Chambersburg PA
CBHW071826270326
41929CB00013B/1907